Essays for Colin Tapper

Essays for Colin Tapper

EDITED BY

Peter Mirfield

and

Roger Smith

LexisNexis™ UK

Members of the LexisNexis Group worldwide

United Kingdom	LexisNexis UK, a Division of Reed Elsevier (UK) Ltd, Halsbury House, 35 Chancery Lane, LONDON, WC2A 1EL, and 4 Hill Street, EDINBURGH EH2 3JZ
Argentina	LexisNexis Argentina, BUENOS AIRES
Australia	LexisNexis Butterworths, CHATSWOOD, New South Wales
Austria	LexisNexis Verlag ARD Orac GmbH & Co KG, VIENNA
Canada	LexisNexis Butterworths, MARKHAM, Ontario
Chile	LexisNexis Chile Ltda, SANTIAGO DE CHILE
Czech Republic	Nakladatelství Orac sro, PRAGUE
France	Editions du Juris-Classeur SA, PARIS
Germany	LexisNexis Deutschland GmbH, FRANKFURT, MUNSTER
Hong Kong	LexisNexis Butterworths, HONG KONG
Hungary	HVG-Orac, BUDAPEST
India	LexisNexis Butterworths, NEW DELHI
Ireland	Butterworths (Ireland) Ltd, DUBLIN
Italy	Giuffrè Editore, MILAN
Malaysia	Malayan Law Journal Sdn Bhd, KUALA LUMPUR
New Zealand	LexisNexis Butterworths, WELLINGTON
Poland	Wydawnictwo Prawnicze LexisNexis, WARSAW
Singapore	LexisNexis Butterworths, SINGAPORE
South Africa	LexisNexis Butterworths, DURBAN
Switzerland	Stämpfli Verlag AG, BERNE
USA	LexisNexis, DAYTON, Ohio

A CIP Catalogue record for this book is available from the British Library.

ISBN 0 406 96439 4

Typeset by Doyle & Co, Colchester
Printed by Antony Rowe Ltd, Chippenham, Wilts

Visit LexisNexis UK at www.lexisnexis.co.uk

Foreword by The Rt Hon Lord Hoffmann

There is only one reason why I think it may be appropriate that I should have been given the honour of writing a foreword to this collection of essays for Colin Tapper and that is that we shared, at more or less the same time, the enormous intellectual influence of being taught by Rupert Cross. Colin, being a Magdalen man, had it in greater measure than I, as a Queensman, who was sent to Rupert by Tony Honoré to learn torts, legal history and, of course, evidence. But we both felt the power of Rupert's forcefulness and clarity and I think I can say for both of us that it not only stimulated a life-long interest in the law of evidence but moulded the way we thought and wrote about the law. Later we both had the privilege of assisting Rupert at the seminars on evidence which he gave for the BCL students and receiving his encouragement and help in our own academic work.

It was Colin, however, who held to the true faith and not only went on to edit Rupert's book but devoted almost the whole of his working life to writing and teaching, while I defected to the Bar. Perhaps this too was because he was a Magdalen man and felt the strong attraction of those other powerful intellects, his predecessors and then colleagues, like John Morris and Guenter Treitel, who made the college so famous among lawyers. But he has certainly maintained the great tradition of combining world-class scholarship with the intimacy of the tutorial relationship with generations of undergraduates and graduate students.

For me, therefore, it is both a privilege to introduce these essays and a pleasure, which I am sure many will share, to have read them.

Leonard Hoffmann
House of Lords

April 2003

Foreword by Sir Guenter Treitel

Forewords to books of this kind should be written by admiring pupils; so that, as Colin Tapper's retired former tutor, I suffer from at least one disqualification for writing this one. Perhaps my doing so can be justified on the ground that, as will appear, I can claim to have been not only Colin's tutor, but also his pupil.

Colin's distinguished career as an undergraduate and as a BCL student at Magdalen is a matter of record, the details of which need not be repeated here. But some personal recollections may be of interest; mine of his first Oxford tutorial are particularly vivid. He had been asked to deal with a number of the usual hypothetical problem cases, and the way in which he tackled the task set the pattern for things to come. First he gave the arguments on one side, then those on the other and finally a reasoned conclusion. Was that, he asked with the shyness of a beginner, the right way of conducting a legal discussion? There could be only one reply. By the time he reached his third year, Colin may (though I rather doubt this) have begun to give some credence to the persistently laudatory reports on his work which his tutors made at the end of each term to the President of the College (the only note of complaint that ever crept into one of my reports was that Colin had dealt so fully with each of the weekly topics that there was nothing left for his tutor to say). At any rate, by this time the beginner's shyness had been dissipated. I remember trying, in a class on the Roman law of delict (may God forgive me), to explain the difference between economic loss and physical harm by reference to (I believe) a Digest text which raised the intriguing question into which of these categories one would put the case of a gold coin thrown into the sea and so lost. 'What nonsense' was Colin's *sotto voce* but quite audible comment; and how right he was, even if the early habit of presenting and evaluating the arguments on both sides seemed to have been temporarily abandoned.

After five years at the LSE, Colin returned to Magdalen as Fellow and Tutor in Law. He has been there ever since and it is good to know that the College has found a way of retaining the benefit of his services even after his having in 2002 reached the age of compulsory retirement. Meanwhile he had become All Souls Reader in English Law in 1979 and an *ad hominem* Professor in 1992. These promotions recognised his growing academic distinction: he had become, and continues to be, the leading scholar in England in the law of Evidence and in various aspects of the law relating to computers. In the present age of increased academic specialisation, to have attained this level of distinction in two such important topics is, in itself, a huge achievement. It is a further tribute to Colin's work in the former subject that he was chosen by Sir Rupert Cross as editor of that great work, *Cross on Evidence*; sadly, Rupert's early death prevented the appearance of the joint edition that was planned before Colin was to take over as sole editor. My early flirtations with that subject leave me in no doubt about the value of Colin's work in what is now justly styled *Cross and Tapper*, to which I invariably turn for guidance in the subject. As for Colin's work on law computers and computer law, it is best for me to steer clear of those deep waters, in which I could scarcely survive. But the importance of Colin's pioneering work in the subject is well known even to those who are electronically *incapax*, and it forms the basis of his international reputation in it.

One other aspect of Colin's work in relation to computers and the law should be recorded, since there is some danger of its being forgotten. When the machinery for electronic retrieval of legal information was first installed in the Bodleian Law Library, Colin, on an entirely voluntary basis, spent an immense amount of time in instructing both students and members of the law faculty in its use; the debt owed to him in this respect is immense. It was at this stage that our original relationship was reversed in the sense that I became his pupil. Fortunately, no reports on my progress, or rather the lack of it, were submitted to the head of my College. Had such reports existed, their tone would necessarily have been very different from that of mine about Colin's undergraduate work. Colin has been very tolerant of my ineptitude and has for many years been so kind as to supply me with materials available only through these means, when my own attempts at electronic retrieval had ended, as they usually did, in ignominious defeat at the first fence or (even more distressingly) in the 15th round. He has also been of immense help in other ways: particularly in putting to me a series of questions which he has disarmingly called 'simple' about contract law. Those are always the most difficult, and the most thought-provoking, ones. I have little doubt that he has, with similar brain-teasers, helped many other academics across a wide range of legal (and other) subjects.

All lawyers know that even the most firmly established rules are subject to exceptions; and I shall here make an exception to that most sacred of general rules, that one should not quote in print from a reference given in connection with a job application. I venture to justify the exception by stating my firm belief that neither the author of the reference (were he still with us) nor its subject would object to my quoting here from what was written about Colin nearly forty years ago, when he had applied for a Fellowship at Magdalen. 'This young man' (the passage went) 'has fire in his belly. You should grab him if you can.' We did and we could not possibly have made a better decision.

GHT

April 2003

Preface

To mark the retirement of Colin Tapper from his Chair in Oxford at the end of September 2002, a number of his friends and colleagues decided to seek to commission a collection of essays in his honour, on subjects in which he has specialised. (It will be no surprise to anyone that knows him that Colin views retirement as an opportunity to spend more, not less, time upon his academic interests.) The scholars invited to contribute essays most readily agreed to do so, and, as editors, we are extremely grateful to them, and not least for the fact that they met our publishing deadlines with grace. We are also most grateful to LexisNexis UK for so willingly agreeing to publish this collection.

With many other distinguished scholars, contributions would inevitably gather closely around a particular branch of the law. It is a mark of the range of Colin Tapper's scholarship that these essays span evidence, intellectual property, computer law and computer applications. It will be apparent from the list of his works to be found in this volume that we could certainly have spread the net more widely, for example to include legal theory.

The contributors themselves are spread over three continents. It will not go unnoticed that many of them are Colin's former students, that several are his present colleagues at Oxford, and that some are both. The two Forewords are written by Lord Hoffmann, a fellow student at Oxford, and by Sir Guenter Treitel, one of his tutors at Magdalen, both of whom we thank most warmly. We know that this unbroken line of academic connection will please Colin greatly, but that it will please him no less that some of his many other friends and colleagues are included among those who contributed so eagerly.

Peter Mirfield
Jesus College, Oxford

Roger Smith
Magdalen College, Oxford

April 2003

Contents

List of contributors

Andrew Ashworth is Vinerian Professor of English Law and a Fellow of All Souls College, Oxford. He is a member of the Sentencing Advisory Panel and of the Criminal Committee of the Judicial Studies Board.

Roderick Bagshaw is Fellow and Tutor in Law at Magdalen College, Oxford. He first studied the law of evidence in tutorials taught by Colin Tapper in Autumn 1991.

Jon Bing dr juris (Oslo) 1982, dr juris hon causae (Stockholm 1997 and Copenhagen 1998), Computer Law Pioneer Award (San Diego 1993), was Visiting Professor, King's College (London) 1997-99 and is currently Professor, Norwegian Research Center for Computers and Law, a department of the Faculty of Law, University of Oslo. Former offices include among others Council of Europe Committee on Legal Data Processing (chair).

William (Bill) Cornish is Herchel Smith Professor of Intellectual Property Law at Cambridge University, where he is a Fellow of Magdalene College and has been its President (1998-2001). In November 2002 he delivered the Clarendon Lectures in the Oxford Law Faculty on *Intellectual Property: Omnipresent, Distracting, Irrelevant?* to which the essay in this volume adds some reflections. He is an External Member of the Max Planck Institute for Intellectual Property in Munich and plays a part in various international associations for the subject. He has interests in modern legal history and restitution; and he directs a course of study in English and EU law in Warsaw University and elsewhere in Central and Eastern Europe.

Katharine Grevling is Fellow and Tutor in Law at Magdalen College, Oxford where she teaches Criminal Law, Contract, Trusts and Evidence. Colin Tapper was her doctoral supervisor and she is a co-editor of *Phipson on Evidence.*

Sue McNicol is an Associate Professor of Law at Monash University, Australia where she has served as Associate Dean (Teaching) of the Law Faculty. She is the author of

Law of Privilege (1992), co-author of *Evidence* (2001) and has written a Report for the Australian Taxation Office entitled 'Access and Privilege in the Taxation System'.

Peter Mirfield is Zeitlyn Fellow and Tutor in Law at Jesus College, Oxford. He also serves as the College's Estates Bursar. He has been a visiting professor on a number of occasions at Florida State University and at Santa Clara University in the United States.

Roger C Park is James Edgar Hervey Professor of Law, University of California, Hastings College of Law. He taught for 22 years at the University of Minnesota Law School, and has been a visiting professor at the Michigan, Stanford, and Boston University law schools.

Richard Susskind OBE is an independent adviser to international professional firms and to national governments. He is IT Adviser to the Lord Chief Justice of England, Gresham Professor of Law at Gresham College, London, and is also a Professor at the Centre for Law, Computers and Technology at the University of Strathclyde. His books include *The Future of Law* (1996) and *Transforming the Law* (2000).

David Vaver is Reuters Professor of Intellectual Property and Information Technology Law at Oxford University and the Director of the Oxford Intellectual Property Research Centre at St Peter's College, Oxford, where he is a professorial fellow. Before coming to Oxford, he was a Professor at Osgoode Hall Law School, York University, Toronto, with prior stints at the law faculties of the University of Auckland and the University of British Columbia.

C R Williams holds the Sir John Barry Chair of Law, Monash University. He is a Fellow of the Academy of the Social Sciences in Australia, and holds the degree of Doctor of Laws from Monash University. He is the author of *Property Offences* (3rd edn, 1999); *Criminal Law Text and Cases*, with L Waller (9th edn, 2000) and *Evidence Commentary and Materials*, with P Waight (6th edn, 2002).

Table of statutes

References in the right-hand column are to page numbers.
Page references printed in **bold** type indicate where the statute is set out in part or in full.

Table of European statutes

References in the right-hand column are to page numbers.
Page references printed in **bold** type indicate where the statute is set out in part or in full.

Table of foreign statutes

References in the right-hand column are to page numbers.
Page references printed in **bold** type indicate where the statute is set out in part or in full.

Table of cases

References in the right-hand column are to page numbers.

A

B

C

D

E

F

G

H

I

J

K

L

M

N

O

P

S

T

U

W

Z

Silence, lies and vicious circularity

Katharine Grevling

We live in an age in which jury directions have become lengthy, copious and complex and hence a fertile ground for appeal. Challenges to instructions concerning two types of evidence have been particularly fruitful.[1] One is the use to which the accused's pre-trial silence may be put, particularly under the terms of s 34 of the Criminal Justice and Public Order Act 1994 (CJPOA). The other concerns lies told by the defendant, the Court of Appeal having recently noted 'the steady and almost unstoppable stream of reported decisions and appeals to this Court on the subject'.[2]

The scope of s 34 is severely restricted by the factual preconditions which must be satisfied before an adverse inference can be drawn. Most of these raise interesting or difficult issues that fall outside the scope of this paper.[3] The accused must have failed to mention a fact, when being questioned under caution or charged with an offence, that he could reasonably have been expected to mention at the time, and relies upon the fact in his defence at trial. In addition, he must have had access to legal advice if he has requested it.[4] The purpose of s 34 is to enable the jury to make use of the accused's pre-trial silence, but silence in the face of police questioning is highly ambiguous, particularly when the caution is taken into account. This affects the adverse inferences that may be drawn by the jury and the topic remains full of uncertainty. In certain respects the law relating to lies is the better developed and it may cast some light on problems that have arisen under s 34 or else highlight deficiencies in the wording of the statute.

The issue of lying lurks just below the surface in many criminal trials. The prosecution will ask the jury to believe their witnesses, a process which may necessarily entail the conclusion by the jury that the accused is lying.[5] It becomes more prominent when the defence case is contradicted by prosecution evidence presented in such a way as to make it necessary for the prosecution to say that the defendant's account is untrue and indeed deliberately and knowingly false.[6] If a direction on lies were required whenever there was a straightforward conflict of evidence, it would be delivered in almost every case.[7] This would be confusing to the jury and do more harm than good,[8] and the defence might not find it helpful to have the jury reminded that the accused could be a liar. A lies warning is desirable only when there is some real danger of inappropriate reasoning by the trier of fact. Elsewhere it should suffice to direct the jury that, should they reject the defence version of events as false or mistaken, they must not jump straight to the conclusion that the accused must be guilty.

Directions about lies and silence under s 34 may be given in the same case, and can even relate to the same response. This overlap provides an opportunity to explore the characteristics of lies and silence. It also highlights the differing character of the tests which the jury is directed to apply. Before an adverse inference can be drawn under s 34, the jury must decide that the accused might reasonably have been expected to mention in interview the fact he later relied upon. In the case of lies, the possibility of there being an innocent explanation for the lie must first be eliminated. The danger of circular reasoning can arise at several points of the reasoning process. For example, it may be impossible to determine whether the accused is actually lying independently of determining the issue of guilt. This has a parallel under s 34 when the question whether the accused had a good reason for not mentioning a fact in interview is, in the circumstances, indistinguishable from the fact relied upon at trial, or indeed the ultimate issue of guilt. The distinction between evidence going to credibility and evidence relevant to guilt can break down entirely when the issue to be decided by the jury is also the matter about which the defendant is said to have told lies or, in the case of s 34, the matter which he failed to mention in interview.

Before any of these issues is discussed, it is necessary to give a brief description of the law relating to pre-trial silence and lies directions.

1 Silence at common law

Section 34 is concerned with pre-trial silence, more specifically the failure to mention a matter which is later relied upon in defence. In order to appreciate how this provision has changed the law,[9] as well as the ambiguity of evidence of silence in the face of police questioning, the probative force of silence at common law will be briefly described.[10] The four possible uses to which silence can be put also give an idea of the type of adverse inferences that may be available under s 34:

1. Silence can be regarded as tantamount to an implied admission when a proposition is put, and silence is taken to be acquiescence in and affirmation of the truth of the relevant proposition. Here silence operates like consent or adoption of an accusation.[11] This inference cannot normally be drawn from silence in a police interview because the suspect has usually been cautioned and in any case is not on even terms with his accuser.[12]
2. Behaviour such as silence, telling lies, fleeing the scene of the crime, tampering with evidence, or conspiring to kill a witness[13] might be said to display consciousness of guilt[14] and provide circumstantial evidence of the accused's culpability for that crime. It is commonly admitted to show that an accused person has acted in a manner which, based on human experience and logic, is consistent with the conduct of a guilty person and inconsistent with the conduct of an innocent person. Evidence of this kind is introduced to show that the accused was aware of having committed the crime in question and acted for the purpose of evading detection and prosecution. This may be difficult to determine except in retrospect and thus such evidence can be highly ambiguous.[15] The courts[16] have expressed caution or outright disapproval of evidence of silence being used in this fashion. Apart from the ambiguity of silence in the face of police interrogation, the courts were concerned that the caution, which advised a suspect that he did not have to say anything unless he wished to do so, would be turned into a trap.[17] The term 'consciousness of guilt' and the psychological theories underpinning it have also been the subject of criticism.[18] The phrase has been said to suggest a conclusion about the conduct in question which undermines the presumption of innocence and may prejudice the accused in the eyes of the jury.

3. Silence can be regarded as strengthening the evidence for the prosecution. However, the suggestion that evidence of silence during interrogation could amount to corroboration was finally rejected in *R v Littleboy*.[19] Here the court was using the term 'corroboration' in its technical sense[20] and thus the evidence had to be from an independent source, and not simply show that some part of the suspect testimony was true (ie be generally supportive) but also tend to prove the fact in issue.
4. Silence during police questioning can be used to weaken a defence raised at a later stage. Though the cases are far from consistent, it was permissible at common law for a judge to remind the jury that a defence was being raised for the first time at trial,[21] and even comment that it was unfortunate that the defence was not set up at an earlier date so as to afford the opportunity of it being tested. Occasionally, the jury was also invited to take this into account when assessing the weight to be given to the explanation.[22]

2 Silence under s 34 of the Criminal Justice and Public Order Act 1994

Section 34 is not specific about the adverse inferences that can be drawn from silence at the police station, using the phrase 'such inferences from the failure as appear proper'.[23] Two different adverse inferences have been identified[24] which fall clearly within the fourth category described above. The original and more commonly cited in the cases is that the fact later relied upon is a recent fabrication or invention.[25] The second suggests that the suspect did have a story in reserve at interview but was not prepared to have it questioned or investigated at the time and so did not mention it.[26] Both inferences affect the weight to be attached to the evidence of the 'fact' later asserted, suggesting that it is less credible. As these inferences point to the fact relied upon being false, there could be a small implied lie issue entailed in every s 34 direction, but it will be seen that it takes more than this to trigger a specific direction to the jury on lies.

Silence under s 34 can be used not just to weaken the defence case by undermining the credibility of its evidence but also to strengthen the prosecution case. This is reflected in an element of the Judicial Studies Board's specimen direction, which says that a failure to mention:

> 'is something which [the jury] are entitled to take into account when deciding whether his evidence about this matter is true, ie [the jury] may take it into account as some additional support for the prosecution's case.'

Birch contends[27] that the Judicial Studies Board specimen direction confines silence under s 34 to a supporting role of 'corroboration in all but name', making the prosecution's case look more persuasive. Mirfield argues that it should now be possible to extend the principle in *Christie* to silence in the face of an accusation made during police interview.[28] But the suspect is warned of the risks in silence only if he later relies upon a defence at trial.[29] Judges have in the past been reluctant to allow the caution to be used as a trap; they might now say that this practice would breach art 6 of the European Convention on Human Rights. Can silence be used as evidence of guilt in its own right?[30] Any such use would be restricted by the fact that the Act provides that a defendant cannot be convicted on the basis of silence alone.[31] It may also be incompatible with the right to a fair trial under art 6 for a conviction to be based mainly on evidence of silence.[32] The role of the caution is another consideration. Despite these factors and the reluctance of the courts to equate silence with consciousness of guilt, jurors might still conclude that the failure of the accused to mention a matter crucial to his defence, when it could reasonably have been expected that he would do so, must spring from this source. Section 34 almost invites such inference in these circumstances.

In practical terms, a significant function of s 34 has been to enable the prosecution to undermine the credibility of evidence relating to matters raised for the first time at trial. The accused's silence has also been used to bolster the prosecution case, 'an evidential poly-filler for cracks in the wall of incriminating evidence which the prosecution has built around the accused'.[33] In the case of lies, one can also distinguish between evidence going to credibility and that probative of guilt. It must be acknowledged, however, that even judges can find it hard[34] to distinguish between evidence going to credibility and that directly probative of guilt, and some have come close to rejecting the distinction altogether.[35] Others doubt that such directions are generally understood by the jurors, let alone observed in their deliberations.[36] In the case of lies, the line between the two begins to blur almost immediately.[37]

Lies can be relied upon indirectly to prove guilt, by demonstrating that the defendant is a person of dubious credibility. If a lie is not related to any matter in the charge,[38] it can be relevant only to credibility and this of course is contingent on his giving evidence at trial. A wide range of lies,[39] including evidence of dishonesty in relation to other matters in the past or a conviction for perjury, may be taken into account when assessing the weight to be given to the defendant's evidence. A lie on a matter pertinent to the offence may also be relied upon to encourage the jury to scrutinise with more care other testimony given by the accused.[40] Where it is clear to the jury that any suggestion that the defendant has lied is relied upon as at most a matter affecting credibility, no special direction is called for[41] and it may be counterproductive to give one.[42] The primary function of lies, however, is as evidence of guilt.

3 Lies as probative of guilt – the *Lucas* direction

It has long been recognised that there is a particular danger of the jury attaching excessive or irrelevant significance to lies told by the accused[43] where this is used by the Crown as evidence of guilt, as opposed to going to credibility. This is aggravated because the lie may be inconsequential, trivial or associated with a peripheral issue in a case. As with similar fact evidence or evidence of bad character, there are 'special risks of illogical intuitive reasoning'[44] or 'forbidden reasoning',[45] that were succinctly described by Lord Devlin on behalf of the Privy Council in *R v Broadhurst*:[46]

> 'There is a natural tendency for a jury to think that if an accused is lying, it must be because he is guilty, and accordingly to convict him without more ado. It is the duty of the judge to make it clear to them that this is not so.'

The standard direction on lies has its origins in the case of *R v Lucas*.[47] This case addressed the circumstances in which the accused's lies could amount to corroboration of the evidence of an accomplice, but the Court of Appeal held in *R v Goodway*[48] that it should be given whenever lies are relied upon by the prosecution or might be used by the jury as evidence supportive of guilt. The direction is to the effect that a lie can be supportive of guilt only if the jury is satisfied that the lie is deliberate; that it relates to a material issue; and that the motive for the lie is the realisation of guilt and a fear of truth. For it to amount to corroboration the statement must clearly be shown to be a lie by evidence other than that of the witness who is to be corroborated.[49]

Reference must also be made to *R v Burge and Pegg*,[50] in which Kennedy LJ gave further guidance concerning a *Lucas* direction. It is required only where the jury may treat a conclusion that the accused has been telling lies as probative of guilt. The direction would normally be needed in four situations:

1. where the defence has raised an alibi;
2. where the judge considers it is desirable or necessary for the jury to look for support or corroboration of one piece of evidence from other evidence in the case, and amongst that evidence draws attention to lies told, or allegedly told by the defendant;[51]
3. where the prosecution seek to show that something said, either in or out of the court, in relation to a separate and distinct issue was a lie, and to rely on that lie as evidence of guilt in relation to the charge which is sought to be proved;
4. where although the prosecution have not adopted that approach, the judge reasonably envisages that there is a real danger that the jury may do so.[52]

His Lordship went on to suggest that where the direction was required, it should make two basic points:[53]

> '1. that the lie must be admitted or proved beyond reasonable doubt; and
> 2. that the mere fact that the defendant lied is not in itself evidence of guilt, since defendants may lie for innocent reasons, so only if the jury is sure that the defendant did not lie for an innocent reason can a lie support the prosecution case.'

Both elements of this direction warrant further examination.

(a) Proving that the accused has lied

Establishing that a statement is a lie requires more than persuading the jury to reject it. If the accused does not admit that he has lied, proving that he has done so may be no easy task. The prosecution may rely upon its own evidence to prove that the accused has lied, or else on clear inconsistencies in statements made by the accused.[54] In some circumstances, which will be discussed in some detail, it may be impossible to establish that the accused has lied independently of resolving the issue of guilt. The line between guilt and credibility in such cases is so thin as to be indiscernible. The requirement that the lie be proved beyond reasonable doubt leads to consequences that will be discussed under the heading of 'circularity'.

(b) Innocent reasons for lying

The evidential value of a lie, as with silence, turns on the reason underlying the behaviour and the jury must be satisfied that there is no innocent explanation for the defendant's falsehood before it moves on to the stage of drawing an adverse inference. The jury should be reminded that some people lie in an attempt to bolster a just cause, or out of shame, or through a wish to conceal disgraceful behaviour. This limb of the direction is to be given even if the defence has not raised an innocent reason as to why he lied.[55] Pattenden[56] observes that whilst a judge is free to make speculative suggestions to the jury about innocent explanations for potential lies, the Court of Appeal has held[57] that this is not appropriate in the case of the statutory provisions on drawing adverse inferences from silence,[58] nor can defence counsel advance reasons for silence at trial in the absence of supporting evidence.[59] This means that in a case requiring both a *Lucas* and a s 34 direction[60] where the defence has not provided any evidence to explain this behaviour, the trial judge may outline possible innocent reasons for the accused's lies, but not his silence, a contrast which must be to the detriment of the defence on the s 34 point.

Pattenden's view is that there is no justification for this difference in approach towards speculative reasons for the accused's behaviour. While the state of the law would probably be improved were it to be abandoned, the distinction may have one small merit. Lying is inherently reprehensible in a way that failing to mention a fact later relied upon is not – the right to silence is recognised in law[61] and reflected in the police caution.[62] There may therefore be a greater need to impress upon the jury the possibility of there being a non-incriminating explanation for the lie, especially as the evidential value to the prosecution of a lie may exceed that of an adverse inference drawn from silence.[63]

4 The problem of circularity

We have already seen that evidence of lies can be used to undermine the accused's credibility as a witness in his own defence, and that, unlike silence, it is also capable of amounting to corroboration. The third element of the *Lucas* test is clearly premised on the notion that the decision to lie may indicate consciousness of guilt and therefore amount to circumstantial evidence of guilt.[64] Some judges detect an element of circularity in this reasoning[65] because the jury is invited to consider whether a lie was told because of guilt and then to decide whether the Crown case became strong enough to prove such guilt. Brennan J in *Edwards v R*[66] suggested that the relevant inference under *Lucas* is not that the accused realised his guilt but that, in making his statement, he was unable to account innocently for the evidence that has been given against him. The majority of the High Court of Australia in *Edwards v R*[67] took the view that a lie would normally form part of the body of evidence to be considered by the jury in reaching their conclusion according to the required standard of proof. It did not have to conclude that the accused was guilty beyond reasonable doubt to accept that a lie exhibited consciousness of guilt.

As *Burge and Pegg* requires the jury to be satisfied beyond reasonable doubt that the accused has lied before drawing any adverse inference, there is a danger of the jury engaging in circular reasoning when trying to follow the terms of a *Lucas* direction. A similar problem arises in the context of s 34, namely whether, if the jury cannot decide if the defendant could reasonably have been expected to mention the fact at the time, it can nevertheless proceed to draw an adverse inference from his silence. These two problems will now be discussed in some detail, and it will be argued that an adverse inference should not be drawn in either case for reasons of circularity. However, there is nothing in the wording of s 34 to prevent the jury adopting an approach akin to that advocated by the majority in *R v Edwards* in relation to lies. It can treat the silence as provisionally suspicious and of some worth in determining guilt.

5 Lies and silence as issues independent of the ultimate question

(a) Lies and circularity

It is sometimes the case that no distinction can be drawn between guilt and lies; the issue before the jury is the same issue that is the subject of the allegation that the defendant was telling lies. *R v Harron*[68] is one example of this situation. The defendant's conviction for assault occasioning actual bodily harm was based on identification evidence provided by two non-independent witnesses (the victim and his girlfriend) who knew the defendant well enough to be able to recognise him in a night club. Their evidence was in direct and irreconcilable conflict with the accused's defence of alibi. Neither witness actually saw who mounted the attack, but their testimony as to the defendant's close proximity at the crucial moment, that he had said something to the girlfriend earlier in the evening that could be construed as a vague threat against the victim, combined with the nature of the attack, could suffice to establish all the elements of the crime and rule out such possibilities as accident or self-defence. The judge directed the jury to consider whether there was any room for the prosecution witnesses to be mistaken in their identification and, if not, whether there was any chance of a deliberately false identification. The Court of Appeal rejected the contention that he should also have directed the jury on the issue of lies. In these circumstances the judicial consensus is that even a limited direction warning of possible innocent explanations for a defendant telling lies, is otiose[69] and is not required,[70] even though a *Lucas* direction is usually to be given where the defence has raised an alibi.[71] The need arises only where, on some collateral matter[72] or due to some change of evidence or change of account given by the defendant,[73] there is scope for drawing an inference of guilt from the fact that the defendant has told lies at the trial or on an earlier occasion.

It is submitted that there are two different reasons why a direction on lies is unnecessary, and that most cases fall more easily into one category than the other. The more common explanation, applicable to *Harron* itself, is the need to avoid circular reasoning. It is succinctly put by the Court of Appeal in *R v Higgins*:[74]

> 'Lies which call for a *Goodway* direction are those which the prosecution maintains support its case and which can be proved to be lies independently of proof of its case. If that were not so, the exercise would be circular, proof of guilt proving the lie, and the lie unnecessarily being advanced as evidence of guilt.'

If we explore the relationship between the lie and the eye-witness evidence in *Harron*, the problem of circularity becomes apparent. In finding Harron guilty, the jury must have been satisfied beyond reasonable doubt that he had been in the night club that evening, which he had denied, and very close to the victim at the time of the assault. It follows that the rejected alibi must have been a lie,[75] but this factor was not relied upon by the prosecution in order to prove something in the case. This may partly explain why a *Lucas* direction was unnecessary[76] but this lack of reliance was not simply the product of prosecutorial tactics or discretion. The lie simply did not have any evidential value to the prosecution, nor was there was any danger of the jury misusing it to engage in a false line of reasoning. The alibi could not be used to corroborate the evidence of the eye-witnesses because its falsity could not be established independently of their testimony and was therefore no more than self-corroboration[77] – not that there was any need for corroboration, since the jury must already have been convinced of their reliability.[78] Nor was the lie one from which an adverse inference might be drawn. In order to make use of the lie, the jury would first have found the prosecution case established.[79] If he was lying he was already guilty, so there was no question of having to draw an adverse inference.[80]

The courts have wisely adopted a common sense view of when lies and guilt are indistinguishable from each other.[81] It suffices that the lie is not a separate matter from the main issue upon which the jury is invited to determine guilt.[82] In *Harron* there were conceivably a few innocent explanations for the false alibi consistent with the accepted prosecution story that he was on the scene.[83] Nor did his lie cover all the elements of the offence; but the courts tend to focus on whether the lie was critical to his defence.[84] Strictly speaking, an alibi can be discounted as a lie as soon as the jury is certain that the defendant committed the actus reus. It might not yet have established beyond reasonable doubt the other elements necessary for guilt[85] but the dispute in *Harron* was a straightforward clash between the prosecution and defence. The issues of mens rea and defences were relatively unproblematic and were resolved almost automatically upon accepting the contentious point, that the accused had wielded the weapon in the circumstances described by the witnesses. The relationship between guilt and lies can be very stark in some cases where the resolution of a single issue determines the outcome, such as *R v Ball*,[86] where it was whether the defendant was the driver or passenger when charged with a motoring offence, or *R v Landon*,[87] where the only issue in dispute in a rape trial was that of consent.

Harron was a case in which guilt was probably determined by reference to the reliability of the prosecution's story rather than dubious nature of the defence's. Therefore, for the jury to leap from the fact that he lied to the conclusion that he was guilty would not entail 'a forbidden chain of reasoning', but this would be circular because it must already have concluded his guilt beyond reasonable doubt from the prosecution evidence. A jury cannot normally conclude that because the accused is wrong the prosecution version of events is necessarily correct, although an adverse inference from a lie can be used to support the prosecution case. There are some exceptional cases, however, in which the conclusion that the accused is lying really leaves the jury with little option but to accept the prosecution case and convict – the scenario advanced in *Dehar* and *Goodway*. A direction on lies is unnecessary, not for reasons of circularity but because it would be otiose. This time the trier of fact is moving in the opposite direction, from the conclusion that the accused is lying to the conclusion that he is guilty. It does not need to be reminded that there may be innocent reasons for lies because in these circumstances there can be none:

> 'Where the accused denies the crime, or makes some assertion whose truth is critical to his defence, it makes no sense to direct the jury that proof of a lie is not proof of guilt and that people may lie for innocent reasons, since in such a case once the jury are sure that the denial or other assertion *is* a lie, they are *ipso facto* sure of guilt; there is no room for a *Lucas* direction.'[88]

To be satisfied that the accused is lying[89] simply removes any doubt that the jury might have had about his guilt, or leaves the prosecution case as the only plausible version of events. The lie is not the foundation for the drawing of an adverse inference which bolsters the prosecution case, although the jury might feel more comfortable about convicting if it was used as evidence in that way. Such cases are relatively rare because the lie has to be established independently of the prosecution's case (otherwise it is a case of circularity) and, moreover, the rejection of the defence must leave the jury with little alternative but to accept the prosecution's version of events. Examples again include classic situations in the law of evidence where the difference between questions going to credit and questions going to the issue are reduced to vanishing point.[90] Thus if the jury is absolutely certain that the defendant is lying about consent on a charge of rape (*Landon*), or that he is lying about not being the driver of the car when charged with a motoring offence (*Ball*) and there is no other point of dispute, the defendant must be guilty. The case of *R v Barsoum*[91] is another example of this type. It is worth giving a brief account of some of the facts of the case in order to understand the reasoning process that should be adopted in assessing whether the accused's assertion has any evidential value to the prosecution or the jury. It will later be argued that this analysis is capable of being extended to a small group of s 34 cases where a parallel problem arises.

Barsoum was prepared to plead guilty to simple possession of drugs but was convicted of possession with intent to supply. The police arrested an individual outside a flat where he had just bought some cocaine.[92] When they attempted to enter the flat, the door was slammed shut and the police had to break it down. When they gained entry they discovered that it contained various drug-dealing paraphernalia. They searched the appellant and found a large amount of cash and some cocaine in his pockets, and a man who was tried as a co-accused (and acquitted of the only count with which he was charged) with a prostitute in another room. In his defence the appellant claimed that the flat was not his and that he had only been there in order to fix the central heating.[93] While admitting possession, Barsoum denied having any intention to supply drugs to anyone else. He claimed that the door had been slammed, though not by him, in order to allow another man, named Michael, who was the dealer, to escape from the back of the building. The purchaser of the drugs testified that the accused had sold the cocaine to him and so either he or Barsoum must have been lying on this central issue. The Court of Appeal confirmed that a direction on lies was unnecessary in these circumstances and that if Michael had been present the appellant was entitled to be acquitted.[94] If Michael was an invention, then it automatically followed from the rejection of his explanation that the appellant must be guilty.[95]

It has been demonstrated that where the issues of lying and guilt are inextricably intertwined any direction on lies is unnecessary. Guilt will be established either on the basis of the prosecution evidence or from the rejection of the defence. To give the jury a direction on lies would be confusing and add complexity,[96] since it might encourage the jury to engage in unnecessary circular reasoning or to draw adverse inferences which should be bypassed in favour of a direct finding of guilt. One should be careful, however, not to over-generalise about the circumstances in which a *Lucas* direction is unnecessary, as happened in the recent decision of *R v Middleton*.[97] The Court of Appeal called for the purpose of giving a *Lucas* direction to be analysed in the context of the individual case. While this is laudable, it is respectfully submitted that the court went too far in asserting that a *Lucas* direction was 'inherently unlikely' to be appropriate where the jury might conclude that the defendant told them lies in his evidence.[98] In many cases this might indeed be adequately covered by general directions of law on the burden and standard of proof, but *Lucas* itself was concerned with the danger of testimonial lies being used by the jury in an inappropriate fashion.[99] The ambit of its remarks is unclear and, on the facts of the case, any lies would have been collateral in nature, rather than falling within the *Dehar* and *Goodway* exception.[100] Thus a *Lucas* direction should have been given even though the prosecution's case was relatively strong. Although the Court of Appeal emphasised that it was not attempting to reformulate principle or undermine existing authorities, the case of *Middleton* casts unnecessary doubt over a relatively clear and sensible aspect of the law relating to lies.

(b) Circularity in the context of s 34

The case law which has developed around lies that cannot be proved independently of establishment of the prosecution case may also be pertinent to one problem which has arisen in relation to silence under s 34 of the CJPOA, although the parallels between the two situations have not been the subject of judicial comment. It first arose in *R v Mountford*,[101] the facts of which are not dissimilar from those in *Barsoum*. In the execution of a search warrant the police entered a flat belonging to one Williams, where the appellant was also staying. Only the appellant and Williams were present when the police came in and the flat was full of drug-dealing apparatus and signs that they were in current use. The appellant was seen to drop a package from one of the windows which, when recovered, was found to contain heroin. The s 34 point arose because the defendant, who had given a 'no comment' interview, now claimed at his trial for possession with intent to supply that Williams was the drug dealer and he was simply there to purchase drugs. Williams had thrown the package to him just as the police broke in. The defendant might have been expected to mention in interview the 'fact' that Williams was the dealer and his explanation for this failure was that he was trying to protect Williams; had he known that Williams accused him of being the dealer it would have made a 'big difference'[102] to whether or not he answered the police questions.

The Court of Appeal thought it difficult for the jury to reject his 'innocent explanation' without also rejecting the truth of the fact. Moreover, 'the fact' not revealed in interview was the central issue in the case – who was doing the dealing. It concluded, with impeccable logic, that:

> 'this element of circularity could only be resolved by a verdict founded not in any way upon the section 34 point but upon the other evidence in the case. A verdict of "guilty" would obviously establish "the fact" not mentioned was untrue and accordingly that the explanation for not mentioning it was equally untrue. In this case, as it seems to us, the evidence which resolved the section 34 issue was the very evidence which resolved the issue in the case and therefore determined the verdict. There was, in our judgment, no evidential basis upon which the section 34 issue could have been resolved as an independent issue in the case, thus permitting an ensuing adverse inference to be used as some additional support for the prosecution's case.'

Although *Mountford* was applied in *R v Gill*,[103] it has been the subject of academic criticism to the effect that the decision represents an unnecessary judge-made restriction upon the operation of s 34, and that the 'element of circularity' that concerned the Court of Appeal does not in fact exist.[104] The decision in *Mountford* has generally not been followed in the Court of Appeal.[105] At best, it might be said to be confined to its own very particular facts, but the judges now seem intent on eliminating it entirely. The Court of Appeal recently said in *Daly*[106] that it had difficulty following the reasoning in *Mountford*, and in *Gowland-Wynn*[107] Lord Woolf advocated that *Mountford* and *Gill* be 'consigned to oblivion'. The fate of *Mountford* has probably been sealed, but it is worth pausing to consider whether the attacks made upon it in the Court of Appeal were justified. It is suggested that the reasoning process applied in the counterpart lies cases provide support for the logical, step-by-step approach to the s 34 point advocated in *Mountford* itself. Moreover, the lies cases can assist us in defining the narrow factual situations over which *Mountford* could have governed without doing any serious harm to the utility of s 34.

It is striking how easily *Mountford* could have been argued as a lies case; the appellant might well have been lying when he testified that Williams was the dealer and had thrown the package of drugs to him. If the facts are changed so that Mountford raised this defence during interview, the s 34 question[108] evaporates. The issue of lying would have been almost identical to that in *Barsoum*, save that the existence and presence of the second person, the alleged dealer, was open to doubt in the latter case. If *Mountford* is viewed as a lie case on its original facts, the defendant's testimony at trial would certainly not have attracted a *Lucas* or *Goodway* warning. Either the jury could not have decided that his story of the other man being the dealer was a lie independently of accepting the prosecution case for guilt, or alternatively the defence could have been rejected,[109] leading inevitably to the conclusion that he was guilty of drug dealing.

The reasoning process in *Mountford* concerning the defence was characterised in similar terms in *Hearne* but the operation of s 34 may be slightly more circuitous and complicated. As was pointed out in *Hearne*, it is not the truth or otherwise of the fact which is the chief concern of the jury, so much as whether he could reasonably have been expected to mention it when interviewed. Thus any explanation for his silence advanced by the defence must be scrutinised by the jury, which, if it rejects the excuse, may draw such inferences as are appropriate, probably that the fact relied upon is a recent invention and indeed false. In most situations the jury would go on to use that inference to bolster the prosecution case[110] but in *Mountford* itself resort to an adverse inference would be superfluous or circular.[111]

The element of circularity identified by *Mountford* has been denied by Munday,[112] but this rejection is founded upon a willingness to allow a jury to draw adverse inferences from silence, thus 'topping up' the prosecution's case, before it is certain beyond reasonable doubt that the accused had no innocent reason for not mentioning the fact earlier. The approach of Court of Appeal in *Mountford* is based on the assumption that each element of the s 34 test must be resolved before the next one is tackled. The crucial step in *Mountford* was to assess the validity of the innocent explanation for silence, which the court held could not be resolved independently of determining the prosecution case. The Court of Appeal in *Daly*[113] asserts that nothing in the wording of the statute requires that the s 34 issue be capable of resolution as a separate issue in the case.[114] This is so, but if the jury cannot decide whether the defendant could reasonably have been expected to mention the fact at the time, it is preferable for it not to proceed to draw an adverse inference from his silence.

Birch also suggests that s 34 permits the jury simply to treat such silence as a provisionally suspicious fact and add it to the other evidence, but does not regard this approach as entirely satisfactory. Nor is it; the task of the jury is a highly complex one, whereas *Mountford* advises the jury to forget about s 34 and abandon any attempt to draw an adverse inference. Nothing much may be lost. Since the conflict between the two sides is fundamental and stark, it is unlikely that applying the *Daly* approach to s 34 would enable the jury to eliminate the last vestiges of doubt and thus push the prosecution's case over the line. If the sides are evenly balanced, it is difficult to imagine that any adverse inference that the jury could provisionally draw would be sufficiently strong to have any discernible effect on the outcome.

Now that two possible styles of reasoning under s 34 have been described, and a case made for the 'step-by-step' approach of *Mountford* over the more generally advocated one of 'topping up', parallels can be drawn with the position regarding evidence of lies. It was mentioned earlier in[115] that only a few years before *Mountford* the High Court of Australia in *Edwards v R*[116] had addressed concerns that the *Lucas* direction entailed a similar element of circularity. The majority view in *Edwards* was that a jury can treat the defendant's lie as exhibiting consciousness of guilt even if it has not been proved beyond reasonable doubt. This is consistent with the approach advocated by Munday and Birch, as well as the Court of Appeal in *Daly*. In England, however, the requirement laid down in *Burge and Pegg* that no adverse inference may be drawn from a lie which has not first been proved beyond reasonable doubt, may face review in the light of the attacks on the *Mountford* style of reasoning. This restriction may, however, survive given that the *Lucas* direction is to a large extent protective of the accused and seeks to limit the use that can be made of evidence of lies.

The judicial reaction to *Mountford* is understandable, particularly the anxiety that it should not be extended so as to defeat the intended width of s 34 and that the provision should have a pivotal role in cases such as this, where there has been a failure to mention a fact which implies complete innocence. It should be remembered, though, that *Mountford* is a very unusual case in that neither the fact relied upon at trial nor the innocent explanation for it not being mentioned in interview could be resolved independently of the issue of guilt. If it were to survive, *Mountford*'s area of operation should be confined to a distinct, easily identifiable and narrow subset of cases, where the truth of the explanation for the silence, or the fact relied upon, or perhaps even both these issues, cannot be resolved independently of the issue in the case.

(c) What is a lie? What is silence?

There is little discussion in the cases of what a lie actually is, though two prerequisites for drawing an adverse inference mean that the untruth must be deliberate and relate to a material issue. Despite the attempts of the Court of Appeal in *Lucas* and *Burge and Pegg* to define the situations in which a jury direction will normally be required, the boundary of lying remains undefined. A purposive approach is of limited use. A court can identify circumstances in which there is a danger that the jury may draw an unjustifiable inference that the accused was implicated in the offence from the fact that he has lied, but the question remains: when is it open to the jury to find that he has lied on a material matter?[117] No court seems to have determined whether telling the truth, but not the whole truth, is something which a jury might construe as a lie.[118] For instance, if a suspect in a murder that was committed around midnight says that he left the person in question alive and well at 10.00 pm, and fails to mention that he saw him again at 11.00 pm, this would probably be a lie if he had specifically been asked the last time he saw the deceased alive.[119] If he was not asked that question, his statement to the police, though accurate in itself, seems calculated to deceive and is thus suspicious, even if his story at trial is that the victim was still alive when he finally left at 11.15 pm. The prosecution would probably argue that this second version amounts to a fact later relied upon under s 34. Because a s 34 direction highlights the discrepancies in the two statements, it might become desirable for the judge to add a *Lucas* direction.[120] At some point lying must abut or overlap behaviour encompassed by s 34. While that provision may have been inspired by the classic 'no comment' interview, it is not concerned with silence per se but with the failure to mention something later relied upon, which can occur if the accused lies and later changes his story. If a lie can be created only and entirely by words uttered by the defendant, then complete silence in interview does not have the potential to trigger a *Lucas* direction.

The absence of such issues in the law reports[121] may be attributable to the practice of the Crown identifying specific statements which it relies upon as lies,[122] and the judge considering with counsel, before speeches and summing up, whether, in the instant case, a *Lucas* direction is required, and if so, how it should be formulated.[123] This should weed out evidence incapable of bearing the construction of a lie. Things are more likely to go wrong if the trial judge errs in not giving a *Lucas* direction at all. It is submitted that *R v Rodrigues*[124] is an example of this type of error. The prosecution relied upon two discrepancies in the evolution of the appellant's defence that were straightforward candidates for a direction on lies. For example, he gave a different alibi at interview from the one relied upon at trial. Despite this, nowhere in the summing up did the judge give a *Lucas* direction or any direction to the jury as to the way to approach the possibility that they might conclude at one time or another that the appellant had told lies. This was particularly unfortunate because the prosecution also highlighted a third discrepancy which, it is submitted, should not have been presented to the jury as a potential lie. The appellant was interviewed on suspicion of having tampered with the brakes of his ex-wife's car, their unhappy marriage having ended in an acrimonious divorce. The appellant was asked to account for the fact that his ex-wife said she had found his business card with his handwriting on it on her driveway around the time of the offence. The appellant said she might have obtained the card from the rubbish outside his restaurant or from his pocket, whereas he testified at trial that he thought she had taken it from his car when it was broken into. On appeal the defence contended that the appellant was not lying but simply guessing at explanations as to where his ex-wife might have obtained the business card.[125] The Court of Appeal does not explore the matter further but it is certainly arguable that he was simply speculating, in which case the changes in his explanations were unimportant. If he were innocent, he could hardly be expected know how the card had come into his ex-wife's possession and indeed all his suggestions might be untrue. The more difficult issue is whether it was open for the jury to conclude that they were certain that he was lying. This surely turns not on the changes in his evidence but on whether he knew at the time that his various explanations were false and therefore lies rather than mere speculation. This consciousness would most probably spring from the realisation or fear that he had actually dropped the card while tampering with her car. In this case, as in many others, the fact that the accused was lying could probably be established only in retrospect through the jury returning a verdict of guilty based on the other evidence in the case.

(d) Combining silence directions and Lucas *directions in the same case*

It may be ironic, but it would seem that the introduction of s 34 is a significant new cause of the telling of lies by suspects during police interview. A recent Home Office study on the impact of the Criminal Justice and Public Order Act 1994[126] records the increase in 'the flannel factor' and illustrates it with striking quotations from police officers:

> 'Well, I would say that there has been a vast change in the number of people who normally remain quiet in interview – it has in the main diminished statistically. What we tend to get now is a pack of lies, given as an explanation initially as opposed to people saying "no reply" to every question.
>
> They always give you a story now, they always give you a story no matter how cock-and-bull it is. In fact they probably lie a little better now, instead of saying "no comment".'

What these suspects can discover if they are brought to trial is that their tactics have badly misfired, with the Crown seeking to make use not only of their failure to mention a fact now relied upon in their defence, but also their proven out of court lies.[127] It can only be a matter of time before a defendant gives as an innocent explanation for lying to the police that he thought this a better thing to do than remaining silent. After all, suspects are not expressly cautioned that their lies may later be used in evidence against them. On the other hand, one popular reason given for not answering questions during interview, that the defendant was acting on legal advice given in good faith,[128] is unlikely to be advanced in the case of a lie.

The Court of Appeal has held that a direction under s 34 can be combined with a *Lucas* direction as to lies,[129] and while their precise terms may require some thought and input from counsel, this does not pose intrinsic problems where the evidence relates to different matters in the case. But where the line of defence changes over time, perhaps in response to developments in the police investigation, the prosecution may rely on the same response in interview as both a lie and a failure to mention a fact when he might reasonably have been expected to do so. In these circumstances, a misdirection on one issue may be amplified by the presence of the other direction. Thus in *Rodrigues*[130] the Court of Appeal said that the failure of the trial judge to give the jury the guidance of a *Lucas* direction in relation to inconsistencies in what the appellant said at interview and his evidence in the witness box was aggravated by a s 34 direction on the same matter which further highlighted these discrepancies to the jury. Some mention should be made of the overlap between lies and the accused's failure to give evidence in court. The Court of Appeal in *R v Napper*[131] has held that there is nothing inconsistent with the *Lucas* direction in the standard direction on silence at trial under s 35 approved in *Cowan.* As a consequence, the trial judge was correct to warn the jury not to hold lies against the defendant if they thought there was a possibility of an innocent explanation. But if they thought that his failure to give evidence in court was to be explained only on the basis that he could not give an innocent explanation for the lies, then it was open to them to draw such an adverse inference under s 35.[132]

(e) Silence and lies directions arising from a single response

The potentially close relationship between *Lucas* and s 34 directions is best illustrated by the case of *R v O.*[133] The defendant was convicted of the rape of his stepdaughter, who had become pregnant. He said in his police interview that he had never had sexual intercourse her.[134] When he testified he said that he had had consensual intercourse with the girl once, some weeks later than alleged by her, a time which could well have caused the pregnancy. He explained that at interview he was being asked about, and had therefore confined his answers to, the earlier period of time. The Court of Appeal upheld the conviction and the judge's decision to give both sets of directions. It held that it was for the jury to determine whether the accused had lied. This would seem the less difficult question of the two. Blood tests established that he had had intercourse with his stepdaughter, and his assertion that he had never had sexual intercourse with her was inconsistent with any assertion that he was confining his responses to the weeks under investigation. Unless he had forgotten that they had had intercourse or not realised that it had taken place, through drunkenness perhaps, his denial could be treated as a lie.[135] The jury would then have to decide in effect whether he lied because he had raped her, ruling out the possibility that he lied in a misguided attempt to avoid trouble with her mother or the police.

As to the s 34 point, while it was fairly clear that the accused was now relying upon the consensual nature of the intercourse, the question for the jury was whether he might reasonably have been expected to mention this matter during an interview concerning a rape which had apparently occurred at least a fortnight earlier. Leng[136] contends that s 34 has been used to impose a normative standard on suspects, namely that people being interviewed by the police should normally answer questions. It puts pressure on suspects to speak in interview, and breach of the norm is informally sanctioned by the drawing of adverse inferences. He further suggests that there is an ambiguity in the phrasing of the s 34 reasonable expectation test. The reasonableness of an expectation[137] can be assessed normatively or by reference to what usually happens, although he acknowledges that the latter approach has not been generally accepted. Applying these two approaches to s 34 to the facts of *O*, he suggests that the jury might conclude that O could have been expected to mention the fact that he had slept with the girl because interviewees should be expected to answer questions. If the jury adopts an expectation of normality, and it decides that many men in O's position would not have told the police that they had had sex with their stepdaughter, or might simply not want to supply any information to the police, then they might conclude that O could not have been expected to mention the intercourse.

Perhaps people ought generally not to lie in police interviews, and it may be that many of them would resort to lies in the circumstances confronting the suspect in *O*. The operation of the *Lucas* direction, however, is not normative in the ways identified by Leng with regard to s 34. Any values a jury might hold about people not lying in interviews have probably been violated at the point at which the *Lucas* direction begins. The precondition for drawing an adverse inference from lies is that the jury is satisfied that he did not lie for a reason which does not denote guilt. It cannot dismiss the possibility of an innocent explanation for this behaviour on normative grounds, that they expected O not to deny the fact of intercourse because interviewees should tell the truth. The task of the jury under s 34 is to decide whether the defendant's behaviour at interview met a statutorily prescribed expectation of reasonableness when he did not mention a fact that he later relied upon. One might add that although adverse inferences can be drawn from lies, this is less of an informal sanction for breaching the norm than is the case with s 34. The prospect of a later *Lucas* direction does not put as much pressure on suspects not to lie in the police station because they are not specifically warned of this possibility. Moreover, while the defence never complains about the absence of a s 34 direction,[138] it frequently appeals on the ground that a *Lucas* direction should have been given, because it can be helpful to its cause that the jury is reminded that people lie for reasons unconnected with guilt.

To conclude, while many parallels can be drawn between silence and lies as evidence against the accused, the distinctive characters of the *Lucas* direction and s 34 should not be overlooked, nor the impact of the caution upon the suspect's decision to remain silent. In cases where the lie or silence at interview relates to a crucial element of the accused's later defence, it seems natural to hold this against him, but in those rare instances where it cannot be distinguished from the ultimate issue in the case, this temptation is better resisted.

NOTES

1 The academic literature is similarly extensive. On lies, see Heydon 'Can Lies Corroborate?' (1973) 89 LQR 552; Mathias 'Lies Directions' [1995] NZLJ 307; Palmer 'Guilt and the Consciousness of Guilt: the Use of Lies, Flight and Other "Guilty Behaviour" in the Investigation and Prosecution of Crime' (1997) 21 MULR 95. On silence, see Birch 'Suffering in Silence: A Cost-Benefit Analysis of Section 34 of the Criminal Justice and Public Order Act 1994' [1999] Crim LR 769; Greer 'The Right to Silence: A Review of the Current Debate' (1990) 53 MLR 709; Jackson 'The Right to Silence: Judicial Responses to Parliamentary Encroachment' (1994) 57 MLR 270; Mirfield *Silence, Confessions and Improperly Obtained Evidence* (1997); Pattenden 'Inferences from Silence' [1995] Crim LR 602; 'Silence: Lord Taylor's Legacy' (2001) 2 E&P 141.

2 *R v Middleton* [2001] Crim LR 251, Lexis. Five years earlier it had said that appeals on lie directions had reached epidemic proportions: *R v Hill* [1996] Crim LR 419, Lexis.

3 Birch [1999] Crim LR 769 at 782–786.

4 *Murray v United Kingdom* (1996) 22 EHRR 29; Youth Justice and Criminal Evidence Act 1999, s 58. This will require the reintroduction of the old-style caution in situations where the suspect has requested but not yet received legal advice.

5 The jury's rejection of a person's account does not necessarily entail a finding that it is a lie.

6 This was described as a 'run of the mill case' in *R v Burge and Pegg* [1996] 1 Cr App Rep 163 at 172.

7 At its most extreme, it could be argued that the defendant simply pleading not guilty raises the question of lying.

8 *R v Burge and Pegg* [1996] 1 Cr App Rep 163 at 173. This passage was relied upon by Lord Hobhouse in the Privy Council case of *Rahming v R* [2002] UKPC 23, [2002] All ER (D) 304 (May) at [12], though the reason for not giving a *Lucas* direction in that case does not seem compelling.

9 The common law is explicitly preserved by CJPOA, s 34(5).

10 The fourfold classification is adopted from *Cross and Tapper on Evidence* (9th edn, 1999) p 38.

11 *R v Christie* [1914] AC 545; *Hall v R* (1971) 55 Cr App Rep 108, PC; *Parkes v R* (1977) 64 Cr App Rep 25, PC. The common law is preserved by CJPOA, s 34(5)(b) and discussed by Mirfield 'Two Side-Effects of Sections 34 to 37 of the Criminal Justice and Public Order Act 1994' [1995] Crim LR 612.

12 See *R v Chandler* (1976) 63 Cr App Rep 1, which qualifies *Christie*. The parties were said to be on even terms because of the presence of the accused's solicitor.

13 *R v Tran* (2001) 150 CCC (3d) 481.

14 This use of silence, as distinct from an implied admission, was discussed by the High Court of Australia in *Woon v R* (1964) 109 CLR 529, 537.

15 *R v White* [1998] 2 SCR 72, 86.

16 *R v Tune* (1944) 29 Cr App Rep 162; *R v McNamara* (1988) 87 Cr App Rep 246.

17 *R v Leckey* [1944] KB 80.

18 See the lies case of *Zoneff v R* (2000) 172 ALR 1 at 19 per Kirby J, who prefers the more neutral phrase 'evidence of post-offence conduct' adopted by the Supreme Court of Canada in *R v White* [1998] 2 SCR 72 at 85.

19 [1934] 2 KB 408. See also *R v Whitehead* [1929] 1 KB 99; *R v Charavanmuttu* (1930) 22 Cr App Rep 1. Cf *R v Feigenbaum* [1919] 1 KB 431.

20 *R v Baskerville* [1916] 2 KB 658; *R v Beck* [1982] 1 WLR 461.

21 *R v Ryan* (1967) 50 Cr App Rep 144, specifically rejected in *R v Gilbert* (1977) 66 Cr App Rep 237 at 244.

22 *R v Ryan* (1964) 50 Cr App Rep 144 at 148.

23 Thus reversing *R v Gilbert* (1977) 66 Cr App Rep 237. The Act also allows the prosecution to comment on the accused's silence.

24 Birch [1999] Crim LR 769, 775; Dennis 'Silence in the Police Station: the Marginalisation of s 34' [2002] Crim LR 25, 33; Judicial Studies Board specimen direction on s 34, n 12.

25 *R v Condron* [1997] 1 Cr App Rep 185, 197.

26 *R v Daniel* [1998] 2 Cr App Rep 373; *R v Beckles and Montague* [1999] Crim LR 148, Lexis. Another possibility is that the defendant is unwilling to reveal the details of his defence to the police for fear that they will try to tamper with his witness.

27 [1999] Crim LR 769, 774.

28 *Silence, Confessions and Improperly Obtained Evidence* (1999) p 272; [1995] Crim LR 612, 615–617.

29 Leng 'Silence Pretrial, Reasonable Expectations and the Normative Distortion of Fact-Finding' (2001) 5 E&P 240, 243–244.

30 See Mirfield *Silence, Confessions and Improperly Obtained Evidence* (1997) p 315; Pattenden (2001) 2 E&P 141, 162.

31 CJPOA, s 38. The jury should be so directed (*R v Abdullah* [1999] 3 Arch News 3), and also that it must find a prima facie case made out before considering an inference from silence (*R v Gill* [2001] 1 Cr App Rep 160).

32 *Murray v United Kingdom* (1996) 22 EHRR 29 at 60.

33 Pattenden [1995] Crim LR 602 at 607.

34 In the context of lies, see Kirby J's remarks in *Zoneff v R* (2000) 172 ALR 1 at 18 and also *R v Hill* [1996] Crim LR 419, Lexis.

35 *Petty and Maiden v R* (1991) 173 CLR 95 at 105, per Brennan J; and cf Dawson J at 120.

36 (1991) 173 CLR 95 at 100–101 per Mason, Deane, Toohey and McHugh JJ.

37 Under s 34 the issue of credibility is directly concerned with the weight to be placed on evidence relating to the matter which was not mentioned in interview; the defendant may choose not testify.

38 See *Edwards v R* (1993) 178 CLR 193.

39 Here the falsehood need not be deliberate. The witness's credibility would still be affected if the lie could be attributed simply to inaccuracy or forgetfulness.

40 The trial judge may require the prosecutor to clarify the way in which the lies should be used by the jury. See JSB specimen direction No 27: Defendant's Lies to the Police and Others. See also *Zoneff v R* (2000) 172 ALR 1 at 22 and *Osland v R* (1998) 159 ALR 170 at 182.

41 *R v Goodway* [1993] 4 All ER 894 at 900–902; *R v Landon* [1995] Crim LR 338, Lexis; *R v Smith* [1995] Crim LR 305, Lexis. Cf *R v Tucker* [1994] Crim LR 683, Lexis, where, exceptionally, there was a risk that the jury might think the accused was guilty because he had lied, and *Zoneff v R* (2000) 172 ALR 1. There the trial judge had mentioned the possibility of lies constituting evidence of consciousness of guilt when this had not been raised by the Crown.

42 *R v Burge and Pegg* [1996] 1 Cr App Rep 163 at 173.
43 Or an important witness in the accused's case as in *R v Ball* [2001] EWCA Crim 3037, [2001] All ER (D) 54 (Dec), Lexis.
44 *Zoneff v R* (2000) 172 ALR 1, 21.
45 Commentary on *R v Smith* [1995] Crim LR 940; *R v Middleton* [2001] Crim LR 251.
46 [1964] AC 441, 21.
47 (1981) 73 Cr App Rep 159.
48 [1993] 4 All ER 894.
49 The passage relates to out of court lies as corroboration, but a lie told in court may also provide corroboration and be the subject of a *Lucas* direction: *R v Lucas* (1981) 73 Cr App Rep 159 at 163; *Edwards v R* (1993) 178 CLR 193 at 200.
50 [1996] 1 Cr App Rep 163 at 173.
51 Where the lie is relied upon as corroboration or as support, *Lucas* requires that the lie must be established by evidence other than that of the witness who is to be corroborated.
52 As in *R v Robinson* [1996] Crim LR 417.
53 [1996] 1 Cr App Rep 163 at 174.
54 This in itself raises the interesting question of which of two inconsistent statements should be regarded as a lie.
55 See also *R v Goodway* [1993] 4 All ER 894 at 900 and *R v Richens* (1994) 98 Cr App Rep 43 at 51. The JSB specimen direction lists further innocent explanations for lies and its notes acknowledge that this aspect of the direction may need to be modified depending on the circumstances of the case.
56 (2001) 2 E&P 141, 154.
57 *R v Cowan* [1996] QB 373 at 386.
58 Cf the approach advocated by Greer in (1990) 57 MLR 729 at 730.
59 [1996] QB 373 at 383. This is also the case with defence explanations for lies which are not underpinned by prosecution or defence evidence: *R v Bateson* (1991) Times, 10 April 1991, Lexis. See Pattenden (2001) 2 E&P 141, 157.
60 This topic will be discussed later.
61 In fact it encompasses a disparate group of immunities: see *R v Director of the Serious Fraud Office, ex p Smith* [1993] AC 1 at 30–31. Although the right to silence is not expressly mentioned in the European Convention, the European Court of Human Rights has recognised it as an important aspect of art 6. See *Murray v United Kingdom* (1996) 22 EHRR 29; *Condron v United Kingdom* (2000) 31 EHRR 1.
62 Pattenden (2001) 2 E&P 141, 154 points out that the accused is formally cautioned about the consequences of remaining silent but not of lying. This difference can never be entirely eliminated, since lies probative of guilt may be told other than in court or during police interview.
63 Bucke, Street and Brown *The Right of Silence: the Impact of the Criminal Justice and Public Order Act 1994* Home Office Research Study 199 (2001) p 35.
64 In *R v Richens* (1994) 98 Cr App Rep 43 the accused's lies could have been attributed to consciousness that he had committed manslaughter following provocation rather than murder. Where the only issue is provocation, the Court of Appeal in *R v Taylor* [1998] Crim LR 822 suggests that the jury be told that the accused's lies can support the prosecution case only if it were certain that the lies were told to conceal the fact that he had murdered the victim, rather than merely to conceal his connection with the death. The risk of circular reasoning in these circumstances is apparent.
65 *Zoneff v R* (2000) 172 ALR 1 at 18; Mathias [1995] NZLJ 307, 308.
66 *Edwards v R* (1993) 178 CLR 193 at 199.
67 (1993) 178 CLR 193 at 209–210.
68 [1996] 2 Cr App Rep 457, [1996] Crim LR 581, applying *R v House and Meadows* (8 March 1994, unreported), CA.
69 *R v Goodway* [1993] 4 All ER 894 at 902.
70 *R v Dehar* [1969] NZLR 763 at 765; *R v Goodway* [1993] 4 All ER 894 at 901; *R v Landon* [1995] Crim LR 338; *R v Barsoum* [1994] Crim LR 194, Lexis; *R v House and Meadows* (8 March 1994, unreported); *R v Higgins* (1995) Times, 11 August, Lexis; *R v Patrick* [1999] 6 Archbold News 4, Lexis; *R v Quang Van Bui* [2001] EWCA Crim 1, Lawtel; *R v Mourot* [2002] EWCA Crim 1517, Lexis; Judicial Studies Board direction on lies.
71 *R v Burge and Pegg* [1996] 1 Cr App Rep 163. Both *R v Harron* and *R v Patrick* were alibi cases.
72 Ie a lie concerning a something not directly relevant to the issue in the case. Cases held not to fall within the so-called *Dehar* exception include *R v Wood* [1995] Crim LR 154, Lexis; *R v Gordon* [1995] Crim LR 306, Lexis; *R v Holman* [1995] Crim LR 80, Lexis; *R v Genus* [1996] Crim LR 502, Lexis and *R v Rodrigues* [2001] EWCA Crim 444.
73 As in *R v Rodrigues*, where the accused gave two different versions of his alibi in a situation where even if the Crown proved that the alibi was not established, it would not necessarily prove the guilt of the appellant.

74 (1995) Times, 11 August, Lexis.
75 Although the jury need not have decided that the appellant was lying.
76 Birch commentary [1996] Crim LR 581, 583.
77 Had the witnesses been independent, they could have corroborated each other.
78 If the jury had been less certain of the identification evidence, it could not have used a fairly strong suspicion that the accused was lying to bolster the prosecution case and so bring it up to the standard of proof because this too would amount to circular self-corroboration. The accused would have had to be acquitted in these circumstances.
79 The burden of proof lay on the prosecution to disprove the appellant's alibi.
80 And for the jury to leap from the fact that he lied to the conclusion that he was guilty would not entail 'a forbidden chain of reasoning' because it must already have concluded guilt from the prosecution evidence.
81 Thus in *R v Patrick* (18 March 1999) Lexis, the Court of Appeal 'had no hesitation' in agreeing with the trial judge's comment that, if the appellant had been correctly identified by a witness, thus destroying his alibi as regards the time of the fire, they might feel sure that the person who was around the house at 10.30pm was the same person who set fire to the pigeon loft some hours later.
82 *R v Higgins* (1995) Times, 11 August.
83 If H had been at the night club, he could not have lied out of embarrassment at being in an awkward third location, perhaps with his mistress or robbing a bank. Perhaps he felt that a defence of being present but not the attacker was less believable than claiming to be uninvolved by virtue of being elsewhere altogether. Alternatively, it is conceivable that his being at the night club could in itself have been sufficiently embarrassing (for reasons other than guilt) to cause him to lie as to his whereabouts. There are a variety of 'innocent' explanations for a false alibi in the *Harron* situation. The function of the lie may be to *bolster* a weak but true defence (such as H's non-involvement in the glassing though being present at the scene). Alternatively, a defendant may use the lie as a *stronger substitute* for what he fears will be seen by the jury as a weak defence, even though it is actually true (eg that the glassing was attributable to duress, automatism, accident or self-defence).
84 As in *R v Quang Van Bui* [2001] EWCA Crim 1, paras [27]–[30]. It is interesting to note in that case that the Court of Appeal appeared to use the same test in order decide there was no room for a *Lucas* direction, and that a direction under s 34 of CJPOA had been appropriate. In both cases it distinguished between assertions collateral and essential to the defence, but this is too stringent a test for whether the accused has relied upon a fact for the purposes of s 34.
85 Once it gets to that stage, and probably at some point before, it would become apparent to the jury that the only reason H lied is because he was conscious of his guilt.
86 [2001] EWCA Crim 3037, [2001] All ER (D) 54 (Dec), Lexis.
87 [1995] Crim LR 338.
88 *R v Quang Van Bui* [2001] EWCA Crim 1.
89 Which does not entail first accepting the prosecution case – the sheer implausibility of the defence might suffice.
90 *Cross and Tapper on Evidence* (9th edn, 1999) p 313.
91 [1994] Crim LR 194, Lexis.
92 The Court of Appeal held that as someone involved in drug dealing, if not an accomplice, his evidence should have been the subject of a judicial warning. There was, however, quite a lot of evidence against the accused.
93 This was somewhat implausible, as the only suitable tool found in the flat was a pair of pliers.
94 It is conceivable that the untraceable Michael could have been present but Barsoum still been the dealer.
95 The Court of Appeal assumes that the other man in the flat with Barsoum, found with a prostitute, could not have been the dealer.
96 Where a *Lucas* direction is required in relation to the evidence of two co-defendants, some form of direction in the case of a third co-defendant whose alleged lies are very much more closely related to the issues at the centre of the case may be unavoidable: *R v Burley* [2001] EWCA Crim 731, [2001] All ER (D) 262 (Mar).
97 [2001] Crim LR 251, Lexis. *Middleton* was subsequently endorsed in *R v Ogundipe* [2001] EWCA Crim 2576, [2001] All ER (D) 313 (Nov) and *R v Barnett* [2002] EWCA Crim 454, Lexis.
98 The danger being that to give a *Lucas* direction to the jury about lies told by the defendant in his evidence will often be circular and therefore confusing. This danger is undoubtedly a real one, discussed in the introductory section of this article and acknowledged in leading cases such as *R v Burge and Pegg* [1996] 1 Cr App Rep 163 at 173. Nevertheless, in some circumstances, a jury could reason inappropriately from testimonial lies if a *Lucas* direction were not given.

99 As corroboration in circumstances where the defendant's lie had not been established by independent evidence. See above n 49 and accompanying text. This use of lies falls within category (2) of the Court of Appeal's account in *Burge and Pegg* of when a *Lucas* direction is normally required. There may be a possibility in these circumstances that, even though the prosecution does not also seek to rely upon that lie as evidence of guilt (*Burge and Pegg*'s category (3)) the judge envisages that there is a real danger that the jury may do so (category (4)).
100 Neither these nor any of the related cases were cited, the Court of Appeal remaining true to its own advice in not 'laboriously trailing through hosts of reported and unreported cases and learned commentaries'. Cf *R v Barnett* [2002] EWCA Crim 454.
101 [1999] Crim LR 575, Lexis.
102 The implication is that he would have told the police in interview that Barsoum was the dealer, thus eliminating any issue under s 34.
103 [2001] 1 Cr App Rep 160 at 163–164. Its facts were almost identical to *Mountford* but the court's attention had not been drawn to the attack recently mounted on *Mountford* in *Hearne and Coleman.*
104 Munday [2002] 2 Archbold News 6, 7. See also Birch [1999] Crim LR 769, 777–778 and Dennis [2002] Crim LR 25, 31–32.
105 *R v Hearne and Coleman* (4 May 2000, unreported), Casetrack; *R v Milford* [2001] 2 All ER 609, Lexis; *R v Daly* [2001] EWCA Crim 2643, [2002] 2 Cr App Rep 201, Casetrack; *R v Gowland-Wynn* [2001] EWCA Crim 2715, [2002] 1 Cr App Rep 569, Casetrack.
106 [2001] EWCA Crim 2643, [2002] 2 Cr App Rep 201 at [10].
107 [2001] EWCA Crim 2715, [2002] 1 Cr App Rep 569 at [9].
108 Including the problematic point about whether there was an innocent explanation for delay.
109 The suspicion that it was a lie because of recent fabrication, which entails rejecting the explanation for the delay as a subsidiary lie.
110 *Hearne* and *Milford* were cases where the inference of recent invention did not lead inevitably to the conclusion of guilt.
111 A finding that the story was untrue meant that he was inevitably guilty of the offence. Alternatively, if they found that he was guilty of the offence, it inevitably followed that the explanation was untrue.
112 Munday [2002] 2 Archbold News 6, 7–8.
113 [2001] EWCA Crim 2643, [2002] 2 Cr App Rep 201 at [10].
114 A point made earlier by Birch in her commentary on *Mountford* in [1999] Crim LR 575. See also Munday [2002] Archbold News 6, 7 who argues that the CJPOA envisaged that a prosecution case calling for an answer could if necessary be 'topped up' to a level of proof beyond reasonable doubt by the addition of an adverse inference. This should apply in all categories of case, including the *Mountford* situation where the tribunal's rejection of the reason for not promptly mentioning a fact ineluctably leads to the rejection of the fact itself.
115 See n 66 above and accompanying text.
116 *Edwards v R* (1993) 78 CLR 193 at 199.
117 The explanation for *R v Adams* [1997] Crim LR 292, Lexis must lie elsewhere. The Court of Appeal concluded: 'it appears to us that the circumstances in which a defendant, with the benefit of legal advice, decides to serve an alibi notice which he knows to be false are so entirely different from the circumstances in which a defendant tells lies in interviews with police or others soon after an offence is committed that it is not necessary for a judge to give a jury a *Lucas* direction in relation to a false alibi if he or she considers it inappropriate in all the circumstances.'
118 But see *R v Hill* [1996] Crim LR 419, in which counsel contended that the jury ought to be given a general warning about lies where 'an accused person has told lies to the police or has omitted to tell the whole truth'.
119 See *R v O* [2000] Crim LR 617, Lexis.
120 *R v Rodrigues* [2001] EWCA 444, Lexis.
121 *Hksar v Mo Shiu Shing* [1998] HKCA 478 is a rare example of a court using a dictionary to define a lie, although the *New Shorter Oxford English Dictionary's* definition is simply 'an intentional false statement; an untruth'.
122 See the JSB specimen direction on lies.
123 The JSB direction contains a note to this effect based on *R v Burge and Pegg* [1996] 1 Cr App Rep 163.
124 [2001] EWCA 444.
125 In the context of s 34, it was said in *R v Milford* [2001] Crim LR 330 that the term 'fact' was to bear its normal dictionary meaning of something that is actually the case. It has been held not to include an explanation proffered at trial as a theory or a possibility: *R v Nickolson* [1999] Crim LR 61; *R v B(MT)* [2000] Crim LR 181. These cases were not cited in *Rodrigues* and the Court of Appeal said in that case: 'It may be that a s 34 direction could be given in relation to the appellant's evidence respecting the business card on the lines that even if the jury did not take the view that he was lying in the witness box they might take the view that his allegations against his

ex-wife that she had broken into his car in order to obtain his card was something that he might have mentioned to the police when he was being interviewed.'

126 Bucke, Street and Brown, Home Office Research Study 199 (2001).

127 These cases include *R v Kerr and Roulstone* (13 January 2000, unreported), Casetrack; *R v O* [2000] Crim LR 617, Lexis; *R v Quang Van Bui* [2001] EWCA Crim 1, Lawtel; *R v Rodrigues* [2001] EWCA 444; *R v Morgan* [2001] EWCA Crim 445, [2001] All ER (D) 363 (Feb), Lexis; *R v Walcott*; *R v Sylvester* [2002] EWCA Crim 1327, [2002] All ER (D) 517 (May) Lexis.

128 *R v Condron and Condron* [1997] 1 Cr App Rep 185; *R v Betts and Hall* [2001] EWCA Crim 224, [2001] 2 Cr App Rep 257. See Dennis [2002] Crim LR 25, 33–35.

129 *R v O* [2000] Crim LR 617.

130 *R v O* [2000] Crim LR 617.

131 *R v Napper* [1996] Crim LR 591.

132 An interesting combination of the *Lucas* approach to lies and adverse inferences drawn from the defendant's failure to give evidence in civil proceedings against him arose in *Francisco v Diedrick* (1998) Times, 3 April, Lexis. Both were used as evidence which supported the plaintiff's civil action that the defendant had murdered her daughter.

133 [2000] Crim LR 617.

134 DNA tests established paternity, but (the facts as reported are not entirely clear) this information seems not to have been available to the police at the time of interview. If the police had received the results but kept this a secret during the interrogation, it might be a matter for the judge's discretion under s 78 of the Police and Criminal Evidence Act 1984, though their silence might be distinguished from flagrant lying to the accused or his solicitor, as happened in *R v Mason* [1987] 3 All ER 481. As far as s 34 is concerned, it was stated in *R v Imran and Hussein* [1997] Crim LR 754 that the only obligation is that the police should not actively mislead the suspect; they do not have to present the whole of the evidence against the suspect prior to the interview.

135 Similarly, in *R v Walker* [2001] 2 NZLR 289 the accused, when confronted by the complainant's friends and in the course of police interview, maintained that there had been no act of intercourse. On trial for rape, he did not give evidence but mounted a defence of consent. This was held by the Court of Appeal, overruling the trial judge, to make him vulnerable to the conclusion that his out of court statements contained deliberate falsehoods.

136 (2001) 5 E&P 240, 245–247.

137 It is for the jury to resolve such factual preconditions such as whether the accused might reasonably have been expected to disclose the matter: *R v Argent* [1997] 2 Cr App Rep 27.

138 Perhaps it should, since its utility to the prosecution can be relatively minor and it is so often botched, to the defence's long-term advantage.

Approaches to similar fact evidence: England and Australia

C R Williams*

1 Introduction

Attempts over the past three decades to re-formulate the similar fact evidence rule have achieved little. A commentator is now tempted to look back with some nostalgia to the days when judges tended to do little more than repeat Lord Herschell's formulation of the rule in *Makin v A-G for New South Wales*,[1] and apply it often on the basis of intuition rather than analysis. This essay will seek to bring a greater measure of clarity to the nature of the conflict of principle that characterises the admissibility of similar fact evidence, and determine the manner in which the rule can most helpfully be formulated. Particular attention will be given to sexual offence cases. These cases raise in the strongest form the conflict between the desire of the prosecution to admit evidence often crucial to its case and of significant probative value and that of the defence to exclude evidence that may be of substantial if not damning prejudice.

2 Terminology

(a) Similar fact evidence

The expression 'similar fact evidence' is used to refer to all evidence which shows or tends to show that on some other occasion the accused acted in a way more or less similar to the way in which the prosecution alleges the accused acted on the occasion the subject of the present charge.[2] This definition adopts what is sometimes termed a 'disclosure' approach, rather than a more limited 'purpose' approach. The purpose approach is adopted in *Cross and Tapper on Evidence*, where the expression 'similar fact evidence' is limited to evidence which is tendered to show the bad disposition of the accused.[3] A wide definition focuses attention on the vice of similar fact evidence, which is its potential for prejudice. All evidence which shows that the accused performed broadly similar acts on other occasions possesses this potential for prejudice and is therefore brought within the expression.[4]

(b) Prejudice

The term 'prejudice' is here used in the sense adopted by Wigmore, that is:

> '(1) the over-strong tendency to believe the defendant guilty of the charge merely because he is a likely person to do such acts;
> (2) the tendency to condemn, not because he is believed guilty of the present charge, but because he has escaped unpunished from other offences; both of these represent the principle of undue prejudice.'[5]

The first form of prejudice noted by Wigmore is the danger that the jury may give similar fact evidence undue weight. The fact that the accused has acted similarly in the past almost always possesses some degree of relevance, but that relevance varies. There is, however, always the danger that the jury will adopt a simplistic line of reasoning to the effect that since the accused is prone to the commission of crimes similar to the one presently charged, he or she must on this occasion be guilty. The second form of prejudice noted by Wigmore refers to the risk that the jury may reason that the accused, even if not clearly shown to be guilty of the crime charged, none the less deserves to be punished. The Law Commission calls prejudice of the former kind 'reasoning prejudice', and prejudice of the latter kind 'moral prejudice'.[6]

Two further forms of prejudice or potential unfairness may also arise in the context of similar fact evidence. In cases where the truth of the similar facts is not admitted or clearly established, there is a danger that the jury's attention may be misdirected in focusing on the question of whether the similar facts have been proved and, if this question is answered adversely to the accused, the jury may then precipitately reach the conclusion that the instant offence is also proven. Finally, the very number of allegations of discreditable conduct may work to the disadvantage of the accused, particularly where the accused is charged on a number of counts, evidence of each one of which is admissible in respect of the others; a jury may reason that the accused must be guilty of some of the counts.[7]

(c) Probative force

The probative force of evidence is its weight, ie the extent to which it tends to render the inference it is led to establish more likely than would otherwise be the case. The problem of estimating the probative value of evidence is one that has received surprisingly little attention. Relevance and weight are generally treated as matters of common sense or experience both by judges and by academic commentators.[8] In this way the difficulties associated with what is in fact the key concept in the law of evidence are largely glossed over. It is, of course, impossible ever to estimate the probative value of evidence with any degree of exactitude. The degree of relevance possessed by an item of evidence is dependent upon an almost infinite number of variables. A number of the more crucial considerations may, however, be isolated.

The first factor is the extent to which the similar facts are themselves established by the evidence. In some cases they are clearly established. They may be admitted,[9] or they may have resulted in criminal convictions the correctness of which, if not expressly admitted, is at least not denied. In other cases the evidence which is led to establish the similar facts may be unreliable or insufficient.[10]

Secondly, regard must be had to the way in which it is sought to use the similar fact evidence. The more common form of reasoning in similar fact cases is along the following lines: 'the accused if shown to have committed the previous acts is more likely to have committed the act the subject of the present charge.'[11] In Australia, under the Evidence Act 1995 (Cth and NSW), evidence possessing this form of relevance is termed 'tendency evidence'.[12] In a number of cases, however, the line of reasoning takes the following quite different form: 'A number of similar transactions have occurred. Each of these transactions has involved the accused, and in respect of each the accused may or may not have committed a crime. The number of transactions involved, and/or their nature, however, suggests that in the absence of a remarkable coincidence the true explanation is criminal activity on the part of the accused.'[13] Under the Evidence Act 1995 (Cth and NSW) evidence possessing this form of relevance is termed 'coincidence evidence'.[14] It was reasoning of this form which was involved in *Makin*[15] below, where it was not established that the Makins had murdered any of the 12 other infants whose bodies were found in the grounds of premises occupied at various times by the Makins.[16] In general it would seem that in cases of this latter kind sufficient relevance to justify admissibility will only be established where the number of transactions involved is considerable, as in *Makin*, or where the innocent explanation itself smacks strongly of implausibility, as in the case of 'brides in the bath Smith'.[17]

Thirdly, the cogency of similar fact evidence may be affected by that which it is tendered to prove. If, for example, the evidence is tendered to prove the actus reus of the crime charged it may possess a quite low degree of probative value establishing no more than that the accused belongs to a class of persons likely to have committed the crime. If, however, it is tendered to prove the mens rea it may possess a high degree of probative value as negating the possibility of the accused having acted in such a way with an innocent intent.

(d) Relevance via propensity and relevance other than via propensity

Evidence is relevant via propensity if the chain of reasoning by which its relevance is demonstrated necessarily involves reaching a point at which it is asserted 'the accused is the sort of person likely to behave in this manner'. Relevance other than via propensity is reasoning that does not involve this step. The distinction may be illustrated by a simple example. Assume that the accused is charged with burglary. Evidence that the accused on some previous occasion broke into another house with intent to steal possesses relevance via propensity only. It shows no more than that the accused has a propensity for dishonesty or, at most, a propensity for burglary. Assume, however, that at the scene of the second burglary an article left by the burglar is found. Assume, further, that it is established that the article was taken from the first house which was burgled. When the facts are changed in this way, evidence that the accused committed the first burglary becomes relevant in a quite different way to show the accused committed the second burglary. The evidence now possesses relevance other than via propensity. The evidence is now relevant in the same sort of way as evidence that a wallet honestly acquired and belonging to the accused was discovered at the scene of the second burglary.

3 Approaches to similar fact evidence

Prior to the decision in *DPP v Boardman*,[18] the leading case on similar fact evidence was *Makin v A-G for New South Wales*.[19] The accused, a husband and wife, were charged with the murder of a baby. Its body was found buried in their garden, and they were proved to have agreed to adopt it in return for payment of a small sum by its parents. The defence of the accused was that the child had died through natural causes. The prosecution case was that the child had been killed by the Makins pursuant to a scheme whereby they took charge of infants in return for payments to be used in the infant's support, killed the infant and retained the sums paid. In support of this case the prosecution led evidence that the bodies of 12 other infants had been discovered in the grounds of premises occupied at various times by the Makins. The accused were convicted and appealed unsuccessfully to the Privy Council. Delivering the advice of the Privy Council, Lord Herschell LC stated:

> 'It is undoubtedly not competent for the prosecution to adduce evidence tending to shew that the accused has been guilty of criminal acts other than those covered by the indictment, for the purpose of leading to the conclusion that the accused is a person likely from his criminal conduct or character to have committed the offence for which he is being tried. On the other hand, the mere fact that the evidence adduced tends to show the commission of other crimes does not render it inadmissible if it be relevant to an issue before the jury, and it may be so relevant if it bears upon the question whether the acts alleged to constitute the crime charged in the indictment were designed or accidental, or to rebut a defence which would otherwise be open to the accused.'[20]

Over the next 80 years this statement was repeated in most of the cases on the subject, and its authority never doubted. The difficulty with Lord Herschell's formulation, however, is that it contains an internal logical contradiction which renders it unworkable.[21] The first sentence states a rule of exclusion. The second sentence states a rule of inclusion, but a rule of such width as to render the rule of exclusion of no effect. It is not possible to say that evidence of a particular class is inadmissible, and then to say that such evidence is admissible 'if it be relevant to an issue before the jury'. To be admissible any item of evidence must be relevant to an issue before the jury. If evidence relevant to an issue before the jury is to be admissible notwithstanding the rule of exclusion, then the rule of exclusion is of no effect.

One approach to the problem of giving a workable meaning to Lord Herschell's formulation is to treat the first sentence as containing a rule of exclusion and the second sentence as referring to classes of exception to the general rule. Although adopted in many of the older textbooks,[22] such an approach largely ignores the true factors that ought to determine whether an item of similar fact evidence should be admitted or rejected.

A more sophisticated approach focuses upon the distinction between relevance via propensity and relevance other than via propensity. If the evidence is relevant only via propensity, it is excluded by the first sentence of Lord Herschell's formulation. If the evidence possesses a relevance other than via propensity, it is admissible as falling within the second sentence of Lord Herschell's formulation. In such case the evidence is admissible notwithstanding that it also possesses relevance via propensity.[23] It is only if the evidence possesses no substantial relevance other than via propensity that it is inadmissible as falling within the first limb of Lord Herschell's formulation.[24]

The difficulty with an approach based upon the distinction between relevance via propensity and other relevance is that in many cases undoubtedly admissible similar fact evidence derives its only relevance from an argument via propensity. A particularly clear illustration is *R v Straffen*.[25] The accused was charged with the murder by manual strangulation of two little girls at Bath. He was found unfit to plead by reason of insanity, and committed to Broadmoor. A year later the accused escaped, and was at liberty for a period of approximately four hours. During the period the accused was at large a small girl, Linda Bowyer, was murdered by strangulation. The accused was seen near the place where the body was found, but there were other passers-by who might have committed the crime. When questioned by police the accused admitted killing the two girls at Bath but denied he was responsible for the murder of Linda Bowyer.

The accused was tried for the murder of Linda Bowyer. The trial judge admitted evidence of the statements made by the accused to the police, and also evidence of the circumstances surrounding the killing of the little girls at Bath. The following points of similarity existed between the two earlier killings and the killing of Linda Bowyer:

1. In each case the victim was a young girl.
2. Each of the children was killed by manual strangulation.
3. In no case was there any attempt at sexual interference or any apparent motive for the crime.
4. In no case was there any evidence of a struggle.
5. In no case was any attempt made to conceal the body, although that could easily have been done.

The accused was convicted, and appealed to the Court of Criminal Appeal. The court dismissed the appeal, holding that the similar fact evidence had been properly admitted. Clearly the court was correct. The evidence was of the highest possible probative value, and it would have been absurd to hold it inadmissible. The sole relevance of the evidence was, however, via propensity. The similar fact evidence established that the accused possessed a propensity of the most unusual kind; he was a strangler of small girls, in peculiar circumstances, and for no apparent motive. The unusual nature of the propensity gave the evidence its great probative value and rendered it admissible. *R v Straffen* is in no way highly unusual in this regard. In many cases the only relevance of undoubtedly admissible similar fact evidence is by virtue of an argument via propensity.[26]

A modified form of this approach recognises that there are many cases where evidence relevant solely via propensity is admissible, but none the less insists on the importance of the distinction. This is the approach taken in *Cross and Tapper on Evidence*.[27] Evidence which possesses a relevance other than via propensity is legally admissible but, because of its potential for prejudice may be rejected by the judge in the exercise of discretion. Evidence relevant solely via propensity is normally inadmissible, but may be admissible if it is of exceptional probative value. This analysis develops a framework by which the decided cases may be satisfactorily explained. If however evidence relevant other than via propensity may be rejected because of prejudice, and evidence relevant only via propensity may be received when it is of sufficient probative value, then it becomes difficult to see a persuasive reason for insisting upon the primacy of the distinction between relevance via propensity and relevance other than via propensity.

It is submitted that the preferable approach is to treat the balance between probative value and risk of prejudice in each case as the key to determining the admissibility of similar fact evidence. On such analysis, the question whether the evidence derives its relevance from an argument via propensity or from an argument other than via propensity is regarded as largely incidental. This approach involves treating Lord Herschell's formulation not as containing two conflicting rules, one of exclusion and one of inclusion, but rather as referring to two competing principles.[28] The first sentence refers to the principle that evidence which shows the accused to be of bad character or disposition is not admissible to establish guilt of the crime charged. The second sentence refers to the principle that relevant evidence that does not fall within a recognised rule of exclusion ought to be admitted. What Lord Herschell's formulation requires is that these two competing factors, the probative value of the evidence and the risk of prejudice, be weighed one against the other. If the risk of prejudice is great and the probative value small by comparison, the evidence should be rejected. If the probative value is great and the risk of prejudice slight by comparison, the evidence should be admitted.

4 Formulations of the similar fact rule

The decision of the House of Lords in *DPP v Boardman*[29] and that of the High Court of Australia in *Perry v R*[30] gave considerable support to the view that the *Makin* formulation involves a comparison of probative value and prejudice in the context of each particular case.[31] Such an approach gives frank recognition to the real issues involved in determining whether similar fact evidence is admissible, and leaves the judge with a wide measure of discretion in determining whether to admit similar fact evidence in particular cases.[32] Subsequent attempts at refinement, however, have left matters less straightforward.

(a) DPP v Boardman and Perry v R

In *DPP v Boardman*[33] the accused was convicted on one count of buggery with S, aged 16, and one count of buggery with H, aged 17. Both boys were pupils at a language school at which the accused was headmaster. Each of the boys gave evidence that the accused came to his dormitory late at night, and asked him to come with him for the purpose of homosexual intercourse. In each case the boy said the accused invited him to take the active role while he, the accused, assumed the passive. In each case the particular occasion to which the charge related was not the only incident affecting that boy. At the trial the judge directed the jury that the evidence of S on the count concerning him was admissible as corroborative evidence in relation to the count concerning H, and vice versa.[34] The accused appealed unsuccessfully, first to the Court of Appeal and then to the House of Lords.

Although their Lordships continued to insist that the rule to be followed is expressed adequately in the formulation of Lord Herschell in *Makin*, the decision in *DPP v Boardman* marked a significant change in judicial approach to the admissibility of similar fact evidence. Their Lordships declined to treat the issue as turning on whether the evidence fell within a recognised category of admissibility. Likewise, the majority of their Lordships declined to give significance to the question of whether the evidence was relevant solely via propensity or whether it possessed some relevance other than via propensity. Only Lord Hailsham continued to stress the primacy of this distinction.[35] Instead, perhaps more clearly than in any previous case, their Lordships treated the admissibility of similar fact evidence as turning solely upon a balancing of the probative value of the evidence against its potential for prejudice. Thus Lord Wilberforce stated:

> 'Whether in the field of sexual conduct or otherwise, there is no general or automatic answer to be given to the question whether evidence of facts similar to those the subject of a particular charge ought to be admitted. In each case it is necessary to estimate (i) whether, and if so how strongly, the evidence as to other facts tends to support, ie to make more credible, the evidence given as to the fact in question, (ii) whether such evidence, if given, is likely to be prejudicial to the accused. Both these elements involve questions of degree.'[36]

The House of Lords held that because of the 'striking similarity' in the accounts given by the boys S and H, the evidence of each boy was admissible in respect of the count relating to the other. Their Lordships did, however, have some reservations as to the sufficiency of the probative value of the evidence of the two boys.

Lord Wilberforce stated that the case, if regarded as an example, 'may be regarded as setting the standard of "striking similarity" too low'.[37] Lord Cross remarked that he regarded the case as very much a 'border-line' one.[38] The trial judge had taken the view that the fact that an adult had induced an adolescent boy to play the active, while he played the passive, part in the acts of buggery was itself a sufficiently unusual feature to justify the admission of the evidence. The majority of their Lordships declined to accept this view.[39] There was no evidence on the point presented, and the assumption that this was the more unusual form for such acts to take between a middle-aged man and an adolescent was pure speculation.[40] The majority held, however, that when the other similarities in the stories of the two boys, in particular the nocturnal visits of the accused to the dormitories, was added to the particular nature of the homosexuality of the accused, the evidence was sufficiently probative to be admissible.[41]

In *Perry v R*[42] the accused was tried in the Supreme Court of South Australia on two counts of attempting to murder Mr Perry, her third husband. The prosecution case was that she had administered poison to her husband with intent to kill him. Mr Perry had become seriously ill as a result of poisoning by lead and arsenic. The accused, who was living with him at the time, had the opportunity to administer the poison, and stood to benefit financially from his death under a number of policies of insurance. The defence was that Mr Perry had accidentally ingested the poison, possibly when he came in contact with rat or insect poison in the course of renovating some old musical instruments. Mr Perry himself gave evidence for the defence and asserted the innocence of his wife. The prosecution led evidence which, it contended, showed that three other persons with whom the accused had a close relationship had died of poisoning. In each case the accused had had the opportunity to administer the poison. The first of these was the second husband of the accused, Constable Haag. He had died 18 years previously while married to the accused. There was evidence that the cause of death was arsenical poisoning, and the accused had stood to benefit from insurance policies on his life. An inquest had been held at the time, but no charges were laid against the accused. The second person to die was the brother of the accused, Montgomerie. His death occurred a year following that of Haag, and the cause of death was again arsenical poisoning. The accused did not, however, stand to benefit financially from his death. There was evidence that he was an alcoholic and suffered from depression, and the defence argued that the circumstances of his death were consistent with suicide. The third person was a former de facto husband of the accused, Duncan. His death occurred eight years after that of Montgomerie. Duncan died from an overdose of barbiturates, having swallowed about 20 tablets. Insurance policies on his life had been arranged by the accused and she received payment under them on his death. The accused was convicted on both counts, and appealed unsuccessfully to the South Australian Court of Criminal Appeal. She then appealed to the High Court of Australia.

The similar fact evidence relating to the death of Constable Haag would seem of considerable probative value. His relationship with the accused was the same, the method of poisoning the same and the suggested motive of financial gain the same. The evidence relating to the death of Mongomerie was of lesser probative value. While the cause of death was again arsenical poisoning, the accused did not stand to gain financially from his death, and he was the brother rather than the husband of the accused. The evidence relating to the death of Duncan would seem to have possessed little real relevance. While the accused benefited financially from his death, it was difficult to see how she could have caused it. Arsenic is easily administered surreptitiously, and this is the reason why it is traditionally a poisoner's choice. It is difficult, however, to see how the accused could have either tricked or forced Duncan to ingest 20 barbiturate tablets.

The High Court allowed Mrs Perry's appeal, and ordered a re-trial.[43] Four judgments were delivered.[44] Gibbs CJ held the evidence relating to Constable Haag to be admissible as a matter of law while leaving open the possibility that it might be rejected by the judge in the exercise of discretion. His Honour held the evidence relating to the deaths of Montgomerie and Duncan was inadmissible. Murphy J held evidence of all three deaths to be inadmissible. Wilson J held the evidence relating to Constable Haag admissible. His Honour described the evidence relating to Montgomerie as 'borderline', but was not prepared to hold it was inadmissible, and held the evidence relating to Duncan was inadmissible. Brennan J held the evidence relating to deaths of Haag and Montgomerie was admissible and that relating to the death of Duncan inadmissible.

Gibbs CJ considered and rejected the interpretation that the *Makin* formula requires the judge to determine admissibility by weighing the prejudicial effect of the evidence against its probative value. His Honour held that to be admissible similar fact evidence must tend to show other than via propensity that the accused committed the act which forms the subject of the charge. The evidence must further possess a strong degree of probative force other than via propensity, and the judge in the exercise of discretion may still reject it where these requirements are satisfied.[45] It is difficult to see how Gibbs CJ was able in the context of *Perry v R* to insist on the primacy of the distinction between relevance via propensity and relevance other than via propensity. The similar fact evidence derived its only relevance from propensity; its significance was that, if accepted, it tended to establish a propensity to poison family members for financial gain. The problem with the evidence was its lack of sufficient probative value. The similar facts were not sufficiently established, and the propensity not sufficiently particular.

Wilson J and Murphy J adopted the approach that what is involved in determining the admissibility of similar fact evidence is a balancing of probative value against prejudice. Wilson J stated:

> 'The view has been expressed that the effect of *Boardman* is to interpret the classic statement of Lord Herschell in *Makin* not in terms of a rule of exclusion with certain categories wherein exceptions may be found, nor in terms of mere propensity or something more, but as requiring the court to compare, in the context of each case, the probative value of the evidence with the risk of prejudice it conveys. To be admissible, the evidence must have a sufficiently high degree of probative force to outweigh the inevitable prejudice flowing from the nature of the evidence. It is a question of degree in each case, since probative value will vary with the nature of the similar fact evidence itself, the issues, and the other evidence in the case ... In my opinion, there is much to be said for this reconciliation of the twin principles stated by Lord Herschell, although there is no reason to treat any particular formulation as exclusive. In some cases, the categorisation of exceptions will continue to be helpful.'[46]

Murphy J adopted the view that the criteria for excluding and admitting the evidence expressed in Lord Herschell's formulation are contradictory, and that what is required is a consideration of the probative value of the particular similar fact evidence.[47] His Honour set a high standard for admissibility, stating that 'evidence of any other alleged poisoning must be excluded unless taken with all the other evidence it could justify a finding beyond reasonable doubt that the accused was guilty in relation to that poisoning'.[48]

The remaining judge, Brennan J, delivered a judgment in which he carefully analysed the evidence in issue but did not commit to a particular theoretical approach to admissibility.

(b) England: the 'just' test

In *DPP v Boardman* the House of Lords had used the expression 'striking similarity' to describe the similarity between the accounts given by the two boys,[49] and this similarity was what gave the evidence its probative force and led to admissibility. This expression would seem to have been intended as no more than a method of expressing the probative force of the evidence in the particular case. Its alliterative attractiveness no doubt helped it to become regarded as itself the test for admissibility of similar fact evidence.[50] The matter was re-considered by the House of Lords in *DPP v P.*[51] The accused was charged with rape and incest against each of his two daughters, B and S. The trial judge rejected an application for severance on the basis that the evidence of each girl was admissible in respect of the counts relating to the other girl. The accused was convicted on one count of rape and all counts of incest in respect of each girl. There was no particular similarity in the course of conduct followed by the accused in respect of each girl. On appeal the Court of Appeal felt constrained to allow the appeal, while stating there was force in the suggestion that the sexual domination exercised by the accused over his daughters might in itself provide a sufficient hallmark to render the evidence of one girl admissible in the case of the other.[52]

The prosecution appealed successfully to the House of Lords. Delivering the judgment of their Lordships, Lord Mackay LC stated that it is not appropriate to single out 'striking similarity' as an essential element in every case of similar fact evidence. His Lordship stated:

> 'The essential feature of evidence which is to be admitted is that its probative force in support of the allegation that an accused person committed a crime is sufficiently great to make it just to admit the evidence, notwithstanding that it is prejudicial to the accused in tending to show that he was guilty of another crime. Such probative force may be derived from striking similarities in the evidence about the manner in which the crime was committed and the authorities provide illustrations of that of which *R v Straffen* and *R v Smith* provide notable examples. But restricting the circumstances in which there is sufficient probative force to overcome prejudice of evidence relating to another crime to cases in which there is some striking similarity between them is to restrict the operation of the principle in a way which gives too much effect to a particular manner of stating it, and is not justified in principle.'[53]

His Lordship held that the sexual domination of a father over his daughters, which always takes some particular form, might itself be regarded as sufficiently uncommon or distinctive to warrant admissibility as similar fact evidence. His Lordship stated:

> 'In the present case the evidence of both girls describes a prolonged course of conduct in relation to each of them. In relation to each of them force was used. There was a general domination of the girls with threats against them unless they observed silence and a domination of the wife that inhibited her intervention. The defendant seemed to have an obsession for keeping the girls to himself, for himself. The younger took on the role of the elder daughter when the elder daughter left home. There was also evidence that the defendant was involved in regard to payment for the abortions in respect of both girls. In

> my view these circumstances taken together gave strong probative force to the evidence of each of the girls in relation to the incidents involving the other, and was certainly sufficient to make it just to admit that evidence notwithstanding its prejudicial effect.'[54]

The particular problems posed by evidence of this kind will be considered further below. As a means of describing the situation where the probative force of evidence is sufficient to warrant admissibility, the word 'just' is appropriate. There is a real danger, however, that if regarded as a test rather than a word used to describe a situation where admissibility is warranted, it will come to serve as a substitute for factual analysis and may perhaps lead too readily to admissibility. Thus, in *Cross and Tapper on Evidence* it is noted that it is not suggested in *DPP v P* that the evidence should achieve a particularly high degree of probative value, and that the decision represents an erosion of the standard required for admissibility.[55]

(c) Australia: the 'no rational view of the evidence consistent with innocence' test

In a series of decisions following *Perry v R*, the High Court sought to refine its approach to similar fact evidence by expressing in various ways the nature and extent of the probative force required to justify admissibility.[56] A clear view emerged with the decisions in *Hoch v R*,[57] below and *Pfennig v R*.[58] In *Pfennig v R* the accused was charged with the murder of a 10-year-old boy. The boy's body was never located, but his bicycle and clothes were found at a reserve on the Murray River close to another reserve where he had last been seen. It was established that on the day of the boy's disappearance the accused had driven his van to the other reserve and had there spoken with the missing boy. Expert evidence established that there was only a remote possibility that if the boy had drowned his body would not have been found. There was evidence that the boy did not go swimming at the reserve where his clothes were found, and did not have his bathers with him on the day of his disappearance. The Crown led similar fact evidence that 12 months later the accused had abducted and raped another boy. Upon securing this boy in his van the accused had left the boy's bicycle near a cliff, presumably to lay a false trail of his disappearance. On this occasion the boy escaped, and the accused was convicted of his abduction and rape. The trial judge ruled that as there was no reasonable possibility that the missing boy had accidentally drowned, the similar fact evidence was admissible in proof of the identity of the boy's abductor and killer. The judge directed the jury that if it rejected drowning as a reasonable possibility and accepted the boy had been abducted, then it was open to them to consider the similar fact evidence in deciding whether the Crown had proved its case of murder against the accused. The accused was convicted and appealed unsuccessfully first to the South Australian Court of Criminal Appeal and then to the High Court.

The decision of the trial judge to admit the evidence was, it is submitted, clearly correct. The relevance of the evidence is similar to that in *Straffen*, and rests on the improbability of another person with propensities similar to those of the accused being in the vicinity at the time of the abduction and murder. In dismissing the appeal the majority, comprising Mason CJ, Deane and Dawson JJ expressed the requirement for admissibility as follows:

> 'Because propensity evidence is a special class of circumstantial evidence, its probative force is to be gauged in the light of its character as such. But because it has a prejudicial capacity of a high order, the trial judge must apply the same test as a jury must apply in dealing with circumstantial evidence and

> ask whether there is a rational view of the evidence that is consistent with the innocence of the accused. Here "rational" must be taken to mean "reasonable" and the trial judge must ask himself or herself the question in the context of the prosecution case; that is to say, he or she must regard the evidence as a step in the proof of that case. Only if there is no such view can one safely conclude that the probative force of the evidence outweighs its prejudicial effect. And, unless the tension between probative force and prejudicial effect is governed by such a principle, striking the balance will continue to resemble the exercise of a discretion rather than the application of a principle.'[59]

The formulation of no 'rational view of the evidence that is consistent with the innocence of the accused' comes from the elaboration of the criminal standard of proof sanctioned by the courts for directing the jury in cases of circumstantial evidence.[60] Thus, as a criterion of admissibility the judge is required to determine whether the similar fact evidence satisfies her or him beyond reasonable doubt of the guilt of the accused. Such a test is unsatisfactory for three reasons. First, it is difficult to see how a judge can be so satisfied when the evidence is sought to be led as part of the prosecution case. At this stage the judge may not be aware of the evidence to be called by the defence. Secondly, if applied literally the test would be far more restrictive in its operation than other judicial formulations of the similar fact rule.[61] A requirement that similar fact evidence establish guilt beyond reasonable doubt is far more demanding that that similar fact evidence possess 'striking similarity' or 'sufficient probative value to justify admissibility notwithstanding its potential for prejudice'. Finally, it is unsatisfactory to require the judge to ask herself or himself when considering admissibility precisely the same question the jury is to ask itself in determining guilt. Questions must arise as to the perceived impartiality of the judge as the trial progresses if, in admitting similar fact evidence, the judge has effectively said he or she is satisfied beyond reasonable doubt as to the guilt of the accused.

In Victoria, legislation was introduced in 1997 with the intention of overturning *Pfennig*. Section 398A of the Crimes Act 1958 (Vic) follows the language of *DPP v P*, stating that propensity evidence relevant to facts in issue in a proceeding is admissible 'if the court considers that in all the circumstances it is just to admit it despite any prejudicial effect it may have on the person charged with the offence'.[62]

(d) Australia: the Evidence Act 1995 (Cth and NSW)

The provisions of the Evidence Act 1995 (Cth and NSW) require the court to engage in a balancing of probative value and potential for prejudice. Section 97 deals with 'tendency evidence', ie evidence tendered to prove 'that a person has or had a tendency (whether because of the person's character or otherwise) to act in a particular way, or to have a particular state of mind'. Section 98 deals with 'coincidence evidence', ie evidence that two or more related events occurred tendered to prove that 'because of the improbability of the events occurring coincidentally, a person did a particular act or had a particular state of mind'. The test prescribed for admissibility is the same for both classes of evidence. Tendency evidence and coincidence evidence are not admissible if 'the court thinks that the evidence would not, either by itself or having regard to other evidence adduced or to be adduced by the party seeking to adduce the evidence, have significant probative value'. The striking of a balance between probative value and risk of prejudice is achieved by s 101 which provides that tendency evidence or coincidence evidence about an accused that is adduced by the prosecution cannot be used against the accused 'unless the probative value of the evidence substantially outweighs any prejudicial effect it may have on the [accused]'. The balancing process incorporates a bias against admissibility by requiring that the probative value of the evidence must both be significant and must 'substantially' outweigh any prejudicial effect it might have on the accused.

In New South Wales the view has been taken that s 101 incorporates the *Pfennig* test for admissibility.[63] This view seems incorrect in principle. The Acts pre-date the decision in *Pfennig*[64] and re-state one interpretation of the pre-*Pfennig* common law. *Pfennig* involved a significant, and it is submitted unsatisfactory, change in that law. There has been a developing trend in Australia to seek where possible to achieve uniformity between the common law of evidence and that contained in the Evidence Act 1995 (Cth and NSW).[65] Consistency between the Acts and the Australian common law is desirable. It should not, however, be pursued by seeking to read the Acts as incorporating clear changes in the common law made after they were drafted. This is particularly so when those changes are themselves open to serious question.

(e) Recommendations of the English Law Commission

As part of its general review of the law of evidence in criminal cases, in October 2001 the Law Commission published its final report on *Evidence of Bad Character in Criminal Cases*.[66] The report deals with all aspects of character in criminal cases, and in the case of the accused whether such evidence is led as part of the prosecution case or put to the accused in cross-examination. A draft Bill accompanies the report. In relation to similar fact evidence, the proposals would not seem to involve a substantial departure from existing practice.

Evidence of bad character is defined widely as evidence that shows or tends to show that a person has committed an offence, or has behaved, or is disposed to behave, in a way of which a reasonable person might disapprove.[67] A distinction is drawn between the central set of facts in a trial about which relevant evidence may be adduced without constraint, including evidence of bad character, and evidence of bad character which falls outside this category which can only be admissible if the court gives leave for it to be adduced.[68] Evidence of the bad character of the accused will be admissible if it has to do with the offence charged, or is evidence of misconduct in connection with the investigation or prosecution of that offence.[69] In other cases evidence of bad character is admissible only with the leave of the court, and leave may only be given if the evidence falls within one of seven listed exceptions.[70] Two exceptions relate to evidence that the prosecution seeks to lead as part of its case in chief. First, leave may be given to adduce evidence of the bad character of the accused if it has substantial explanatory value and the interests of justice require it to be admissible, even taking account of its potentially prejudicial effect (evidence of substantial explanatory value).[71] Secondly, leave may be given to adduce evidence of the bad character of the accused if the evidence has substantial probative value in relation to a matter in issue (other than whether the accused has a propensity to be untruthful) which is itself of substantial importance in the context of the case as a whole, and the interests of justice require it to be admissible, even taking account of its potentially prejudicial effect (evidence of substantial probative value).[72] The draft Bill lists factors to which the court must have regard in assessing the probative value of the evidence. The court is to consider the nature and number of the events to which the evidence relates; when those events are alleged to have occurred; the nature and extent of similarities between alleged instances of misconduct; and the extent to which the evidence tends to show the same person was responsible for alleged incidents of misconduct.[73]

Evidence admissible as having to do with the offence charged would match the existing res gestae inclusion exception,[74] or alternatively could be viewed as a class of situation where a balancing of probative value and risk of prejudice would always warrant admissibility. Evidence of misconduct in connection with the investigation or prosecution of the offence is an expression that has the potential to be interpreted unduly widely. The Commission intended it to cover such matters as an accused absconding in the course of the proceedings, or seeking to dissuade a witness from testifying.[75] The Commission stated it could not be used, for example, to enable a police officer to testify that the officer interrogated known offenders including the accused.[76]

Evidence of substantial explanatory value and evidence of substantial probative value can only be admitted with the leave of the court. For leave to be given, the evidence must meet an enhanced relevance test of being 'substantial', and the court must be satisfied that the interests of justice require it to be admitted notwithstanding its potential for prejudice. Thus, a balancing of probative value against potential for prejudice is required, with the expression 'the interests of justice' re-stating the *DPP v P* test. The division between substantial explanatory value and substantial probative value is of analytical significance only, since the same test applies in both cases. Evidence of explanatory value is evidence that provides essential background that, in the Commission's view, is not strictly evidence of probative value.[77] The proposed model draws no distinction between evidence the relevance of which is via propensity and evidence that possesses relevance other than via propensity. What is important is the value of the evidence against its potential for prejudice and not the nature of the reasoning process by which the evidence derives its value. The model differs from the Australian legislation both in structure and in requiring merely that the probative value outweigh the potential for prejudice. Section 101 of the Evidence Act 1995 (Cth and NSW) requires that the probative value must 'substantially' outweigh the danger of prejudice.[78] The approach taken by the Law Commission seems preferable. To require that the evidence possess substantial explanatory or substantial probative value, and that its value substantially outweigh the risk of prejudice, seems unduly awkward. The words chosen by the Law Commission have considerable open texture, and consideration of the extent to which probative value must exceed prejudice may be left to the judge in determining what the interests of justice require.

(f) Criminal Justice Bill 2002

The Criminal Justice Bill was introduced in the House of Commons on 21 November 2002.[79] In contrast to the recommendations of the Law Commission, the Bill effectively abolishes the similar fact exclusion principle.[80] Clause 84 provides that evidence of the bad character of the accused is to be admissible in eight situations, of which three relate to evidence that the prosecution seeks to lead as part of its case in chief. Clause 84 provides:

> '(1) In criminal proceedings evidence of the defendant's bad character is admissible if, but only if –
>
> > ...
> >
> > (c) it is important explanatory evidence,
> >
> > (d) it is evidence of the defendant's conviction for an offence of the same description, or of the same category, as the one with which he is charged,
> >
> > (e) it is relevant to an important matter in issue between the defendant and the prosecution,
> >
> > ...

> (2) The court must not admit evidence under subsection (1)(d), (e) or (h) if, on an application by the defendant to exclude it, it appears to the court that the admission of the evidence would have such an adverse effect on the fairness of the proceedings that the court ought not to admit it.'

The expressions 'bad character',[81] 'important explanatory evidence',[82] offences 'of the same description' or 'of the same category',[83] and 'matter in issue between the defendant and the prosecution'[84] are defined in the Bill.

Clause 84(1) is wide in its operation. Paragraph (c) is derived from the recommendation of the Law Commission.[85] Paragraph (d) is sufficient to cover all cases of similar fact evidence taking the form of a criminal conviction. Paragraph (e) poses a test of simple relevance to an important matter in issue between the accused and the prosecution. The operation of the provision is thus to render similar fact evidence admissible in the first instance in virtually all cases, casting on to the accused the obligation of showing that admission would have such an adverse effect on the fairness of the proceedings that the court ought not to admit it. Admissibility becomes the norm, with only a limited discretion reposed in the court to exclude such evidence in exceptional cases.

The similar fact exclusion principle was developed by the common law in order to protect accused persons from wrongful conviction occurring as a consequence of the prejudice inherent in this class of evidence. Where the probative value of the similar fact evidence is sufficient, it should be received notwithstanding its potential for prejudice. Achieving a correct balance between the competing claims for admission and exclusion is a difficult task. Reducing the operation of the principle of exclusion to that of a discretion to be exercised only in exceptional cases gives insufficient weight to the importance of protecting the accused from unwarranted and unnecessary prejudice. It is submitted that the approach adopted in the Bill is incorrect in principle. The recommendations of the Law Commission, on the other hand, achieve a satisfactory balance between the competing arguments of principle favouring admission and exclusion, and it is hoped that these recommendations may be returned to.

5 Sexual offence cases

Sexual offence cases are those where similar fact evidence is very often most crucial to the prosecution. The need is particularly great where the victim is a child. Sexual offences against children usually take place in private, and there are no independent witnesses to what occurred. Victims of paedophiles and incest offenders are typically fearful and reluctant to report what has occurred. In consequence, many child sexual abuse cases are conducted months or years after the event. In such cases there will be no medical evidence corroborating the victim's account of abuse. If the only evidence directly incriminating the accused is the evidence of the victim and the accused denies the victim's testimony, it is difficult for the prosecution to establish its case beyond reasonable doubt. If, however, there is admissible evidence of similar acts committed by the accused, the victim's account becomes much more credible and the chances of conviction are significantly increased.

On the other hand, the dangers inherent in similar fact evidence generally are greatly enhanced in sexual offence cases.[86] The relevance of similar fact evidence in sexual offence cases is almost always via propensity, and the subject matter is one where the passions of a jury are likely to be at its highest. Accordingly, in such cases the defence is particularly anxious to exclude similar fact evidence.

In Australia, two arguments that create substantial difficulties for the prosecution have been accepted by the High Court. The House of Lords has rejected both arguments. The first is that in sexual cases similar fact evidence of other victims is not admissible if there exists a possibility of concoction between the victims. In *Hoch v R*[87] the accused was convicted on three counts of sexual molestation of boys aged under 14. The counts were joined in one indictment and an application for separate trials was refused. On appeal it was submitted that the evidence of each boy was inadmissible as similar fact evidence on the basis that, because of demonstrated association between the boys and their antipathy towards the accused, there was a real chance that their evidence was concocted. The High Court accepted the submission and allowed the appeal of the accused. In a joint judgment, Mason CJ, Wilson and Gaudron JJ posited the test of 'no other rational view of the evidence', and held that 'the possibility of concoction – not a probability or real chance of concoction' was sufficient to render the evidence inadmissible.[88] Their Honours stated:

> 'In cases where there is a possibility of joint concoction there is another rational view of the evidence. That rational view – viz joint concoction – is inconsistent both with the guilt of the accused person and with the improbability of the complainants having concocted similar lies. It thus destroys the probative value of the evidence which is a condition precedent to its admissibility.
>
> Thus, in our view, the admissibility of similar fact evidence in cases such as the present depends on that evidence having the quality that it is not reasonably explicable on the basis of concoction.'[89]

In *R v H*[90] the House of Lords rejected the *Hoch* 'no possibility of concoction' test of admissibility. The accused was charged with sexual offences committed upon his adopted daughter and his stepdaughter. There were similarities in each complainant's accounts as to the nature of the alleged assaults, but in cross-examination they denied that they had collaborated in concocting a false story. The judge directed the jury that it was for the prosecution to satisfy the jury that the girls were in fact telling the truth, and that the evidence of one girl could support the evidence of the other only if the jury was sure that the girls had not collaborated to concoct a false story against the accused. The accused was convicted, and his conviction upheld by the Court of Appeal (Criminal Division). The accused appealed unsuccessfully to the House of Lords. Their Lordships held that the possibility of collusion is a consideration that goes to weight, not to admissibility. Lord Mackay, with whom the other members of the House of Lords agreed, stated:

> 'Where there is an application to exclude evidence on the ground that it does not qualify as similar fact evidence and the submission raises a question of collusion (not only deliberate but including unconscious influence of one witness by another) the judge should approach the question of admissibility on the basis that the similar facts alleged are true and apply the test set out by this House in *Director of Public Prosecutions v P* accordingly. It follows that generally collusion is not relevant at this stage.'[91]

His Lordship stated that where evidence of similar facts has been admitted and circumstances are adduced in the course of the trial which indicate that no reasonable jury could accept the evidence as free from collusion, the judge should direct the jury that it cannot be relied upon for any purpose adverse to the defence. His Lordship continued:

> 'Where this is not so but the question of collusion has been raised the judge must clearly draw the importance of collusion to the attention of the jury and

> leave it to them to decide whether, notwithstanding such evidence of collusion as may have been put before them, they are satisfied that the evidence can be relied upon as free from collusion and tell them that if they are not so satisfied they cannot properly rely upon it as corroboration or for any other purpose adverse to the defence.'[92]

The view taken by the House of Lords in *R v H* is, it is submitted, preferable to that adopted by the High Court of Australia in *Hoch v R*. In Victoria and in Queensland *Hoch v R* has been overturned by statute. Section 398A of the Crimes Act 1958 (Vic)[93] provides that in deciding whether it is just to admit similar fact evidence the possibility of a reasonable explanation consistent with the innocence of the accused is not relevant, although such a consideration is relevant when considering the weight of the evidence or the credibility of a witness. Section 132A of the Evidence Act 1977 (Qld) provides that similar fact evidence, the probative value of which outweighs its potentially prejudicial effect, must not be ruled inadmissible on the ground that it may be the result of collusion or suggestion.[94] The general *Pfennig* test has been criticised, above, and the 'no possibility of concoction' application of that test is at the least equally unsatisfactory. If applied it would clearly have led to rejection of the evidence in *DPP v Boardman* and, indeed, in cases where the evidence is far stronger than in *Boardman*. It is difficult to see how the test can be applied, since the issue of possible concoction must be determined before the evidence is tested. The proposition that evidence must be totally convincing in order to be admitted is contrary to the general rule that facts which are a condition precedent to admissibility must be established to the standard of the balance of probabilities.[95] In England a confession will only be admissible if the prosecution establishes beyond reasonable doubt that it was not obtained by oppression,[96] but this may be regarded as an exception to the general principle. In any event, an analogy from confessions can hardly support *Hoch v R*, since in Australia the conditions precedent to the admissibility of a confession need only be established to the standard of the balance of probabilities.[97] The effect of the decision in *Hoch v R*, if literally applied, would be to render similar fact evidence inadmissible in virtually all cases of incest with multiple family members. There is no inherent objection to some measure of collaboration between victims in such cases. In incest cases, discussion between victims as a precursor to making a formal complaint might be expected. Where collaboration is or may be present it would be an easy thing for the defence to allege concoction which, even in the absence of any supporting evidence, would be likely to prevent the evidence from satisfying the *Hoch* 'no possibility of joint concoction' test.

The Law Commission considered and approved the approach taken in *R v H*, while emphasising the power of the judge to direct an acquittal.[98] The Commission recommended that where evidence of the bad character of the accused has been admitted, and the judge becomes satisfied that the evidence is contaminated such that a conviction would be unsafe, the judge should be required to discharge the jury or direct the jury to acquit.

Secondly, in *De Jesus v R*[99] the High Court held that were an accused is charged with a number of sexual offences and the evidence is not cross-admissible, separate trials should be ordered. This view was rejected by the House of Lords in *R v Christou*.[100] The accused was charged with rape, buggery and indecent assault against each of two younger female cousins. The accused had been living in the same household as his cousins at the time of the alleged offences. The trial judge held that the evidence of the girls was not cross-admissible, but refused an application that the counts relating to each girl be tried separately. The accused was acquitted on the counts of rape and buggery, but convicted of counts of indecent assault against each girl. On appeal the House of Lords upheld the judge's decision not to order severance of the counts in respect of each girl. Their Lordships held that s 5(3) of the Indictments Act 1915 (Eng) gives the judge a discretion to order severance or not, and that the discretion should be exercised having regard to the circumstances of the particular case. Their Lordships expressed doubts as to the correctness of the judge's view that the evidence of the girl's was not cross-admissible, but declined to rest their decision on that basis. Lord Taylor stated:

> 'Looking specifically at sexual abuse of children ... cases can vary greatly. A defendant may, for example, be indicted for discrete incidents of sexual abuse of different children in different places at different times, so that the allegations in respect of each count are in "watertight compartments". By contrast, when, as here, the allegation is of a continuous course of conduct within one household involving two or more children over the same period and in similar circumstances, joint trial of all the counts may well be appropriate. Indeed, in such cases the principles laid down in *Director of Public Prosecutions v P* will often render the evidence of one child admissible to support the evidence of the other.'[101]

The decision in *R v Christou* is, it is submitted, preferable to that in *De Jesus v R*. In cases of multiple offences committed against a large number of victims over many years, a requirement of automatic severance would create a substantial imposition on public resources. The Crown would be encouraged to proceed only with a selection of charges, denying vindication to other victims. In Victoria, *De Jesus v R* has been overturned by statute. Section 372 of the Crimes Act 1958 (Vic) creates a presumption against severance in sexual offence cases, and specifically states that the presumption is not rebutted merely because evidence on one count is inadmissible on another count.[102] The Law Commission considered and approved the *Christou* approach, subject to the proviso that it must be clear that the overriding proviso is that the accused must receive a fair trial.[103] The Commission accordingly recommended that where an accused is charged with more than one offence, evidence of the bad character of the accused is admissible on one of the offences charged but inadmissible on another, and the accused applies for the offences to be tried separately, that application should be granted unless the court is satisfied that the accused can receive a fair trial.[104]

In the United States, Rule 413 of the Federal Rules of Evidence removes the prohibition on similar fact evidence in sexual offence cases. Rule 413(a) provides that in sexual assault cases 'evidence of the defendant's commission of another offence or offences of sexual assault is admissible, and may be considered for its bearing on any matter to which it is relevant'. Such a blanket abolition of the principle of exclusion is unwarranted.[105] A persuasive argument for greater admissibility of similar fact evidence in sexual offence cases must focus on the probative value of the evidence, together with legitimate difficulties faced by the prosecution in particular types of sexual offence case if it is prevented from leading similar fact evidence.

The relevance and probative value of similar fact evidence varies greatly in sexual offence cases, depending on the evidence itself and the nature of the offence and of the offender. Sexual offence cases in which an issue of similar fact evidence is likely to be raised fall into three major classes.

First, cases of serial stranger attacks. The victim and offender are either not known to one another or have only a loose association. The accused is alleged to be a serial offender who has acted in a similar fashion on occasions other than that the subject of the current charge. In such cases there is rarely an issue as to whether an offence has been committed, and the issue in contest is whether the accused is the offender. The relevance of the similar fact evidence is most commonly as establishing a specialised propensity or modus operandi, and reasoning that since this method of offending has been followed by the accused on other occasions and by the offender on the occasion in question, the accused and the offender are one and the same person. The example given by Lord Hailsham in *Boardman v DPP* is apposite.[106] If the accused was charged with a rape committed by an offender wearing a native American head-dress, similar fact evidence that the accused had committed previous rapes while wearing such head-dress would be of great probative value and would be admissible. *Straffen* and *Pfennig*, although murder cases, are examples of this type of case and this form of reasoning.

Secondly, cases of incestuous paedophilia. These are cases where an adult preys upon a number of his children or members of an extended family. Here there is no dispute as to identity, and the issue is usually whether the allegations made against the accused are founded in fact or malicious concoctions. In some cases there may be peculiarities in the manner in which the offences are alleged to have been committed, but more often the accusations will be of more or less typical incestuous paedophilia.

Thirdly, cases of predatory sexual offenders. These cases normally involve an adult who consistently, often over many years, preys upon a particular class of victim. Most commonly the class of victim is children, but this is not always the case. The offender will commonly pursue a career (school teacher, priest or social worker) or social activities that place him in frequent contact with, and invest him with a degree of power over, the chosen class of victim.

Whichever class of case is involved, the fact that the offence charged and the similar fact evidence exhibited an abnormal sexual preference is not of itself sufficient to render similar facts admissible. In England in the first half of the twentieth century, an exception to the first branch of Lord Herschell's formulation developed to the effect that in cases of abnormal sexual activity similar fact evidence is admissible, the so-called 'hallmark' doctrine.[107] In *DPP v Boardman* the House of Lords firmly rejected the doctrine.[108] The hallmark doctrine developed in relation to homosexuality, which could now no longer be regarded as sufficiently uncommon to justify its application. The rejection of the doctrine, however, is also correct in relation to such sexual abnormalities as paedophilia, sadism and incest. While the percentage of members of the community prepared to engage in such practices is quite limited, membership of such a class cannot of itself be regarded as sufficiently probative without more to justify the admissibility of similar fact evidence.[109]

Evidence of other offences committed against the same victim is, however, normally admissible.[110] Here the evidence possesses significant probative value as showing a passion directed towards a particular victim, and is relevant also as bearing on the nature of the relationship between victim and accused.[111] Such other offences must, however, be established by evidence that is not limited to the testimony of the victim. Testimony by the victim as to other offences, if unsupported by other evidence, does not possess sufficient probative weight to justify admissibility having regard to its significant potential for prejudice.[112]

In cases of serial stranger attack the defence will typically accept that an offence has occurred but dispute that the accused was the offender. In such cases similar fact evidence must possess considerable probative force in order to mark the accused out as the person who most likely committed the crime.[113] In *Sutton v R*[114] the accused was charged on eight counts of rape and attempted rape. The offences involved three victims, with no particular similarity in the nature of the sexual acts performed. There were a number of similarities in the attacks, in that in each case the victim was a young girl and the assailant operated alone and approached on foot. The trial judge rejected an application for separate trials, on the basis that the similarities deposed to by the three victims were sufficiently striking that the evidence relating to each was admissible in respect of the other two. The accused was convicted and appealed unsuccessfully to the South Australian Court of Criminal Appeal and then to the High Court. The key factors relied upon by the High Court were that each attack took place within a limited area and over a limited period of time, and that in each case the victim was abducted and conducted to a school (the same school in respect of two of the attacks), where the assaults took place. That two rapists may have been operating in the same area and choosing to commit offences in a schoolyard was sufficiently unlikely to justify admissibility.

It is suggested that an insufficiently strict approach was taken by the Court of Appeal in *R v John W*.[115] The accused was charged with false imprisonment and indecent assault upon a 25-year-old woman and false imprisonment of a 13-year-old girl two weeks later. The offences took place in the vicinity where the accused was living at the date of each assault, and the issue in both cases was identity. The trial judge refused to order severance on the basis that the evidence in respect of each victim was cross-admissible, and the Court of Appeal upheld that decision. Both incidents involved sexual attacks that were in no way unusual. The court held there is no special rule in identification cases requiring striking similarity, and that the circumstances of both offences were such as to provide sufficient probative support for the conclusion that the defendant committed both offences to render it fair for the evidence to be used for this purpose. The similar fact evidence, however, showed no more than a general propensity to commit sexual attacks, and this, without more, cannot be sufficient for admissibility on the issue of identification.

The requirement for a significant level of relevance in cases where identity is in issue was recognised by the Victorian Court of Appeal in *R v Tektonopoulos*.[116] The accused was convicted of entering premises as a trespasser with intent to commit a sexual assault and with indecent assault. The accused was identified by the complainant, but denied he was the offender. Evidence was tendered that, three days after the date of the offences, the accused, whilst under police surveillance, was seen to enter premises in the same vicinity, attempt to open a window and then leave the premises. The trial judge admitted the evidence, relying on s 398A of the Crimes Act 1958 (Vic). The Court of Appeal held that the evidence should not have been received. Winneke P, with whom Charles and Batt JJA agreed, noted that the test provided by s 398A(2) 'is not far removed from the test that was customarily applied in Australia before *Hoch*'.[117] His Honour stated that similar fact evidence will only be received 'with great caution', and continued:

> 'This is particularly so in cases where the evidence is tendered for the purpose of establishing the identity of the accused as the offender. In such cases the risk is high that the jury will reason, from the mere fact of established criminal propensity, that the accused is the offender. That is why the courts have insisted in such cases that there should be something in the evidence, in the nature of "striking similarity" with the offences charged, which strongly points to the accused as the offender.'[118]

His Honour examined the evidence, and concluded that the similar fact evidence revealed no striking similarity with the alleged offences which made it objectively improbable that the offences charged were not committed by the accused.

Different considerations apply in cases where identity is not in issue. The fact that the accused possesses a propensity for incest, paedophilia or rape will not of itself be sufficient to justify admissibility. To insist, however, that there must be some 'striking similarity' or peculiar modus operandi raises the bar for admissibility unduly high, and posits a test that is not suitable for resolution of the issues involved. This is illustrated by the decision of the Supreme Court of Canada in *R v Litchfield*.[119] The accused, a physician, was charged with 14 counts of sexual assault involving seven female patients. The accused applied to have the counts severed. The judge hearing the application ordered three different trials, depending on the part of the complainants' body that was involved in the assault. Therefore, there was to be one trial for allegations involving the complainants' genitalia, one trial for allegations involving the complainants' breasts and another trial for any other matters. The effect of this was that in some cases there would be separate trials relating to a single visit by a complainant. The prosecution appealed to the Supreme Court of Canada. The court held the judge had proceeded on a misapprehension about the nature of the offence of sexual assault in holding that an improper touching of one part of the body during the same medical examination was inadmissible in considering the propriety of a touching of another part of the body. Further, the court held that evidence from one complainant should be admissible in relation to allegations involving another complainant, even if the body parts touched were not identical. Iacobucci J stated:

> '... the evidence provided information highly relevant to understanding the context in which the alleged offences occurred and shed light on the nature of the respondent's relationship with his patients, particularly the standard of medical treatment he provided. The evidence provided a different perspective on the alleged assaults from that afforded by the medical evidence. The evidence going to the severed counts, if accepted by a jury, would also tend to show a distinct pattern of behaviour engaged in by the respondent.'[120]

DPP v P and *R v H* likewise illustrate this form of relevance. The significance of the evidence is that it goes beyond establishing a propensity for indecency or for incest, and demonstrates a pattern of behaviour on the part of the accused. Further, that of the others supports the testimony of each victim. Were a single allegation made by a daughter against her father or by a patient against her doctor, a jury might be disinclined to accept the possibility of a father or doctor conducting himself in such a manner. Where there are a number of such allegations, the evidence of each witness provides powerful support for that of the others. Such evidence may, of course, raise issues of possible concoction on the part of the alleged victims, and careful directions on this possibility must be given to the jury. Given the privacy and the absence of other evidence which is characteristic of this type of offence, however, not to recognise the force of this form of reasoning as supporting the case for admissibility may be tantamount to rendering the accused immune from successful prosecution.

The Ontario Court of Appeal adopted similar reasoning in *R v B (L)*.[121] The decision involved two appeals heard together. In the first case the accused was convicted of sexual assault against his stepdaughter. At trial evidence was received of sexual incidents involving his two natural daughters and the younger sister of his first wife. In the second case the accused was a teacher convicted of offences against former students. At trial evidence was received of incidents involving other former students of the accused. In each case the incidents comprising the similar fact evidence took various and in no way unusual or distinctive forms. The court dismissed the appeals of both accused. Delivering the judgment of the court, Charron JA stated:

> 'Focusing on the specifics of the allegation assists in the assessment of the extent to which the evidence of prior discreditable conduct supports the inference that the complainant's allegation is true. It stands to reason that, in

> this type of case, the more similar the complaints are, the higher the probative value ... It is also important to consider which similarities are truly compelling. In cases of sexual assault, the similarities or dissimilarities between the sexual acts that are alleged are, of course, relevant, but often not as compelling as the circumstances surrounding the incidents. This stands to reason, particularly where there is nothing unusual about the sexual acts in question. In most circumstances, the fact that one complainant was kissed as compared to the other being fondled may not have a whole lot of significance. The allegations all pertain to acts of a sexual nature. In the same way, and again depending on the circumstances, the fact that assault occurred in the basement as opposed to the other in the bedroom may not be of consequence on the question of probative value. The different location may simply be attributable to a different opportunity for privacy.'[122]

The significance of this line of approach is illustrated by the two cases of *R v Glennon.*[123] The accused had been a Catholic priest and youth worker who was alleged, over the period between 1970 and 1980, to have taken advantage of his position of authority systematically to abuse sexually adolescent males and females in his charge. In the first case the trial took place in 1991, prior to the enactment of s 398A of the Crimes Act 1958 (Vic). The trial judge directed the jury that, in respect of a number of counts evidence relating to other counts could be used as similar fact evidence. The Court of Criminal Appeal upheld the decision of the trial judge, applying the 'striking similarity' test. The decision of the court was correct. The evidence established a pattern of behaviour on the part of the accused, and that of the others supported the evidence of each boy. It seems forced, however, to achieve the result of admissibility through application of the 'striking similarity' test. The offences did not exhibit significant features distinguishing them from the normal run of cases involving an adult in a position of authority and power using that position to exploit sexually young people in his charge.

The second case was on appeal from convictions at two trials, the first of which involved 29 counts of various sexual assaults against six separate complainants. The judge ruled that evidence in respect of each of the counts was mutually admissible, and refused an application for severance of the counts involving one particular complainant from the counts involving other complainants. The accused was convicted on 24 counts, and appealed unsuccessfully to the Court of Appeal. The cross-admissibility of the evidence relating to the various counts was now governed by s 398A of the Crimes Act 1958 (Vic). The Court of Appeal held that severance was properly not ordered if all the evidence was mutually admissible, and that the ruling of the trial judge on mutual admissibility was correct. Callaway JA stated:

> 'The applicant was known to each of [the complainants] as a priest and in other leadership roles ... In all those roles the applicant was in a position to exercise, and did exercise, strict discipline over children of a vulnerable age. He was in a position of trust derived from his personal standing, as well as his standing as a priest, with the children's families. The evidence of the complainants, taken together, pointed strongly to a pattern of conduct on the part of the applicant, involving the systematic exploitation of vulnerable children within his domain in a similar manner. The probative value of the evidence lay in the improbability of six complainants giving such connected accounts unless those accounts were true.'[124]

A similar case is *R v Liddy.*[125] The accused was a magistrate and coach of junior surf lifesavers. It was alleged he had, over a period of years, used his position of authority sexually to molest young boys. The accused was charged on 15 counts involving five boys between the ages of 8 and 13 years and convicted of nine counts involving four of the boys. No issue of possible joint concoction arose, the complaints being made years later when the victims were adults and no longer associated with one another. The trial judge refused to order severance and held the evidence on the counts cross-admissible. The Supreme Court of South Australia upheld the decision of the judge. Mullighan J summarised the significance of the evidence as follows:

> 'It is capable of negativing innocent association between the appellant and each of the boys. It is capable of amounting to corroboration or confirmation of the evidence of each complainant about each charged act relating to him. The evidence is capable of proving that the incidents occurred and all complaints relating similar events is not a matter of pure coincidence. It is capable of proving the objective improbability of each of the complainants giving accounts of sexual conduct by the appellant unless those accounts are true and there is no reasonable view of the evidence other than as supporting an inference that the appellant is guilty of the charge under consideration. The evidence could negative innocent association. Furthermore, it is capable of establishing a sexual attraction on the part of the appellant to the complainants and to put their evidence into true context. Also, the evidence is capable of establishing that he used the group of boys and the activities which he provided for them as the opportunity for his offending.'[126]

In *R v Glennon* and *R v Liddy* the court was able to hold the similar fact evidence admissible, notwithstanding the strictness of the *Pfennig* test. These cases do, however, demonstrate that the test posited in *DPP v P* and s 398A of the Crimes Act 1958 (Vic) is more satisfactory than other formulations of the similar fact rule. It does not impose restrictions on the manner in which the similar fact evidence derives its probative force, and consideration of whether it is just to admit the evidence permits the judge to have regard to the legitimate difficulties in prosecuting paedophiles and sexual predators if such evidence is not received.

6 Conclusion

In seeking a satisfactory formulation of the similar fact rule, a significant level of generality is desirable. What the rule has always required is a comparison of probative value against risk of prejudice, and this task calls for careful consideration of the factual nuances of the particular case and the process by which relevance is demonstrated. Insistence on the primacy of the distinction between relevance via propensity and relevance other than via propensity directs attention away from the crucial issues involved in this process. A test of 'striking similarity' may be a suitable way of describing some cases where the probative value of similar fact evidence is high, but in other situations it is an inappropriate test. The test of 'no rational view of the evidence consistent with innocence' developed by the High Court of Australia is both in principle incorrect, and sets the bar to admissibility unduly high. The approach adopted in the Evidence Act 1995 (Cth and NSW) is to be preferred, but a requirement that probative value must 'substantially' outweigh prejudice may also raise the bar to admissibility unduly high.

The approach taken by the House of Lords in *DPP v P* and adopted in s 398A of the Crimes Act 1958 (Vic) is, it is submitted, the most suitable. The test requires the judge to weigh probative value against risk of prejudice and decide whether in the circumstances of the case it is just to admit the evidence. The test recognises the wide measure of discretion called for in determining the admissibility of similar fact evidence, and enables the judge to have regard to the necessities of the particular type of case in which the issue arises. Thus the need for the prosecution to rely upon similar fact evidence in prosecuting paedophiles and other predatory sexual offenders becomes a proper consideration in deciding whether the admission of similar fact evidence is just. The recommendations of the English Law Commission, while providing a new structural framework for determining admissibility, essentially re-state the *DPP v P* test. Similar fact evidence will be admissible if it has substantial explanatory value or substantial probative value, and if the interests of justice require it to be admitted notwithstanding its potential for prejudice. These recommendations represent a far more satisfactory approach than that adopted in the English Criminal Justice Bill 2002.

NOTES

* I am grateful to Emeritus Professor Louis Waller and Associate Professor Sue McNicol of Monash University for reading this essay, and for their comments and suggestions.

1 [1894] AC 57 at 65.

2 In Australia the expression 'propensity evidence' is gaining favour as a more suitable description of this class of evidence; *Pfennig v R* (1995) 182 CLR 461; Crimes Act 1958 (Vic), s 398A.

3 Tapper *Cross and Tapper on Evidence* (9th edn, 1999) p 335. See also Law Commission, *Evidence of Bad Character in Criminal Proceedings* (Law Com No 273, 9 October 2001) para 2.4.

4 In *R v Best* [1998] 4 VR 603 at 606 Callaway JA defined 'propensity evidence' in this broad manner, but then subdivided propensity evidence into 'relationship evidence' (where the victim is the same) and 'similar fact evidence' (where the victim is different). See also *KRM v R* [2001] HCA 11, per McHugh J. This subdivision does not seem to offer any clear benefit, and may create uncertainty as to the principles governing the admissibility of relationship evidence; see Clough, 'Section 398A of the *Crimes Act* 1958 (Vic): *Pfennig* Resurrected?' (2000) 24 Crim LJ 8.

5 Wigmore *Evidence* (1940) vol 1, p 650.

6 Note 3 above, paras 6.33, 7.23.

7 Note *R v Bailey* [1924] 2 KB 300 at 305, per Lord Hewart CJ. In Tapper *Cross and Tapper on Evidence* (9th edn, 1999) pp 356–357 the general rule of exclusion is also supported by reference to what is termed 'secondary prejudice'. It is argued that if similar fact evidence was more generally admitted, prosecutors would rely on such evidence more and more, police and prosecutors would base their decisions to prosecute more strongly upon the previous records of suspects, and accused persons who had criminal records would be placed under greater pressure to plead guilty. Although this argument has validity, it does not appear to influence the courts in their approach to the subject. In determining whether to accept or reject similar fact evidence, the courts focus solely on the notion of prejudice in its primary sense of giving rise to a risk that the accused might be improperly convicted.

8 These concepts are dealt with in detail in Eggleston *Evidence, Proof and Probability* (2nd edn, 1983).

9 As in *R v Straffen* [1952] 2 QB 911, below.

10 As in *Perry v R* (1982) 150 CLR 580, below.

11 Note Acorn 'Similar Fact Evidence and the Principle of Inductive Reasoning: Makin Sense' (1991) 11 OJLS 63.

12 Section 97.

13 For elaboration of this form of reasoning, see Eggleston *Evidence, Proof and Probability*, above n 8, ch 2; E J Imwinkelried 'A Small Contribution to the Debate over the Proposed Legislation Abolishing the Character Evidence Prohibition in Sex Offence Prosecutions' (1993) 44 Syracuse L Rev 1125, 1134.

14 Section 98.

15 [1894] AC 57.

16 It is suggested that in *Harris v DPP* [1952] AC 694 the House of Lords failed to appreciate the significance of this form of reasoning, and in consequence incorrectly allowed the appeal of the accused.

17 *R v Smith* (1915) 11 Cr App Rep 229.

18 [1975] AC 421.
19 [1894] AC 57.
20 [1894] AC 57 at 65.
21 The two sentences of Lord Herschell's formulation constitute an example of what Professor Julius Stone has termed 'Legal Categories of Competing Reference' in *Legal System and Lawyers' Reasoning* (1964) pp 248–252.
22 Eg *Cross on Evidence* (3rd edn, 1967) pp 292–324; *McCormick on Evidence* (2nd edn, 1972) pp 447–454; *Phipson on Evidence* (12th edn, 1976) ch 11.
23 What Wigmore termed the doctrine of 'multiple admissibility' is applicable, ie 'when an evidentiary fact is offered for one purpose, and becomes admissible by satisfying all the rules applicable to it in that capacity, it is not inadmissible because it does not satisfy the rules applicable to it in some other capacity and because the jury might improperly consider it in the latter capacity': Wigmore *Evidence* (1940) vol 1, p 300.
24 This distinction forms the basis of many judicial interpretations of the similar fact rule. See eg the judgment of Lord Hailsham LC in *DPP v Boardman* [1975] AC 421 at 453, and the judgments of Gibbs CJ in *Perry v R* (1982) 150 CLR 580 at 585 and in *Sutton v R* (1984) 152 CLR 528 at 533.
25 [1952] 2 QB 911.
26 Leading English cases in which the similar fact evidence was relevant solely via propensity include: *R v Ball* [1911] AC 47; *Thompson v R* [1918] AC 221; *DPP v Boardman* [1975] AC 421; *DPP v P* [1991] 2 AC 447; *R v H* [1995] 2 AC 596. Leading Australian cases in which the similar fact evidence was relevant solely via propensity include: *Griffith v R* (1937) 58 CLR 185; *O'Leary v R* (1946) 73 CLR 566; *Perry v R* (1982) 150 CLR 580; *Sutton v R* (1984) 152 CLR 528; *Hoch v R* (1988) 165 CLR 292; *Harriman v R* (1989) 167 CLR 590; *Pfennig v R* (1995) 182 CLR 461.
27 Tapper *Cross and Tapper on Evidence* (9th edn, 1999) ch VIII. See also 'The Admissibility of Evidence of Similar Facts: A Re-Examination' in Cowen and Carter *Essays on the Law of Evidence* (1956) p 106; Ligertwood *Australian Evidence* (3rd edn, 1998) p 109.
28 On the distinction between rules and principles, see Dworkin *Taking Rights Seriously* (1977) chs 2 and 3.
29 [1975] AC 421.
30 (1982) 150 CLR 580.
31 A similar approach has been adopted by the Canadian courts: see *Alward and Mooney v R* (1977) 35 CCC (2d) 392; *R v Green* (1988) 40 CCC (3d) 333; *R v B (CR)* (1990) 55 CCC (3d) 1; *R v B (FF)* (1993) 18 CR (4th) 261; *R v Litchfield* (1994) 86 CCC (3d) 97; *R v B (L)* (1997) 116 CC (3d) 481; *R v Arp* (1998) 129 CCC (3d) 321; *R v Rulli* (1999) 134 CCC (3d) 465; *R v Batte* (2000) 145 CCC (3d) 449.
32 See generally, Hoffman 'Similar Facts after Boardman' (1975) 91 LQR 193; Williams 'The Problem of Similar Fact Evidence' (1979) 5 Dalhousie LJ 281; Piragoff *Similar Fact Evidence: Probative Value and Prejudice* (1981); Mirfield 'Similar Facts – Makin Out?' [1987] CLJ 83; Zuckerman *The Principles of Criminal Evidence* (1989) ch 12; Mirfield 'Similar Facts in the High Court of Australia' (1990) 106 LQR 199; Tapper 'The Probative Force of Similar Fact Evidence' (1992) 108 LQR 26; Palmer 'The Scope of the Similar Fact Rule' (1994) 16 Adel LR 161; Nair 'Weighing Similar Fact and Avoiding Prejudice' (1996) 112 LQR 262.
33 [1975] AC 421.
34 The decision of the House of Lords two years earlier in *DPP v Kilbourne* [1973] AC 729 had established that, where similar fact evidence is admissible, it may constitute corroboration.
35 It is difficult to see how Lord Hailsham was, in the context of *DPP v Boardman*, able to insist on the importance of this distinction. The similar fact evidence had no major relevance other than via propensity; a propensity to homosexuality with adolescent partners, the accused preferring the passive role.
36 [1975] AC 421 at 442. See also per Lord Cross at 457.
37 [1975] AC 421 at 445.
38 [1975] AC 421 at 461.
39 Lord Morris, [1975] AC 421 at 442; Lord Hailsham, at 447 and 455; Lord Cross, at 461 and Lord Salmon, at 467. Lord Wilberforce, while expressing doubts on the point, accepted the view taken by the trial judge, at 445.
40 See in particular the judgments of Lord Salmon, [1975] AC 421 at 463 and Lord Cross, at 460.
41 The appeal was allowed and a new trial ordered on other grounds.
42 (1982) 150 CLR 580.
43 The prosecution ultimately decided not to proceed with a re-trial.
44 The fifth member of the court who heard the appeal, Aickin J, died before delivering judgment.
45 (1982) 150 CLR 580 at 585–589. For elaboration of this approach, see also his Honour's judgment in *Sutton v R* (1984) 152 CLR 528.

46 (1982) 150 CLR 580 at 604.
47 (1982) 150 CLR 580 at 592.
48 (1982) 150 CLR 580 at 600.
49 [1975] AC 421 at 441, per Lord Morris; at 444, per Lord Wilberforce; at 455, per Lord Hailsham; at 460, per Lord Cross; at 462, per Lord Salmon.
50 See *R v Inder* (1977) 67 Cr App Rep 143; *R v Clarke* (1977) 67 Cr App Rep 398; *R v Scarrott* [1978] QB 1016; *R v Lunt* (1986) 85 Cr App Rep 241; *R v Brooks* (1990) 92 Cr App Rep 36.
51 [1991] 2 AC 447.
52 [1991] 2 AC 447 at 453.
53 [1991] 2 AC 447 at 460.
54 [1991] 2 AC 447 at 461.
55 Tapper *Cross and Tapper on Evidence* (9th edn, 1999) pp 338–339. See also Tapper 'The Probative Force of Similar Fact Evidence' (1992) 108 LQR 26.
56 *Sutton v R* (1984) 152 CLR 528; *De Jesus v R* (1986) 68 ALR 1; *Hoch v R* (1988) 165 CLR 292; *Harriman v R* (1989) 167 CLR 590; *S v R* (1989) 168 CLR 266; *Thompson v R* (1989) 169 CLR 1; *B v R* (1992) 175 CLR 599.
57 (1988) 165 CLR 292.
58 (1995) 182 CLR 461. For discussion of *Pfennig v R* see Tapper 'Dissimilar Views of Similar Facts' (1995) 111 LQR 381.
59 (1995) 182 CLR 461 at 482–483.
60 *R v Hodge* (1838) 2 Lew CC 227; 168 ER 1136; *Grant v R* (1975) 11 ALR 503; *Barka v R* (1974) 133 CLR 82; *Sutton v R* (1984) 152 CLR 528; *Shepherd v R* (1990) 170 CLR 573.
61 Note *R v Best* [1998] 4 VR 603 at 608–609, per Callaway JA.
62 Section 398A provides:
(1) This section applies to proceedings for an indictable or summary offence.
(2) Propensity evidence relevant to facts in issue in a proceeding for an offence is admissible if the court considers that in all the circumstances it is just to admit it despite any prejudicial effect it may have on the person charged with the offence.
(3) The possibility of a reasonable explanation consistent with the innocence of the person charged with an offence is not relevant to the admissibility of evidence referred to in sub-section (2).
(4) Nothing in this section prevents a court taking into account the possibility of a reasonable explanation consistent with the innocence of the person charged with an offence when considering the weight of the evidence or the credibility of a witness.
(5) This section has effect despite any rule of law to the contrary.
For discussion of this provision, see *R v Best* [1998] 4 VR 603; *R v Tektonopoulos* [1999] 2 VR 412; *R v Mateiasevici* [1999] 3 VR 185; *R v Cogley* [1999] 3 VR 366.
63 *R v AH* (1997) 42 NSWLR 702; *R v Ogd* (2000) 50 NSWLR 433. Cf *W v R* (2001) 189 ALR 633.
64 The decision in *Pfennig* was handed down on 17 February 1995. The Commonwealth Act was passed on 2 February 1995 and came into force on 18 April 1995. The New South Wales Act was passed on 19 June 1995 and came into force on 1 September 1995. The Bills had gone before the Parliaments in 1993 and were based upon draft legislation contained in a report of the Australian Law Reform Commission, *Evidence*, Report No 38 (1987).
65 See *Esso Australia Resources Ltd v Federal Comr of Taxation* (1999) 168 ALR 123.
66 The Law Commission *Evidence of Bad Character in Criminal Proceedings* (Cm 5257, October 2001). A consultation paper, *Evidence in Criminal Proceedings: Previous Misconduct of a Defendant*, was published in 1996. For general discussion of the Law Commission Report, see McEwan 'Previous Misconduct at the Crossroads: Which "Way Ahead"?' [2002] Crim LR 180.
67 Para 8.19; cl 1 of the draft Bill.
68 Para 1.2.
69 Para 8.31; cl 2 of the draft Bill.
70 Para 8.32; cll 3 and 6 of the draft Bill.
71 Para 10.12; cl 7 of the draft Bill.
72 Para 11.46; cl 8 of the draft Bill.
73 Para 7.19; cll 8(4) and 5(2) of the draft Bill.
74 *O'Leary v R* (1946) 73 CLR 566; *R v O'Malley* [1964] Qd R 226; *R v Ciesielski* [1972] 1 NSWLR 504; *R v Vicic* (1986) 43 SASR 176.
75 Para 8.28.
76 Para 8.27.
77 Para 10.7.
78 This matter is discussed at paras 11.23–11.30.
79 The government, in its paper *Justice for All* (Cm 3362, July 2002), foreshadowed introduction of substantial reforming legislation.

80 Cl 82 specifically abolishes the common law rules governing the admissibility of evidence of bad character.

81 Cl 81 provides:

'(1) For the purposes of this Chapter, evidence of a person's bad character is evidence which shows or tends to show that –

(a) he has committed an offence, or

(b) he has behaved, or is disposed to behave, in a way that, in the opinion of the court, might be viewed with disapproval by a reasonable person.

(2) But references in the Chapter to evidence of a person's bad character do not apply to evidence which –

(a) has to do with the alleged facts of the offence with which the defendant is charged, or

(b) is evidence of misconduct in connection with the investigation or prosecution of that offence.'

82 Cl 85 provides:

'(1) For the purposes of section 84(1)(c) evidence is important explanatory evidence if –

(a) without it, the court or jury would find it impossible or difficult properly to understand other evidence in the case, and

(b) its value for understanding the case as a whole is substantial.'

83 Cl 86 provides:

'(1) For the purposes of section 84(1)(d) –

(a) two offences are of the same description as each other if the statement of the offence in an information or indictment would, in each case, be in the same terms;

(b) two offences are of the same category as each other if they belong to the same category of offences prescribed for the purposes of this section by an order made by the Secretary of State.

(2) A category prescribed by an order under this section must consist of offences of the same type.

(3) Only prosecution evidence is admissible under section 84(1)(d).'

84 Cl 87 provides:

'(1) For the purposes of section 84(1)(e) the matters in issue between the defendant and the prosecution include –

(a) the question whether the defendant has a propensity to commit offences of the kind with which he is charged, except where his having such a propensity makes it no more likely that he is guilty of the offence;

(b) the question whether the defendant has a propensity to be untruthful, except where it is not suggested that the defendant's case is untruthful in any respect.

(2) Only prosecution evidence is admissible under section 84(1)(e).'

85 Considered above.

86 That prejudice is at its strongest in sexual cases, and particularly those involving children is supported by research carried out by Dr Lloyd Bostock on mock juries; Law Commission, consultation paper, *Evidence in Criminal Proceedings: Previous Misconduct of a Defendant* (1996), Appendix D, referred to in Law Commission, final report, above n 66, paras 6.37–6.42. Further research addressing the effect of such evidence on magistrates revealed a similar pattern, Law Commission, final report, Appendix A.

87 (1988) 165 CLR 292.

88 (1988) 165 CLR 292 at 296.

89 (1988) 165 CLR 292 at 296–297. In *R v Colby* [1999] NSWCCA 261 the New South Wales Court of Appeal interpreted *R v Hoch* narrowly as requiring a real danger of concoction.

90 [1995] 2 AC 596

91 [1995] 2 AC 596 at 612.

92 [1995] 2 AC 596.

93 Set out above, n 62.

94 For discussion of this provision, see *Cross on Evidence* (6th Australian edn, 2000) pp 611–612.

95 *Wendo v R* (1963) 109 CLR 559; *R v Savage* [1970] Tas SR 137; *R v Attard and Mifsud* [1970] 1 NSWR 750 at 758; *R v Browne-Kerr* [1990] VR 78; *DPP v Alexander* (1990) 120 ALR 673 at 682. Note Evidence Act 1995 (Cth and NSW), s 142.

96 Police and Criminal Evidence Act 1984 (Eng), s 76(2).

97 *Wendo v R* (1963) 109 CLR 559; *R v Donohoe* [1963] SRNSW 38; *R v Hagan* [1966] Qd R 219.

98 *Evidence of Bad Character in Criminal Proceedings*, above n 66, paras 15.26, 15.37; cll 13, 14 of the draft Bill.

99 (1986) 68 ALR 1. See also *Sutton v R* (1984) 152 CLR 528; *Hoch v R* (1988) 165 CLR 292.

100 [1997] AC 117.

101 [1997] AC 117 at 129. Note also *R v Wright* (1989) 90 Cr App Rep 325; *R v Cannan* (1990) 92 Cr App Rep 16; *R v Musquera* [1999] Crim LR 857.

102 See *R v TJB* [1998] 4 VR 621; *R v KRA* [1999] 2 VR 708; *R v GAE* [2000] 1 VR 198; *R v Loguancio* [2000] 1 VR 235.
103 *Evidence of Bad Character in Criminal Proceedings*, n 66 above, para 16.12.
104 Para 16.21; cl 12 of draft Bill.
105 See K K Baker 'Once a Rapist? Motivational Evidence and Relevancy in Rape Law' (1997) 110 Harv LR 563.
106 [1975] AC 421 at 454.
107 *Thompson v R* [1918] AC 221; *R v Sims* [1946] KB 531; *R v Hall* [1952] 1 KB 302; *R v King* [1967] 2 QB 338.
108 [1975] AC 421; see in particular the judgments of Lord Hailsham at 455–456 and Lord Wilberforce at 443.
109 *R v Flack* [1969] 2 All ER 784; *R v Clarke* (1977) 67 Cr App Rep 398; *R v Wright* (1989) 90 Cr App Rep 325; *R v BA* [1997] 2 Cr App Rep 88; *R v Glennon* [1993] 1 VR 97.
110 *R v Ball* [1911] AC 47; *R v Gellin* (1913) 13 SRNSW 271; *R v Etherington* (1982) 32 SASR 230; *R v Dolan* (1992) 58 SASR 501; *B v R* (1992) 175 CLR 599; *R v Beserick* (1993) 30 NSWLR 510; *R v AH* (1997) 42 NSWLR 702; *R v Josifoski* [1997] 2 VR 68; *R v Wackerow* [1998] 1 Qd R 197; *R v Grech* [1997] 2 VR 609; *R v Nieterink* (1999) 76 SASR 56; *KRM v R* (2001) 178 ALR 385. Cf per Gaudron J in *Gipp v R* (1998) 194 CLR 106; *R v Young* [1998] 1 VR 402.
111 This might not, however, be enough to satisfy the *Pfennig* test of admissibility. In *KRM v R* (2001) 178 ALR 385 McHugh J sought to resolve this difficulty by suggesting the *Pfennig* test is not applicable to 'relationship' evidence. See also *R v Nieterink* (1999) 76 SASR 56; *Conway v R* (2000) 172 ALR 185.
112 *Gipp v R* (1998) 194 CLR 106.
113 See Pattenden 'Similar Fact Evidence and Proof of Identity' (1996) 112 LQR 446.
114 (1984) 152 CLR 528. See also *Griffith v R* (1937) 58 CLR 185; *R v Morris* (1969) 54 Cr App R 69; *R v Barrington* [1981] 1 All ER 1132.
115 [1998] 2 Cr App Rep 289.
116 [1999] 2 VR 412. See also *R v Tricoglus* (1976) 65 Cr App Rep 16.
117 [1999] 2 VR 412 at 416.
118 [1999] 2 VR 412 at 418.
119 (1994) 86 CCC (3d) 97. I am grateful to Jill Witkin of my graduate Evidence class for drawing the recent Canadian cases to my attention.
120 (1994) 86 CCC (3d) 97 at 116–117.
121 (1997) 116 CCC (3d) 481.
122 (1997) 116 CCC (3d) 481 at 499–500.
123 *R v Glennon* [1993] 1 VR 97; *R v Glennon* [2001] VSCA 17.
124 [2001] VSCA, para [101]. Application for leave to appeal to the High Court was refused on 15 February 2002.
125 (2002) 81 SASR 22.
126 (2002) 81 SASR 22 at 45.

Implications of the human right rationale for legal professional privilege – the demise of implied statutory abrogation?

Sue McNicol

Legal professional privilege is a fundamental principle of the common law in the majority of the jurisdictions of the Commonwealth.[1] It provides that, in civil and criminal cases, confidential communications passing between a lawyer and her or his client, which have been made for the dominant purpose of seeking or being furnished with legal advice or for the dominant purpose of preparing for actual or contemplated litigation, need not be disclosed in evidence or otherwise revealed. This rule also extends to communications passing between a lawyer or client and third parties if made for the purpose of actual or contemplated litigation.

The first head of legal professional privilege protects lawyer-client communications made for the purpose of obtaining legal advice or for the purpose of obtaining information necessary for use in litigation. Traditionally, the rationale behind this head has been the encouragement and fostering of trust and candour in the lawyer-client relationship.[2] This rationale has been described variously as the instrumental or utilitarian view of the privilege.[3] However, more recently judgments in most Commonwealth jurisdictions have expanded the rationale for the common law privilege as one giving effect to or safeguarding rights, fundamental rights or human rights.[4]

The second head of legal professional privilege protects communications passing between third parties and the lawyer or the client if made in contemplation of litigation. The rationale for this head of the privilege was based on the importance in the conduct of litigation of keeping from the other side any information which a party or lawyer had gathered for an action.[5] It has become customary to conflate this rationale for the third-party litigation head of privilege with the instrumental rationale for the legal advice privilege. On this view:

> 'One is left with a broad rationale which furthers and promotes both the administration of justice and an effective adversary system of litigation. Legal professional privilege is said to achieve both these objectives by, first, fostering candour and trust in the lawyer-client relationship, and secondly, protecting the information of each party from disclosure to the other side.'[6]

Obviously the conflating of these two rationales is expedient, tidy and convenient but it also leaves the rights rationale unaccounted for.[7] It is the aim of this paper, inter alia, to explore some of the implications of the rights-based rationale for the privilege. In particular, it is intended to focus on the description of legal professional privilege as not merely one of the many rights and immunities embedded in the common law but on the description of legal professional privilege as a fundamental *human right*.

Some of the consequences of specifying legal professional privilege as a human right are as follows. First, the human right rationale for the privilege has dramatically impacted upon the possibility of statutory abrogation of the privilege. The balance between the common law and statute has shifted, with some of the rules of statutory construction being rendered nugatory in the face of a fundamental common law human right. Indeed, describing legal professional privilege as a fundamental human right imports a gravitas to the privilege which will mean that the possibility of statutory abrogation will be extremely remote, if not impossible. Legal professional privilege can only be abrogated or displaced by the manifestation of a clear legislative intention. This intention may be demonstrated by express words or necessary implication. It will be submitted that not only abrogation by 'necessary implication' will be extremely rare but so also will express abrogation by Parliament.

It is proposed to consider the area of statutory abrogations from the privilege in the context of two recent decisions from different jurisdictions which approach a similar issue from different perspectives and which reach very different results. First, the House of Lords decision in *R (on the application of Morgan Grenfell & Co Ltd) v Special Comr of Income Tax*[8] will be considered and, second, the Full Federal Court of Australia's decision in *Australian Competition and Consumer Commission v Daniels Corpn International Pty Ltd*[9] will be analysed. These two decisions have been chosen by the present author as illustrations of the more general argument that the starting point in cases dealing with the possible statutory abrogation of legal professional privilege may greatly influence the outcome in the case. Since writing this paper, the High Court of Australia has allowed an appeal by the Daniels Corporation against the decision of the Full Federal Court.[9a] In the present author's view, this High Court decision does not affect (and in fact supports) the general argument made in this paper. Lord Hoffmann in the *Morgan Grenfell* decision began his speech with the proposition that legal professional privilege 'is a fundamental human right long established in the common law' whilst, in contrast, all three judges in the *Daniels* decision began their judgments with an analysis of the statutory provision (s 155 of the Trade Practices Act 1974 (Cth)) which it was argued displaced legal professional privilege by necessary implication. In the author's opinion, this 'common law' starting point for Lord Hoffmann greatly influenced his Lordship's ultimate decision that s 20(1) of the Taxes Management Act 1970 (UK) did not impliedly abrogate legal professional privilege. Similarly, the 'statutory' starting point for Wilcox, Moore and Lindgren JJ in the Federal Court also greatly influenced their Honours' ultimate decision that s 155 of the Trade Practices Act 1974 (Cth) did impliedly abrogate legal professional privilege. The Full Federal Court added that the purpose for which the power is conferred by s 155 would be hampered or defeated if legal professional privilege were to apply.

Second, if legal professional privilege is a 'fundamental human right', then it is difficult to see how a corporation could continue to claim it.[10] If 'human' in the phrase 'human right' is defined literally as something that is enjoyed by human beings, then the privilege rule will have to be narrowed so that only human clients of lawyers can enjoy the benefit of it. This was presumably unintended and, as Gleeson CJ in the High Court of Australia recently commented, 'no one has ever suggested that legal professional privilege is not available to corporations'.[11] Alternatively, the courts could recast the rationale more broadly in this context in order to allow corporations to continue to use it.[12] Third, the human rights rationale does not sit well with the crime-fraud exception. It will be argued below that it is extremely difficult to justify the crime-fraud exception as one which operates to quash a human right of a client to receive confidential legal advice from their lawyer.[13]

It is proposed to consider below how the human right rationale has impacted on the possibility of statutory abrogation of the privilege. There will follow a brief discussion of corporations and the human right rationale. It is then proposed to consider the crime-fraud exception to privilege in the context of the human right rationale. Although a full discussion of the crime-fraud exception is outside the scope of this paper, it remains important to include it briefly. In particular, if the thesis below is correct that either form of legislative abrogation of the privilege[14] will be extremely remote in the future, then areas such as the crime-fraud exception will become an important focus as one of the few remaining avenues for attenuating or eroding the scope of the privilege.[15]

1 Statutory abrogation of the privilege and a human right rationale

In this section, the House of Lords decision in *R (on the application of Morgan Grenfell & Co Ltd) v Special Comr of Income Tax*[16] will be considered and then the Full Federal Court of Australia's decision in *Australian Competition and Consumer Commission v Daniels Corporation International Pty Ltd*[17] will be analysed. Both decisions involved the question whether a particular statutory provision, which did not expressly abolish the privilege, could be read as impliedly displacing the privilege. In the *Morgan Grenfell* case, s 20(1) of the Taxes Management Act 1970 (UK) empowers an inspector of taxes to require a person, by notice in writing, to deliver to him such documents as were in that person's possession or power and, in the inspector's opinion, contained information relevant to any taxation liability to which the person might be subject or the amount of such liability. The Revenue contended that Parliament had provided, in other provisions of the Taxes Management Act 1970, a number of specific safeguards and restrictions for the protection of the taxpayer, including an express preservation of legal professional privilege for documents in the possession of a barrister, advocate or legal advisor, and that accordingly no wider qualification of the general words of s 20(1) had been intended.[18] In the *Daniels* decision, s 155(1) of the Trade Practices Act 1974 (Cth) empowers a member of the Australian Competition and Consumer Commission (ACCC) to require a person, by notice in writing, to furnish to the Commission such information or documents (or appear to give evidence orally or in writing) where the Commission has reason to believe that the person is capable of furnishing information, producing documents or giving evidence relating to a matter that constitutes, or may constitute, a contravention of the Act. Section 155(5) makes it an offence for a person to refuse or fail to comply with a notice under sub-s (1) 'to the extent that the person is capable of complying with it'. Section 155(7) expressly abolishes the privilege against self-incrimination by providing that a person is not excused from furnishing information or producing a document under this section on the ground that the information or document might incriminate the person but use-immunity for the answers is also provided in any criminal proceedings other than proceedings under this section.

Hence, both provisions (that is, s 20(1) of the Taxes Management Act 1970 (UK) and s 155(1) of the Trade Practices Act 1974 (Cth)) were silent on legal professional privilege but other provisions in both Acts indicated that Parliament had considered privilege at some point.[19] When exploring the rationale for legal professional privilege, there is a suggestion by Auburn that 'not too much should be taken from the line of taxation cases on the issue of the rationale, as the relevant statutory provisions of the Taxes Management Act 1970 conferred the privilege in some situations but not others'.[20] In the present author's view, it is artificial to separate the privilege cases which are dealt with in a legislative context from the privilege cases which are dealt with in a non-legislative context. Indeed, the true force and effect of the common law privilege can be gleaned from the cases that have arisen since the advent of legislation giving executive bodies, police, regulators and administrators the power to compel testimony or the production of documents.[21] Some of the statutes may be silent altogether on the privilege whilst others may mention the privilege elliptically in some provisions but not others.[22] This, of course, makes the task of deciding whether the privilege applies more difficult,[23] but it still should not affect the central issue of the characterisation of the privilege itself. It is now proposed to analyse both decisions in detail.

2 The *Morgan Grenfell* decision

The facts of the case were as follows. During the 1990s, Morgan Grenfell marketed a simple tax avoidance scheme to create chargeable gains for clients who had available capital losses. An issue arose between Morgan Grenfell's tax advisors and the Revenue in the case of a scheme which had been sold to Tesco. Morgan Grenfell contended that a premium paid by them for a long lease of property held by Tesco was a payment on revenue account and the Inland Revenue disagreed, arguing that the purchase of the lease was a capital asset. There was no dispute that Morgan Grenfell were completely open about the way the scheme operated. Nevertheless, an inspector of taxes asked to see documents relating to the advice that the taxpayer had obtained from leading counsel and solicitors about whether the scheme would work. The taxpayer objected on the ground, inter alia, that the documents were protected by legal professional privilege. On 28 September 1999 the inspector issued a notice under s 20(1) of the Taxes Management Act 1970 demanding a wide range of documents relating to the advice Morgan Grenfell had sought and received in connection with the Tesco transaction. Section 20(1) of the Taxes Management Act 1970 relevantly provides:

> 'subject to this section, an inspector may by notice in writing require a person (a) to deliver to him such documents as are in the person's possession or power and as (in the inspector's reasonable opinion) contain, or may contain, information relevant to — (i) any tax liability to which the person is or may be subject, or (ii) the amount of any such liability ...'

The taxpayer applied for judicial review to quash the notice, contending, inter alia, that the 1970 Act upon its true construction did not entitle the inspector to require delivery of documents subject to legal professional privilege. That contention was rejected by the Divisional Court, which dismissed the application. The Court of Appeal affirmed that decision, and the taxpayer appealed to the House of Lords. In seeking to uphold the decisions below, the Revenue contended that Parliament had provided, in other provisions of the Taxes Management Act 1970, a number of specific safeguards and restrictions for the protection of the taxpayer, including an express preservation of legal professional privilege for documents in the possession of a barrister, advocate or legal advisor, and that, accordingly, no wider qualification of the general words of s 20(1) had been intended.

The House of Lords held that on its true construction, s 20(1) of the Taxes Management Act 1970 did not entitle an inspector of taxes to require a taxpayer to deliver to him material that was subject to legal professional privilege.

Lord Hoffmann stated that two of the principles relevant to the construction of the 1970 Act are not in dispute. First:

> 'Legal professional privilege is a fundamental human right long established in the common law. It is a necessary corollary of the right of any person to obtain skilled advice about the law. Such advice cannot be effectively obtained unless the client is able to put all the facts before the advisor without fear that they may afterwards be disclosed and used to his prejudice.'[24]

Secondly:

> 'the courts will ordinarily construe general words in a statute, though literally capable of having some startling or unreasonable consequence, such as overriding fundamental human rights, as not having been intended to do so. An intention to override such rights must be expressly stated or appear by necessary implication.'[25]

Lord Hoffmann noted that s 20(1) contains no express reference to legal professional privilege and the question is therefore whether its exclusion must necessarily be implied and for this purpose it is necessary to examine s 20(1) in its context.[26] Lord Hoffmann referred to the Revenue's argument that Parliament has provided a number of specific safeguards and restrictions for the protection of the taxpayer and that it necessarily follows that no wider qualification of the general words of s 20(1) was intended. His Lordship had no trouble dismissing the first four safeguards as not 'coming anywhere near'[27] giving rise to an implication that legal professional privilege was intended to be excluded. As a result, the Revenue stands or falls by the express reference to legal professional privilege in ss 20B(8) and 20C(3). Lord Hoffmann explained the Revenue's argument on ss 20B(8) and 20C(3) as simple:

> 'If Parliament intended to preserve legal professional privilege in general, why did it specifically provide for its preservation in respect of documents in the possession or power of a lawyer? The inescapable inference is said to be that legal professional privilege was not intended to be preserved for documents in the possession or power of the Taxpayer.'[28]

Lord Hoffmann rejected this argument, commenting that it would have been irrational for Parliament to have preserved legal professional privilege for documents in the hands of the lawyer but not for documents (which might well be copies or originals of the same documents) in the hands of the taxpayer. Legal professional privilege was a single privilege for the benefit of the client, whether the documents were in his hands or those of his lawyer.[29]

Lord Hoffmann then asked why Parliament should have dealt expressly with documents in the hands of the lawyer but not with those in the hands of the client. In his Lordship's opinion, the answer was bound up with the decision of the Court of Appeal in *Parry-Jones v Law Society*.[30] In that case, his Lordship stated, the reasoning suggests that any statutory obligation to disclose documents will be construed as overriding the duty of confidence which constitutes the client's only protection.[31] Lord Hoffmann disapproved of this reasoning, commenting that:

> 'It is not the case that legal professional privilege does no more than entitle the client to require his lawyer to withhold privileged documents in judicial or quasi-judicial proceedings, leaving the question of whether he may disclose

> them on other occasions to the implied duty of confidence. The policy of legal professional privilege requires that the client should be secure in the knowledge that protected documents and information will not be disclosed at all.'[32]

Lord Hoffmann then surmised that Parliament, as a result of the *Parry-Jones* decision, would want to make it clear that any disclosure by a lawyer to a tax or other authority (under ss 20(3) or 20A(1)) could not be done without the client's consent. On the other hand, no such provision would be required in the case of documents of the client himself.[33]

Lord Hoffmann concluded his judgment by stating that it is open to Parliament, if it considers that the Revenue require powers to override legal professional privilege, to enact them in unambiguous terms.[34] His Lordship cautioned, however, that the Human Rights Act 1998 should be borne in mind and that the European Court of Human Rights has said that legal professional privilege is a fundamental human right which can be invaded only in exceptional circumstances.[35] Further, Lord Hoffmann 'very much doubted' that the public interest in the collection of the revenue could provide the necessary justification. Lord Hoffmann concluded with the observation that if new legislation is passed, it will have to be seen whether it is limited to cases in which the interference with legal professional privilege can be shown to have a legitimate aim which is necessary in a democratic society.[36]

Lord Hobhouse delivered a separate judgment agreeing with Lord Hoffmann. Lord Hobhouse used a passage from the *Simms* case[37] (which dealt not with legal professional privilege but with human rights) where Lord Hoffmann had stated that 'in the absence of express language or necessary implication to the contrary, the courts therefore presume that even the most general words were intended to be subject to the basic rights of the individual'.[38] Lord Hobhouse added that the protection given by the common law to those entitled to claim legal professional privilege is a basic tenet of the common law as has been reaffirmed by *B*'s case.[39] Lord Hobhouse concluded that in this case the statute does not contain any express words that abrogate the taxpayer's common law right to rely on legal professional privilege and that the statutory language falls a 'long way short' of showing a necessary implication to that effect.

In his book, *Legal Professional Privilege; Law and Theory,* Auburn describes what he considers to be 'the move from the traditional Wigmorean "instrumental" justification for the privilege to the more recent recognition of a "common law right to privilege" in most Commonwealth jurisdictions'.[40] Auburn challenges Wigmore's accepted instrumental rationale for the privilege which he describes as:

> 'absolute confidentiality in legal communications being necessary for the maintenance of good lawyer-client relations; a goal taken to be important for the effective administration of justice.'[41]

It is interesting to test Auburn's thesis that there has been a move from the instrumental rationale for the privilege to the common law right rationale against the actual decision of the House of Lords in the *Morgan Grenfell* case. In the latter case Lord Hoffmann has made a clear statement about the rationale for legal professional privilege in the following passage:

> 'Legal professional privilege is a fundamental human right long established in the common law. It is a necessary corollary of the right of any person to obtain skilled advice about the law. Such advice cannot be effectively obtained unless the client is able to put all the facts before the advisor without fear that they may afterwards be disclosed and used to his prejudice.'[42]

In the present writer's view, Lord Hoffmann is here touching on the Wigmorean instrumental rationale by referring to the importance of the client being able to put all the facts before the advisor without fear that they may afterwards be disclosed and used to his prejudice. But Lord Hoffmann is also referring to legal professional privilege as being a 'fundamental human right' and a 'necessary corollary of the right of any person to obtain skilled advice about the law'. Auburn has noted that commentaries which talk about the demise of the utilitarian rationale and the rise of rights-based theories are problematic because the extent to which a rights-based privilege is also designed to give effect to instrumental concerns is not clear, and has received little attention.[43] In the present writer's view, Lord Hoffmann's passage, above, highlights this unexplored connection between the instrumental and rights-based rationales.

But Lord Hoffmann's passage is also much more focused than many other discussions on the new rationale in that it describes legal professional privilege as not merely 'rights-based' – it specifies the privilege as a 'fundamental human right'. It is submitted that the latter description of the privilege, with its different emphasis, may lead to different consequences compared with a description of the privilege as a 'common law right'.[44]

There are numerous references in both Lord Hoffmann's and Lord Hobhouse's judgments to the fact that *human rights* can 'be invaded only in exceptional circumstances' and to the principle of construction that 'the courts will ordinarily construe general words in a statute, though literally capable of having some startling or unreasonable consequence, such as overriding fundamental *human rights*, as not having been intended to do so'.[45] Lord Hobhouse acknowledged that the earlier speech of Lord Hoffmann relied upon from the *Simms* case[46] was speaking of human rights but Lord Hobhouse added:

> 'the principle of construction is not new and has long been applied in relation to the question whether a statute is to be read as having overridden some basic tenet of the common law.[47] The protection given by the common law to those entitled to claim legal professional privilege is a basic tenet of the common law as has been reaffirmed by *B*'s case.'[48]

Auburn has remarked that there are numerous dicta in most Commonwealth jurisdictions stating that the privilege at common law gives effect to or safeguards 'rights, fundamental rights or human rights'.[49] He goes on to point out that no distinction appears to have been drawn between the various formulations and that the terminology used in expositions of this area is often vague and imprecise.[50] In the argument before the High Court in *Daniels Corpn International Pty Ltd v Australian Competition and Consumer Commission*,[51] several of the Australian High Court judges grappled with some of the problems associated with describing legal professional privilege as a fundamental human right. For instance, Gleeson CJ stated:

> 'The [*Morgan Grenfell*] case referred to a citizen's fundamental human right to obtain advice about the Tax Act from a lawyer. Has anyone ever inquired whether citizens have a corresponding right to obtain advice about the Tax Act from an accountant? Why is confidentiality a fundamental human right when it comes from a lawyer and not when it comes from an accountant?'[52] … If a farmer in a country town goes to a lawyer, a country solicitor … to ask whether a particular receipt constitutes assessable income he is exercising a fundamental human right, and if he asks the local accountant he is not. Is that the position? … Once legal professional privilege moved out of the context of the administration of justice and into the area of receiving advice

about your legal rights, you have got into this problem … that is to say, it is not only lawyers who give you advice about your legal rights.' [53]

3 The *Daniels* decision

The facts of this case were as follows. The applicant, the Australian Competition and Consumer Commission (ACCC) was investigating the first respondent, the Daniels Corporation International Pty Ltd, to determine whether it had engaged in conduct which contravened the Trade Practices Act 1974 (Cth). As part of the investigation the ACCC served the Daniels Corporation with a notice to produce documents and information, pursuant to s 155 of the Trade Practices Act 1974 (Cth). The Daniels Corporation referred the notice to its solicitors, the second respondents. The second respondents produced some documents but refused to produce others, arguing those documents were protected from disclosure by legal professional privilege. The ACCC then served the second respondent with a notice to produce information and documents pursuant to s 155 of the Trade Practices Act 1974 (Cth). The information sought by the notice included information about communications during 1998 between the second respondent solicitors and Daniels in respect of a particular subject. The applicant, the ACCC, applied to the court for declarations that: (i) The power granted to it by s 155 is not subject to legal professional privilege; or (ii) the particular documents requested by the notice were not covered by the privilege. The primary judge, Wilcox J, directed the issue raised in (i) be dealt with separately as a preliminary question. As this issue was purely a question of law and was likely to be appealed regardless of the result before a single judge, Black CJ directed it to be dealt with by a Full Court exercising original jurisdiction pursuant to s 20(1A) of the Federal Court of Australia Act 1976 (Cth).

The Full Federal Court (Wilcox, Moore and Lindgren JJ) granted the declaration and held that legal professional privilege is not a valid answer to a notice served under s 155 of the Trade Practices Act 1974 (Cth). Accordingly, the court ordered and declared that the second respondent was not entitled to refuse to comply with the notice issued by the applicant on the ground of legal professional privilege.

Section 155 of the Trade Practices Act 1974 (Cth) relevantly provides:

> '(1) Subject to subsection (2A), if the Commission, the Chairperson or the Deputy-Chairperson has reason to believe that a person is capable of furnishing information, producing documents or giving evidence relating to a matter that constitutes, or may constitute, a contravention of this Act … a member of the Commission may, by notice in writing served on that person, require that person:
> (a) to furnish to the Commission, by writing signed by that person or, in the case of a body corporate, by a competent officer of the body corporate, within the time and the manner specified in the notice, any such information;
> (b) to produce to the Commission, or to a person specified in the notice acting on its behalf, in accordance with the notice, any such documents; or
> (c) to appear before the Commission at a time and place specified in the notice to give any such evidence, either orally or in writing, and produce any such documents.
>
> (2) …
>
> (2A) …

(3) The Commission may require evidence referred to in paragraph (1)(c) to be given on oath or affirmation and for that purpose any member of the Commission may administer an oath or an affirmation.
(4) …
(5) A person shall not:
(a) refuse or fail to comply with a notice under this section to the extent that the person is capable of complying with it;
(b) in purported compliance with such a notice, knowingly furnish information on the evidence that is false or misleading; or
(c) obstruct or hinder an authorized officer acting in pursuance of subsection (2).
(6) …
(6A) A person who contravenes subsection (5) or (6) is guilty of an offence, punishable on conviction:
(a) in the case of a person not being a body corporate – by a fine not exceeding $2,000 or imprisonment for 12 months; or
(b) in the case of a person being a body corporate – by a fine not exceeding $10,000.
(7) A person is not excused from furnishing information or producing or permitting the inspection of a document in pursuance of this section on the ground that the information or document may tend to incriminate the person, but the answer by a person to any question asked in a notice under this section or the furnishing by a person of any information in pursuance of such a notice, or any document produced in pursuance of such a notice or made available to an authorized officer for inspection, is not admissible in evidence against the person:
(a) in the case of a person not being a body corporate – in any criminal proceedings other than proceedings under this section; or
(b) in the case of a body corporate – in any criminal proceedings other than proceedings under this Act.
(7A) …
(8) …
(9) …'

All three judges held that the requirement in s 155(5)(a) that a person shall not 'refuse or fail to comply with a notice under this section to the extent that the person is capable of complying with it' is inconsistent with legal professional privilege.[54] Further, all three judges held that applying legal professional privilege would prevent s 155 from operating as intended. Indeed, they emphasised that the purpose for which the power is conferred by s 155 would be *hampered*[55] or *defeated* if legal professional privilege were to apply. Wilcox and Moore JJ decided that the practical and policy problems arising from claiming the privilege against self-incrimination, which greatly influenced the High Court in *Pyneboard's* case,[56] would be 'equally apposite'[57] to legal professional privilege. Wilcox J stressed that the ACCC would be unable properly to perform its statutory investigative function if legal professional privilege were available, particularly in the following passage:

> 'Conduct that involves a contravention of the Act often comprises many separate acts, some of which may be effected through lawyers. Without information about contacts between the person under investigation and that person's lawyer, it may be *impossible* for the ACCC to see the whole picture.'[58]

Wilcox J began his judgment by setting out s 155 of the Trade Practices Act, the facts and the proceedings. His Honour then proceeded to summarise and discuss the 'more important decisions focusing on the obligations imposed by s 155 and the nature and ambit of legal professional privilege'.[59] First, the High Court decisions. In *Pyneboard,*[60] the five justices were unanimously of the opinion that a person cannot refuse to comply with a notice under s 155 of the Trade Practices Act on the ground that the information or documents required to be furnished might lead to exposure to a penalty. However, their Honours differed in their reasoning. Wilcox J referred first to certain passages of Mason ACJ, Wilson and Dawson JJ, including the following:

> '... It is necessary to bear in mind the general principle that a statute will not be construed to take away a common law right unless the legislative intent to do so clearly emerges, whether by express words or by necessary implication.'[61]

Although remarking that the comments by Mason ACJ, Wilson and Dawson JJ in *Pyneboard* related to self-incrimination and not to legal professional privilege,[62] Wilcox J referred to the following important passage from Mason ACJ, Wilson and Dawson JJ's judgment:

> 'It is significant that sub-s (5) makes it an offence for a person to refuse or fail to comply with a notice under sub-s (1) "to the extent that the person is capable of complying with it" for these words in themselves are quite inconsistent with the existence of a privilege entitling the recipient of a notice to refuse to comply, whether on the ground that compliance might involve self-incrimination or otherwise. Moreover, it is apparent that the purpose of conferring the power and imposing the obligation is to enable the Commission to ascertain whether any contravention of the Act has taken place, or is taking place, and to make the information furnished, the documents produced and the evidence given admissible in proceedings in respect of contravention of the Act, a purpose which would be *defeated* if privilege were available. As in *Mortimer* the comment may be made that the provision is *valueless* if the obligation to comply is subject to privilege. Without obtaining information, documents and evidence from those who participate in contraventions of the provisions of Pt IV of the Act the Commission would find it *virtually impossible* to establish the existence of those contraventions. The consequence would be that the provisions of Pt IV could not be enforced by successful proceedings for a civil penalty under s 76(1).[63]

It is submitted by the present author that the above passage played the most significant influence on Wilcox J's ultimate decision that legal professional privilege could not be claimed in response to a notice served under s 155 of the Trade Practices Act. Next, Wilcox J referred to *Baker v Campbell*,[64] where the High Court by a 4:3 majority (Murphy, Wilson, Deane and Dawson JJ, withi Gibbs CJ, Mason and Brennan JJ dissenting) held that the doctrine of legal professional privilege is not confined to judicial and quasi judicial proceedings and that the Crimes Act did not evince an intention to oust the privilege. Wilcox J quoted some passages from the judgments which strongly supported the importance of legal professional privilege and suggested that any statutory mandate to impair or destroy that privilege should be framed in 'express and unambiguous terms'[65] or 'unmistakably'.[66] Wilcox J cited *Yuill*'s[67] case, where the High Court by a 3:2 majority (Brennan, Dawson and Toohey JJ, with Gaudron and McHugh JJ dissenting) held that legal professional privilege cannot be claimed in response to the power to require information under the now defunct s 295(1) of the Companies (NSW) Code. Here Wilcox J again emphasised the fact identified by Brennan J in the majority in *Yuill's* case that 'it would frequently be *impossible* for an inspector to carry out his function without disclosure of communications between the corporation and its legal advisers'.[68]

Second, Wilcox J referred to the Federal Court decisions. The Income Tax Assessment Act cases were considered first. In *Federal Comr of Taxation (Cth) v Citibank,*[69] the Full Court held that the power conferred upon the Commissioner of Taxation by s 263 of the Income Tax Assessment Act 1936 (Cth) to have access to books, documents and papers for any of the purposes of the Act, is subject to the doctrine of legal professional privilege. Next, in *Stergis v Boucher*[70] Hill J held that the privilege against self-incrimination cannot be claimed in response to a notice issued under s 264 of the Income Tax Assessment Act 1936 (Cth). In coming to his conclusion, Hill J drew attention to 1984 amendments to the Taxation Administration Act 1953 (Cth) inserting ss 8C and 8D. These sections create offences, respectively, of failing to comply with a request to produce documents and failing to comply with a request to give evidence, in each case 'to the extent that the person is capable of' doing so. Hill J noted this was the same formula as was used in s 155 of the Act and considered in *Pyneboard.*

Next, in *Fieldhouse v Comr of Taxation,*[71] Lockhart J held that legal professional privilege was an available response to a s 164 notice (notwithstanding the lack of argument on the point), whilst Burchett and Hill JJ assumed that legal professional privilege was available.[72] Next, in *Donovan v Comr of Taxation*[73] Wilcox J held that the privilege against self-incrimination cannot be claimed in response to a notice issued under s 264 of the Income Tax Assessment Act 1936 (Cth). *Stergis* and *Donovan* were then approved by a Full Court in *Comr of Taxation (Cth) v De Vonk.*[74] Wilcox J referred to that part of Foster J's judgment in *De Vonk* where he indicated that the phrase 'to the extent that a person is capable of doing so' achieves the result by impliedly excluding the privilege against self-incrimination.[75] Wilcox J also highlighted an important passage from the joint judgment of Hill and Lindgren JJ in *De Vonk* which pointed out that it would be *impossible* for the Commissioner to interrogate a taxpayer about sources of income if the taxpayer could claim the privilege against self-incrimination and that 'such an argument would totally *stultify* the collection of income tax'.[76]

Finally, Wilcox J mentioned *Comr of Taxation v Coombes,*[77] where the Full Court stated that s 264(1)(a) is subject to legal professional privilege but there was no argument, no reasons given and no authority cited.

Wilcox J then distinguished the corporations and bankruptcy cases of the Federal Court as of little assistance for two significant reasons. First, neither the Corporations Law nor the Bankruptcy Act contained the formula 'to the extent that the person is capable of doing so', as in s 155 of the Trade Practices Act or ss 8C or 8D of the Taxation Administration Act. Second, neither the Corporations Law nor the Bankruptcy Act requires a suspicion of wrongdoing before a notice requiring information is issued. In contrast, a notice may be given under s 155 of the *Trade Practices Act* only where the ACCC has reason to believe the recipient is capable of furnishing information 'relating to a matter that constitutes, or may constitute, a contravention of the Act'.[78] Wilcox J concluded this section with six general propositions that are said to emerge from the authorities. In the present author's view the sixth is the most important in the present case, namely:

> '(vi) in determining whether the grounds used by Parliament impliedly exclude legal professional privilege, in a particular case, it is necessary to have regard to the nature of the relevant statutory functions and powers and the extent (if any) to which legal professional privilege might *impede* the discharge of those functions of the exercise of those powers.'[79]

Wilcox J then identified the 'critical question' in the present case, as:

> 'the meaning of the words, in s 155(5)(a) of the Act, 'to the extent that the person is capable of complying with it', reading those words in the context of the s 155 as a whole. If the natural meaning of those words, in that context, is such as to exclude the doctrine of legal professional privilege, that is the end of the matter. If it is not, legal professional privilege is available in this case.'[80]

Wilcox J applied the *Pyneboard* reasoning to these words, noting that Mason ACJ, Wilson and Dawson JJ in *Pyneboard* had stated that the words 'to the extent that the person is capable of complying' were 'quite inconsistent with the existence of a privilege entitling the recipient of a notice to refuse to comply, whether on the ground that compliance might involve self-incrimination *or otherwise*' (emphasis added).[81]

Wilcox J concluded that Mason ACJ, Wilson and Dawson JJ must have intended that the emphasised words 'or otherwise' were referring to legal professional privilege and as such their Honours' observations 'command great weight'. This was so despite the fact that legal professional privilege was not in issue in *Pyneboard* and hence any observations on the relationship between legal professional privilege and s 155 were obiter.[82] Wilcox J found support for the *Pyneboard* interpretation of the words 'is capable of complying with it' in the judgment of Hill J in *Stergis*[83] which held that the adoption of the same formula in ss 8C and 8D of the Taxation Administration Act was effective to exclude the privilege against self incrimination. Wilcox J helpfully explained that the word 'capable' in its natural meaning refers to what a person is *able* to do and is not limited by reference to what a person is entitled not to do.[84] Finally, Wilcox J analogised between legal professional privilege and the privilege against self-incrimination in so far as both privileges could present themselves as substantial obstacles to the ACCC in carrying out their investigative functions and 'seeing the whole picture'.[85]

The second judgment was delivered by Moore J. After setting out the facts, s 155 of the Trade Practices Act and related sections, Moore J commenced with the meaning of the words 'is capable of complying' in s 155(5) of the Trade Practices Act. Moore J first considered the meaning of those words in ss 8C and 8D of the Taxation Administration Act 1953 (Cth), referring to the fact that the legislature enacted ss 8C and 8D (changing the formulation from 'just cause and excuse' to 'capable') the year following the judgment of the High Court in *Pyneboard*.[86] Moore J noted that both Wilcox J in *Donovan v Deputy Comr of Taxation*[87] and Hill and Lindgren JJ in *Comr of Taxation v De Vonk*[88] had observed that the drafter of the amendment had most likely relied on the *Pyneboard* interpretation that the words 'capable of complying' evidenced an intention to exclude the privilege against self incrimination.[89] Moore J decided that 'capable of complying' in s 155(5) comprehends circumstances where the recipient is physically able to comply as the second respondent solicitors were in the present case.[90]

Moore J then considered the passage (referred to in Wilcox J's judgment) from *Pyneboard* where Mason ACJ, Wilson and Dawson JJ stated that the words 'capable of complying' in s 155(5) are quite inconsistent with the existence of a privilege entitling the recipient to refuse to comply, whether on the ground of self incrimination *or otherwise*.[91] Moore J inclined towards the view that Mason ACJ, Wilson and Dawson JJ had legal professional privilege in mind when using the words 'or otherwise'.[92] However, his Honour conceded that *Pyneboard* cannot be treated as authoritative and binding on the relationship between s 155 and legal professional privilege. Nevertheless, Moore J added that the *Pyneboard* decision 'must be taken to indicate the expression "is capable of complying" imposes an obligation that is unlikely to permit of any exceptions'.[93]

Moore J then considered the scope of s 155 and held that the principle of *contemporanea expositio est optima et fortissima in lege* (a statute should be interpreted according to its meaning at the time at which it was enacted) is inapplicable in Australia (except perhaps in the case of archaic words and/or very old statutes) and should not be applied to s 155.[94] His Honour noted that the language of s 155(5) is emphatic and requires compliance if the recipient of the notice is capable, notwithstanding the fact that doing so is in derogation of a common law right.[95] Further, Moore J concluded that the purpose of the power under s 155 may be *hampered, fettered* or *stultified* if it were subject to legal professional privilege.[96] This is particularly so where the aims of the investigation include the prosecution of offences and the institution of civil proceedings. There follows an interesting comparison between legal professional privilege and the privilege against self-incrimination in terms of which privilege would be more likely to stultify the statutory purpose for which s 155 was enacted. Moore J conceded that documents and information resisted on the grounds of the privilege against self-incrimination may be thought, in the ordinary course, to be likely to have a greater bearing on the question of whether there had been contravention of the Trade Practices Act[97] Nevertheless, in relying on certain observations regarding legal professional privilege from Dawson J in *Corporate Affairs Commission (NSW) v Yuill*,[98] Moore J concluded that legal professional privilege would create a significant practical impediment to investigations under s 155 and the practical problems arising from a claim of privilege based on self-incrimination adverted to in *Pyneboard* would be no less if the asserted privilege were legal professional privilege.[99] Hence Moore J concluded that the power granted by s 155 is not subject to legal professional privilege.

The third and final judgment was that of Lindgren J. His Honour agreed with the reasons of Wilcox and Moore JJ and held that a client served with a notice under s 155 of the Trade Practices Act is not rendered not 'capable of complying with it' for the purpose of sub-s (5)(a) by reason of the fact that he/she enjoys the common law legal professional privilege. Lindgren J further held that solicitors served with a notice under s 155 also cannot refuse to do so on the ground that they owe their client a duty to attempt to protect their client's privilege: they can be in no better position than their client.[100] Lindgren J agreed that 'capable' means at least 'immediately physically able without unreasonable practical difficulty and without in any respect acting unlawfully or committing a legal wrong'[101] and noted that the court was not called upon to decide whether 'capable' refers to nothing more or less than physical capacity, or, on the other hand, imports a reference to legal concepts, such as contravening a statutory provision or breaching a court order.[102]

4 Which comes first, statute or common law? – the demise of statutory abrogation

In the argument before the High Court in the *Daniels* case, Kirby J stated:

> '… you really have to start with the statute and construe the statute. It is a statute of the Federal Parliament. It has a higher democratic legitimacy than the common law and if it is constitutionally valid and if it is clear, then we have no right to refuse to give it effect. The purpose of this whole exercise is to find what is the meaning of the federal statute, not to find what is the common law.'[103]

In the author's opinion, it is indeed important to start with the statute, but once it is recognised that legal professional privilege is a fundamental human right, no amount of consideration of the purpose of the statute will alter the fact that general words of a statute will not be read as impairing or impeding the fundamental human right. Furthermore, it can be seen from the discussion of the *Morgan Grenfell* decision above that the courts do not always 'start with the statute'. The *Morgan Grenfell* and the *Daniels* decisions are diametrically opposed in their approach to what are almost identical issues.[104] The Federal Court in *Daniels* has taken a logical, step-by-step approach concentrating almost exclusively on the relevant provisions of the Trade Practices Act. There is barely any mention of the status or rationale of the doctrine of legal professional privilege at common law.[105] In contrast, it is submitted that Lord Hoffmann has 'locked himself in' to the view that legal professional privilege is virtually immutable or untouchable[106] by starting with the proposition that, at common law, legal professional privilege is a fundamental human right.

An appellate court which is today faced with a similar decision on possible abrogation of the privilege by necessary implication has a stark choice. It could start with a concentration on the common law human right that is now said to be the basis of legal professional privilege or it could start with a focus on the words of the statute and the overall purpose of the legislation.[107] For example, to take the facts of *Daniels*' case as an illustration, an appellate court could take either of two routes. It could take the following three steps, starting with the statute. The first step would be to consider the meaning and effect of s 155(1), together with the meaning of the words 'to the extent that the person is capable of complying with it' in s 155(5)(a) of the Trade Practices Act. The latter involves taking into account existing authority such as *Stergis*[108] and *De Vonk*,[109] where similar words used in ss 8C and 8D of the Taxation Administration Act 1953 (Cth) were interpreted as meaning 'physically capable' and not being limited by what a person is entitled not to do. These cases also held that the words 'capable of complying' (and the change of formulation from 'just cause and excuse' to 'capable') reveal an intention on the part of Parliament to exclude as a defence, inter alia, the privilege against self-incrimination.[110] The next step would be to consider whether those words would also operate to exclude legal professional privilege. This involves deciding whether there are any differences between the privilege against self-incrimination and legal professional privilege where both are regarded as having the potential to stultify the purpose for which the investigative power is conferred.[111] The third and final step would necessarily involve considering the overall purpose of the legislation (here the Trade Practices Act) and deciding whether legal professional privilege would operate as just as much a substantial impediment to the operation of the Trade Practices Act as (the High Court decided that)[112] the privilege against self-incrimination does. For example, in *De Vonk's* case, Hill and Lindgren JJ considered the language and character of the coercive statutory power (s 264) as well as the wider issue of the overall purpose of the legislation (the Income Tax Assessment Act 1936 (Cth)). Their Honours stated:

> 'If the argument were to prevail that the privilege against self incrimination was intended to be retained in tax matters it would be impossible for the Commissioner to interrogate a taxpayer about sources of income since any question put on that subject might tend to incriminate the taxpayer by showing that the taxpayer had not complied with the initial obligation to return all sources of income. Such an argument would totally stultify the collection of income tax.'[113]

Alternatively, an appellate court could start with the common law and stress the importance of legal professional privilege as an entrenched common law right. It could then consider the relevant words of the statute and the overall purpose of the legislation and decide whether the purpose of conferring the power and imposing the obligation would be rendered valueless, stultified or hobbled if the privilege were to apply. In the author's view, this latter task of considering the words of the statute and the overall purpose of the legislation is both redundant and artificial if the court has started with the proposition that legal professional privilege is a fundamental human right. The principle of statutory construction that 'fundamental human rights cannot be overridden by general or ambiguous words'[114] will dominate the exercise and dictate the result that privilege will persist. Indeed, Lord Hoffmann describes the possibility of general words of a statute overriding fundamental human rights as 'startling or unreasonable'.[115] Although the House of Lords has recently conceded that a 'fundamental right such as the common law right to legal professional privilege would very rarely be held to be abolished by necessary implication',[116] it is submitted that it is more accurate to concede that the fundamental *human* right to legal professional privilege will never be abolished by necessary implication.[117] The whole concept of abrogation by necessary implication is artificial and irrelevant in this context. It simply cannot and will not happen. Once the perspective of legal professional privilege as a fundamental human right embedded in the common law is embarked upon, it is a sham to suggest that an at best equivocal statutory provision or statute as a whole will operate to displace the privilege.

As to the possibility of abrogation by express words, it is submitted that this too is most unlikely. Lord Hoffmann throws open the challenge to Parliament to abolish legal professional privilege by express words in the following passage:

> '... it is of course open to Parliament, if it considers that the Revenue require such powers, to enact them in unambiguous terms. But there is also the Human Rights Act 1998 to be borne in mind ... if new legislation is passed, it will have to be seen whether it is limited to cases in which the interference with legal professional privilege can be shown to have a legitimate aim which is necessary in a democratic society.'[118]

In the author's view, Lord Hoffmann is actively discouraging Parliament from enacting legislation that would expressly abolish legal professional privilege and His Lordship appears to suggest that even if such an unlikely event were to occur,[119] the courts may be prepared to limit the application of such a statute.[120] The constraints upon Parliament in legislating contrary to fundamental principles of human rights are, of course, ultimately political not legal.[121] There is, however, a positive benefit in recognising that abrogation of the privilege by necessary implication will not occur in the future. This is that Parliament will be forced to act if it wishes to abolish the privilege and the 'principle of legality will mean that Parliament must squarely confront what it is doing and accept the political cost'.[122] It also means that Parliament can confer immunity and other protections against the use of confidential material. It is submitted, however, that it will remain extremely unlikely that Parliament will act, especially to abolish expressly a fundamental human right. As a result, legal professional privilege will only be challenged or attenuated at common law and judges will be confined to areas such as the crime-fraud exception and the doctrine of waiver of privilege if there is a perceived need to narrow the scope of the privilege.[123]

5 Corporations and a human right rationale

The issue of whether corporations should be entitled to the benefit of privilege highlights the importance of identifying and clarifying the rationale for legal professional privilege. If the instrumental rationale of encouraging candour and trust in the lawyer-client relationship is the favoured rationale, then in the author's view, clearly corporations should be entitled to the benefit of legal professional privilege. The objective of maximising lawyer-client relations would clearly embrace clients who are corporations. There is no reason why corporate clients should not be encouraged to be candid and open with their legal advisers. If, however, the human right rationale for privilege is treated as the predominant rationale, it is less clear that corporations should be entitled to the benefit of the privilege.

In a similar context dealing with the privilege against self-incrimination, a 4:3 majority of the High Court of Australia[124] had no difficulty in deciding that when the self-incrimination privilege is viewed as an internationally recognised human right protecting personal freedom, privacy and human dignity,[125] it obviously does not apply to corporations. The majority referred to Lord Denning's view that a corporation has 'no body to be kicked and no soul to be damned'[126] and hence would not be exposing itself to the danger of any physical punishment if it were compelled to incriminate itself.[127] In contrast, the minority considered that the privilege cannot be considered to rest exclusively upon notions of personal freedom and human dignity. Rather the privilege reflects a much broader context in which the inquisitorial approach is emphatically rejected and where there is a 'deep-seated belief that those who allege the commission of a crime should prove it themselves and should not be able to compel the accused to provide proof against himself'. Their Honours emphasised that this broader justification does apply to corporations and to make an exception in the case of corporations merely because a corporation 'has no body to be kicked or soul to be damned' is not a sufficient reason.[128] At least one member of the High Court of Australia, Kirby J has recognised that, in the context of legal professional privilege, a corporation 'may not be entitled to all of the rights described as fundamental human rights'.[129] This may necessitate a reconsideration of the view that legal professional privilege is a human right.

There is also the suggestion that legal professional privilege should not be described as a 'human right', if corporations were to remain entitled to claim it. It has been suggested by Gummow J in *Propend*'s case,[130] that traditional common law rights or constitutional rights 'do not have to be explained in terms of human rights. It [legal professional privilege] is just a fundamental right of citizens, natural and legal persons in our country, that you can get the very useful advice of a lawyer.[131] The convenience of describing legal professional privilege as a 'fundamental right of citizens, natural and legal persons' rather than a *human right* is obviously so that corporations can continue to claim the privilege. However, in the author's view, merely broadening the description of the rationale of the privilege is not answering the deeper question of what the nature of the privilege is or should be. If a 'rights-based' rationale continues to be used in the future (whether it is described as a human right or the right of all legal persons), the courts need to confront the issue of whether corporations are entitled to the same rights as individuals. In the meantime, in order for corporations to continue to claim the benefit of legal professional privilege, it is preferable that the instrumental rationale is the dominant rationale for the privilege.[132]

6 The crime-fraud exception and a human right rationale

It was established in the old case of *R v Cox and Railton*[133] that communications between a lawyer and client which are made in the furtherance of a crime or fraud are not privileged. Stephen J justified the exception on the basis that such communications are outside the scope of the lawyer-client relationship and therefore no privilege arises.[134] His Honour explained that legal professional privilege only covers situations where there is 'professional confidence' and 'legitimate professional employment' between the lawyer and the client. Furthermore, legal professional privilege 'cannot include the case of communications, criminal in themselves, or intended to further any criminal purpose'.[135] Hence, Stephen J concluded that the privilege will be destroyed whenever the communication is made to facilitate the commission of a crime or fraud, whether or not the solicitor is ignorant of the criminal or fraudulent purpose.[136] More recently, the Australian Federal Court has followed English authority in extending the crime-fraud exception to a situation where the relevant illegal or improper purpose was that of a third party.[137]

The crime-fraud exception is difficult to reconcile with both the instrumental rationale and the human rights rationale. For example, the instrumental rationale encourages candour, openness and honesty in the client. If the client is genuinely unaware of the illegality of her planned activities, the instrumental rationale would still dictate that the client seek the advice of her lawyer. Yet such a communication might come dangerously close to falling outside the scope of the lawyer-client relationship. Similarly, if the client has a human right to seek the confidential advice of her lawyer, it is difficult to see why the crime-fraud exception should operate to strike down the right if the communication is used for the purpose of evading the law. And the more the crime-fraud exception is expanded, for example, to cover situations where the illegal or improper purpose was that of a third party, the more difficult it is to see how the privilege was ever operating as a human right. In *Francis & Francis (a firm) v Central Criminal Court*[138] Lord Goff, in extending the crime-fraud exception in this way, stated:

> 'most important of all, it seems to me that the disclosure of the third party's iniquity must, in the interests of justice, prevail over the privilege of the client, innocent though he may be.'[139]

It is submitted that it is extremely difficult to justify the crime-fraud exception in this situation as one which operates to quash a human right of the client. What is more likely is that a broad public interest is operating to quash a privilege which also appears to be resting on a competing (albeit imperfect) public policy rationale of promoting confidential lawyer-client relations.

7 Conclusion

In 1976, the High Court of Australia expressed a now oft-repeated concern that legal professional privilege was 'travelling beyond the underlying rationale to which it is intended to give expression'.[140] Accordingly, the High Court decided to limit the doctrine of legal professional privilege to a 'sole purpose' test because the court feared that the privilege was being too easily claimed by corporate litigants and corporate clients. It has been argued in this paper that today, over 25 years later, the reverse may well be occurring, namely, the underlying rationale is travelling beyond the necessary application of the privilege. In his book, *Legal Professional Privilege: Law and Theory*,[141] Auburn asserts that the advent of the rights rationale for the privilege is 'inextricably bound up in the extension of evidentiary compulsion beyond the curial realm, and the need for courts to find a principle to justify the privilege's further reach'.[142] This may well be correct but it has been submitted in this paper that the advent of the rights rationale has developed now to the stage where legal professional privilege is being treated as not merely one of the many interrelated rights and immunities which have become woven into the common law[143] but as a quite specific and fundamental *human right*.[144] It is likely that, with the advent of human rights legislation in all the Commonwealth jurisdictions apart from Australia mentioned above,[145] the human right rationale for the privilege will continue to be popular and used indiscriminately as a stated rationale for the privilege without a thorough analysis of whether it is appropriate. It has even been recently conceded by some members of the Australian High Court that certain statements on statutory construction in *Pyneboard's* case[146] 'sound like a voice from another era' because there is 'no mention of fundamental rights' and that 'from 1987 onwards human rights has moved on and the High Court has given much more emphasis to the right of the individual'.[147] Furthermore, the new human right rationale has brought with it (or will, in some cases, bring with it) a new debate about the balance between the courts and Parliament as well as a number of other problems which are yet to be resolved.[148] Obviously the rationale should provide the foundation, the justification and the explanation for the privilege. There should be a happy marriage between the privilege and its rationale, so that when the privilege is looking to be delimited or extended by the courts, the rationale can be resorted to as a solid foundation against which to test the proposed delimitation or extension. If consistency cannot be achieved between the proposed delimitation or extension of the privilege on the one hand and the enshrined rationale on the other, then a strong case should be made out before the scope of the privilege is altered. In the author's view, it is unfortunate that not much of this is occurring. On the contrary, the courts are tinkering with the rationale which now does not appear to sit well or firmly as a base for the common law privilege. In other words, there is emerging a lack of synchronisation between the privilege itself and the more recently articulated human right rationale.

Recently the High Court of Australia, when referring to its own decision in *Esso Australia Resources Ltd v Federal Comr of Taxation*,[149] stated:

> 'it is one thing to say … that the common law may develop by analogy to the enacted law. It is another proposition that the common law should stand still because the legislature has not moved.'[150]

It has been predicted above that legislative inactivity will be inevitable with regard to legal professional privilege. But has the common law been 'standing still' when it labels legal professional privilege a human right and then applies the rule of construction that it is highly improbable that the legislature would infringe such rights without expressing its intention with 'irresistible clearness'?[151] In the present author's opinion, the common law is only 'standing still' in the sense that the rule of privilege is held not to be abrogated by necessary implication. But in other more abstruse and indirect ways, the common law is moving – it is recasting the rationale for the privilege, it is throwing down the gauntlet to Parliament by inviting it to act and it is making the task more unpleasant for Parliament by insisting it confront the legal and political ramifications of what it is doing openly and expressly.

In conclusion, it is hoped that if the human right rationale for the privilege continues to be used, as is likely given the recent global interest in humanitarian law and human rights, then the judges who articulate it will at least concede and explore some of the following issues. Judges should acknowledge that this rationale has effectively been imposed over the top of the traditional instrumental rationale; that its own origins and links to the privilege are imprecise and uncertain; that the rationale is often ill-served to justify some of the rules which are ingredients of the privilege and that the long-term effect of subscribing to this rationale is to 'set in concrete' the doctrine of legal professional privilege which will require an extremely robust Parliament to abolish or attenuate it.

NOTES

1 The Commonwealth jurisdictions referred to are England, Australia, Canada, New Zealand and South Africa, although some slight variations occur. European and US law could also be covered by this discussion in a general sense, despite differing descriptions of the privilege, eg 'attorney-client' privilege in the US.

2 See *Grant v Downs* (1976) 135 CLR 674 at 685.

3 Wigmore stressed the importance and acceptance of the instrumental view: see J H Wigmore and J T McNaughton *Evidence in Trials at Common Law* (Boston: Little, Brown & Co, 1961) pp viii, 542–545; D W Louisell 'Confidentiality, Conformity and Confusion: Privileges in Federal Court Today' (1956) Tulane LR 101, 111, cited in J Auburn *Legal Professional Privilege: Law and Theory* (Oxford Hart Publishing, 2000) p 15.

4 *R (on the application of Morgan Grenfell & Co Ltd) v Special Comr of Income Tax* [2002] UKHL 21, [2002] 3 All ER 1 at 4–5, where Lord Hoffmann described the privilege as 'a fundamental human right long established in the common law'; *Baker v Campbell* (1983) 153 CLR 52 at 120, where Deane J described the importance of legal professional privilege in protecting individual rights of the citizen from the intrusion of the state; *Esso Australia Resources Ltd v Federal Comr of Taxation* (1999) 201 CLR 49 at 92, where Kirby J described the rationale for the privilege as founded on human rights; see Auburn, above n 3, at p 16, but note that the judicial support for the rights-based rationale does not extend to South Africa (*see Andresen v Minister for Justice* 1954 (2) SA at 481D; *Mandela v Minister of Prisons* 1983 (1) SA 938 at 957–958 (AD); Auburn, above n 3, p 23) and some United States jurisdictions (*Upjohn Co v United States* 449 US 383 at 389 (1981 SC); *Swidler & Berlin v United States* 118 S Ct 2081 at 2086 (1998 SC); Auburn, above n 3, p 28–29).

5 See *Baker v Campbell* (1983) 153 CLR 52 at 120, per Deane J.

6 S McNicol *Law of Privilege* (Law Book Co, 1992) pp 48–49 as quoted in Auburn, above n 3, pp 33–34.

7 In the United States it has been argued that there is a movement back from the rights rationale to the instrumental/utilitarian rationale: Comment 'Attorney-Client and Work Product in a Utilitarian World: An Argument for Recomparison' (1995) 108 Harv LR 1697, 1703.

8 [2002] UKHL 21, [2002] 3 All ER 1

9 (2001) 108 FCR 123.

9a See *Daniels Corpn International Pty Ltd v Australian Competition and Consumer Commission* (2002) 192 ALR 561.

10 In the High Court decision in *Daniels Corpn International Pty Ltd v Australian Competition and Consumer Commission* (2002) 108 ALR 561 Kirby J at 587 states: 'Daniels is not a human being', and at s 84, para 86, Kirby J states: 'I am conscious of the fact that Daniels is a corporation. As such, it may not be entitled to all of the rights described as fundamental human rights'.

11 See the argument before the High Court in *Daniels Corpn International Pty Ltd v Australian Competition and Consumer Commission* S27/2002 (18 June 2002) at p 50 of 75.

12 Eg the phrase 'human right' could be read loosely as something that can be enjoyed by all legal persons, including corporations. This has been the approach recently in Canada: see *R v Big M Drug Mart (1985)* [1985] 1 SCR 295 where, although freedom of conscience and religion is a right which, although guaranteed to 'everyone' by s 2(a) of the Charter of Rights 1982, cannot apply to a corporation, because a corporation has no conscience and no religion. Nevertheless, in that case, a corporation, Big M Drug Mart Ltd, successfully invoked the right to freedom of religion as a defence to a criminal charge. See also *Irwin Toy v A-G of Quebec* [1989] 1 SCR 927, where a corporation argued that a Quebec law (which prohibited advertising directed at children) infringed s 7 of the Charter of Rights 1982, which provided that 'everyone' has the right to 'life, liberty and security of the person'. The court refused to address the argument on its merits that a corporation by its nature cannot enjoy 'life, liberty and security of the person'. See also *Canadian Egg Marketing Agency v Richardson (1998)* [1998] 3 SCR 157: see P Hogg *Constitutional Law of Canada* (Carswell: Thomson Professional Publishing, 3rd edn, Looseleaf, 2001) pp 56–12 to 56–17.

13 Fourth, the third-party litigation head of privilege is difficult to justify on the basis of a human right rationale. It is difficult to see, for example, how a communication between a lawyer and a third party (such as an accountant or valuer) for the purpose of contemplated litigation would be

protecting a fundamental human right of the client from intrusion from the state. See Deane J in *Baker v Campbell* (1983) 153 CLR 52 at 120. The litigation privilege will not be considered in this paper. See also Auburn, above n 3, p 32, who suggests other areas (such as the rule that privilege survives the death of the client) where parts of the rules that go to make up the privilege are inconsistent with the rights rationale.

14 That is, abrogation of the privilege by express words or by necessary implication.

15 The other remaining area with some potential to limit the privilege is the doctrine of waiver: see *Mann v Carnell* (1999) 201 CLR 1.

16 [2002] UKHL 21, [2002] 3 All ER 1

17 Above n 9.

18 On provisions protecting lawyers only, see S McNicol *Law of Privilege*, above n 6, pp 132–135.

19 Sections 20B(8) and 20C(3) of the Taxes Management Act deal specifically with legal professional privilege, but only in relation to documents in the possession of the lawyer. Section 155(7) of the Trade Practices Act deals specifically with the privilege against self incrimination.

20 Above n 3, p 26. Unfortunately, Auburn chooses not to consider statutory abrogations from the privilege in his book which in the present author's view is a significant omission from an otherwise scholarly treatise: see S McNicol 'Book Review: J Auburn, Legal Professional Privilege: Law and Theory (Oxford: Hart Publishing, 2000)' (2001) 1 OUCLJ 115 at 116.

21 See eg *Baker v Campbell* (1983) 153 CLR 52; *IRC v West-Walker* [1954] NZLR 191.

22 See eg the 'reasonable excuse' provision considered in *Corporate Affairs Commission (NSW) v Yuill* (1991) 100 ALR 609 and the detailed consideration of the phrase 'to the extent that the person is capable of complying' in *Australian Competition and Consumer Commission v Daniels Corpn International Pty Ltd* (2001) 108 FCR 123.

23 Other issues arise also, for example, the complaint of inconsistency due to the fact that statutes expressly removing privilege contain greater protections (such as use immunity) than statutes interpreted by the courts as impliedly removing privilege. See S McNicol *Before the High Court: Australian Competition and Consumer Commission v Daniels Corpn International Pty Ltd* (2002) 24 Syd L Rev 281 at 293.

24 [2002] UKHL 21, [2002] 3 All ER 1 at 4–5. Lord Hoffmann here referred to the cases collected in the speech of Lord Taylor *in R v Derby Magistrates' Court, ex p B* [1996] AC 487. His Lordship added that legal professional privilege has been held by the European Court of Human Rights to be part of the right of privacy guaranteed by art 8 of the European Convention for the Protection of Human Rights and Fundamental Freedoms (see *Campbell v United Kingdom* (1992) 15 EHRR 137; *Foxley v United Kingdom* (2000) 8 BHRC 571) and held by the Court of Justice of the European Communities to be part of Community law (see *AM & S Europe Ltd v EC Commission* Case 155/79 [1983] 1 All ER 705).

25 [2002] UKHL 21, [2002] 3 All ER 1 at 5. Lord Hoffmann here referred to the speeches of Lord Steyn and himself in *R v Secretary of State for the Home Department, ex p Simms* [2000] 2 AC 115 in the context of human rights.

26 [2002] UKHL 21, [2002] 3 All ER 1.

27 [2002] UKHL 21, [2002] 3 All ER 1 at 6.

28 [2002] UKHL 21, [2002] 3 All ER 1 at 7.

29 [2002] UKHL 21, [2002] 3 All ER 1 at 7–8, relying on a passage from Advocate General Slynn in *AM & S Europe Ltd v EC Commission* Case 155/79 [1983] 1 All ER 705 at 733.

30 [1969] 1 Ch 1.

31 [2002] UKHL 21, [2002] 3 All ER 1 at 9.

32 [2002] UKHL 21, [2002] 3 All ER 1, adding that it is unfortunate that the Court of Appeal in *Parry-Jones* was not referred to valuable judgments of the Supreme Court of New Zealand in *IRC v West-Walker* [1954] NZLR 191.

33 [2002] UKHL 21, [2002] 3 All ER 1 at 9–10. Lord Hoffmann then went on to comment that the reasoning of Bingham LJ in *R v IRC, ex p Taylor (No 2)* [1990] 2 All ER 409 at 413–414 was too broad and that the decision of Millett J on a similar point in *Price Waterhouse (a firm) v BCCI Holdings (Luxembourg) SA* [1992] BCLC 583 was wrong.

34 [2002] UKHL 21, [2002] 3 All ER 1 at 11. His Lordship commented that the Revenue's argument that it is important for them to have access to the taxpayer's legal advice in those cases in which liability may turn upon the purpose with which he entered into a transaction or a series of transactions is not thought a sufficient reason for overriding legal professional privilege. The court must infer the purpose from the facts.

35 In *Foxley v United Kingdom* (2000) 8 BHRC 571 at 581; [2002] UKHL 21, [2002] 3 All ER 1 at 11.

36 [2002] UKHL 21, [2002] 3 All ER 1 at 11.

37 *R v Secretary of State for the Home Department, ex p Simms* [1999] 3 All ER 400 at 412.

38 [2002] UKHL 21, [2002] 3 All ER 1 at 12.

39 *B (a minor) v DPP* [2000] 1 All ER 833 ([2002] UKHL 21, [2002] 3 All ER 1 at 13).

40 Auburn, above n 3, p 35. Auburn argues that judges have assumed that new applications of the privilege require a new rationale. Hence the rights rationale in Australia, South Africa and possibly England and Wales is 'inextricably bound up in the extension of evidentiary compulsion beyond the curial realm, and the need for courts to find a principle to justify the privilege's further reach' (p 35).

41 This rationale is occasionally recast by Auburn from being completely objective and neutral as between lawyer and client (eg the instrumental goal of 'maximising lawyer-client communications' (p 105) and the 'global advantage accruing to the entirety of legal relations' (p 114)) to being almost exclusively client-driven (eg 'maintaining client confidence in the secrecy of legal communications' (p 78)).

42 [2002] UKHL 21, [2002] 3 All ER 1 at 4–5. Lord Hoffmann here referred to the cases collected in the speech of Lord Taylor *in R v Derby Magistrates' Court, ex p B* [1996] AC 487. His Lordship added that legal professional privilege has been held by the European Court of Human Rights to be part of the right of privacy guaranteed by art 8 of the European Convention for the Protection of Human Rights and Fundamental Freedoms (see *Campbell v United Kingdom* (1992) 15 EHRR 137; *Foxley v United Kingdom* (2000) 8 BHRC 571) and held by the Court of Justice of the European Communities to be part of Community Law (see *AM & S Europe Ltd v EC Commission* Case 155/79 [1983] 1 All ER 705). Lord Hoffmann later added that 'legal professional privilege does not involve the balancing of interests. It is absolute and is based not merely upon the general right to privacy but also upon the right of access to justice' ([2002] UKHL 21, [2002] 3 All ER 1 at 6). In the argument before the High Court in *Daniels Corpn International Pty Ltd v Australian Competition and Consumer Commission* High Court of Australia Transcript S27/2002 (18 June 2002), Gaudron J remarks that the House of Lords in the *Morgan Grenfell* case importantly put legal professional privilege 'on a different basis from the European Convention which locates legal professional privilege merely as an aspect of the right to privacy. Legal professional privilege has always been located on much more important principle than that' (p 24 of 75).

43 Above n 3, p 16.

44 Eg if legal professional privilege is a 'fundamental human right', then it is difficult to see how a corporation could continue to claim it. This is discussed below.

45 [2002] UKHL 21, [2002] 3 All ER 1 at 5 (emphasis added). Lord Hoffmann referred to the European Court of Human Rights decision in *Foxley v United Kingdom* (2000) 8 BHRC 571 at 581, which described legal professional privilege as a fundamental human right which 'can be invaded only in exceptional circumstances' ([2002] UKHL 21, [2002] 3 All ER 1 at 11) and both Lord Hoffmann and Lord Hobhouse referred to *R v Secretary of State for the Home Department, ex p Simms* [1999] 3 All ER 400 at 412, where Lord Hoffmann stated that the courts 'presume that even the most general words were intended to be subject to the basic rights of the individual'. See also *Coco v The Queen* (1994) 179 CLR 427, where the High Court of Australia refers to the principle that general words are not read as having their literal ambit if that would impede or impair fundamental rights ([2002] UKHL 21, [2002] 3 All ER 1 at 5).

46 *R v Secretary of State for the Home Department, ex p Simms* [1999] 3 All ER 400 at 412.

47 Citing *Viscountess Rhondda's Claim* [1922] 2 AC 339 and *B (a minor) v DPP* [2000] 1 All ER 833 ([2002] UKHL 21, [2002] 3 All ER 1 at 13).

48 *B (a minor) v DPP* [2000] 1 All ER 833 ([2002] UKHL 21, [2002] 3 All ER 1 at 13).

49 Above n 40, p 16.

50 Above n 40, p 16, n 19.

51 Above n 11, High Court of Australia Transcript S27/2002 (18 June 2002).

52 Above n 11, pp 16–17 of 75.

53 Above n 11, p 21 of 75. Kirby J also notes that 'the fundamental human right against self incrimination is in the instruments, whereas you have to do a bit of work to find the fundamental human right to legal advice' (p 24 of 75).

54 Paras 51–56, 60, 67–71, 81, 90, 97.

55 Above n 9 at 146, para 83 (Lindgren J).

56 *Pyneboard Pty Ltd v Trade Practices Commission* (1983) 152 CLR 328.

57 Above n 9, at 137, para 57 (Wilcox J) and at 146, para 84 (Moore J).

58 Above n 9, at 137, para 57.

59 Above n 9, at 128, para 14.

60 (1983) 152 CLR 328.

61 Above n 9, at 128, para 18 (above n 56, at 341).

62 Above n 9, at 129, para 20. Also the comments made in *Mortimer v Brown* (1970) 122 CLR 493 were in respect of the privilege against self incrimination on a public examination of company directors: above n 9 at 129, para 20.

63 Above n 9, at 129, para 20 (above n 56, at 343) (emphasis added). See also the reference by Wilcox J to the passages of Brennan J's judgment in *Pyneboard*, where Brennan J refers to the purpose of investigating suspected contraventions of Pt IV as being 'frustrated by a qualification which makes the statute ineffective' and the privilege being rendered 'relatively valueless' if the penalty privilege were allowed and the investigation being 'so hobbled' as to render much of Pt IV 'unenforceable' ((1983) 152 CLR 328 at 356 above n 9, at 130, para 25).
64 (1983) 153 CLR 52.
65 (1983) 153 CLR 52 at 116–117 (Deane J), above n 9, at 131, para 28.
66 (1983) 153 CLR 52 at 90 (Murphy J), above n 9, at 131, para 29.
67 (1991) 172 CLR 319.
68 (1991) 172 CLR 319 at 323, above n 9, at 132, para 32.
69 (1989) 20 FCR 403.
70 (1989) 20 ATR 591.
71 (1989) 25 FCR 187.
72 (1989) 25 FCR 187 at 191 (Lockhart J), at 203 (Burchett J) and at 208 (Hill J).
73 (1992) 34 FCR 355.
74 (1995) 61 FCR 564.
75 (1995) 61 FCR 564 at 567.
76 (1995) 61 FCR 564 at 583 (emphasis added).
77 (1999) 92 FCR 240.
78 Above n 9, at 135, para 48. In the present author's view, it should also have been noted here that the Income Tax Assessment Act is more like the Corporations Law and the Bankruptcy Act in relation to the second reason, ie there is also no requirement of some suspicion or wrongdoing for a notice to be issued under s 264 of the Income Tax Assessment Act.
79 Above n 9, at 136, para 49 (emphasis added).
80 Above n 9, at 136, para 51.
81 Above n 56, at 343.
82 Above n 9, at 136, paras 53–54.
83 *Stergis v Boucher* (1989) 20 ATR 591.
84 Above n 9, at 137, para 56.
85 Above n 9, at 137, para 57.
86 Above n 9, at 140, para 65.
87 (1992) 34 FCR 355 at 364.
88 (1995) 61 FCR 564 at 583.
89 Above n 9 at 140, para 65.
90 Above n 9 at 141, para 67, relying on Carr J's decision on this point in *De Vonk v Comr of Taxation (Cth)* (1995) 59 FCR 203.
91 (1983) 152 CLR 328 at 343; Above n 9 at 141–142, paras 69–71.
92 Above n 9 at 142, para 70.
93 Above n 9 at 142, para 71.
94 Above n 9 at 142–144, paras 72–77.
95 Above n 9 at 145, para 81.
96 Above n 9 at 146, para 83.
97 Above n 9.
98 (1991) 172 CLR 319 at 333. Note that the High Court in *Daniels* distinguished *Yuill* for various reasons, with Kirby J noting that 'there are weaknesses and difficulties in the majority opinions of this court' (above n 9a, at 584, para 89): see above n 9a, at 567, paras 19–22 (Gleeson CJ, Gaudron, Gummow and Hayne JJ) at 576, paras 53–55 (McHugh J), at 584–585, paras 69–71 and 88–92 (Kirby J) and at 599, para 142 (Callinan J).
99 Above n 9, at 146, para 84.
100 Above n 9, at 148, para 96.
101 Above n 9, at 147, para 90.
102 Above n 9, at 148, para 95.
103 Above n 11 at p 23 of 75. Kirby J later reinforced this point in the High Court decision in *Daniels*, above n 9A at 578, para 67, at 580, para 73 and at 588, paras 104–105.
104 The Australian Taxation Office has similar provisions to s 155 of the Trade Practices Act in the combined effect of s 264 of the Income Tax Assessment Act 1936 (Cth) and ss 8C and 8D of the Taxation Administration Act 1953 (Cth). However, unlike s 155 of the Trade Practices Act, there is also no requirement of some suspicion or wrongdoing for a notice to be issued under s 264 of the Income Tax Assessment Act. (Note, however, the argument that s 155 is not confined to circumstances where there is suspected to be a contravention of the Act: see High Court decision in *Daniels*, above n 9a, at 569, para 26.) See U Torresi 'Does s 264 of the Income Tax Assessment Act 1936 Abrogate Legal Professional Privilege?' (2001) 30 ATR 117, who argues that 'when one properly understands the context in which the Commissioner performs his functions

and discharges his duties and that claims of legal professional privilege will not stultify the Commissioner in his factual inquiry, it is clear that ss 8C and 8D do not abrogate legal professional privilege'. Note that the Income Tax Assessment Act also contains access powers in s 263 (as does s 155(2) of the Trade Practices Act, which subsection was not referred to by the Federal Court in the *Daniels* decision) and the Australian Commissioner of Taxation has granted an administrative concession to professional accountants to withhold certain confidential advice to their clients: see Access to Professional Accounting Advisors' Papers: *Guidelines for the Exercise of Access Powers* (*One.Tel Ltd v Deputy Comr of Taxation* [2000] FCA 270). An abrogation of legal professional privilege for the purpose of a notice issued under s 264 is arguably inconsistent with the maintenance of the privilege where physical access powers are used under s 263 (see *Federal Comr of Taxation (Cth) v Citibank* (1989) 20 FCR 403) and inconsistent with the ability of accountants to suppress documents in response to powers under both ss 263 and 264.

105 Wilcox J quoted some passages from the judgments in *Baker v Campbell* (1983) 153 CLR 52 which strongly supported the importance of legal professional privilege and suggested that any statutory mandate to impair or destroy that privilege should be framed in 'express and unambiguous terms' (at 116-117, Deane J), above n 9, at 131, para 28, or 'unmistakably' (at 90, Murphy J), above n 9, at 131, para 29.

106 On the argument that judges should not always regard the privilege as absolute (in a non-legislative context) and hence judges should be encouraged to engage in rule balancing in order to recognise new derogations from the privilege, see Auburn, above n 3, p 117.

107 In High Court decision in *Daniels*, Kirby J states that 'the correct starting point for analysis is the language of s 155, not pre-existing doctrines of the common law. Where valid legislation has been enacted, the function of a court is to give effect to it, not to common law rights as if the partliament had not spoken: above n 9a, at 580, para 73.

108 *Stergis v Boucher* (1989) 20 ATR 591.

109 *Comr of Taxation (Cth) v De Vonk* (1995) 61 FCR 564.

110 (1995) 61 FCR 564 at 583. As Hill and Lindgren JJ said in *De Vonk*, 'the context of the legislation combined with the terms of ss 8C and 8D lead to the conclusion that the privilege has been abrogated' (at 583); above n 9 at 134, para 45.

111 It is submitted by the present author that when the two privileges are considered in the broader context of whether they operate to stultify the operation of the Trade Practices Act, there are no differences between them. It is conceded that in other contexts, legal professional privilege and the privilege against self-incrimination are not treated similarly. In 1993 it was decided by the High Court of Australia that corporations, unlike a natural person, cannot claim the privilege against self-incrimination: see *Environment Protection Authority v Caltex Refining Co Pty Ltd* (1993) 178 CLR 477. No such equivalent change has occurred with legal professional privilege. Further, there has been a considerable expansion of legal professional privilege beyond its original definition. For example, in Australia, legal professional privilege has been extended to copies of unprivileged documents: *Comr, Australian Federal Police v Propend Finance Pty Ltd* (1997) 188 CLR 501 and the exception to the legal professional privilege in respect of documents which further the defence of an accused has been abolished at common law in England and Australia: *R v Derby Magistrates' Court, ex p B* [1963] AC 487 and *Carter v Northmore Hale Davey & Leake* (1995) 183 CLR 121. Note that s 123 of the Evidence Act 1995 (Cth) reverses the common law position in Australia and see also the strong criticism of the House of Lords decision in the *Derby Magistrates'* case by C Tapper in 'Prosecution and Privilege' (1996) Int J Evidence and Proof 1. There has also been a growth of legal professional privilege via the doctrines of joint privilege and common interest privilege: see S McNicol 'Professional Privilege Spreads its Wings' (1996) 70 LIJ 32, as well as the more recent replacement by the High Court of Australia of a dominant purpose test for a sole purpose test: *Esso Resources Australia Ltd v Federal Comr of Taxation* (1999) 201 CLR 49. There has been no equivalent expansion of the privilege against self-incrimination. In fact, the statute books are replete with examples of the abrogation of the privilege against self-incrimination, whereas there are very few examples of abrogation (or even mention) of legal professional privilege by statute.

112 In *Pyneboard Pty Ltd v Trade Practices Commission* (1983) 152 CLR 328.

113 (1995) 61 FCR 564 at 583; Above n 9, at 134, para 45: note that there have been various reports and papers suggesting that privilege be attenuated in the Taxation system: see eg 'Taxation and Privilege: A Proposed New Structure' Govt Discussion Paper, May 2002, Wellington, New Zealand; 'In the Public Interest? A consultation by the Lord Chancellor's Department following the OFT report on Competition in Professions' (London, July 2002); Taxation Administration Bill 2001 (WA) cl 94.

114 *R v Secretary of State for the Home Department, ex p Simms* [1999] 3 All ER 400 at 412. As McHugh J states in the High Court decision in *Daniels*, 'It is an elementary rule of statutory construction that courts do not read general words in a statute as taking away rights, privileges and immunities that the common law or the general law classifies as fundamental unless the

context of subject matter of the statute points irresistibly to that conclusion': above n 9a, at 572, para 39.

115 Above n 4.

116 *R (Daly) v Secretary of State for the Home Department* [2001] 3 All ER 433 at 438–439, per Lord Bingham, citing *R v Secretary of State for the Home Department, ex p Leech (No 2)* [1993] 4 All ER 539 at 550.

117 There is a suggestion that there may be a type of hierarchy of rights in the *Daniels* argument before the High Court, above n 11, p 10 of 75, where counsel argues that the presumption that 'you construe a statute so as not to disturb the existing legal situation' be confined to 'what are truly recognised to be fundamental rights'.

118 [2002] UKHL 21, [2002] 3 All ER 1 at 11.

119 In the recent paper by the Lord Chancellor's Department entitled 'In the Public Interest? A consultation by the Lord Chancellor's Department following the OFT report on Competition in Professions' (July 2002), it is stated that 'while Parliament would be free to restrict legal professional privilege, the Government should (on policy grounds) be circumspect about bringing forward any such proposals unless it was satisfied that there was such a need', at para 120, p 51.

120 It is, of course, important to stress that the courts must give effect to the clear words of the statute.

121 *R v Secretary of State for the Home Department, ex p Simms* [1999] 3 All ER 400 at 412.

122 [1999] 3 All ER 400 at 412, as cited in the *Morgan Grenfell* case, above n 4, at 12.

123 Eg where the application of the privilege appears to be producing unjust results: see Auburn, above n 40, p 261.

124 *Environment Protection Authority v Caltex Refining Co Pty Ltd* (1993) 178 CLR 477. See S McNicol 'Corporations and the Privilege Against Self Incrimination: The High Court Rules' (1996) 70 LIJ 32.

125 Citing art 14(3), (9) of the International Covenant on Civil and Political Rights.

126 *British Steel v Granada Television* [1981] AC 1096 at 1127.

127 This view was preferred to that of du Parcq LJ that although a company 'cannot suffer all the pains to which a real person is subject', it can still be 'convicted and punished, with grave consequences to its reputation and its members': *Triplex Safety Glass Co v Lancegaye Safety Glass (1934) Ltd* [1939] 2 KB 395 at 409. Brennan J in particular pointed out that the privilege against self-incrimination was never designed to ameliorate any of these specific 'pains' which a company can suffer.

128 (1993) 178 CLR 477 at 493, per Deane, Dawson and Gaudron JJ.

129 In the High Court decision in *Daniels*, above n 9a, at 584, para 86.

130 *Comr Australian Federal Police v Propend Finance Pty Ltd* (1997) 188 CLR 501 at 564–565.

131 As referred to by Kirby J in the argument before the High Court in *Daniels*, above n 11 at p 50 of 75.

132 In V Waye 'The Corporation and Legal Professional Privilege' (1997) 8 Aust J Corp Law 25, 47 the author observes that legal professional privilege has been applied to corporations with little debate and that this reflects the assumption that it is a necessary adjunct to the administration of justice. The author adds, however, that there remains some doubt as to how far down the privilege applies within the corporate hierarchy and the scope of agency between a corporation and a third party required to attract legal advice privilege.

133 (1884) 14 QBD 153.

134 An alternative rationale for the crime-fraud exception is that, as a matter of public policy the law will not shield communications used for the purpose of evading the law: see Auburn, above n 3, p 155. On the distinction between 'privilege not arising' (which has become popular with the courts' treatment of the crime-fraud and other exceptions) and 'arising but being overridden' see Auburn, above n 3, pp 123–193, where the author argues forcefully that in reality the privilege does arise but is being overridden by the crime-fraud rule.

135 (1884) 14 QBD 153 at 167. See also *Re Moage Ltd (in liq), Sheahan v Pitterino* (1998) 26 ACSR 726.

136 *John Fairfax Publications Pty Ltd v Abernathy* [1999] NSWSC 826; *Baker v Evans* (1987) 77 ALR 565.

137 See *Clements, Dunne & Bell Pty Ltd v Comr Australian Federal Police* (2002) 188 ALR 515, where North J in the Federal Court of Australia expressed agreement with the view of Lord Goff in *Francis & Francis (a firm) v Central Criminal Court* [1988] 3 All ER 775. See also *Capar v Comr of Police* (1994) 34 NSWLR 715.

138 [1988] 3 All ER 775.

139 [1988] 3 All ER 775 at 800.

140 *Grant v Downs* (1976) 135 CLR 674 at 688.

141 Above n 3. Auburn argues that there has been a move from the Wigmorean instrumental rationale for the privilege to the common law right rationale in Commonwealth countries.

142 Above n 3, p 35. Other commentators have explained the advent of the rights rationale as due to the twentieth century experience of totalitarianism and a subsequent interest in humanitarian principles and human rights: see J Gardner 'A Re-evaluation of the Attorney-Client Privilege' (1963) 8 Vill LR 279 at 285, cited in Auburn, above n 40, p 35.

143 This description was given of the privilege against self-incrimination by the minority of the High Court of Australia in *Environmental Protection Authority v Caltex Refining Co Pty Ltd* (1993) 178 CLR 477.

144 See eg the speech of Lord Hoffmann in *Morgan Grenfell* and the judgment of Kirby J in *Esso Australia Resources v Federal Comr of Taxation* (1999) 201 CLR 49 and in *Daniels*, above n 9a, at 583, para 86.

145 Human Rights Act 1998 (UK). Auburn states, in the author's view correctly, that the way in which the common law privilege doctrine fits in with this new rights framework has never been adequately settled, above n 3, p 17. Auburn predicts that significant parts of the privilege will be taken over by arts 6 and 8 of the European Convention on Human Rights which have been incorporated into domestic law by the Human Rights Act 1998, above n 3, p 27; see J Wadham and H Mountfield *Blackstone's Guide to the Human Rights Act* 1998 (London: Blackstone Press, 1999); Bill of Rights Act 1990 (NZ), see P A Joseph 'The Zew Zealand Bill of Rights Experience' in P Alston (ed) *Promoting Human Rights Through Bills of Rights* (Oxford: OUP, 1999); 1993 Constitution (SA), s 35, see D van Wyk, J Dugard, B de Villiers and D Davis *Rights and Constitutionalism: The New South African Legal Order* (Oxford: Clarendon Press, 1996); Charter of Rights 1982 (Canada), see Hogg, above n 12.

146 Above n 56, at 355.

147 McHugh J in the *Daniels* argument before the High Court, above n 11, at p 49 of 75.

148 Such as whether there can be a human right of corporations, how the human rights rationale is consistent with the extension of the crime-fraud exception, and whether the human rights rationale can subsist with the third-party litigation limb of the privilege.

149 (1999) 201 CLR 49.

150 *Hollis v Vabu Pty Ltd (t/as Crisis Couriers)* (2001) 181 ALR 263 at 280, per Gleeson CJ, Gaudron, Gummow, Kirby and Hayne JJ.

151 *Bropho v Western Australia* (1990) 171 CLR 1 at 18, citing *Potter v Minahan* (1908) 7 CLR 277 at 304.

Legal proof of knowledge

Roderick Bagshaw

A person's knowledge is so often an object of proof that it would be impractical, and probably pointless, to catalogue all the legal contexts where it is regularly a matter of dispute. This essay considers some of the issues raised for the law of evidence by common methods of proving a person's knowledge.[1] But as a preliminary it pays some attention to the definition of knowledge and how it is to be distinguished from other closely related states of mind. Definitions of knowledge in legal contexts are, of course, likely to reflect assumptions about what distinctions the law of evidence will allow a court to draw in practice. Furthermore, assumptions may have to be made about both what admissible evidence is likely to be available and how it is likely to be distributed.

1 What is knowledge?

Some of the problems which would face a philosopher asked to define knowledge can be ignored by lawyers. For instance, lawyers are generally willing to accept that an external world exists and that it is both possible for propositions about that external world to be true and for such propositions to be proved to be true.[2] Thus if a court of law asks 'did Q know f at the pertinent time (t)?' and we asked it to rephrase the question, it might say that it wanted proof as to whether Q knew that proposition f was true at t. If this is how such a question should be understood then three difficulties invite further discussion: (a) whether proof that Q knew f was true at t requires proof that Q was contemplating the truth of f at t; (b) how to deal with situations where Q knew that f was probably true but was not certain that it was true; and (c) whether there is any stable distinction between knowledge that f was true and belief that f was true.

(a) Knowledge and contemplation

It seems clear that people are commonly said to know things that they are not presently contemplating.[3] Thus when a textbook insists that to commit the offence of handling stolen goods a recipient of the goods must have had knowledge that they were stolen goods at the moment when he received them, the author does not intend that the handler must have been thinking about their provenance at that moment. Glanville Williams argued that it would be too lenient to treat a person as knowing only that which was 'present to the mind at the moment in question' and stated that probably the correct test was: 'was the defendant capable of recalling the fact at the moment in question, if he had addressed his mind to it?'[4] It is worth going a little deeper, however, into 'capacity to recall'.

(i) Forgetfulness

Suppose that in January R told S, a regular handler, that he had acquired a lorry load of stolen confectionery and would send him a sample so that he could consider whether to purchase it. In August S received a box of chocolates through his letterbox with no accompanying card. He was baffled as to who had delivered it or why, but decided that if he ate the chocolates immediately then, even if the delivery was a mistake, he would not have to give them back. As he swallowed the last chocolate, he recalled the conversation with R and shortly afterwards the police knocked on his door. Can S be convicted of handling stolen chocolates?

This case raises a difficult question about the relationship between knowledge and memory. Glanville Williams's test would not be easy to apply to it, since although S was unable to recall the pertinent fact when he actually addressed his mind to the problem (on receipt of the chocolates), he later proved able to recall it, and it is not clear that his 'capacity to recall' altered between those two times. Of course, it is possible that his 'capacity to recall' *did* alter between those times since capacity may vary with external environment, and internal state or mood.[5] But it seems more likely that he simply found an appropriate retrieval cue. Glanville Williams suggests that his test might be made workable in practice by asking whether the average person could have remembered. It seems, however, that what a person can recall from his store of knowledge is dependent on the length of time he is offered to carry out the task, since with extra time it is possible to try a wider range of retrieval strategies. Moreover, another important variable influencing the capacity to recollect is the 'depth', 'richness' or 'breadth' of processing when the fact was initially learned.[6] But one might expect that courts asked to apply Glanville Williams' test would often have very little evidence about how long the forgetful person had to try to remember the pertinent fact or how deeply he originally processed the information.

Given the practical difficulties in applying a 'capacity to recall' test, we might ask whether it is obvious that the person who honestly fails to recall that which a reasonable person would have been able to recall should be convicted. It is certainly possible to argue that such a person should not be convicted. A parallel can be drawn with the person who makes an honest but wholly unreasonable mistake. This suggests that the case for employing a 'capacity to recall' test may reflect reasons other than a desire to convict the unreasonably forgetful. A principal reason might be that the makers of the law were concerned that fact finders might struggle to distinguish the honestly forgetful from those who dishonestly claim forgetfulness. This concern gains weight from the fact that many of the forms of evidence which are commonly relied on to prove knowledge are incapable of disproving forgetfulness. In particular, many of the forms of evidence go no further than proving a 'capacity to know'.[7]

(ii) Failures to reason

Alongside those who claim not to have known f at t because of forgetfulness we may also consider those who claim not to have known f at t because they never carried out the simple reasoning processes necessary to allow them to conclude that f was true. It seems clear that not all of the propositions which we know to be true are propositions which we have perceived and then memorised.[8] There is another class of propositions which we conclude are true by means of inference, using simple reasoning processes. For instance, I know it is unsafe to cross the road at this moment, even though I have never previously seen this particular set of positionings and speeds of cars and trucks. So we must consider how to treat those who claim that they never reached the conclusions which were available to them. One possibility worth considering is whether because *in law* people are taken to know that which they had a 'capacity to recall' we should also say that they know that which they had a 'capacity to infer'.

There are passages in the case law which point away from a 'capacity to infer' test. For instance, in *R v Hall*,[9] the Court of Appeal discussed the position of a person who thought: 'I cannot say I know for certain that these goods are stolen but there can be no other reasonable conclusion in the light of all the circumstances, in the light of all that I have heard and seen' and held that this person did not know that the goods were stolen.[10] This strongly suggests that people are not *always* treated *in law* as knowing that which they had a 'capacity to infer'.

The apparent rejection of a 'capacity to infer' test may cast doubt on the previous suggestion that the attraction of the 'capacity to recall' test reflects a concern that evidence can rarely disprove forgetfulness, because evidence will also only rarely enable a litigant to prove whether another carried out various reasoning processes. A possible explanation for the divergence, however, may be that cross-examination can be more effective in revealing whether a denial of reasoning processes is honest. This is because we think that people are more likely to have something useful to say about *why* they did not reason to a particular conclusion than about *why* they did not recall, and consequently a person might be expected to offer a reason for his failure to infer. For instance, in *R v Forsyth*[11] the defendant explained that she had not drawn the inference that seemed obvious with the benefit of hindsight because of the degree of trust and confidence that she had in the integrity of Asil Nadir.

If people whose knowledge is in issue are expected to offer explanations for any failure to infer then evidence may be available which will allow the law to treat *different reasons for failing to infer* differently. In particular, it may be possible to distinguish between those who failed to infer that f was true by neglecting to formulate any conclusions, and those who failed to infer that f was true because they reasoned towards a conclusion in an unreasonable way. But before saying more about reasons for failing to infer it is necessary to say something about conclusions subject to doubts.

(b) Doubts

Can we say that the defendant who concludes that 'there is a very high chance that the goods are stolen but the seller's story about them being an unwanted gift might possibly be true' knows that the goods are stolen? Clearly it would be too generous to defendants to say that they could avoid being fixed with knowledge of f if they could produce any reason for doubting f, since even a direct perception of f might be unreliable. In *R v Hall*[12] the Court of Appeal asserted that 'A man may be said to know that goods are stolen when he is told by someone with first-hand knowledge (someone such as the thief or the burglar) that such is the case'. But clearly in such a situation there would still be scope for doubts; the thief might be lying or have forgotten that he owned the goods or have hallucinated the theft.

It seems obvious that the law cannot insist that Q only knows f if Q believes that there is no possibility whatsoever of f being untrue. Such an approach would suggest that 'knowledge of f' was defined far more narrowly in legal contexts than it is in everyday speech and, given the difficulty of proving knowledge, this would be unsatisfactory. A more satisfactory approach would be for the law to say that Q knows f provided that Q is 'practically certain' that f is true. This seems to reflect how the word 'know' is used in everyday speech.

Unfortunately, however, 'practical certainty' is not easy to define because it is context sensitive. For instance, the degree of certainty that an engineer will require before she asserts that she knows that the bridge has been designed to withstand a grade 6 earthquake is likely to be far more that the degree of certainty that I will require before I assert that I know that I switched off the kitchen light before leaving for work. If, as seems likely, 'practical certainty' is an essential element in any practical definition of 'knowledge', but the degree of certainty required for 'practical certainty' varies with the amount at stake in the particular context, this may help to explain why English courts have struggled to define 'knowledge' in several criminal contexts. For instance, we may doubt if most purchasers of cheap goods *gain* anything from the goods *actually* being stolen goods. Consequently, they have no reason to consider how much they 'have at stake' or what degree of certainty they might want in order to pronounce themselves 'practically certain'. Without any guidance as to what the relevant actors in a particular social context themselves consider as 'practically certain', courts are left to invent standards, apparently arbitrarily, as the Court of Appeal had to in *R v Hall.*[13]

Regardless of whether the standard is arbitrary, law makers seeking to define 'knowledge' in substantive law will have to define what degree of doubt is nonetheless compatible with 'practical certainty' in the particular context that they are making law for. But, having done this, such law makers may also want to consider whether to include within the margins of the substantive law two further groups of people who have only reached conclusions subject to doubts (and not 'practical certainty'). First, there are those who have reached their conclusions subject to doubts and then decided not to seek the further information that would have allowed them to proceed to 'practical certainty'. This group is discussed below under the heading 'blind eye knowledge'.[14] Second, there are those who have reached their conclusions subject to doubts only by unreasonable chains of reasoning.[15] A member of the second group is likely to face an uphill struggle to persuade a fact finder that she actually followed the unreasonable chain of reasoning that she claims to have followed, but if her story is accepted it seems appropriate that she should not be classed as 'knowing'. As in other contexts, a genuine but unreasonable mistake reduces culpability.

(i) Blind-eye knowledge

A problem arises where a person claims that he was ignorant as to the truth of f even though he could have easily discovered its truth. In many contexts, but not all,[16] English law deals with this problem by treating 'blind-eye knowledge' as equivalent to actual knowledge. What then is 'blind-eye knowledge' of f? The answer seems to be that Q has 'blind-eye knowledge' of f if Q suspects that f may be true and chooses to make no further inquiries in order to avoid the possibility of having this suspicion confirmed.

In *Manifest Shipping Co Ltd v Uni-Polaris Shipping Co Ltd*[17] the House of Lords concluded that such knowledge requires proof of three elements: (i) 'at least a suspicion of a truth about which you do not want to know';[18] (ii) 'a deliberate decision not to inquire';[19] and (iii) the reason for not inquiring 'was because he did not want to know for certain'.[20] Stage (iii) of the test explains why 'blind-eye knowledge' is often bracketed with actual knowledge for the purposes of moral evaluation. Lord Hobhouse offered a list of reasons for not inquiring which would not satisfy stage (iii) of the test; if a person 'did not inquire because he was too lazy or he was grossly negligent or believed there was nothing wrong'.[21] This seems to imply that Lord Hobhouse believed that fact finders could expect evidence to be available about a person's reasons for failing to reason. As was suggested above, we might expect that such evidence would have to come from the person who failed to reason.

In contexts where 'blind-eye knowledge' is not treated as equivalent to actual knowledge courts none the less sometimes state that actual knowledge can be inferred from 'blind-eye knowledge'.[22] For instance, in *Griffiths*,[23] a case of handling stolen goods, James LJ stated that:

> 'To direct the jury that the offence is committed if the defendant, suspecting the goods were stolen, deliberately shut his eyes to the circumstances as an alternative to knowing or believing the goods were stolen is a misdirection. To direct the jury that, in common sense and in law, they may find that the defendant knew or believed the goods to be stolen because he deliberately closed his eyes to the circumstances is a perfectly proper direction.'

It is not clear, however, that finding the three elements said to constitute 'blind-eye knowledge' in *Manifest Shipping* would make it more probable that that person actually reached the conclusion that he did not wish to reach. Of course, a failure to make inquiries *might* support an inference that they were not made because the person was *already* satisfied as to the conclusion. But such an inference (of actual knowledge) would only be proper if the fact finder rejected the contention forming stage (iii) of the *Manifest* test, that the inquiries were not made because he did not wish to reach any absolute conclusions.[24]

(c) Knowledge and belief

The relationship between knowledge and belief can be illuminated through consideration of s 22 of the Theft Act 1968. This provision defines the offence of handling stolen goods and states that to be convicted the accused must have handled the goods 'knowing or believing them to be stolen'. It has been generally assumed that in this context 'knowing' and 'believing' are two different states of mind.[25]

One obvious distinction between knowing and believing is that a person can only know what is true, but can believe what is untrue. But this is clearly not the distinction which the legislature intended to invoke in s 22 since the goods must have been stolen.

Philosophers tend to regard 'people who know f' as a subset of 'people who believe f', and if informed that lawyers were seeking a distinction (other than that for knowledge of a fact the fact must be true) they might state that knowledge must be justified whilst belief need not be.[26] When Q mistakenly thinks that he sees R, his old friend from Australia, going into the Bodelian Law Library, Q cannot know that R is visiting Oxford, even if R is indeed visiting Oxford (although he has been nowhere near the Bodelian Law Library). Q may, however, believe that R is visiting Oxford. Thus the presence of 'or believing' in s 22 might have permitted the conviction of a handler who believed that a calculator was stolen because he mistakenly thought that he had witnessed his friend stealing it a few minutes before, even if he actually received from his friend a different calculator stolen some weeks earlier. Lawyers certainly seem to have no sympathy for the defendant who receives stolen goods believing them to be stolen but without a sufficient justification for that belief.[27] But it also seems clear that the legislature did not intend the provision to plug *this* gap.[28]

The Criminal Law Revision Committee illustrated the 'serious defect' that the provision was needed to plug by reference to a 'man who buys goods at a ridiculously low price from an unknown seller whom he meets in a public house'.[29] The Committee thought that such a man might not know that the good were stolen, especially if he asked no questions, but might none the less believe that they were stolen. The suggestion behind this is apparently that a person can reach belief that a fact is true more easily that knowledge that a fact is true. Or, to put the same point in other words, that 'believe' appropriately describes a state of mind accommodating a greater degree of doubt than 'know'.

It is not easy to know whether the word 'believe' is used in this way in general public discussion, because any such pattern of usage may be masked by the fact that a person cannot 'know' what is untrue. Thus, it is certainly true that if a student unexpectedly asked in a lecture when the last edition of *Cross and Tapper* was published I would probably reply 'I believe that it was published in 1999' rather than 'I know that it was published in 1999'. But there is a possible reason for this choice of words *other than* that I choose 'believe' because it better accommodates my degree of doubt. This other reason is that the choice reflects the rule that one can only know that which is true. So in a context where a person speaks about his or her state of mind towards a fact *prior* to it being established whether that fact is true, it is safer to use the word 'believe'. In a context where the discussion takes place *after* it has been established that the fact is true, it seems to be just as easy to choose the word 'know': if the student opens the cover of the book and reports that 'it was published in 1999' then I would be as likely to say 'I knew that' as 'that's what I believed'.

One of the difficulties faced by the law relating to handling stolen goods is that it (often[30]) involves asking in a context *after* it has been established that the fact is true (the goods were stolen goods) about the defendant's state of mind with regard to that fact *prior* to its being established that the fact was true. Thus a fact finder which asks itself how *the accused* might *at the time of receipt* have honestly described his state of mind might use the word 'belief' more readily than the same fact finder if it asks itself how *it* would *now* describe the defendant's state of mind at the time of receipt.

The Committee's use of the word 'believe' suggests that it thought that the level of 'practical certainty as to the truth of f' necessary for a claim to 'know f' is higher than the level of 'practical certainty as to the truth of f' necessary for a claim to 'believe f'. This way of presenting the Committee's understanding of 'believe' can be illustrated by analysing the position of the person who it thought might 'believe' even if he did not 'know', 'the man who buys goods at a ridiculously low price from an unknown seller whom he meets in a public house'. It seems that such a man would have to admit that he 'was aware that there was a very high chance that the goods were stolen' and might also assert that he could not discount other possibilities entirely. But in analysing this situation it is important to note that the defendant's admission does not directly reveal his state of mind as to the crucial fact: whether the goods were stolen. Instead, it informs us of his state of mind as to *another* fact: whether there was a very high chance that the goods were stolen. With regard to this other fact the man could *equally well* have said 'I *believed* that there was a very high chance that the goods were stolen' or 'I *knew* that there was a very high chance that the goods were stolen'. But a statement that he believed that there was a very high chance that the goods were stolen might tell us indirectly about his state of mind as to whether they were stolen. This is because, in most legal contexts, his statement would imply that he also believed that there was a slim chance that the goods were *not* stolen. But if this belief is sufficient to prevent a conclusion of 'knowledge' that the goods were stolen but not a conclusion of 'belief' that the goods were stolen then that must be because the level of 'practical certainty as to the truth of f' necessary for a claim to 'know f' is higher than the level of 'practical certainty as to the truth of f' necessary for a claim to 'believe f'.

We have already seen, however, that it is difficult for a court to set the level of 'practical certainty' necessary for a claim of knowledge in a context where the person whose state of mind is in issue (like other participants in the same context) has no interest in establishing what level of 'practical certainty' is necessary for a claim of knowledge. And we might anticipate that it will be equally difficult for courts to set the level of 'practical certainty' necessary for a claim of belief in such a context. More importantly, so far as such difficulties stem from the fact that there are no stable conventions as to what level of certainty a person who does not care whether f is true must reach as to the truth of f in order to claim that he 'knew f' or 'believed f', it is clear that such difficulties cannot be resolved by asking a fact finder to pay attention to the 'ordinary meaning' of 'belief'.

(d) Knowledge and belief: case law

The argument above predicts that courts applying s 22 of the Theft Act 1968 will struggle to define a consistent boundary between 'knowledge' and 'belief'. Whilst it would be tedious to demonstrate the accuracy of this prediction by trawling through all the inconsistencies in the case law, even a brief survey is sufficient to give a flavour of the problems.

In *Hall* the Court of Appeal described 'believing' as 'the state of mind of a person who says to himself: "I cannot say I know for certain that these goods are stolen but there can be no other reasonable conclusion in the light of all the circumstances, in the light of all that I have heard and seen."'[31] But this example proved problematic, since it was not clear whether it involved a person who had reached a conclusion about the status of the goods, but at a level of 'practical certainty' insufficient for a claim of knowledge, or a person who had refused to reason to the only conclusion which was reasonable. The latter understanding may be supported by the fact that, two sentences later in the judgment, Boreham J confirmed that a defendant who had said to himself 'despite all that I have seen and all that I have heard, I *refuse* to believe what my brain tells me is obvious'[32] was a defendant who 'believed' for the purposes of s 22.

This interpretation of 'believing', however, was inconsistent with the judgment of the Court of Appeal in *Moys*,[33] in which Lord Lane CJ[34] had stated that: 'suspicion that [the goods] were stolen, even coupled with the fact that he shut his eyes to the circumstances, is not enough, although these matters may be taken into account by the jury when deciding whether or not the necessary knowledge or belief existed.' Subsequently, in *R v Forsyth*[35] the Court of Appeal declared that *Hall* contained 'potential for confusion' and urged judges to follow *Moys*. The *Forsyth* court made clear that 'belief' was not equivalent to 'suspicion', even 'great suspicion'.[36] Further, it stated that 'between suspicion and actual belief there may be a range of awareness'.[37] The phrase 'range of awareness' is opaque, but might sensibly be taken to mean 'range of assessed degrees of likelihood'.[38] The *Forsyth* court, however, did not offer any useful guidance on what degree of likelihood is necessary for a responsible claim of 'belief', or how 'belief' relates to 'knowledge'. Indeed, it stated that 'the ordinary meaning of belief is the mental acceptance of a fact as true or existing',[39] which, because it ignores the crucial issue of 'degree of likelihood', could equally do service as a definition of 'knowledge'.

2 How is knowledge proved?

In the absence of a confession, the obvious methods rely on either betrayal or an inference from opportunity. An easy example of betrayal is provided by the importer of video tapes who presents them to Customs Officers in packaging taken from other videos he had recently purchased in the airport shop then dumped in a lavatory.[40] A more difficult one is the girl who throws a lighted match into a puddle of white spirit (rather than throwing a clothes-peg or a screwdriver).[41] Examples of opportunity are provided by proof that information was published in a newspaper to which the relevant person subscribed[42] and proof that the defendant knew the claimant well and was thus likely to know that the statements about him were untrue.[43]

(a) Betrayal

Reliance on betrayal as a method of proving Q's knowledge of f can raise the problems of hearsay[44] and indeterminacy.[45]

(i) Hearsay

The hearsay problem involves three elements. First, there is the question whether the utterance or conduct which is thought to betray knowledge is being used testimonially. Second, there is the question whether, even if it is not being used testimonially, such circumstantial use undercuts the hearsay rule to such an extent that it should be prohibited. Third there is the question whether some exception to the hearsay rule applies.

The first and second questions can be confronted through considering use of Q's statement 'a powerful mobile phone may trigger this type of airbag' to establish that Q knew of that defect in a car prior to an accident. The first question demands whether such use would be testimonial, that is would it involve use of the statement to establish 'some fact narrated by the words'.[46] Recent opinion seems to have coalesced around the view that the hearsay rule should be reserved for use of out-of-court statements to prove that which it was the speaker's intention to convey to another.[47]

There is certainly a strong case for removing from the ambit of the hearsay rule statements and conduct which were not intended to communicate anything to anybody, because in such circumstances an intention to mislead is negatived. But an intention-based approach can lead to unsatisfactory conclusions when applied to situations where a person makes a statement which is intended to communicate one thing, but which also simultaneously communicates another. This is often the situation where a statement incidentally communicates the speaker's state of mind. For instance, a party anxious to use Q's statement to prove his knowledge might reasonably state that Q intended to convey to his audience that it was possible that the airbag had the defect concerned, but that it was no part of Q's project to communicate the fact that he *knew* about the defect. The awkward problem that such an example raises for supporters of an intention-based approach is that even if Q did not intend to communicate anything about his state of knowledge this *does not mean* that what he did incidentally communicate about his state of knowledge was reliable. This is because the reliability of what he did not intend to communicate none the less *depends on* the reliability of what he did intend to communicate. For instance, if Q made the statement in order to persuade customers to buy a different brand of airbag, and without any belief in the existence of the defect, then the statement would not be reliable evidence of his knowledge of the defect. And, obviously, the fact that a party may have no interest in using the statement to prove the existence of the defect (because that can be established by other evidence) and merely wants to use it to prove Q's knowledge will not make the statement reliable evidence of Q's knowledge.

Is there a solution to the problem identified short of preserving *Kearley*[48] and leaving 'the law of hearsay in England to wallow in a parochial morass of technicality'?[49] The happiest compromise might be to confine the hearsay rule to use of statements in order to prove what the speaker intended to assert or in order to prove that which is to be inferred from the content of an intended assertion. This would permit evidence to be given of the sea captain's boarding following inspection[50] whilst not permitting Q's statement to be admitted to establish his knowledge of the defect.[51]

Even if supporters of the intention-based approach reject the compromise proposed above, they must accept that it is often not straightforward to identify what a speaker did intend to assert. The difficulties can be illustrated by a brief reference to the use of Q's utterance 'I am Napoleon' to establish Q's insanity.[52] The first move in analysis of this use must be to establish the chain of reasoning leading from the utterance to the inference of insanity, and in particular whether the chain proceeds through Q's 'belief' that he is Napoleon. If the fact-finder is merely asked to weigh the improbability of a sane person ever using the sequence of words 'I am Napoleon' then the use is circumstantial.[53] But if the fact-finder is asked to conclude that Q believed that he was Napoleon, and that this belief suggests insanity, then it is necessary to ask if Q intended to communicate this belief. Here much will turn on whether one is willing to allow intentions to be expressed narrowly or not. An evidence lawyer willing to allow persons to describe their intentions narrowly might accept the answer: 'no, Q did not intend to communicate his state of mind (belief), but only to communicate the objective fact of his own identity.' Other evidence lawyers less tolerant of any faint whiff of sophistry might argue that for Q to deny that he intended to communicate his belief would be equivalent to a man choosing to walk to the shops in the rain then denying that he intended to get the soles of his shoes wet. In other words, they would insist that a person cannot claim not to have intended the known and necessarily inseparable accompaniments to fulfilment of his project. In its report on the hearsay rule in criminal cases the Law Commission expressly recommends adoption of the narrow approach to the description of intentions.[54] The reasoning supporting this recommendation, however, seems to have been influenced by the Commission's erroneous opinion that unintended communications are reliable even when inferred from intended communications. It is difficult for a person who believes that it is an error to delimit the hearsay rule in terms of intentions alone to offer constructive[55] advice on whether intentions should be defined broadly or narrowly. But enough has been said in this paragraph to establish that those who reject the proposed compromise must confront this further choice.

The second question asks whether circumstantial use of a statement can undercut the hearsay rule to such an extent that it should be prohibited. The answer seems straightforward. Even if a legal system accepts that Q's statement can be admitted to prove his knowledge (because he did not intend to communicate his knowledge), it would be inappropriate to go further and invite a fact finder to infer from the knowledge that the defect actually existed .

But if one assumes that the unintended communication of the state of mind is reliable because it was unintended,[56] then the objection to this chain of reasoning cannot be that it is unreliable. Rather the objection must be that it allows the hearsay rule to be undercut or circumvented in too many cases. This problem of over-circumvention has been recognised in some jurisdictions where hearsay is admissible under an exception in order to prove a state of mind. Thus under r 803(3) of the Federal Rules of Evidence the hearsay rule does not exclude a statement of 'the declarant's then existing state of mind, emotion, sensation, or physical condition (such as intent, plan, motive, design, mental feeling, pain, and bodily health)', but there is an exception to this exception so that it cannot be used to admit 'a statement of memory or belief to prove the fact remembered or believed unless [the exception to the exception to the exception] it relates to the execution, revocation, identification, or terms of declarant's will'.[57] The problem of undercutting which necessitates such a provision, however, is equally great whether the evidence of memory or belief is admitted under an exception to the hearsay rule or because it is thought never to fall within the scope of the rule. Despite this, the problem does not seem to have been addressed by the Law Commission in its proposed reforms to the hearsay rule in criminal cases.[58] As will be noted below, the technique which English law uses to prevent the current English version of the state of mind exception from undercutting the hearsay rule will not necessarily translate to a situation where the evidence is defined as beyond the scope of the hearsay rule altogether.

The third question asks about exceptions to the hearsay rule. Where a relevant state of mind is betrayed by a defendant in a criminal case it will often be admissible as an admission.[59] Where the relevant matter is the knowledge of a person other than the defendant then the most obviously useful exception is that covering declarations as to a contemporaneous state of mind.[60] This exception requires the state of mind to be contemporaneous with the declaration. Thus it is inapplicable when a person declares that he or she had a particular state of mind at an earlier time; for instance, that he was angry when he came into the room two hours ago.[61] But often a declaration of a current state of mind will allow an inference of that same (or some other) state of mind earlier or later. For instance, past knowledge may be inferred from a betrayal of current knowledge.

The justification for the state of mind exception to the hearsay rule is obscure. Early cases seem to have treated evidence of a relevant state of mind as part of the *res gestae*,[62] and the exception is still put under that sub-heading in *Cross and Tapper*.[63] But the reason for the persistence, and perhaps expansion, of the exception seems to have had more to do with necessity and convenience.[64] Although the existence of the exception is not in doubt,[65] as mentioned above, it has the capacity to undercut the hearsay rule to a substantial extent.[66] English law has limited this threat in two ways. First, where an out-of-court statement details a state of mind and explains the circumstances leading to the formation of that state of mind, English law has excluded the explanation of the circumstances.[67] Second, where the evidence of the state of mind has been offered in order to support an inference as to the circumstances leading to the formation of that state of mind, courts have often asserted that the state of mind is insufficiently relevant for the exception to be relied on.[68] Although no English case has expressly recognised an exception to the exception similar to that found in r 803(3) of the Federal Rules of Evidence,[69] it seems likely that any attempt to use the exception to prove memory and hence to support an inference as to the truth of what was remembered could be stifled by the response that the memory itself was insufficiently relevant. Some slim support for an express English exception to the exception can be found in *Thomas v Connell*,[70] where Parke B stated that evidence of a bankrupt's statement that he was insolvent was inadmissible to establish his insolvency but was admissible to establish his knowledge of his insolvency *after* his insolvency had been proved by other evidence.[71]

(ii) Indeterminacy

The problem of indeterminacy is one which arises where the person's utterance or conduct is consistent with more than one possible state of mind. It is particularly acute when the person's absence from the witness box leaves the fact-finder with no reliable basis for deciding which of the possible states of mind he or she should infer. An example may assist.

Suppose that a dilapidated ship has sunk, drowning its captain, and a dispute arises over whether an insurance company should pay a sum to his relatives which would not be due if he consciously exposed himself to an unreasonable risk. The insurance company offers the evidence that the captain examined the ship carefully before boarding as evidence that he was conscious of the extreme risk he was taking by boarding such a dilapidated vessel. The relatives argue that the same evidence establishes that he was not conscious of the risk. As it stands[72] there is a strong argument for declaring that the evidence is irrelevant in the special sense that it does not render either contention more likely relative to the other contention.[73]

It might be thought that the example is in some way exceptional. But in fact in many cases where behaviour is said to betray knowledge it is equally consistent with a non-absolute mental state. For instance, the purchaser of silverware who buries it in the garden could be betraying knowledge that it was stolen, but could equally be betraying the state of mind that 'there is a significant chance that it might be stolen, and it would be embarrassing to have to explain things if it turns out to be, so I'll reduce my risk of embarrassment whilst waiting for things to become clearer'. There are obvious parallels with the problems which arise when the prosecution seeks to use flight or evasive lying to try and prove guilt of a serious offence when the person now claims that he was only trying to conceal a less serious offence which he is now willing to admit.[74]

Attempts to rely on utterances or actions which were not intended to be communicative as evidence also give rise to a further related problem of indeterminacy. The related problem stems from the fact that a person who was not intending to communicate will not necessarily have used the ordinary conventions which allow communications to be understood. Thus any decoding of the unintentionally communicated message may be unreliable. The person who claps his hands when he thinks that nobody is watching may not have the same state of mind as the person who intends to communicate by clapping his hands.

The difficulty in drawing the correct inferences from utterances and actions which were not intended to be communicative provides ammunition for those who believe that the hearsay rule should extend further than use of out of court utterances and actions to prove what the speaker or actor intended to communicate. In terms of hearsay dangers the problem posed by non-communicative utterances and actions is that even if the danger of insincerity is low the danger of ambiguity is high.

(iii) Conclusions on betrayal

The purpose of this section is not to advocate retention of an extensive hearsay rule. Rather it cautions against any reformulation of the hearsay rule to permit proof of Q's knowledge of f by reference to an out-of-court statement made by Q simply because Q did not intend to assert his knowledge of f. The section suggests that such a reformulation of the hearsay rule cannot be justified by the assumption that such inferences will necessarily be reliable,[75] may require the creation of a further doctrine to avoid undesirable undercutting of the hearsay rule, and may increase the already existing problem of indeterminacy.

(b) Opportunity

It seems straightforward that a second strategy for proving that Q knew f at t is to demonstrate that Q had an opportunity to discover the truth of f before that time. Wigmore, with usual thoroughness, explains the strategy as involving the proof of 'external circumstances, calculated by their presence or occurrence to bring about the state of mind in question'. He then classifies relevant circumstances into four typical categories, with the weight of the evidence depending on (a) the probability that the circumstances caused Q to receive an impression of any fact at all, and (b) the probability that Q gained an impression as to the specific fact.[76] The present essay will make no attempt to assess how well the English cases illustrate the merits of Wigmore's classification. Instead, it will make a few general points about how the law of evidence seeks to regulate inferences from opportunity.

(i) Why regulate inferences from opportunity?

Although it is a broad generalisation, it is probably possible to defend the opinion that a majority of modern evidence scholars are sceptical about regulation of the substantive process of proof other than to ensure that only relevant evidence is admitted and prejudicial and unfair material is excluded. But such sceptics tend to overlook the insight that not all facts are equally provable. There are some facts about which very little external evidence is likely to exist. Moreover, what external evidence there is may be unevenly distributed between the parties that have an interest in establishing the fact concerned. In circumstances where it is likely to be difficult or costly for one party to find evidence about a particular fact, courts may choose to amend the substantive law in order to maintain balance[77] or may develop informal rules about what quality of evidence the party with the easier task must introduce before it calls for an answer or how far the party with the harder task can depend on presumptions.

A person's knowledge seems to be a fact about which little external evidence is likely to exist, with what evidence there is being unevenly distributed.[78] This observation may be of assistance in explaining some of the arcane doctrines surrounding proof of knowledge by use of evidence of opportunity. The next three paragraphs will consider how far the cases that are often mentioned in general discussions of legal proof of knowledge support this observation. Discussion will then move on to two special situations involving proof of knowledge by means of proof of opportunity to acquire knowledge: the 'doctrine of recent possession' and proof of knowledge by means of proof of similar conduct on other occasions.

(ii) Regulation of inferences from opportunity

It would be reasonable for courts to be cautious about admitting weak evidence of opportunity where it might leave Q with the unenviable practical burden of trying to prove a negative, that is trying to prove that despite the opportunity he did not discover the truth. This practical burden might be particularly awkward in situations where Q was unavailable to deny acquiring knowledge or where any such denial by Q would now be regarded as self-serving and entitled to little weight. In such circumstances a judge might seek to avoid admitting evidence of opportunity pointing only faintly towards knowledge. An example may be provided by *Harding v Crethorn*,[79] where Lord Kenyon was unwilling to accept that witnessing a document tended to prove knowledge of its contents, and further evidence had to be given that the document had been read to the witness.

In many contexts where a party seeks to rely on weak evidence that Q had an opportunity to discover the truth of f, it is difficult to determine where the substantive law ends and the law of evidence begins. For instance, in *Mackintosh v Marshall*[80] a claimant on an insurance policy had made a representation to an underwriter which was inconsistent with the contents of Lloyd's List. A dispute arose as to whether the List should have been admitted as evidence to prove that the underwriter was aware of the truth, and consequently not misled by the misrepresentation. Lord Abinger CB held that the List should have been admitted, but that the judge should have also told the jury that in the circumstances it was obvious that the underwriter would not have taken the premium if he had been aware of the contents of the List so the presumption that he had looked at the List was entirely rebutted. In *Bates v Hewitt*[81] the Queen's Bench reached a similar conclusion on substantive grounds, holding that a claimant on an insurance policy who was alleged to have failed to disclose a material fact could not avoid that defence simply by establishing that an underwriter of ordinary intelligence and knowledge of his business would have known the fact anyway. Although it is difficult to draw a neat line between substantive and evidentiary points, these cases tend to suggest that courts will be more stern about use of weak evidence of opportunity to prove knowledge where a party is seeking to prove the knowledge of another in order to avoid the consequences that would normally attach to his own wrongful acts.

The cases discussed above offer some very faint support for the view that where it would be difficult for one party to provide convincing evidence of lack of knowledge then the other party might sometimes be prevented from proving knowledge by use of weak evidence of opportunity to acquire knowledge. There is a further group of cases, however, involving situations where one party's knowledge is in issue and it would be almost impossible for the other party to provide any evidence of knowledge *other than* evidence of opportunity. In some of these situations it might be unfair (and could lead to serious uncertainty) to allow the party which had the opportunity to acquire the knowledge to later deny it, and thus to demand other evidence. Consequently, in such circumstances courts may choose to treat the evidence of opportunity as conclusive evidence of knowledge. Thus in *Guardhouse v Blackburn*[82] Sir J P Wilde held that if a will had been read to a capable testator and then executed, that should 'be held conclusive evidence that he approved as well as knew the contents thereof'. Similarly, in *Re Cooper*,[83] Jessel MR held that there was 'a presumption of law that when a man signs a deed he is acquainted with its contents'[84] and in *Cooper v Law*[85] a vestryman was presumed to have known of the contents of parish books to which he had access.[86]

(iii) Recent possession

Where a person is proved to have been in possession of recently stolen goods, and either offers no explanation for his possession of them or offers an explanation which the fact finder is satisfied is untrue, the fact finder *may* infer that he stole the goods or handled them 'knowing or believing' them to be stolen.[87] Professor Sir John Smith has argued forcefully that this 'doctrine' 'is nothing more than the application to this constantly recurring situation of the ordinary principles of circumstantial evidence'.[88] But this opinion risks masking the fact that, particularly in cases involving handling, negative evidence, the absence of a satisfactory explanation, plays an important part in establishing the case against the accused.[89] The fairness of directing the fact finder's attention to the negative evidence may, of course, reflect the difficulty faced by the prosecution in securing positive evidence of 'knowledge'. Indeed, where there is positive evidence relating to the circumstances in which the goods came into the accused's possession the doctrine will not apply.[90]

One oddity of the doctrine is that the negative evidence is only considered sufficient to ground an inference of guilt when the accused was in possession of *recently* stolen property.[91] Thus it seems that possessors of *recently* stolen property are thought to be more likely to know its status than possessors of property stolen longer ago. This view must draw its strength from the belief that those who obtain property shortly after a theft are more likely to be associated with the thief or otherwise to have had a better opportunity to discover the status of the property. Indeed, it seems that the likelihood of an inference can be increased by improving the evidence of opportunity, for instance, by introducing evidence of a relationship of trust and confidence between the thief and the person accused of handling.[92]

(iv) Similar conduct

Section 27(3) of the Theft Act 1968 permits the admission of evidence of possession of stolen goods on other occasions and previous convictions for handling in order to prove 'knowledge or belief'. The risk that it might lead to the admission of evidence likely to be used in the chains of reasoning restricted by the 'similar fact' rule has led to the emasculation of the subsection by narrow interpretation and the invention of an exclusionary discretion.[93] Were it not for this emasculation, the subsection might have been used to introduce evidence of the surrounding circumstances of previous transactions with stolen goods where those circumstances are likely to have enhanced the accused's opportunity to acquire knowledge about the status of current goods. For instance, previous transactions might have taught the accused not to trust a particular source or how to identify the status of a particular class of goods. It seems likely, however, that the emasculation of the subsection will not prevent the prosecution from arguing that such evidence is admissible at common law if it is sufficiently strongly relevant to the accused's state of mind.

3 Conclusions

This essay has not taken the form of an argument aimed at reaching specific conclusions. But two suggestions that have been made in the course of the discussion might be thought to have wider significance and to be worth repeating at this stage. First, it has been suggested that the definition of 'knowledge' in substantive law often reflects assumptions about what admissible evidence is likely to be available and how it is likely to be distributed. Second, it has been argued that some of the doctrines relating to legal proof of knowledge demonstrate how the law of evidence may become involved in regulating the admissibility of evidence and the inferences that can be drawn from it in order to respond to difficulties caused by the natural distribution of admissible evidence relating to a particular type of fact.

NOTES

1 To avoid complication, the discussion will concentrate on Q's knowledge of external facts, such as, that the goods were stolen, the funds had been abstracted from a trust, or the girl was under 14 years of age.

2 This assertion is based on the belief that it would be difficult for a lawyer to explain her willingness to become involved in legal practice if she did not accept these propositions.

3 For instance, I know a substantial number of the reported facts of the cases mentioned in this essay, but contemplate them only infrequently.

4 *Criminal Law – The General Part* (2nd edn, 1961) p 170.

5 A D Baddeley *Essentials of Human Memory* (1999) pp 182–186, citing studies showing that material learned underwater was best recalled underwater, material learned when drunk was best recalled when drunk, and happy memories were harder to recall when miserable.

6 Baddeley, above n 5, pp 176–178. Of course, not all facts that are known are 'learned'.

7 See the discussion below of proof of knowledge by proof of the opportunity to acquire knowledge.
8 S Bernecker and F Dretske (eds) *Knowledge – readings in contemporary epistemology* (2000) p 431 divide the basic sources of knowledge into the 'more or less standard categories' of perception, introspection, testimony, memory, reason and inference.
9 (1985) 81 Cr App Rep 260 at 264.
10 The court thought that he believed that the goods were stolen, but held that belief 'is something short of knowledge'.
11 [1997] 2 Cr App Rep 299.
12 (1985) 81 Cr App Rep 260 at 264.
13 (1985) 81 Cr App Rep 260 at 264 (quoted above).
14 There may also be a category of persons who have all the information necessary to reach a conclusion of 'practical certainty' but who after reaching a conclusion subject to doubts decide not to reason any further. There is no certainty that this category exists, since people who decide not to engage in the mental processes necessary to produce a conclusion must be at least as rare as people who can obey the instruction not to think about elephants at any stage during the next ten minutes. So far as the category exists, there seems no harm in treating it identically to the group who reached conclusions subject to doubts then decided not to seek the further information that would have allowed them to reach 'practical certainty'.
15 Of course, it is possible for a person to belong to both sub-groups.
16 Handling stolen goods is thought to be one context where 'blind-eye knowledge' is insufficient. It is often suggested that the insertion of the words 'or believing' into the Theft Act 1968 was an unsuccessful attempt to extend the mens rea to cover 'blind-eye knowledge': See eg J C Smith [1997] Crim LR 591.
17 [2001] UKHL 1, [2001] 2 WLR 170.
18 Per Lord Clyde at [3]. See also at [25] (Lord Hobhouse) and at [115] (Lord Scott). Lord Scott, at [116], went most deeply into the meaning of 'suspicion' in this context: '[s]uspicion is a word that can be used to describe a state-of-mind that may, at one extreme, be no more than a vague feeling of unease and, at the other extreme, reflect a firm belief in the existence of the relevant facts. In my opinion, in order for there to be blind-eye knowledge, the suspicion must be firmly grounded and targeted on specific facts.'
19 Per Lord Scott at [115]. See also at [26] (Lord Hobhouse).
20 Per Lord Hobhouse at [25]. See also at [3] (Lord Clyde) and at [115] (Lord Scott).
21 At [25].
22 This is said expressly by Beldam LJ in *R v Forsyth* [1997] 2 Cr App Rep 299.
23 (1974) 60 Cr App Rep 14.
24 A more complicated argument might be that since 'blind-eye knowledge' is dishonest a person who claims that this was his state of mind is more likely to be lying about other matters, such as the inferences that he drew from the inquiries that he did make.
25 Eg 'This section requires a distinction between two states of mind', J C Smith and B Hogan *Criminal Law* (10th edn, 2002) p 665. Lawyers do not suggest, however, that the two states of mind are exclusive. Thus a person who knows f will also believe f, and a person who believes f *may* also know f.
26 Of course, such philosophers would probably *not* claim that knowledge is adequately defined as 'justified true belief'. Further, some of them might make careers out of disputing what suffices for 'justification'.
27 Glanville Williams expressly dissented from the philosophers' insistence that true belief based on error cannot be classed as 'knowledge'. Thus he would have argued that an offence requiring 'knowledge' would not allow acquittal of an accused with only an 'unjustified but true belief'. Hence there was no such gap for inclusion of 'belief' in s 22 to plug. Less plausibly, he also claimed that even 'untrue belief' could be 'knowledge'. See Williams *Criminal Law – The General Part* (2nd edn, 1961) p 169.
28 At least this was not the gap discussed by the Criminal Law Revision Committee.
29 Criminal Law Revision Committee, Eighth Report *Theft and Related Offences* (Cmnd 2977) para 64.
30 In some trials the accused contests that the goods were actually 'stolen goods' as well as contesting his knowledge or belief as to that fact.
31 *R v Hall* (1985) 81 Cr App Rep 260 at 264.
32 Emphasis added.
33 (1984) 79 Cr App Rep 72 at 76. Following *Griffiths* (1974) 60 Cr App Rep 14.
34 Who was also a member of the court in *Hall*.
35 [1997] 2 Cr App Rep 299. In this case the trial judge had directed the jury that 'It is sufficient to constitute belief even if the defendant says to herself: "Despite all that I have heard I refuse to believe what my brain tells me is obvious".'
36 G Williams 'Handling, Theft and the Purchaser Who Takes a Chance' [1985] Crim LR 432 at 433 stated that he had come to believe that the Criminal Law Revision Committee's insertion of the

words 'or believing' had been a mistake and that he would not have assented to the new words if he had thought they would be interpreted as covering 'strongly suspecting'.

37 [1997] 2 Cr App Rep 299 at 321.

38 The suggestion being that the 'assessed likelihood of f being true' can be less for a responsible claim of 'suspicion that f' than for a responsible claim of 'belief that f' and less still than for a responsible claim of 'knowledge that f'.

39 [1997] 2 Cr App Rep 299 at 320.

40 *R v Forbes* [2001] UKHL 40, [2002] 1 Cr App Rep 1.

41 Of course, throwing the lighted match does not prove conclusively that the girl knew that the spirit was flammable. Perhaps she believed that the fluid would extinguish the lighted match. Or perhaps she was indulging in experimentation; though this would probably be sufficient to establish knowledge of the possibility of flammability. In *Elliott v C (a minor)* [1983] 2 All ER 1005, the accused, who threw two lighted matches onto white spirit in a shed, conceded that she had been aware of the possibility of flammability but the magistrates concluded that she had not considered the possibility of destruction of the shed and would not have appreciated this risk even if she had turned her mind to the matter.

42 *Leeson v Holt* (1816) 1 Stark NPC 186; *Norwich and Lowestoft Navigation Co v Theobald* (1828) Mood & M 151; cf *Rowley v Horne* (1825) 3 Bing 2.

43 *R v Wicks* [1936] 1 All ER 384, CCA, per Du Parcq J, at 387–388: 'The best and often the only way of proving that a statement was known to be false by the person who made it is to prove that he had the means of such knowledge. A jury is then entitled to draw what may be, in some circumstances, the irresistible inference that he had knowledge in fact.'

44 Principally in criminal cases. Though problems may also persist in civil cases if s 1(2)(a) of the Civil Evidence Act 1995 is interpreted narrowly: See *Cross and Tapper on Evidence* (9th edn, 1999) pp 564–565.

45 These are not the only possible problems. It would be possible, for instance, to argue that polygraphs and other lie detectors rely on the betrayal of knowledge, and use of the output of such devices in evidence raises issues other than simple indeterminacy.

46 This is how Lord Wilberforce explained 'testimonially' in *Ratten v R* [1972] AC 378 at 387.

47 Thus in Australia the Evidence Act 1995 (Cth), s 60 states that: 'The hearsay rule does not apply to evidence of a previous representation that is admitted because it is relevant for a purpose other than proof of the fact intended to be asserted by the representation.' *Cross and Tapper on Evidence* (9th edn, 1999) pp 598–599 appears to support this approach, although querying whether the additional refinements recommended by the Law Commission (England and Wales) are necessary: on which see *Evidence in Criminal Proceedings: Hearsay and Related Topics* (Law Com no 245) ch 7.

48 *R v Kearley* [1992] 2 AC 228.

49 Colin Tapper's prediction in the immediate aftermath of *Kearley*, 'Hearsay and Implied Assertions' (1992) 108 LQR 524, 528.

50 The example famously provided by Parke B in *Wright v Doe d Tatham* (1837) 7 Ad & El 313 at 388. It is assumed that this could be admitted because the sea captain had no intention to assert *anything*, thus the inference is not based on the *content* of any intended assertion.

51 Though it would certainly permit Q's statement to be admitted to demonstrate that he was alive at the point of time when he said it, and might perhaps permit it to be admitted to demonstrate his ability to speak English and his familiarity with the existence of mobile phones. The hesitation over these last two examples stems from the fact that 'from the content' is capable of further refinement.

52 *Cross and Tapper on Evidence* (9th edn, 1999) p 546 regards this use as outside the hearsay rule.

53 The suggestion would be that a person who during his lifetime uttered the sequence of sounds 'I am Napoleon' would be more likely to be insane than a person who never uttered this sequence, all other things being equal. Of course, the suggestion is dubious since the sequence of sounds 'I am Napoleon' is almost certainly uttered more often by evidence teachers than by insane people. More seriously, it is difficult to imagine that a jury would be able to rely on the circumstantial chain of reasoning whilst paying no attention to the likelihood that Q believed that he was Napoleon.

54 *Evidence in Criminal Proceedings: Hearsay and Related Topics* (Law Com no 245) para 7.38.

55 The non-constructive advice would be to define intentions broadly since this would reduce the harm done by the error in defining the scope of the hearsay rule.

56 It is argued above that this should not be assumed where the state of mind is inferred from the content of a statement that was intended to be communicative.

57 The exception to the exception was not a creation of the Federal Rules. The necessity for it was recognised by Cardozo J in *Shephard v United States* 290 US 96 at 104–106 (1933) and by E W Hinton 'States of Mind and the Hearsay Rule' (1934) 1 U Chi LR 394, 423 (an article substantially written before the Supreme Court's decision in *Shephard* but published afterwards).

58 *Evidence in Criminal Proceedings: Hearsay and Related Topics* (Law Com no 245).
59 I have nothing to add to the debate over why admissions are not caught by the hearsay rule: See J C Smith 'Exculpatory Statements and Confessions' [1995] Crim LR 280.
60 The usefulness of this exception will clearly be reduced if the scope of the English hearsay rule is pruned so as to allow the use of out-of-court statements to prove that which the speaker did not intend to communicate. If this occurs then the exception will be needed only for out-of-court statements by which the speaker *intended* to communicate the relevant state of mind.
61 If such statements were admissible then defendants would often be able to introduce into evidence (without facing cross-examination) exculpatory statements that they made to police about their states of mind at the time of the alleged crime.
62 Eg *Rawson v Haigh* (1824) 2 Bing 99.
63 *Cross and Tapper on Evidence* (9th edn, 1999) pp 549–554.
64 *Cross and Tapper on Evidence* (9th edn, 1999) p 549, 'a person's statements are the best, and sometimes the only, means of demonstrating his state of mind.'
65 Judicial statements treating its existence as 'elementary' can be found in *R v Blastland* [1986] AC 41 at 54 and *R v Gilfoyle* [1996] 1 Cr App Rep 302.
66 Colin Tapper's masterful account of the 'subversive' qualities of this exception is well known: 'Hillmon Rediscovered and Lord St Leonards Ressurected' (1990) 106 LQR 441.
67 *R v Gloster* (1888) 16 Cox CC 471. Although this case involved the contemporaneous description of physical sensations rather than of a state of mind, the two exceptions run parallel with regard to explanations of the circumstances leading to the sensations or state of mind.
68 Most famously in *R v Blastland* [1986] AC 41, but also in eg *R v Williams (David)* [1998] Crim LR 494. This may also be the best explanation of *R v Gunnell* (1886) 16 Cox CC 154, where a party sought to rely on hearsay to prove that G's solicitor knew of a fact *before* compulsory bankruptcy proceedings in order to show that the information had not been disclosed by G for the first time at those proceedings. Thus it was important for the party to persuade the fact finder to infer that G's solicitor acquired his knowledge through a disclosure by G rather than through a lucky guess or some other source.
69 That is preventing use of 'a statement of memory or belief to prove the fact remembered or believed unless it relates to the execution, revocation, identification, or terms of declarant's will'.
70 (1838) 4 M & W 267.
71 This leaves open the difficult question of what to do when both the truth of the fact allegedly known and the person's knowledge of it are in issue *and* the trial cannot be simply divided into a stage addressing the truth of the fact followed by a stage addressing knowledge.
72 The position might be changed by additional evidence such as that the dangerousness of the ship was obvious to all or the captain was notoriously cautious about risks.
73 It is arguable that the evidence of a third party's early knowledge of the crime in *R v Blastland* [1986] AC 41 was irrelevant in this special sense since there was no rational basis for determining whether that knowledge was acquired as the real perpetrator (the defendant being innocent) or as a witness (the defendant being guilty).
74 Eg *R v Richens* (1994) 98 Cr App Rep 43; *R v Taylor* [1998] Crim LR 822.
75 Only a modified reformulation forbidding inferences from the content of intended communications can be justified in this way.
76 Wigmore *A Treatise on the Anglo-American System of Evidence* (Chadbourn revision), vol II, paras 244–245.
77 It was suggested above that the substantive law on 'capacity to recall' and 'capacity to infer' reflected assumptions about the availability of evidence.
78 The person concerned is, if alive and available, likely to be in a good position to testify as to her knowledge. But if she is a litigant then there is a serious risk that her testimony will be treated as self-serving and entitled to little weight.
79 (1793) 1 Esp 56.
80 (1843) 11 M & W 116.
81 (1867) LR 2 QB 595.
82 (1866) LR 1 P & D 109.
83 (1882) 20 Ch D 611.
84 Though in the case the person who signed the deed was dead and there was no evidence that he had not known of the contents, only an assertion by his mother and sister.
85 (1859) 6 CB (NS) 502.
86 Willes J suggested that the vestryman might have negatived his knowledge of the contents of the books but chose not to. The other three judges, however, did not discuss this possibility. Although there are several other cases, beyond those referred to, which refer to knowledge being 'presumed' from access to documents which might provide the opportunity to acquire it, in most instances it is impossible to determine whether the language of presumption is intended to communicate anything more than that an inference of knowledge can be made.

87 *R v Schama; R v Abramovitch* (1914) 11 Cr App Rep 45. Because an inference of either theft or handling is permitted this doctrine suffers from problems of indeterminacy. The solution suggested by the Privy Council in *A-G of Hong Kong v Yip Kai-foon* [1988] AC 642 is not the solution commended by *Cross and Tapper on Evidence* (9th edn, 1999) p 39.

88 Smith and Hogan, above n 25, p 666.

89 This can be demonstrated by comparing answers to the two questions: (1) What proportion of those in possession of stolen property a few days after it was stolen 'knew or believed' it to be stolen? (2) What proportion of those in possession of stolen property a few days after it was stolen and unwilling to give any explanation of how it was acquired to the court 'knew or believed' it to be stolen?

90 *R v Bradley* (1979) 70 Cr App Rep 200.

91 Because of this limit on the 'doctrine' it may be overtaken in usefulness by the Criminal Justice and Public Order Act 1994, s 36.

92 *DPP v Nieser* [1959] 1 QB 254 at 267.

93 For detail, see Munday [1988] Crim LR 345; *Cross and Tapper on Evidence* (9th edn, 1999) pp 377–379; *Phipson on Evidence* (15th edn, 2000) paras 17-67–17-71.

Empirical evaluation of the hearsay rule

Roger C Park

I am honoured to participate in this festschrift for Professor Colin Tapper, and to join in celebrating his justly deserved international reputation. This article relates to reform of the hearsay rule, one of his many interests.[1] Studies of the value and impact of hearsay should be of continuing importance to scholars and reformers on both sides of the Atlantic. Hearsay reform in the United Kingdom has moved more vigorously than in the United States,[2] but there are still many areas of common interest. Moreover, art 6 of the European Convention on Human Rights seems to guarantee that fundamental hearsay issues will be of enduring interest in criminal cases.[3]

In this article, I will ask what message empirical studies have for policy-makers who are assessing the value of hearsay and cross-examination. In a sense, all writing about hearsay and cross-examination is empirical, because its analysis and prescriptions are based upon inductions about how the real world works. Here, however, I use 'empirical' in the sense that has become common in the law journals. It denotes systematic experiments and field studies, using quantitative methods, or articles that rely upon such studies in drawing conclusions. In this essay I will focus primarily on work based on experimental studies, as opposed to surveys, archival studies, and other field studies.

I will examine two areas of research that contribute to our understanding of the value of hearsay and cross-examination. These are the studies of lie detection by demeanour cues, and studies that examine the value or impact of hearsay evidence.

1 Studies of lie detection by use of demeanour cues

Courts and lawyers have often treated demeanour evidence as an important element in reaching accurate verdicts.[4] One of the ancillary supports for hearsay doctrine is that, in the absence of live testimony, the trier of fact has no opportunity to observe the demeanour of the witness under direct and cross-examination.

Commentators familiar with the social science evidence have doubted that demeanour evidence is helpful in detecting deception. In a useful review published in 1991, law professor Olin Guy Wellborn concluded that the social science literature indicates that judgments of lay people about deception are not improved by the observation of nonverbal behaviour, whether the nonverbal behaviour be facial behaviour, body cues, or paralinguistic cues.[5]

The psychologist Aldert Vrij, himself a prolific experimenter in the area, reached a similar conclusion in a recent book on the subject.[6] He states that 'generally, people are rather good at lying, but not very good at detecting lies'.[7] Vrij found a mean accuracy rate of only 56.6% in his comprehensive survey of studies. When accuracy in detecting known lies is considered separately from accuracy in detecting known truths, Vrij's review shows that 'observers are reasonably good at detecting truths (67% accuracy rate) but particularly poor at detecting lies (44% accuracy rate)'.[8]

Experimental evidence also indicates that lay people have misconceptions about which demeanour clues are important. For example, lay people tend to think that shifty eyes (gaze aversion) are an important cue to lying. But, perhaps because liars know of that view and because the conduct is relatively easy to control, it is not a good indicator.[9]

Admittedly, there are important distinctions between the experimental conditions and trial conditions:

1. The experimental lies were authorised, thus the feeling of guilt and shame would be less than in a courtroom situation.[10]
2. The penalty and benefits of failed or successful lying were less in the experiments than at trial, thus making the fear of detection less.[11] Because the stakes were not high for laboratory liars, they may not have experienced as much stress as courtroom liars, and therefore emotional cues may have been muted.[12]

   It is possible, though difficult to study authentic high-stake lies, but so far not many studies have done so.[13]
3. The liars in the experiments did not have very complicated stories to tell and they did not have to worry about circumstantial contradiction. Consider such real-life situations as the allegedly disabled plaintiff who learns on the witness stand that surveillance tapes show him painting his house, or the witness who learns part way through cross-examination that the opponent secretly taped some of the witness's prior statements. These witnesses would have to think about the import of each answer. Is this something that they might have on record? Is this something that might be disproven? Does this fit in with the rest of my story? If I say I was on the parlour stairs while the murder occurred, will the prosecution have a witness who saw me in the barn? As Ekman notes, in some cases speech pauses can be reliable demeanour evidence.[14] So it may be that with real liars who have high stakes and complicated stories that might be disproven by an adversary, demeanour clues such as speech hesitation, speech errors and diminished use of illustrators may be more pronounced and easier for observers to detect.[15]
4. The lie detectors in the experiments generally had to decide right away whether someone was lying, and they had only a short time to observe the liar, whereas jurors have an opportunity to think and deliberate and often a long time to observe.[16]

Some of the differences listed above might suggest that the courtroom could be a better venue for lay people to use demeanour cues to detect lies than the laboratory. On the whole, however, differences between the experimental conditions and the trial situations militate against the usefulness of demeanour, because:

1. At trial, rehearsal increases confidence and decreases fear of detection.
2. The long time delay blunts emotional reactions and may lead the witness to believe her own false account.
3. The truthful witness comes to trial terrified of being disbelieved. Signs of fear can be misinterpreted.[17]

In the courtroom, as in the experimental conditions, the judge or juror must assess the credibility of a stranger. This can lead to mistakes because the lie detector does not know the base-rate or typical behaviour of the witness. It may be that the witness often averts her gaze, hesitates, gives convoluted answers,[18] or fidgets. In short, the fact that demeanour cues are sometimes useful in everyday life does not mean they will be helpful in the courtroom, although particular conduct cues, such as hesitation (a demeanour cue) when combined with other evidence of deception (for example, evasive content), may be helpful in particular situations.[19] And the experiments do not say anything about the value of demeanour in making judgments about matters other than lying. For example, in child abuse trials it is possible that the jury can draw useful inferences from fear displayed by the child when confronted by the defendant.

On the whole, the experimental evidence indicates that it is unlikely that demeanour cues help fact-finders to detect liars in courts of law; the cues may in fact be harmful.

2 Studies examining the value or impact of hearsay

(a) Review of the literature

Aside from work in the study of rumour that is only tangentially related to hearsay issues,[20] actual experimental work on hearsay law[21] did not start appearing in print until the early 1990s, long after the climate for psychology-law studies was improved by successful work on other topics, notably on the psychology of eyewitness identification and of jury behaviour.

Since 1990, several experiments have scrutinised the weight given to hearsay evidence by participants playing the role of jurors or fact-finders. In the first published study, Landsman and Rakos (1991), 147 participants read a 12-page transcript of a theft trial.[22] The 12 experimental conditions involved four different levels of hearsay strength (from vague hearsay to detailed hearsay based on the declarant's first-hand knowledge) and three different levels of overall evidence strength. Participants filled out a survey instrument giving a verdict and evaluating the strength of the evidence. The researchers concluded that hearsay evidence was heavily discounted by jurors and had little or no influence upon their verdicts.[23]

In another early study, Miene, Park and Borgida (1992) also concluded that the mock juror verdicts were not influenced by the addition of incriminating hearsay evidence.[24] The study is notable for the realism of its trial stimuli. The eyewitness participants observed the apparent theft of a computer monitor. They were then interviewed about the identity of the thief and asked to make an identification from a photo array. The declarant participants witnessed the interview and the identification. The researchers then produced videotaped trials, using practising lawyers and a sitting judge. 186 juror participants viewed one of four videotaped trials. For juror participants in the 'eyewitness' condition, the tape contained testimony of an eyewitness who identified the thief. Juror participants in the 'hearsay' condition viewed a tape in which the declarant who witnessed the identification testified. In the 'all evidence' condition, the tape contained testimony from both the eyewitness and the declarant witness. Finally, in the 'circumstantial evidence only' condition, no testimony of identification was presented.[25] There were statistically significant differences in the verdicts rendered by the juror participants. The conviction rate was 62% in the eyewitness condition (the condition in which an eyewitness testified that the defendant was the thief she had seen, and the circumstantial evidence of possession of the stolen monitor was also admitted, but no hearsay evidence was presented). The conviction rate was significantly lower in the hearsay condition (40%) (the condition in which hearsay evidence that a declarant identified the defendant, plus the same circumstantial evidence of possession, was presented), and only 4% higher than in the condition in which only circumstantial evidence of guilt was offered. In the condition in which all the evidence was presented (circumstantial evidence, eyewitness testimony that the defendant was the thief, plus hearsay evidence that the declarant heard someone else identify the defendant as the thief), the conviction rate was 55%, lower (though not significantly so) than the eyewitness condition.[26]

The two studies above indicated that hearsay had little or no impact. In contrast, Schuller (1995) found hearsay to have a persuasive impact on jurors.[27] In her study, the hearsay came into evidence through the testimony of an expert witness. The study was inspired by the Canadian Supreme Court case of *Lavallee v R* (1990).[28] The *Lavallee* case held that testimony of an expert on battered women would be admissible, including a description of the expert's interviews with the defendant and her mother that were not otherwise admitted into evidence, if the jury was instructed to use the hearsay recounted in the testimony only to evaluate the weight to be given the opinion and not as proof of the facts related. Schuller quite plausibly hypothesised that, although previous studies of non-expert testimony showed hearsay to have little impact, hearsay presented through expert testimony might have greater influence because of paramessage elements of prestige and expertise. In her experiment, Schuller had 100 psychology undergraduates judge a homicide case involving an allegedly battered woman. The trial stimulus was a written trial summary approximately four single-spaced pages long. The experimental conditions were hearsay-with-instructions (an expert provided hearsay testimony which was followed by limiting instructions), two forms of corroborated hearsay (an expert testified, and hearsay of expert was corroborated by live testimony of defendant; or an expert testified, and hearsay of expert was corroborated by a police witness who read defendant's initial statement). She found no significant difference in verdicts in the hearsay with limiting instructions and the admissible hearsay conditions, although both groups generated guilty verdicts more than the no hearsay information group, indicating that the participants do not appear to have discounted hearsay. There was apparently no recall measure asking whether the participants remembered that certain testimony in the written stimulus was presented as hearsay, and the author raises the possibility that the participants failed to note that aspects of the expert testimony were to be treated as hearsay.[29]

In a subsequent experiment involving an audio stimulus with simulated cross-examination, Paglia and Schuller (1998) found that juror subjects apparently disregarded hearsay evidence in reaching their verdicts.[30] In the hearsay condition in that experiment, the hearsay testimony was prosecution testimony by a lay person about statements by a homicide victim describing harassment by the accused. The authors reconcile the results of this study in which jurors found hearsay unpersuasive with Schuller's 1995 study,[31] in which jurors gave more weight to hearsay evidence, by suggesting that there may be a difference between the way that expert and non-expert hearsay is received. The expert's prestige and expertise may have a halo effect on the hearsay. They also distinguish the two experiments by noting that in the 1998 experiment, the in-court witness relaying the hearsay may have been perceived as biased because of her sibling relationship with the declarant, and the testimony by the live witness about the suspect's bad behaviour may have been viewed as showing his behaviour to be more egregious than that described by the hearsay witness because it occurred in the presence of a third party.[32]

In Schuller and Paglia (1999), the authors return to Professor Schuller's interest in expert testimony after the *Lavallee* case.[33] Once again the stimulus was a written trial summary. This time, the amount of hearsay underlying the expert's opinion was varied factorially with the presence or absence of limiting instructions. (The *Lavallee* court had opined that the more the expert relied upon facts not in evidence, the less weight the jury should give to the opinion.) This time, the expert testimony was psychiatric testimony about the defendant's state of mind at the time he allegedly murdered an acquaintance to whom he owed a large sum of money. The researchers concluded that there were no differences in verdicts as a function of the amount of hearsay underlying the expert opinion, though other measures suggested that the participants were able to distinguish between hearsay that was supported by other evidence presented at trial and hearsay that was not supported in that fashion. None the less, the juror participants did regard events as being more likely when they were supported only by hearsay evidence than when they were supported by no evidence.[34] Consistent with Schuller's initial hypothesis, Schuller and Paglia conclude that expert hearsay may have more effectiveness than non-expert hearsay because of expertise and prestige.

Another study indicating that hearsay may be given considerable weight by jurors is Golding, Sanchez and Sego (1997).[35] The authors look at the problem from the perspective of a district attorney trying to decide whether to prosecute a case in which the only evidence of child sex abuse is hearsay evidence. They conclude that hearsay evidence is believable and that victims need not always testify in order to obtain convictions:

> '[M]ock jurors will believe to a considerable degree a hearsay witness who testifies about an alleged child sexual assault in the absence of the alleged victim, and will continue to believe the alleged victim even when she does not testify.'[36]

They reached this conclusion on the basis of two experiments in which participants read a one-page summary of a hypothetical trial. The different experimental conditions varied the age of the child and whether the child testified. There was no cross-examination or final argument and no deliberation by the juror participants. In both experiments, psychology students read summaries of trials in which age, sex of juror and nature of evidence were varied. The variable of interest here, whether the testimony included hearsay, had four levels: live victim testimony, live testimony plus hearsay, hearsay testimony only, and the 'no-witness' condition in which there was no significant evidence of child abuse.[37] There were no significant differences between the guilty verdicts in the hearsay condition and those in the child testimony condition, and both differed significantly from the condition in which no evidence of sex abuse was introduced.[38] The authors note that there were no reliable differences between the live testimony condition and the hearsay condition, and conclude that 'hearsay was believed to a considerable extent'.[39] In Experiment 2, for which hearsay results are described more fully by the authors than in Experiment 1, 85% of the participants in the live witness condition returned a guilty verdict, and 85% of the participants in the hearsay condition also returned a guilty verdict.[40] Measures other than verdict (such as responses to the question whether the participant believed the incident) were consistent with the verdict measures. The authors suggest that hearsay may have had more impact in the context of their study than in other studies because jurors accepted the appropriateness of hearsay testimony in a child abuse case (jurors could understand why the child might be unwilling or unable to testify), they were pro-prosecution jurors because of the repugnant nature of the crime charged, and because they thought the hearsay witness had good character, based on the witness's decision to come forward.[41]

Using a videotaped child sex abuse trial, Ross, Lindsay and Marsil (1999)[42] found that subjects who viewed the the child's testimony were significantly more likely to convict than subjects who viewed the hearsay condition, possibly because the hearsay witness (the child's mother) was perceived as biased because she was in a custody battle with the defendant. In a follow-up experiment, the same researchers presented subjects with conditions in which the hearsay witnesses were a doctor, teacher, neighbour, or mother, and the alleged abuser was a neighbour instead of an ex-husband. Under these conditions, the 'testimony' of the child witness was significantly less likely to lead to guilty verdicts than the testimony of most of the hearsay witnesses. This surprising result might be due to differences in the procedures used in the two experiments (brief written trial summary versus videotaped trial) or in perceptions of the credibility of the hearsay witnesses (doctor, teacher, or mother with no motive to lie versus mother in custody battle).

The studies described above say something about the impact of hearsay testimony, but do not shed any light on whether jurors can use it successfully. They do not attempt to study whether jurors were able to use hearsay to reconstruct events accurately. A study by Kovera, Park and Penrod (1992) does aim at examining, not only the impact of hearsay, but whether it had a harmful or helpful effect.[43] The authors used videotaped stimuli. The declarant participants were asked to watch excerpts of videotaped client interview.[44] They then were interviewed about what they saw, and the videotaped interviews were shown to the juror participants. The different conditions varied the witnessing conditions (how much time elapsed before the declarants were asked to recall what they saw), and the differences in conditions affected the accuracy of the declarants' statements (those who were interviewed after a short delay were much more accurate than those who were interviewed after a long delay). The juror participants were apparently sensitive to these problems, and rated the short-delay testimony as more accurate than the long-delay testimony – and it in fact was more accurate.

In a sophisticated 1999 study, Pathak and Thompson examined whether hearsay helped juror participants reach an accurate verdict about whether a janitor had cleaned toys or played with them in front of a child witness.[45] Thirty-one children were brought individually by their parents to the university to participate in study of memory. The children were left alone in a laboratory room for about ten minutes while performing a task. During the ten minutes, a confederate posing as a janitor came into the room and either cleaned a set of toys or played with them. The children were later questioned by a confederate about whether the janitor had cleaned or played. Some of the interrogators used powerfully suggestive techniques that succeeded in getting the children to change their stories to the opposite of what really happened. Others used non-suggestive interviews and got accurate accounts from the children.

In Experiment 1, 112 college student participants were asked to watch a videotape of one of the 31 children being interrogated. Approximately four participants, randomly assigned, watched each videotape. After being interviewed about what they saw in a way designed to elicit an open-ended account of what the child had said, these participants were asked to respond, on a five-point scale, to questions about whether the janitor had cleaned or played with the toys, and whether the child's report was influenced by the way the child's interviewer had asked the questions. The participants were able to recognise suggestive questioning, but they underestimated its influence in trying to discern what the janitor actually did.[46]

In Experiment 2, the hearsay experiment, 63 of the participants who had watched the child-interview videotape then became hearsay declarants as videotapes of the open-ended interviews of them describing what they had seen were shown to 104 additional participants, the juror participants, recruited from both university and community sources. These juror participants then filled out questionnaires with five-point scales asking whether the children had been influenced by suggestive questioning and whether the janitor had played with the toys or cleaned them. Despite a trend toward saying that the suggestive interviews influenced the children's reports more than the neutral interviews, there was no statistically significant difference between the answers on the first questionnaire, leading the authors to conclude that the juror participants did not realise that the children had been influenced by suggestive questioning.[47] Surprisingly, though, the juror participants were apparently able to use the hearsay accurately, generally disregarding inaccurate accounts produced by suggestive questioning and accepting accurate accounts produced by neutral questioning. The authors conclude, quite plausibly, that this effect was caused by the fact that the children changed their stories during the suggestive questioning – at first they were accurate, and then were influenced to change their accounts – and that the juror subjects, even though perceiving the children's answers at one remove through the accounts of the declarant subjects, detected this inconsistency and discounted the inaccurate testimony.

Thus, the authors concluded that jurors were not misled by the hearsay testimony that recounted false statements elicited by suggestive questioning. Jurors discounted the hearsay and gave neutral answers (approximately halfway between 'cleaned' and 'played' on the five-point scale) when asked what the janitor had done. Jurors who were given accurate hearsay accounts (the product of non-suggestive questioning of children, a condition in which the children were generally quite accurate about what the janitor had done), gave the hearsay weight and generally reached accurate conclusions about what the janitor had done. The authors conclude that 'Those advocating the broader use of child hearsay should find these results encouraging', while conceding that more studies are needed before policy conclusions can be drawn with confidence.[48]

The Kovera, Park and Penrod study and the Pathak and Thompson study are both theoretically driven, in the sense that they test phenomena that psychologists have identified as challenges to eyewitness accuracy, and seek to show whether the problems persist or get worse in the hearsay context. In Kovera, Park and Penrod the challenge was delay, in Pathak and Thomson it was suggestive interviewing. Another interesting and useful study on the effect of suggestion in interviewing is Warren and Woodall (1999).[49] These investigators studied the ability of interviewers to recall their interviews with children. Interviewers trained in questioning children for forensic purposes interviewed children three to five years old who had viewed a magic show and participated in 'silly doctor' play with a confederate at a preschool. The interviewers were good at recalling the substantive content of what the children said, but not good at recalling the mode of interview, such as whether they used leading questions. The authors observe that this may cause concerns for the legal system and recommend detailed documentation of interviews. (Pathak and Thompson suggest that jurors will still be able to distinguish results of suggestive interviews from those of non-suggestive ones, but their experiment differed, among other things, in that neutrals, not the interviewers themselves, described the interviews to jurors; at any rate, the cue that the jurors apparently used in distinguishing between good and poor testimony (the inconsistency of the children) does not exist in every case in which there is suggestive interviewing; children can yield to suggestion without ever giving a contrary story, as illustrated by the transcripts in Warren and Woodall.)

I believe I have described the principal experimental studies. The literature also contains survey studies on use of hearsay in child abuse cases[50] and an intriguing qualitative study on hearsay in custody mediation.[51] There are also several articles reviewing empirical research on hearsay and making suggestions for future inquiry.[52] Finally, there are notable efforts to apply general-purpose psychology studies on memory and perception to issues raised by particular hearsay exceptions.[53]

(b) Value of the experimental studies in assessing three issues of hearsay policy

(i) Whether hearsay should be received when there is a choice between hearsay and live testimony

I will start by distinguishing two issues of hearsay policy. The first is whether hearsay should be admissible *in lieu of* live testimony. The second is whether hearsay should be admissible when live testimony is not available.

When dealing with the first issue, the policy-maker must ask whether justice is harmed by allowing adversaries to substitute hearsay for available live testimony. Probably most jurists would agree that the principal loss, if this substitution were allowed, would be the loss of cross-examination, though the substitution has other consequences, such as avoiding physical confrontation between the witness and the accused in criminal cases, allowing evidence to be received from out-of-court declarants who were not under oath or subject to observation for demeanour cues.

It is risky to allow adversaries to substitute hearsay evidence for cross-examined evidence. Adversaries are tendentious; in fact, their code of ethics normally requires that they be. They will substitute hearsay for live testimony when that substitution helps their case. The situation in which an adversary would choose to forgo the benefits of a vivid live presentation because the adversary does not want to have her witness questioned by the opponent is exactly the situation in which cross-examination might turn up information helpful in finding the truth.[54]

The empirical studies of hearsay simply do not address this issue. They do not simulate the role of adversaries in choosing what evidence to present, or study whether adversaries would choose to present inferior evidence in the absence of a hearsay rule.

Aside from that, the studies do not attempt to examine the value of cross-examination in uncovering new evidence. The experiments focus on the modality of presentation of the evidence, not on whether the trial procedure of cross-examination uncovers useful new information.

To create conditions that are similar in all respects other than the independent variable being tested, the hearsay researchers generally make the evidence in the hearsay condition, in substance, be the same as the evidence in the live testimony condition, except that in one condition the evidence is produced through a live witness, and in the other it is produced through a hearsay witness. For example, in Golding, Sanchez and Sego,[55] the difference between the written trial summaries given to the participants in the two conditions is as follows:

Live testimony condition:

> '[T]he alleged 6-year-old victim testified that while she was staying overnight at her cousin Ann's house, "Uncle John felt me inside of my panties. He kept doing it even though I told him to stop".'

Hearsay condition:

> 'Sandra's mother testified that on the morning of February 28, 1993, Sandra told her that while she was staying overnight at her cousin Ann's house, "Uncle John felt me inside of my panties. He kept doing it even though I told him to stop".'

It is obvious that what is being tested here is the impact of the medium, just as in an experiment comparing the effectiveness of live in-court testimony with the effectiveness of closed-cable TV testimony. There is no attempt to determine whether cross-examination might bring out new facts that would influence the fact-finder or enhance the accuracy of verdicts.

What might cross-examination do in situations such as the one simulated by Golding, Sanchez and Sego? One leading expert on child witnesses suggests several ways in which the cross-examiner may seek to use the procedure to elicit new evidence that favours the defence. He recommends that the cross-examiner display a friendly, low-key demeanour, seeking to establish rapport with the child, while reinforcing answers favourable to the cross-examiner with nods or other signs of approval. This approach might encourage the child to admit that the facts could have occurred differently, or demonstrate suggestibility by leading the child to testify to patently false facts.[56] In one hypothetical example, the cross-examiner induces the child, whose favourite sport is baseball, to assert that he hits a home run every time at bat and that he always pitches no-hitters.[57] Other approaches include getting the child to describe coaching by the prosecution or to repeat testimony verbatim in an effort to show that it has been memorised.[58]

Of course, children are not the only witnesses whose credibility can be undermined by cross-examination. An adult witness may be exposed as a liar by getting him to commit to assertions than can be disproven conclusively, or as a charlatan simply by exposing gaps in expert knowledge. No one knows how often these successes occur, and it is undisputed that cross-examination can backfire badly. But the question of value and effectiveness cannot be assessed without knowing whether cross-examination often brings out useful new information that would not otherwise come to light, and the present collection of laboratory studies does not address that issue.

That is not necessarily a flaw in the studies, it simply limits the inferences that can be drawn from them. For example, a prosecutor who thought that the child would be a good witness – that no detrimental information would come out – but who also wanted to protect the child from trauma might find it useful to know that juries find hearsay evidence acceptable. But that is a long way from saying that hearsay testimony is evidence that helps accuracy, or that cross-examination is not needed for accurate verdicts.

The hearsay studies that seek to say something about the accuracy of hearsay, as opposed to its impact, do not seek to simulate any kind of cross-examination, much less typical cross-examination.[59] Thus it is obvious that they are of limited usefulness in assessing the value of hearsay testimony as a substitute for cross-examined testimony.

(ii) Whether hearsay should be received when there is no choice

A different issue of legal policy is presented when the declarant is not available, so that hearsay testimony is the only way of hearing her account of the facts. For example, suppose that the declarant has been murdered, and the prosecution wishes to put in evidence about a statement that the declarant made before her death, saying that the defendant was stalking her. Here, there is a strong common-sense argument that hearsay is better than nothing at all, that one should not go in the dark because the light is not perfect. But the hearsay rule sometimes bars the testimony even in this situation.[60] The empirical question is whether hearsay evidence is so misleading that it ought to be excluded even when live testimony is not an alternative. Here, empirical studies can be helpful even if they do not simulate adversarial incentives to substitute hearsay for live testimony. None the less, it is difficult to use the existing experiments in reaching conclusions about this issue.

The reason is that the legal policy issue is whether hearsay would be helpful to the jury in reaching the ground truth. In most of the experiments, the ground truth was not known to the experimenter. Either the experiment involved a fictional trial not based on an actual incident, or the experimenter did base the experiment upon a real incident, but did not know what the ground truth was about the incident. The Schuller experiment, for example, tested the impact of an expert witness who testified about things that the defendant told her. Without knowing whether the things the defendant told her were true or not, we cannot assess whether the hearsay would be useful in reaching the ground truth.

In two of the experiments,[61] the investigators did have accurate knowledge of the ground truth. They controlled and recorded the events witnessed by the hearsay declarant and by the person reporting the content of the hearsay statements, and examined the question whether the juror subjects were able to use the second-hand information to reconstruct accurately what actually happened.

Neither of these experiments simulated actual cross-examination in a trial setting. Here it is necessary to distinguish between cross-examination of the declarant and cross-examination of the in-court hearsay witness. If the declarant is not available for cross-examination, the legal policy issue does not turn on whether it would be better to hear from a cross-examined declarant or from a hearsay witness. Cross-examining the declarant is simply not an option. But to make an experiment more generalisable to the legal situation, it would still be useful to simulate the cross-examination, not of the declarant, but of the hearsay witness, the person who testifies to the content of the out-of-court statement by the declarant. The reason is that the cross-examiner could ask questions that might undermine the believability of the hearsay witness. At a minimum these questions would point out that the hearsay witness did not see the event herself, does not know from first-hand knowledge what happened, is relying solely on the declarant, and does not know the witnessing conditions of the declarant (such as whether something was in the way, whether the declarant was paying attention etc).

Also, the two experiments, admirable though they were, did not simulate other features of the legal context, such as instructions about the use of hearsay or deliberation by jurors.

Finally, the two experiments did not make a complete attempt to assure typicality. The participants playing the role of jurors were selected and assigned randomly from a numerous pool, so one can assume they were typical, or at least typical of the student populations from which they were drawn. But the participants who played the role of hearsay declarants and hearsay witnesses were chosen from a small group with no attempt to insure typicality, so one cannot know with satisfaction whether their performance in transmitting data was unusually poor or unusually good.

(iii) Whether erroneous admission of hearsay should be deemed prejudicial error

Appellate courts often encounter the question whether erroneous admission or exclusion of hearsay is prejudicial error. When an evidence error is harmless, in the sense that it was quite unlikely to have affected the result, then the appellate courts refuse to reverse under the doctrine of harmless error.[62] The hearsay studies have relevance to this policy issue even when they do not address the question whether hearsay aids in reaching accurate verdicts. If, as some of the studies suggest, juries heavily discount hearsay, then the erroneous admission of hearsay (at least where it is substituted for live testimony) should less often be considered to be prejudicial error.

The hearsay experiments reach divergent results, some finding that jurors heavily discounted hearsay evidence, others that jurors found it persuasive. To some degree the difference may be accounted for by differences in trial stimuli. In the studies finding hearsay to be as persuasive or nearly as persuasive as live testimony, the trial stimuli consisted wholly of written summaries.[63]

First, it is doubtful that the subjects always realised whether the written account of the trials included hearsay, since they did not actually see or hear the trials, and the recall measures apparently did not ask whether the trials included hearsay. Secondly, even if the subjects knew they were dealing with hearsay, it may not have had the same impact. It is hard to conclude confidently that hearsay has an impact similar to that of live testimony on the basis of experiments that do not use live testimony. Experiments using written stimuli compare hearsay (a written transcript or summary of a trial) with hearsay within hearsay (a written transcript or summary stating that one of the witnesses was repeating what someone else said); they do not compare hearsay with live witnesses. It is hard to judge the impact of live witnesses when the stimuli do not involve live witnesses. (Professor Michael Siegel would extend this criticism to hearsay studies in which the trial stimuli was videotaped, but in the absence of any showing that jurors react differently to videotape than to staged trials, I think that criticism carries it too far.[64])

The divergence in results may also be attributable to the different situations portrayed by the stimuli in the different experiments. Hearsay from an expert may, as Schuller suggested, have more impact than hearsay from a lay witness. Child hearsay may be more acceptable than other hearsay because jurors recognise the need for it. Because there are many different situations in which hearsay can be offered, and different witnesses through whom it can be offered – parties, police, informants, children, experts, to name a few – it is hard to generalise.

There are other problems with generalising from the experiments to the courtrooms. The participants with juror roles are commonly undergraduates; features of the courtroom, such as deliberation, are frequently not simulated; the motives of the participants may be different from those of participants in real trials.

Because of divergent results, the wide range of circumstances in which hearsay issues can arise, and difference between the simulations and the actual courtroom environment, caution must be used in deriving broad policy recommendations from the experiments on hearsay impact. The experiments are useful, but merely a start.

3 Conclusion

(a) Demeanour and the hearsay ban

As I have noted, the experimental evidence indicates that demeanour evidence is of little or no help to lay people in the detection of lies. What conclusion does this lead us to about the value of cross-examination or the wisdom of substituting hearsay for cross-examined testimony? It suggests that one of the ancillary benefits of cross-examination may be exaggerated. Perhaps rules requiring live testimony in lieu of transcripts of trials or depositions should be relaxed. But there are, of course, many possible benefits of cross-examination that have nothing to do with demeanour cues. For example, cross-examination allows the examiner to attempt to commit a lying witness to a story that can conclusively be disproven. Therefore, the research on detection of deception through demeanour cues, useful as it may be for other purposes, has only secondary bearing upon the value of cross-examination.

(b) General assessments of hearsay and cross-examination

I have expressed reservations about whether the current generation of hearsay experiments can confidently be used to draw conclusions about the legal policy issues I have described. I have described those policy issues at a high level of generality. The experiments are a good start in answering more narrow questions. For example, the Warren and Woodhall (1999) experiment suggests a danger of hearsay in the child witness context – that persons interrogating child witnesses do not accurately remember the mode of interrogation – while the Pathak and Thomson (1999) experiment indicates that when the suggestive interrogation causes a complete change of story, the trier of fact may be able to detect the truth even without realising the full danger of suggestiveness. Other experiments may be useful to lawyers making strategic decisions, such as whether to substitute a hearsay witness for a child witness. And, as has been the case with studies of eyewitness testimony, the studies are more likely to be useful as they multiply and converge. Studies examining particular hearsay dangers – the danger of suggestive questioning of child witnesses, for example – in particular specific situations are likely to be more useful than studies that attempt to answer the global question whether hearsay is good evidence. Attitude surveys that ask lawyers, judges and witnesses about whether cross-examination of live witnesses enhances accuracy in particular situations may also come to play a role in assessing its value and in designing experiments.

It may also be possible to draw inferences about the value of cross-examination (and the consequences of using hearsay as a substitute) from studying the precepts that lawyers follow in conducting it. Practice manuals advise taking no risk and not asking a question unless the cross-examiner knows the answer. If lawyers follow this advice, that may limit (though not eliminate) the role of cross-examination in revealing evidence that is not already known. I hope to pursue this topic at greater length in a future article.

Pending further empirical research, legal policy-makers seeking answers to question such as whether the hearsay rule should be abolished or modified will have to rely upon their traditional tools of history, experience and fireside induction. Anecdotal accounts of trial experiences will and should continue to be important. Policy-makers should take care not only to attend to the cross-examination stories of lawyers, but also to the views of others – non-professional expert witnesses, journalists, victims – who have seen cross-examination used or abused.

NOTES

1 Professor Tapper's plenary address on the subject at the Minnesota Hearsay Conference in 1991 taught me about developments in the United Kingdom and the Commonwealth, his article on the *Hillmon* case, *Hillmon Rediscovered and Lord St. Leonards Resurrected* (1990) 105 LQR 441 has caused me to change my way of teaching the subject, and of course Professor Tapper's *Cross and Tapper on Evidence* has long had an honoured place on my bookshelf. Though Professor Tapper's ninth edition jettisoned two chapters in reaction to the more relaxed attitude toward hearsay in the UK, his book still contains a rich treatment of the subject.

2 Colin Tapper *Tapper and Cross on Evidence* (9th edn, 1999) ch XIV (1995 reform of hearsay rule in civil cases).

3 Above n 2, p 538.

4 See authorities cited in James P Timony 'Demeanor Credibility' (2000) 49 Catholic University LR 903.

5 Olin Guy Wellborn III 'Demeanor' (1991) 76 Cornell LR 1075, 1088. See also R C L Lindsay, Gary L Wells and Fergus J O'Connor 'Mock-Juror Belief of Accurate and Inaccurate Eyewitnesses' (1989) 13 Law & Human Behav 333.

6 Aldert Vrij *Detecting Lies and Deceit* (2000) (hereafter Vrij *Detecting Lies and Deceit*). After noting that Kraut's 1980 review found a mean accuracy rate of 57%, Vrij added that he had himself reviewed 39 additional studies done since 1980, and found that 'the majority of the accuracy rates fall in the range 45–60%, and the mean accuracy rate is 56.6%'. This is almost identical to the 57% accuracy rate found by Kraut (1980).

7 Above n 6, p 2.

8 Above n 6, p 69.

9 Eg Aldert Vrij *Detecting Lies and Deceit* pp 58–62; Paul Ekman *Telling Lies* (2nd edn, 1992) pp 141–142 (hereafter Ekman *Telling Lies*).

10 An example of a deception experiment that successfully overcame the motive problem is an ingenious Israeli polygraph experiment in which the subjects, police officers, were given an opportunity to cheat while self-scoring aptitude tests. The tests had been chemically treated to detect changes in answers. The subjects were then told they were suspected of cheating, and asked to take a polygraph examination. See Ekman *Telling Lies* p 213. The studies examining detection of lies by demeanour cues have not generally incorporated realistic motives, with rare exception. See nn 11–13 below.

11 In another exception, again from a lie detector study, two examiners tested 48 inmates in a mock crime situation: 'It was understood that each participant's bonus of $20 [a considerable sum by prison standards] would be withheld if more than ten of the 48 subjects failed the polygraph test. Moreover, the names of the inmates failing the test would be posted in the prison for all to see. That this manipulation was successful is suggested by the fact that several inmates expressed their concern about the consequences of failing and a few actually declined to participate for that reason.' *State v Porter* 698 A 2d 739 at 766 n 52 (Conn 1997) (brackets in original), the prisoner study described in the footnote to *State v Porter*.

12 See Vrij *Detecting Lies and Deceit* p 72; Ekman *Telling Lies* p 91; *State v Porter* 698 A 2d 739 at 765–766 (Conn 1997). Practical and ethical considerations stand in the way of making the stakes high in

the laboratory. For examples of situations in which experimenters nevertheless found themselves able to put subjects in situations where there were substantial penalties for unsuccessful lying, see [the Israeli experiment described in n 10 above, and the prisoner experiment described in n 11 above. In the latter, the prisoners feared ostracism (or worse) from other prisoners if they failed to lie successfully. Both of those experiments were ones in which the investigators sought to test the polygraph, not to test the ability of lay subjects to use demeanour cues.

13 In a recent study, Samantha Mann, Aldert Vrij, and Ray Bull 'Suspects, Lies and Videotape, Analysis of Authentic High-Stake Liars' (2002) 26 L & Human Behav 365, the authors studied lying in a real-life, high-stake situation. They studied videotapes of suspects being interrogated by police. Whether the suspect was lying or telling the truth was determined by other evidence in the case. The 'ground truth' criteria were quite strict. The authors were examining cues in the behaviour of those who were lying and telling the truth, not – in this experiment – the success of lay people in detecting lies, so the study does not directly bear on the topic of this paper. Mann, Vrij and Bull note that insight into behaviour of liars has been obtained almost exclusively through laboratory studies involving low-stake lies (at 365–366).

14 Ekman *Telling Lies* pp 92, 286–287. For example, if a wife asks her husband why the family car was seen parked outside a motel on a night when the husband said he was working late, failure to have an answer right away might justify suspicion about the one that eventually comes.

15 Ekman *Telling Lies* p 332.

16 Vrij *Detecting Lies and Deceit* p 70. Vrij lists other challenges to the external validity of the laboratory experiments that do not seem so troublesome when applied to juristic settings. First, the subjects are passive observers who do not get to ask questions (pp 71–72). (Vrij thinks that this difference between the experimental setting and realistic settings may actually be an advantage. Whether or not that is the case, jurors also are passive observers, so they do not differ from the subjects in this respect.) Second, the observers are asked to detect lies by strangers, and hence are not familiar with the usual behaviour of the liars (pp 72–73). This is also true of jurors. Third, the lie detectors in the laboratory are aware that someone may try to lie to them (as are jurors) (p 73). Fourth, the lie detectors in the courtroom, as in the laboratory (but not as in ordinary life) are free to scrutinise the liar carefully, often from 'head to foot'. Two of Vrij's other observations may apply to some extent to juridical settings, however. First, the laboratory liars are chosen at random and hence may include people quite inexperienced at lying; it is perhaps true that courtroom liars, especially repeat players like police witnesses, are more experienced, and second, that the liars in the laboratory are forced to lie about topics with which they are not familiar; in the courtroom setting it might be possible to restrict lies to topics on which the witness is expert (p 73).

17 Ekman, who generally is more optimistic about the value of demeanour evidence than other scholars, nevertheless has explained eloquently some of the problems of using it in the courtroom:

> 'What I learned in teaching police, judges, and attorneys in the past five years suggested a wisecrack – which I now use in my workshops. The criminal justice system must have been designed by someone who wanted to make it impossible to detect deceit from demeanour. The guilty suspect is given many chances to prepare and rehearse her replies before her truthfulness is evaluated by jury or judge, thus increasing her confidence and decreasing her fear of being detected. Score one against the judge and jury. The directed examination and cross-examination take place months, if not years, after the incident, thereby blunting emotions conditions associated with the criminal event. Score two against the judge and jury. Because of the long time delay before the beginning of the trial, the suspect will have repeated her false account so often that she may start to *believe* her own false story; when that happens she is, in a sense, not lying when she testifies. Score three against the judge and jury. When challenged in cross-examination, the defendant typically has been prepared if not rehearsed by her own attorney, and the questions asked often allow a simple yes or no reply. Score four against the judge and jury. And then there is the *innocent* defendant who comes to trial terrified of being disbelieved. Why should the jury and judge believe her, if the police, prosecutor, and the judge, in pretrial moves for dismissal, did not? The signs of fear of being disbelieved can be misinterpreted as a guilty person's fear of being caught. Score five against the judge and jury.'

(*Telling Lies* pp 291–292) (emphasis in original).

18 For this reason, Ekman disparages a popular newscaster's reliance on verbal content as a cue to lying. When he was an interviewer for NBC's Today Show, Brokaw said 'Most of the clues I get are verbal, not physical. I don't look at a person's face for signs that he is lying. What I'm after are convoluted answers or sophisticated evasions. John Weisman 'The Truth Will Out' TV Guide, 3 September, 1977, p 13, as quoted in Ekman *Telling Lies* p 91. There is some research that support's Brokaw's hunch, though it is inclusive. See Ekman *Telling Lies* p 91 noting that a few studies have found 'that some people when they lied were indirect in their reply, circumlocutious, and gave more information than was requested. Other research studies have shown just the opposite: most people are too smart to be evasive and indirect in their replies'. At any rate, it is dangerous to rely on 'convoluted answers'

as a cue for lie detection without knowing whether the subject has a propensity to give convoluted answers when telling the truth.

19 For a lawyer who believed so, see Amos C Miller (1907) 2 Ill LR 257, quoted in Wigmore *Science* § 268 at 603, who says: 'A witness who is testifying falsely will, as a rule, try to evade, on cross-examination, questions on collateral matters; this, of course, is to avoid the danger of being entrapped. He will frequently ask the cross-examiner to repeat plain, simple questions for the purpose of giving him time to think; or he will answer irresponsively in order to steer the cross-examiner off the track.' Cf Ekman *Telling Lies* (on hesitancy).

20 Allport and Postman *The Psychology of Rumor* (1947). I say that the rumor studies are only tangentially related to hearsay issues because they involve many levels of hearsay, whereas the typical courtroom hearsay issue involves only one level. Moreover, Allport and Postman did not attempt to simulate courtroom conditions.

21 I am not counting law review articles that review psychology literature on memory and perception for purposes of drawing inferences about hearsay law, for example, about whether excited utterances are reliable. Some of these are quite interesting and worthwhile. See n 52 below. Rather, my discussion is limited to empirical work that avowedly studies second-hand information.

22 Stephan Landsman and Richard F Rakos 'Research Essay: A Preliminary Empirical Enquiry Concerning the Prohibition of Hearsay Evidence in American Courts' (1991) 15 Law & Psychol Rev 65.

23 See (1991) 15 Law and Psychology Review 65, 76, noting that even strong hearsay evidence failed to differentially influence the verdicts of the mock jurors in the study.

24 Peter Miene, Roger C Park and Eugene Borgida 'Juror Decision Making and the Evaluation of Hearsay Evidence' (1992) 76 Minn LR 683. The results of this study were also reported in Peter Miene, Eugene Borgida and Roger Park 'The Evaluation of Hearsay Evidence: A Social Psychological Approach' in N John Castellan Jr *Individual and Group Decision-Making: Current Issues* (1993) pp 151–166.

25 In all conditions there was circumstantial evidence apart from the identification, consisting of testimony that the missing computer had been found in an apartment that the accused shared with his roommate.

26 If it is not the product of chance, that trend could be the result of the tainting of the eyewitness evidence by the hearsay evidence; possibly some of the jurors reasoned that there was something lacking in the eyewitness testimony if the prosecution decided to supplement it with weak hearsay evidence.

27 Regina A Schuller 'Expert Evidence and Hearsay: The Influence of "Secondhand" Information on Jurors' Decisions' (1995) 19 L & Human Behav 345.

28 (1990) 55 CCC 3d 97.

29 (1990) 55 CCC 3d 97 at 358.

30 Angela Paglia and Regina A Schuller 'Jurors' Use of Hearsay Evidence: The Effects of Type and Timing of Instructions' (1998) 22 Law & Human Behav 501, 515. They also found limiting instructions ineffective (in fact, they backfired) because they were less likely than those who received limiting instructions to believe the admissible evidence presented by the hearsay witness.

31 Regina A Schuller 'Expert Evidence and Hearsay: The Influence of "Secondhand" Information on Jurors' Decisions' (1995) 19 Law & Human Behav 345.

32 (1998) 22 Law & Human Behav 501, 514.

33 Regina A Schuller and Angela Paglia 'An Empirical Study: Juror Sensitivity to Variations in Hearsay Conveyed Via Expert Evidence' (1999) 23 Law & Psychol Rev 131.

34 (1999) 23 Law & Psychol Rev 131, 147.

35 Jonathan M Golding, Rebecca Polley Sanchez and Sandra A Sego 'The Believability of Hearsay Testimony in a Child Sexual Assault Trial' (1997) 21 Law & Human Behav 299.

36 (1997) 21 Law & Human Behav 299, 318.

37 In the no-witness case, a witness testified that Sandra Johnson, the defendant's niece, stayed overnight at the defendant's house on 27 February 1993. The defendant then testified admitting that his niece stayed overnight, visiting his daughter, but denied any sexual contact with the niece. In Experiment 1, on the basis of this testimony, 45% of the participants found the defendant guilty! (p 308). Either they misread the trial summary or concluded that if the defendant was charged with the crime, he must be guilty. In Experiment 2, fully 44% of the no-witness participants rendered a guilty verdict (p 312); incredibly, when the alleged victim was six years old, 55% of the participants rendered a guilty verdict (p 316).

38 In Experiment 1, 90% of the participants in the live testimony condition returned a guilty verdict, as did 85% of the participants in the hearsay condition; in the no-witness condition, 45% returned a verdict of guilty.

39 (1997) 21 Law & Human Behav 299, 308–309.

40 (1997) 21 Law & Human Behav 299, 312.

41 (1997) 21 Law & Human Behav 299, 318–319.

42 David F Ross, R C L Lindsay and Dorothy L Marsil 'The Import of Hearsay Testimony on Conviction Rates in Trials of Child Sexual Abuse: Toward Balancing the Rights of Defendants and Child Witnesses' (1999) 5 Phych Pub Pol and L 439.

43 Margaret Bull Kovera, Roger C Park and Steven D Penrod 'Jurors' Perceptions of Eyewitness and Hearsay Evidence' (1992) 76 Minn LR 703.

44 The interview came from the movie 'Anatomy of a Murder' (Otto Preminger, 1959).

45 Maithilee K Pathak and William C Thompson 'From Child to Witness to Jury: Effects of Suggestion on the Transmission and Evaluation of Hearsay' (1999) 5 Psych Pub Pol and L 372.

46 See above n 45, at 378, Table 1.

47 See above n 45, at 379–381.

48 See above n 45, at 385–386.

49 Amye R Warren and Cara E Woodall 'The Reliability of Hearsay Testimony: How Well Do Interviewers Recall Their Interviews With Children?' (1999) 5 Psych Pub Pol and L 355.

50 See Myers, Prizmich, Redlich, Goodman and Imwinkelried (1999) (field research in which jurors who had participated in actual child sex abuse trials were questioned about perceptions of hearsay; the investigators found that adult hearsay witnesses were generally viewed as more credible than child witnesses giving non-hearsay testimony. Gail S Goodman, Jodi A Quas and Josephine Bulkley 'Innovations for Child Witnesses: A National Survey' (1999) 5 Psych Pub Pol and L 255 (report on results of survey of prosecutors about innovations relating to child witnesses, ranging from giving children a tour of the courtroom to using hearsay in lieu of live testimony; review of literature on innovations); Helen L Westcott, Graham M Davies and J R Spencer 'Children, Hearsay, and the Courts: A Perspective From the United Kingdom' (1999) 5 Psych Pub Pol and L 282 (review of legal developments, field research and survey research relating to extensive use of live links and videotaped testimony in child abuse cases in the United Kingdom).

51 Kandel (1994) (qualitative field research in three child custody mediation cases; adults able to quote others in telling a story had an advantage).

52 See Richard F Rakos and Stephan Landsman 'Researching the Hearsay Rule: Emerging Findings, General Issues, and Future Directions' (1992) 76 Minn LR 655 and William C Thompson and Maithilee K Pathak 'Empirical Study of Hearsay Rules Bridging the Gap Between Psychology and Law' (1999) 5 Psychology, Public Policy, and Law 456 (reviews of the literature and suggestions for further research); Helen L Westcott, Graham M Davies and J R Spencer 'Children, Hearsay, and the Courts: A Perspective From the United Kingdom' (1999) 5 Psych Pub Pol and L 282 (review of legal developments, field research and survey research relating to extensive use of live links and videotaped testimony in child abuse cases in the United Kingdom); Jean Montoya 'Child Hearsay Statutes: At Once Over-Inclusive and Under-Inclusive' (1999) 5 Psych Pub Pol and L 304 (author argues that child hearsay statutes are over-inclusive in admitting hearsay testimony of prior consistent statements even when victim testifies, and underinclusive in that they apply only to child victims and not to other child witnesses to victimisation; survey of law and empirical literature); David Dunning 'On the Social Psychology of Hearsay Evidence' (1999) 5 Psych Pub Pol and L 473 (review of literature and suggestions for further research; author favours theoretically driven research that pinpoints particular situations in which jurors assess hearsay evidence); Lucy S McGough 'Hearing and Believing Hearsay' (1999) 5 Psych Pub Pol and L 485 (review of the literature and suggestions for further research).

53 See Robert M Hutchins and Donald Slesinger 'Some Observations on the Law of Evidence – Spontaneous Exclamation' (1928) 28 Col LR 432 (noting effect of excitement on accuracy and advocating admission of unexcited contemporaneous statements); Robert M Hutchins and Donald Slesinger 'Some Observations on the Law of Evidence – Memory' (1928) 41 Harv LR 860 (examining experiments on subjects such as forgetting over time and comparison of recognition with recall, and making various recommendations on past recollection recorded and refreshing recollection); I Daniel Stewart Jr 'Perception, Memory, and Hearsay: A Criticism of Present Law and the Proposed Federal Rules of Evidence' (1970) Utah LR 1 (noting experimental evidence of flaws in human perception and memory and arguing that therefore the law should more often require cross-examination of available declarants); Myers, Gordon, Ghetti and Goodman 'Hearsay Exceptions: Adjusting the Ratio of Intuition to Psychological Science' (2002) 65 Law and Contemporary Problems 3 (review of psychology literature relevant to use in child abuse cases of residual exception, exception for statements for medical diagnosis or treatment, and excited utterance exception).

54 Eg the government might wish to put in hearsay statements rather than produce a disreputable and unstable informant who is himself a criminal and is co-operating in return for leniency. The defence might prefer to have the defendant tell his story through the mouth of a psychiatrist who had examined the defendant rather than through his own mouth, thereby avoiding questions that might provoke the defendant to tell lies that can be disproven. Similarly, in situations where the out-of-court statements consist of solicitations of illegal conduct, as where the police occupy premises believed to have been used by the defendant in drug dealing and receive visits and calls from persons seeking to buy drugs, cf *R v Kearley* [1992] 2 All ER 345, HL, the prosecution would almost certainly prefer to incriminate the defendant through testimony of the police officers about the solicitations than to place on the stand the persons who came to ask for drugs.

55 Jonathan M Golding, Rebecca Polley Sanchez and Sandra A Sego 'The Believability of Hearsay Testimony in a Child Sexual Assault Trial' (1997) 21 Law & Human Behav 299.

56 Myers quotes a trial transcript from preliminary hearing in which the cross-examiner induced the child to say that the child had met the cross-examiner before trial, and that the cross-examiner was wearing a red suit with stripes running around the legs; none of those facts were true. John E B Myers 'The Child Witness: Techniques for Direct Examination, Cross-Examination, and Impeachment' (1987) 18 Pac LJ 801, 887.

57 (1987) 18 Pac LJ 801, 891. Pitching a no-hitter is a rare event even for world-class baseball pitchers, and is almost impossible in child's play; and hitting a home run each time at bat would be comparable to being a soccer player who scored a goal on every possession.

58 (1987) 18 Pac LJ 801, 896–896.

59 See the studies by Kovera, Park and Penrod and by Pathak and Thompson cited in nn 42–44, above.

60 Compare Day with Rufo.

61 Kovera, Park and Penrod, above n 42, and Pathak and Thompson, above n 44.

62 See, eg Roger C Park *Trial Objections Handbook* (2d edn, 2002) at § 12:2.

63 See Schuller (1995) n 27 above; Schuller and Paglia (1999) above n 33; Golding, Sanchez and Sego (1997) above n 35.

64 Professor Seigel writes that: '[A]lthough each of the studies purports to examine the ability of human subjects to differentiate and discount hearsay in comparison with witness testimony, they actually measure individuals' abilities to differentiate among different types of hearsay and hearsay within hearsay. Remarkably, the articles are silent on this critical issue concerning their internal design.' Michael L Seigel 'A Pragmatic Critique of Modern Evidence Scholarship' (1994) 88 Nw ULR 995, 1042–1043. As applied to videotaped simulations, this is a barren conceptual criticism. The hearsay rule is actually two rules: the important and consequential rule that a witness cannot report another person's statement if it is used for its truth, and the relatively trivial rule that witnesses testifying to first-hand observations cannot testify by videotape. Because these two rules both share the label 'hearsay' instead of being called the 'second-hand information rule' and the 'videotape rule', Professor Seigel believes that a trial presented by videotape cannot tell us anything about the processing of second-hand information. He does not give any reason why not, except the formal labelling. To be sure, videotaped trials are not real trials, but this challenge to validity is not any more serious in the hearsay context than in any other context using videotaped stimuli, such as studies of the effect of jury instructions.

Exploring the integrity principle in evidence and procedure

Andrew Ashworth*

In recent years the so-called integrity principle has achieved increasing prominence. In broad terms, it is the principle that a court should not act upon evidence obtained by state officials by methods that were so fundamentally wrong that for the court to take the resulting evidence into account would compromise the integrity of the criminal process. Thus, where the main prosecution evidence derived from the activities of an undercover police officer which were held to amount to entrapment, the House of Lords held that the prosecution should be halted in order 'to protect the integrity of the criminal justice system'.[1] Similarly, where a defendant had been brought into the jurisdiction by unlawful methods, the House of Lords held that it would not be fair to try him: 'the rule of law demands that the court take cognisance of that circumstance ... the whole proceeding is tainted.'[2] The integrity principle is often related to the decision to grant a particular remedy, notably a stay of the prosecution on grounds of abuse of process (where the court determines that it is not fair to try the defendant at all in view of what has happened), but it may also be used as a rationale for the exclusion of evidence (where the court concludes that admission of the evidence would have such an adverse effect on the fairness of the trial that it should be excluded).[3]

The purpose of this essay is to explore the theoretical foundations of the integrity principle and to assess its cogency, focusing on the significance of the right violated rather than upon the remedy that might be most appropriate. In exploring the principle's foundations here, references to writings and to judicial decisions will be selective and jurisdictionally promiscuous, in an endeavour to cut through to the essential arguments and counter-arguments. To begin with, two forms of the integrity principle will be distinguished, and the relevance of the European Convention on Human Rights will be explained. Then, at the end of section 1, the contours of the subsequent analysis will be described.

1 Coherence, complicity and the convention

It is surely axiomatic that a system of law should not contain inconsistent rules of conduct:[4] it would be intolerable if it required a person in a given situation to do *X* and to do *not-X* at the same time. The same might be said of rules of adjudication addressed to officials. If they were required to do *Y* and also to do *not-Y* in a given situation, this would be contradictory and would not meet the essentials of the rule of law, since no effective guidance would be given. But how far can this principle of non-contradiction or coherence be taken? There is nothing unusual or objectionable about a legal system that declares principles or even rules that may occasionally come into conflict,[5] and it is often the courts that have to resolve these conflicts in their application to particular situations. The expectation is that the courts will do so in a consistent manner, ie that they will adhere to some principle of non-contradiction or coherence in their own decisions.[6] If they do not do so, then again the law will fail in one of its essential objectives, which is the guidance of human conduct. It will tell citizens or officials that in a given situation the consequences of doing *X* may be either *a* or *b*, depending on the composition and disposition of the court that hears the case. That would be a rare situation, perhaps, and one that would attract much criticism. But there are occasions where the courts come close to adopting such a position, as where they state that the resolution of a particular conflict requires the court to balance factor *P* against factor *Q*, without specifying what weight is assigned to various forms of *P* and of *Q*, and on what basis the metaphorical 'balancing' is to be carried out.[7] More frequently, and more satisfactorily, courts will endeavour to resolve such conflicts by analysing the types of situation in which they arise, and adducing arguments as to why in certain situations the legal consequence of doing *X* will be *a*, whereas in other situations the legal consequence of doing *X* will be *b*. Critics can then debate whether the correct criteria have been used, and whether the dividing line between *a* and *b* has been drawn in the appropriate place.

On the basis of this abstract discussion, we may provisionally draw a distinction between two varieties of the integrity principle. The first is concerned with the integrity of the criminal justice system: the claim is that the administration of criminal justice must carry moral authority, and that this is compromised if agents are supposed to respect certain fundamental rights, and yet when they fail to do so there are either no adverse consequences or insufficient remedial consequences. A failure to protect or re-affirm fundamental rights in such circumstances undermines the coherence and moral authority of the system. It introduces hypocrisy and self-contradiction. It departs from the ideal of a *Rechtstaat*, in which the state upholds and abides by the rule of law. The different elements of these claims will be discussed below: the key point is that the claims relate to the integrity of the whole system, to which both law enforcement agents and the courts belong. The second kind of integrity principle is narrower and might be termed the principle of judicial integrity. The claim here is that by acting on the evidential or procedural results of a violation of a fundamental right, a court would not only compromise its integrity but also become an accomplice to the violation – the complicity arising because the court exercises a choice in recognising, rather than refusing to accept, the results of the violation.

The two variations of the integrity principle have much in common, especially when confined (as in this chapter) to breaches of fundamental rights. The term 'fundamental' will be used to refer to rights with a constitutional or supra-national status, notably the rights declared in the European Convention on Human Rights, to which we now turn. The Convention declares a number of individual rights. Some of them are drafted in such a way as to recognise and manage conflicts: examples of this are readily found in arts 8, 9, 10 and 11, each of which declares a general right (in brief: privacy, religion, expression, assembly) and then goes on to state that interference with the right may be permitted in limited circumstances and if 'necessary in a democratic society'. Some of the rights may occasionally conflict among themselves, and such conflicts will require resolution: one example is the conflict between the defendant's art 6 right to a fair trial and to have witnesses against him examined, and the right of a witness to respect for her private life under art 8.[8]

The second paragraphs of arts 8 to 11 explicitly recognise the protection of the rights of others as a reason for curtailing one of those rights, but the particular interest of this essay lies in potential conflicts that do not appear on the face of the Convention. Article 3 of the Convention declares the right not to be 'subjected to torture or to inhuman or degrading treatment', and art 6 declares the right to a fair trial. If evidence obtained by officials by means of a violation of art 3 forms part of the case for the prosecution, can the trial be fair if the court takes that evidence into account? The Convention is one of many constitutional and international documents that remain silent on this point, saying nothing about the consequences of breaching certain rights. It has therefore been left to the Strasbourg organs to deal with such issues. Remarkably, there appears to have been only one occasion on which this point has had to be confronted, and this was a case before the European Commission on Human Rights (not the Court) over 40 years ago.[9] The Commission decided that the art 6 right to a fair trial would be violated if evidence obtained through a breach of art 3 were used and, although this is merely a decision of the Commission and is rather old, it has been widely adopted as a statement of the correct approach.[10] The decision is manifestly under-theorised, and it leaves open the question whether there would be any element of contradiction or incoherence in reaching the opposite decision.

Before that point is pressed further, attention should be given to the Court's resolution of an apparent conflict between art 8 and art 6. Article 8 declares the right to respect for private life, and allows interference with that right only in certain circumstances. One peremptory requirement of a legitimate interference with art 8 is that it should be 'in accordance with the law'. In *Schenk v Switzerland*[11] evidence had been obtained from the defendant in contravention of Swiss law and in breach of art 8 and was then used at his trial; the Court held that the art 6 right to a fair trial was not violated by the admission of evidence obtained through a breach of art 8. In *Khan v United Kingdom*[12] evidence had been obtained from the defendant without any legal authorisation under English law and in breach of art 8; the Court followed its *Schenk* judgment and held that, so long as the evidence was reliable and the defence had the opportunity to contest it, the trial was not unfair. In *PG and JH v United Kingdom*[13] evidence had again been obtained without any authority in English law and in breach of art 8; again the Court simply followed the *Schenk* approach. However, not all the judges accept the Court's approach: in *Khan* Judge Loucaides dissented, and in *PG and JH* there was a stinging dissent from Judge Tulkens, who pointed out that in this decision and the previous cases the Court had repeatedly avoided facing the key question of coherence. The Court frequently states that the Convention should be interpreted as a whole, and yet here it sees no need to justify its failure to hold that to base a criminal trial on evidence obtained through a breach of art 8 is to violate the right to a fair trial in art 6.

The challenge has now been clearly thrown down. Is there any incoherence in proclaiming a right to respect for private life under art 8, finding that a criminal investigation has breached that right, and yet allowing the fruits of that breach into the criminal trial without declaring the trial unfair under art 6? The issue has particular poignancy because it is not simply a question of the possible contradiction involved when a court bases a criminal conviction on evidence that has been obtained by unlawful means. The articles of the Convention are intended to declare human rights and fundamental freedoms, and there is a significant qualitative difference between the violation of a fundamental freedom and a mere breach of domestic law. The focus here is not upon the broad argument that a criminal trial should be regarded as unfair (and contrary to art 6) whenever any unlawfulness taints a piece of prosecution evidence. It is on the narrower and more powerful argument that a criminal trial should be regarded as unfair whenever a breach of another Convention right taints a piece of evidence on which the prosecution is allowed to rely.[14] The distinction is equally valid when the context is changed from European human rights law to English law. The Human Rights Act 1998 obliges the courts to act compatibly with Convention rights and, so far as possible, to interpret statutes in a way that is compatible with Convention rights. Whether the Human Rights Act has the effect of entrenching the Convention or bestowing upon it a kind of fundamental or constitutional status is not for discussion here.[15] What is clear is that Convention rights are to be accorded special weight by the courts. As Lord Steyn put the point, in relation to a right in a Commonwealth constitution:

> 'The stamp of constitutionality on a citizen's rights is not meaningless: it is clear testimony that an added value is attached to the protection of the right ... [T]he fact that there has been a breach of a constitutional right is a cogent factor militating in favour of the exclusion of the confession. In this way the constitutional character of the infringed right is accorded a high value.'[16]

Consistently with that, our courts ought to take a different view of evidence obtained by breach of a Convention right, compared with evidence obtained merely by unlawful means.

Both varieties of the integrity principle come into play here. It can be argued that for a court to act on such fundamentally tainted evidence involves the criminal justice system in self-contradiction: those who are entrusted with the task of upholding the law are breaching fundamental rights and the system is failing to mark that adequately. Moreover, the courts themselves have the power to refuse to act on such fundamentally tainted evidence, and if they decline to exercise that power they become accomplices in the original violation. If courts are prepared to overlook breaches of fundamental rights by public officers, do they therefore lack the moral standing to make authoritative pronouncements on the value of fundamental rights in other spheres? Whereas others might phrase this question in terms of legitimacy, that concept is probably better avoided because it may (appear to) depend too greatly on public reactions and public opinions. The concept of moral standing, on the other hand, derives from the consistency of courts in their own decisions and judgments, and it is the foundations of this concept that need further exploration. Detailed examination of the underpinnings of the integrity principle will be taken up in section 4 below. Before that, the context of integrity within criminal procedure will be sketched in two brief sections, the first dealing with alternative arguments in favour of regarding it as unfair to try a person on evidence obtained through breach of a Convention right (section 2), and the second dealing with antithetical arguments which deny that such a trial is unfair and put forward other solutions (section 3).

2 Alternative arguments

No assumption is made here that a version of the integrity principle provides the most persuasive rationale for courts refusing to act on evidence obtained by a violation of a fundamental right. It is therefore important to give brief consideration to three alternative arguments that might lead to a similar conclusion. The first claims a different source for the integrity principle, here termed the public confidence thesis; the second is a protective principle; and the third is the disciplinary or deterrent rationale.

(a) The public confidence thesis

In an incisive discussion of versions of the integrity principle, Peter Mirfield has drawn a number of helpful distinctions, including that between 'court-centred integrity', where the basis of the principle lies in 'the moral scruple of the court', and 'public attitude integrity', where the benchmark seems to be public reaction.[17] Whereas 'court-centred integrity' lies very much at the centre of this essay and will be explored in section 4 below, 'public attitude integrity' is really a separate rationale, and it will be dealt with here. It has a considerable pedigree in English criminal procedure. For example, in the leading case of *Connelly v DPP*,[18] where the question was whether it was an abuse of process for a second prosecution to be brought on essentially the same facts as the first, the House of Lords stated that 'it is the courts' duty to conduct their proceedings so as to command the respect and confidence of the public'. But the willingness of judges to refer to the importance of maintaining public confidence in the administration of criminal justice seems not to be accompanied by a willingness to examine its political and empirical foundations. How do we distinguish public reactions from that of politicians and the mass media? The reaction of sections of the public who have access to the media, whether it be Radio 4 or the tabloid press, surely cannot be treated as a barometer of public opinion in general. Moreover, public opinion itself – even if it can be discovered by reliable research methods[19] – may be founded on incomplete information, misconceptions or the failure to consider certain arguments. To rely on public opinion as the benchmark of public confidence is therefore unwise. To refer to the danger of bringing the criminal justice system into disrepute is no better:[20] such a phrase is actually part of the test declared in the Canadian Charter of Rights, and the Supreme Court has veered towards some kind of objective test that refers to the long-term values of informed members of the community.[21] There are certainly those who maintain that the greatest damage to 'public confidence' is done by acquitting the guilty rather than by allowing people to be convicted on evidence obtained by a manifest breach of human rights.[22] So far as popular opinion is concerned, one could certainly assert that a system that greatly lacks public confidence ought to be re-assessed, on account of the dangers arising if people are tempted to try to 'take the law into their own hands'. But even then there may be good reasons for persevering if the policies that give rise to the adverse public reaction can be regarded as the right policies. After all, it seems that an overwhelming proportion of the British public favour capital punishment and might well support the use of torture on terrorist suspects, but that would not be a compelling reason for adopting policies that go against Convention rights.

(b) The protective principle

Another argument in favour of holding that a criminal trial based on evidence obtained through breach of a Convention right is unfair would be the protective principle, arguing that the holder of a right ought to be protected against the consequences of an official's breach of that right.[23] The point is not so much that the criminal courts should use their authority as a check on the misuse of power by the executive, but rather that the courts should ensure that, as it were, the right-bearer does not lose as a result of the violation.[24] This approach has been adopted by the Supreme Court of Ireland;[25] it has some similarity with the exclusion, under Canadian law, of evidence that could not have been obtained but for the unconstitutional participation of the defendant;[26] some of the decisions of the German Constitutional Court can be read in the same way, as ensuring that basic rights of the defendant are safeguarded through the exclusion of the resulting evidence.[27] Another way of expressing it would be to argue that the court should rule in such a way that the state and the citizen are placed in the positions they would have been in, had the Convention not been violated.[28] It may be doubted whether the protective principle should be used in all cases of unlawfully obtained evidence, since remedies such as the exclusion of evidence may be disproportionate to small or merely 'technical' breaches, but its credentials are surely stronger where Convention rights (or, in other legal systems, constitutional rights) are concerned. If a particular right is singled out as a fundamental freedom and human right, this ought to lead to extra protection. Indeed, it may be said to be implicit in the notion of a fundamental right that the law should not simply declare it, but also ensure that the right-bearer does not suffer as a result of a violation of such a right.[29] If the prosecutor wishes to rely on the fruits of the violation in a criminal trial, it surely follows that the protective principle ought to operate so as to prevent that.

(c) The deterrent or disciplinary rationale

Many of the leading decisions in the Supreme Court of the United States have laid emphasis on deterrence as the rationale for the prevailing exclusionary rule, whereby evidence resulting from unconstitutional conduct by officials may be held inadmissible at trial. Thus in *Elkins v United States*[30] the court said that the purpose 'is to deter – to compel respect for the constitutional guaranty in the only effectively available way – by removing the incentive to disregard it'. Likewise, in the landmark decision in *Mapp v Ohio*[31] the court referred to the exclusionary rule as a 'deterrent safeguard without insistence upon which the Fourth Amendment would have been reduced to "a form of words".' This emphasis on the deterrent or disciplinary purpose has continued,[32] but has gradually been used to restrict and re-shape the judicial approach. For example, in *United States v Leon*[33] the court held that the rule should not apply in cases where officers relied in good faith upon a warrant that was defective, since in those circumstances there was no basis for believing that the exclusion of evidence 'would have a significant deterrent effect'. It is to be noticed that the form of deterrence implied by most of these statements is general deterrence, ie the use of the threat of inadmissibility to prevent future violations of the constitution in similar situations. If that is to be the criterion, legal argument will focus on whether or not excluding evidence in this (type of) case is likely to have a significant deterrent effect on police conduct. There is some relevant research evidence,[34] but in many situations the inquiry will be speculative and, it must be said, the prospects of deterrence not necessarily high. Police officers might well believe that the breach of the constitution (or, as the case may be, of a Convention right) may go unnoticed, or that the defendant will plead guilty anyway, or that they will be able to use some countering device or bargaining tool against the defendant so as to suppress the illegality. Thus critics of the deterrent rationale might argue that its focus purely on the consequences of excluding the evidence fails adequately to mark the wrong done through the breach of the fundamental right.

3 Antithetical arguments

From among the various arguments that can be made against the integrity principle, two are selected for brief discussion in this section – first, what may be called the 'separation thesis', which includes the argument that any violation of fundamental rights is an entirely separate matter from the admissibility of evidence in a criminal trial, and also the argument that the actions of the police are entirely separate from those of the judiciary; and secondly, the linked argument that the controlling principle in relation to trials should be the relevance and reliability of evidence. Discussion of these two lines of argument will lead naturally towards the exploration of the integrity principle that follows in section 4.

(a) The separation thesis

A prominent example of this approach is to be found in the decision of the House of Lords in *R v Sang*,[35] where the defence had objected to the use by the prosecution of evidence obtained by means of what the defence described as entrapment. The House unanimously rejected the defence argument and went so far as to deny that there was a judicial discretion to exclude evidence obtained at or before the commission of the alleged offence. A major part of Lord Diplock's reasoning was that it is 'no part of the judicial function' to exclude probative evidence unless it was obtained after the commission of the offence by unconscionable methods. 'However much the judge may dislike the way in which a particular piece of evidence was obtained before proceedings were commenced', that is none of the judge's concern. It is a separate issue that should be addressed through a complaint against the police, police disciplinary proceedings and, if appropriate, an action for damages against the police. The House of Lords has recently re-asserted this approach, relying on *Schenk* and the other Strasbourg decisions set out in section 1 above:

> 'The criterion to be applied is the criterion of fairness in Article 6, which is likewise the criterion to be applied by the judge under section 78. Similarly, the European Court of Human Rights' decision that any remedy for a breach of Article 8 lies outside the scope of the criminal trial and that Article 13 does not require a remedy for a breach of Article 8 to be given within that trial shows that their Lordships were right to say that a breach of Article 8 did not require the exclusion of evidence.'[36]

The separation thesis, vigorously advocated by Wigmore in relation to the Fourth Amendment to the US Constitution on search and seizure,[37] is certainly alive and well.

At the level of practice, questions may be raised about the adequacy of the alternative mechanisms of enforcement that are available – for example, the Strasbourg Court has repeatedly criticised the police complaints system for its lack of independence and impartiality,[38] and actions for damages against the police require considerable perseverance. At the level of principle, moreover, the separation thesis raises deep questions about the relationship between the trial itself and pre-trial events. Is it defensible to say that the concern of the judge should be to regulate events at the trial itself, and that courts should not be concerned with earlier happenings? Support for this position could be garnered from the availability of other remedies for pre-trial violations of rights, whereas the strongest attack on the position derives from the significance of the court hearing. A criminal trial is not simply one of a sequence of events following arrest, charge, plea etc. It is the centrepiece of the criminal process, and the point at which those charged with a criminal offence should have the opportunity for a fair hearing before an independent, impartial and public tribunal. It is a person's right to have a fair trial: there is no justification for state punishment unless the defendant has had a fair hearing, or has indicated an informed waiver of the opportunity.[39] This establishes that the trial is not simply a sealed compartment, not one of a row of separate boxes that go to make up the criminal process. The point becomes stronger if one reflects on the purpose of many of the pre-trial activities of state officials such as the police, other investigative agencies, and prosecutors. That purpose is largely[40] to obtain evidence, or 'leads' that may produce evidence, with a view to constructing a case against a suspect. Whether it is a matter of searching for real evidence, obtaining forensic science evidence, or questioning the suspect and witnesses, the goal is to put together a case that will either yield sufficient evidence for a prosecution or lead the defendant to plead guilty. Thus there can be no true separation between the processes of gathering evidence against a suspect and the subsequent trial, since the latter is linked inextricably with the former.[41]

Another aspect of the separation thesis is that the activities of the police and other investigators are entirely separate from the role of the judiciary, and therefore that the latter should in no way be identified with what may have occurred earlier. This version of the thesis is discussed further in section 4 below. The counter-argument is that the earlier investigations and acts are carried out by officers of the state or of the court, notably the police or other official regulatory agencies, and the Crown Prosecution Service, whose legally qualified members are technically 'officers of the court'. It is therefore entirely fitting that the English courts have long felt it appropriate to take procedural measures against the prosecution when either the police or a prosecutor has acted in an unconscionable manner. It is not merely that the trial has great symbolic significance, as a public event. Nor is it merely the teleological point that the very motivation for almost all pre-trial activities is to prepare the ground for the trial. It is also that the courts have (assumed) the power to review the fairness of what state officials have done in order to prepare for the trial, and that it is right to regard fairness in the pre-trial sphere as intimately bound up with fairness during the hearing itself.

It is well established in European human rights law that the right to a fair trial under art 6 applies to all stages of criminal proceedings, from the time of the initial charge through to the conclusion of the appeals system. Indeed, there are decisions extending the right to a fair trial to official conduct even before any arrest or questioning: in *Teixeira de Castro v Portugal*[42] the applicant, a man with no criminal record, had been approached twice by undercover police officers who asked whether he could obtain some heroin for them. On the second occasion he did so and was arrested. The Strasbourg Court held that this was a plain case of entrapment, concluding:

> 'that the two police officers' actions went beyond those of undercover agents because they instigated the offence and there is nothing to suggest that without their intervention it would have been committed. That intervention and its use in the impugned criminal proceedings meant that, right from the outset, the applicant was definitively deprived of a fair trial.'[43]

In domestic law the House of Lords reached a similar conclusion in *A-G's Reference (No 3 of 2000)*.[44] They held that, where it appears that an accused person had been entrapped into committing the offence (as distinct from merely being given an unexceptional opportunity to commit it), it would be an abuse of the process of the court to allow a prosecution to be launched. Both the House of Lords and the Strasbourg Court therefore posit a firm link between official misconduct in inciting an offence and the concept of a fair trial in a court of law. The conclusion is not that the trial would be unfair but that it would be unfair to try the defendant at all if the offence was caused or created by a police officer or someone else acting on behalf of the state. This rationale applies strongly to cases of entrapment, as well as to cases where force or illegality has been used to bring the defendant into the jurisdiction.[45]

The separation thesis could be applied here, inasmuch as the offending officer could be prosecuted for the crime of incitement, whilst the incitee was still prosecuted for giving way to temptation. After all, if a private citizen had incited the defendant to commit an offence and he had succumbed, there would be no defence except in the few extreme cases where the pressure amounted to duress.[46] But, again, it is the significance of an official's role in creating the offence that is regarded as crucial: opponents of the separation thesis maintain that the courts and the police are both parts of the official machinery of criminal justice, and for the one to act on the other's unconstitutional or fundamental-rights-violating conduct would be to condone the violation and to undermine human rights. This strand of the argument will be examined further in section 4 below.

(b) Reliability as the touchstone

It was Jeremy Bentham who elaborated a system of proof that gave priority to the attainment of reliability and accuracy, or 'rectitude' as he called it.[47] On many occasions, appellate judges too have made statements that place the reliability of evidence above all consideration of the means by which it was obtained. For example, in the early case of *R v Warickshall*[48] it was held that real evidence was admissible, even though the police had been led to it by the accused's revelations during a confession that was held to have been unfairly obtained. Again, in *United States v Payner*[49] the Supreme Court held that the societal interest in allowing the use of probative evidence should be given greater weight than the fact that the evidence was obtained by violation of a constitutional right. It was real evidence, and therefore assumed to be highly reliable. Thus in a sense this is another manifestation of the separation thesis: in his oft-quoted words in *R v Leatham*,[50] Crompton J said, 'it matters not how you get it; if you steal it even, it would be admissible in evidence'. Those words were spoken in relation to evidence of undoubted reliability. On this view the focus of the trial should be on the reliability and accuracy of the evidence. This does not necessarily mean that the way in which it was obtained is irrelevant, because that might cast light on the degree of its reliability, especially where it is oral rather than real evidence (such as a confession). But it does mean that any breach of a fundamental right is of itself irrelevant, except in the rare event that it reflects on reliability. There was hardly any place in Bentham's structure of evidence for notions of rights.[51] Whatever the merits of that position, it is less attractive in the present context of human rights and constitutional declarations. It must stand or fall with the resolution of the conflict between the separation thesis and the integrity principle, to which we now turn.

4 Investigating integrity

Having sketched some of the rival principles and two of the arguments opposing the integrity principle, the time has come to explore the strands of the rationale for the integrity principle (in this section), and then to examine some of the issues arising in the application of the integrity principle (in section 5).

It seems that there are around five strands of reasoning, often interwoven, that are claimed to support the integrity principle. It is argued that any declaration of fundamental rights (such as the European Convention) should be treated as a whole; that the criminal justice system, and those holding office within it, should be treated as a single integrated process; that a fundamental right without a fundamental remedy amounts to nothing more than empty rhetoric; that if a court acts upon evidence obtained by violating a fundamental right it condones that violation and becomes an accomplice in it; and that a court should not act upon any evidence or procedural irregularity that shocks its conscience. The first three arguments relate generally to the integrity of the criminal justice system, whereas the fourth and fifth are specifically concerned with the principle of judicial integrity. Let us explore these rationales further.

The first line of argument is probably the most fundamental. It takes issue directly with one form of separation thesis by treating a declaration of rights such as the European Convention or any national constitution as an integrated whole. This emerges from the early reference of the Supreme Court of the United States to its being 'charged at all times with the support of the Constitution', with the implication that:

> 'to sanction such proceedings [based on an unconstitutional search and seizure] would be to affirm by judicial decision a manifest neglect, if not an open defiance, of the prohibitions of the Constitution, intended for the protection of the people against such unauthorized action.'[52]

This declaration treats the constitutional document as a whole, and not only maintains that it is inconsistent to ensure that some of a defendant's rights are respected (notably the right to a fair hearing in the courts) whilst acting on the results of a breach of one or more of his other rights, but also interprets this as 'sanctioning' the breach. This is exactly the argument used by those judges of the Strasbourg Court who dissented in the *Khan* and *PG and JH* decisions, and who (among other arguments) reminded the majority judges of the general policy of regarding the Convention as an integrated whole.[53] Does this dispose conclusively of the argument that a court could grant a defendant a financial or other remedy for the invasion of the violated right whilst allowing a criminal trial to proceed on the basis of the evidence thereby obtained? Is it not arguable that allowing the conviction to stand does not 'sanction' the breach of a fundamental right, especially if the breach is judicially condemned and a separate remedy granted? The rebuttal of this version of the separation thesis must lie in the two reasons emerging from the quotations from American decisions earlier in this paragraph. One is the function of the courts in upholding fundamental rights and calling the executive to account for breaches of those rights. This is a function that the judiciary exercises under the European Convention and in most national constitutional courts, and the question is whether it requires the court to refuse to act on the tainted evidence or whether it can be satisfied by a separate condemnation and remedy (such as financial compensation). Related to this is the second reason, that it is inconsistent or even hypocritical to evince respect for some fundamental rights and not for others. These reasons lean heavily on the symbolic significance of court judgments, discussed in the paragraph after next. The point is often phrased in consequentialist terms – what the public would think if the courts were to appear to ignore some breaches of fundamental rights – but its principal force is as an argument from coherence.

The second line of argument takes issue with the aspect of the separation thesis discussed in detail in section 3(a) above, by proclaiming that the whole apparatus of the administration of criminal justice should be viewed as a single system. The challenge was laid down by Holmes J in his dissent in *Olmstead v United States*,[54] when he said that:

> 'no distinction can be taken between the Government as prosecutor and the Government as judge. If the existing code does not permit district attorneys to

have a hand in such dirty business, it does not permit the judge to allow such iniquities to succeed.'

The idea of the *government* as judge is probably no more than a manner of speaking: presumably by 'Government' was meant the whole structure of legislature, judiciary and executive. The force of the main argument is focused on district attorneys, who are officers of the law, but the most extensive version of the argument applies to all public officials involved in law enforcement, including the police. The argument does not absolutely require acceptance of the view that the police can be seen as part of the same system as the courts. Its other leg, as it were, is that it is the courts' function to 'supervise' the conduct of the police and other officials and agencies whose actions constitute steps in the process of bringing a criminal case to court. 'Judicial supervision of the administration of criminal justice ... implies the duty of establishing and maintaining civilized standards of procedure and evidence.'[55] The Australian courts have also proclaimed the power of supervision over the whole criminal process, using the inherent jurisdiction to stay prosecutions for abuse of process which has also been called upon by the English courts in various cases.[56] It can be said to be one of the functions of the courts to ensure that violations of rights are remedied in individual cases, and also by their actions to ensure that the officials responsible for such violations are reprimanded. But, again, critics would ask whether it requires the court to refuse to act on the tainted evidence or whether it can be satisfied by separate condemnation and remedy.

This leads into the third strand of the argument – that if a court fails to treat seriously the violation of a fundamental right, it reduces the Convention or constitution to a series of empty words. Forceful expression of this view may be found in US Supreme Court decisions such as *Mapp v Ohio*,[57] asserting the appropriateness of the remedy of excluding all such evidence:

'Just as without the *Weeks* rule the assurance against unreasonable federal searches and seizures would be "a form of words," valueless and undeserving of mention in a perpetual charter of inestimable human liberties, so too, without that rule the freedom from state invasions of privacy would be so ephemeral and so neatly severed from its conceptual nexus with the freedom from all brutish means of coercing evidence as not to merit this court's high regard as a freedom "implicit in the concept of ordered liberty".'

This is, at bottom, an assertion that a right without a remedy is not a right. Since we are discussing only fundamental rights, the ideal of a *Rechtstaat* requires that the courts give some kind of remedy. As with the fourth strand of argument below, it does not conclusively rebut the version of the separation thesis which maintains that the grant of a separate remedy (damages, police disciplinary proceedings, etc) is sufficient and that the fairness of the trial itself is unrelated – although it would insist that the alternatives be practical and effective, rather than theoretical and illusory.[58] Rather, it assumes that the only appropriate remedy is to protect the defendant from the consequences of the violation, by endeavouring to minimise any adverse consequences flowing from it.

The fourth strand of argument, which also applies specifically to judicial integrity, is that for a court to act on the fruits of evidence resulting from the breach of a fundamental right is to condone that breach. The judicial condonation rationale was evident at an early stage in Scotland;[59] it has been adopted by the Supreme Court of Canada and developed in various ways;[60] it has also featured in leading Australian decisions.[61] The US Supreme Court has taken the rationale further, by stating that a conviction resting on evidence obtained by a breach of the Constitution 'cannot be allowed to stand without the courts themselves becoming accomplices in wilful disobedience of a Constitution they are sworn to uphold'.[62] These rationales depend on attributions of symbolic significance to court decisions. By their actions, as much as (or even more than) by their words, judicial decisions carry a certain message. If a judge says that the violation of a fundamental right was a terrible thing, but that the court takes the view that it has no bearing on the overall fairness of the trial, it is not unreasonable to infer that the court has condoned the violation. To add that the court then becomes an accomplice in the violation is merely to add rhetorical force. Proponents of the separation thesis would suggest that there is no condonation if the court states that a remedy may be given for the violation but that this does not affect the fairness of the hearing itself. It is certainly easier to support the condonation rationale if the court ignores the possibility of a remedy for the breach, but of course a civil remedy would have to come from separate proceedings and it may still be insisted that this is not enough to show that the fundamental right is being taken seriously. It is quite unsatisfactory for alternative remedies to require exhausting and time-consuming applications that resemble an obstacle race.[63]

Brief mention may be made of a fifth strand of the argument, that courts should not act upon evidence obtained by means that 'shocks the conscience'.[64] This kind of phrase seems to depart from the violation of a fundamental right as the criterion, and to substitute an uncertain and possibly narrower standard. Its unattractiveness is not confined to its failure to embrace rule-of-law values such as certainty and predictability. It is so flexible as to be reversible: as Robert Bork once observed, 'the conscience of the court ought to be equally shaken by the idea of turning a criminal loose upon society'.[65] This fifth strand of reasoning therefore seems distinctly unpromising.

5 The point of application

Adherents of the integrity principle could argue for a strict exclusionary rule in cases where evidence has been obtained through violation of a fundamental right. Such a rule would, however, leave no flexibility for dealing with difficult cases, and it might well have unwanted consequences such as more frequent police perjury and judicial attempts to circumvent the rule in certain types of case. Adherents of the separation thesis, on the other hand, could argue for the admissibility of all such evidence – leaving alternative remedies to cope with the breaches. However, in almost all jurisdictions the courts have been feeling their way towards some compromise that stops short of embracing either extreme and yet that shows respect both for fundamental rights and for public policies on law enforcement. Colin Tapper has argued that:

> 'It is a mistake to suppose that the choice lies between admitting the evidence and leaving the aggrieved party to pursue such civil or criminal remedies against the wrongdoer as may be available, or rejecting the evidence as a warning to officialdom that convictions cannot be obtained by illegal action.'[66]

Thus the trend is in favour of a judicial discretion to decide, on the facts of each case, whether the balance favours what may be termed a 'criminal process remedy' or favours the separation thesis.[67] However, which factors are to be 'balanced' depends very much on the principles adopted, and many of the judicial discussions of 'balancing' are vague and unconvincing. This is hardly surprising if the metaphor of 'balancing' is scrutinised. As Colin Tapper has argued:

> 'The basic problem is that in everyday life balancing involves the comparison of two different objects by reference to one common factor, that of weight, so as to determine which is the heavier. It commonly includes the use of a precise technique, for example scales, to establish the comparison when cruder forms of comparison may be inappropriate or inaccurate. It is far from clear how this model applies to forensic balancing. It may be true that the things to be compared are similarly apparently diverse, but it is far from clear that they possess a common element, or that the forensic process of comparing them is in any way more precise than that which would have been accorded without reference to balancing at all.'[68]

References to balancing the rights of the individual against the social need to enforce the law and convict the guilty are therefore unlikely to be helpful, not least because they rarely disclose the weight being assigned to the different factors, let alone the reasons behind that assignment.

It is fair to say that the courts in some jurisdictions have striven to identify relevant factors and to assign them some kind of weight or priority, thus trying to do what is necessary to fashion a suitably sensitive approach to these cases of fundamental conflict.[69] Thus, one factor singled out by judges in various jurisdictions as particularly significant when deciding how their discretion ought to be exercised is whether the violation was deliberate or in bad faith, or was innocent and in good faith.[70] On what basis, however, is this relevant? If a disciplinary or deterrent rationale is adopted, then deliberation has a clear relevance, since it might be assumed to be much easier to deter deliberate or conscious wrongdoing than to deter negligent or mistaken breaches. If a version of the integrity principle is adopted, it is possible to argue that a court's integrity would be much more clearly compromised by condoning a deliberate breach than by overlooking a negligent or mistaken breach.[71] But if the protective principle is the favoured rationale, it is hardly relevant whether or not the violation of a right was deliberate: the key issue is that the bearer of the fundamental right should not suffer disadvantage as a consequence of the breach.[72]

Some courts pay attention to an even narrower criterion, such as whether the breach involved coercion or violence,[73] or whether the breach was 'outrageous'.[74] Since it may be assumed that all such breaches would also be deliberate and in bad faith, the above observations apply even more strongly. In particular, it is not relevant on the protective principle that the breach of a fundamental right was non-violent or non-coercive; if it deprived a right-bearer of the declared safeguard, this should be sufficient.

A further factor is whether the breach is minor or 'technical'.[75] It can certainly be argued that judicial integrity is less compromised by a technical than by a substantive breach of a fundamental right. For the protective principle, however, the term 'technical' would have to be interpreted with care, so as to be closely aligned with a harmless breach which did not disadvantage the holder of the right: as argued above, a breach that was unintentional or mistaken may cause substantial disadvantage in some cases. A particular issue concerns the absence of any legal framework for authorising intrusive surveillance in this country prior to the Police Act 1997 and more generally the Regulation of Investigatory Powers Act 2000. On several occasions the Strasbourg Court has found violations of art 8 of the Convention because of the absence of a legal framework, which means that no interference with the right to respect for private life could be 'in accordance with the law' and therefore no interference could be justified.[76] Might one take the view that this was merely a technical breach of art 8, in so far as the police were applying a Home Office circular which set out appropriate criteria and safeguards? Or would it be more persuasive to argue that the absence of a legal framework meant that there was no sufficient notice to citizens and no sufficient safeguards against arbitrariness?

The attraction of the label 'technical' is that it draws attention to the relationship between the nature of the breach and the consequences of the remedy. If the integrity principle or the protective principle is adopted so as to lead to either the exclusion of evidence or a stay of the proceedings, whether mandatory or discretionary in nature, that is an extremely strong remedy which – some will argue – is inappropriate for minor and insubstantial breaches. As many of the judicial statements make plain, one of the powerful considerations is that the courts should strive to ensure the conviction of the guilty.[77] This is the element of public policy or 'public safety' that is often brought into the 'balance' when courts are considering how to respond to a violation of fundamental rights. It is in the nature of rights, particularly fundamental rights, that they are protected claims against general arguments based on public policy. The more fundamental the right, the weaker the argument for allowing it to be overridden in any circumstances. Thus, the right not to be tortured (art 3 of the Convention) is so fundamental that it should never yield to arguments based on the greater good of the greater number.

Another judicial favourite, whether the offence charged is a serious one, is conspicuously unconvincing. It is staggering how frequently judges repeat this point without pausing to consider its foundations. As has been pointed out sharply on more than one occasion,[78] just as the greater seriousness of the crime makes it more of a social priority for the guilty to be convicted, so also the greater seriousness of the crime makes the allegation more crucial for defendants, particularly the innocent, and hence more important that all the fundamental rights are properly secured. Any court that respects human rights must recognise this point: once a right has been accorded fundamental status, the courts should treat it accordingly. Indeed, as Peter Mirfield points out, there is a significant difference here between what he terms 'court-centred integrity' and 'public attitude integrity', because:

> 'where there is a moral panic about a particular kind of offence, say child sexual abuse, the public in general may see nothing objectionable about throwing away the rule-book altogether.'[79]

Reflections of that kind ought surely to be sufficient to consign 'public attitude integrity' to the list of unsatisfactory rationales. They also demonstrate the weaknesses of the metaphor of judicial 'balancing',[80] in so far as it allows weight to be given to factors without a full examination of their credentials, and more generally conceals the degree of weight or preference given to particular factors in particular cases, and the reasons for such weighting.

Judges have been driven towards the notion of 'balancing' by the difficulty of keeping faith with both fundamental rights and public policy on law enforcement. If judicial discretion is thought preferable to a blanket rule of inadmissibility or admissibility, then it seems to be assumed that some kind of balancing is inevitable. However, if fundamental rights are to be taken seriously, there ought to be a presumption that violation of a right leads to the inadmissibility of the evidence resulting from it. Another way of expressing this is a prima facie rule:

> 'unless there is at least a *prima facie* rule against admitting a confession [or other evidence] obtained in breach of constitutional rights, no or virtually no value would be accorded to the incorporation of those rights into a written constitution.'[81]

This presumptive approach can be defended as giving appropriate weight (priority) to rights that are declared to be fundamental, whilst at the same time leaving open the possibility of the opposite conclusion in a case where there were sufficiently strong countervailing factors.

6 Re-assessing the integrity principle

Can it be said that the integrity principle, taking its two varieties together, provides a convincing rationale for a court's refusal to act on evidence obtained through violation of a fundamental right? At their strongest its claims seem to depend on three propositions, each of which has been discussed above:

- that the coherence of the criminal justice system demands this;
- that the position of the courts is such that their decisions have great symbolic significance; and
- that the moral standing of the judiciary depends on their willingness to denounce breaches of fundamental rights and not to condone them.

Although these propositions have a certain unity, there remains the question whether they can really be said to be more persuasive than the rival separation thesis, which argues:

- that pre-trial breaches of rights do not compromise the fairness of the trial itself, especially if separate remedies are available;
- that breaches of rights by the police or other investigatory agencies do not compromise the integrity of the judiciary; and
- that the moral standing of the judiciary will be higher if they usually give priority to the conviction of guilty people on reliable evidence than if they usually acquit guilty people on the grounds of entirely separate violations of their rights.

Each view has a possible weakness. Some proponents of the separation thesis might concede that there may be extreme circumstances in which they would accept that a court should not act on evidence obtained through breach of a fundamental right, notably the right not to be subjected to torture. They might take the view that torture is such an egregious breach of a human right that there can be no question of dealing with it in any other way than to remove the evidence from all official records. No doubt supporters of the integrity principle would then press the point that this should apply whenever evidence has been obtained through a breach of a right that is sufficiently fundamental to be declared in a constitution or an international document such as the European Convention. On the other hand, proponents of the integrity principle might feel compelled to concede that there may be a few 'technical' breaches, even of fundamental rights, that do not warrant a court's refusal to hold the trial fair – for example, where the method by which the judge was appointed is held not to ensure that the court was an 'independent and impartial tribunal' within the meaning of art 6 of the Convention, or where there is no legal framework for authorising intrusive surveillance, although both of these examples are contestable.[82] One point here is that, if there are breaches of fundamental rights that are capable of being characterised as 'trivial' or 'technical', there is something wrong with the way in which the right is defined. Re-definition of the right would then be indicated, although sometimes it is politically impossible.

It was argued at the end of section 5 that the most appropriate approach is to maintain a presumption in favour of the exclusion of evidence resulting from the breach of a fundamental right, allowing the presumption to be outweighed in rare cases where, for example, there was a good faith breach that did not disadvantage the defendant. This approach might be compatible with the integrity principle. But if, as I suspect, there is no utterly convincing reason for rejecting the separation thesis in favour of the integrity principle, my own inclination would be to return to the protective principle – not out of stubbornness[83] but because it chimes better with the notion of human rights. The argument would be that it is incoherent to declare a fundamental right and then to fail to provide a remedy that ensures that a person who suffers a violation of such a right is not placed at a material disadvantage as a result of the violation. It should be noted that this formulation of the protective principle insists that any remedy should be tailored so as to prevent the right-bearer from being disadvantaged by the breach: this ensures that the right is not empty rhetoric and that the interest which it protects is safeguarded by the remedy granted.[84] Application of the protective principle means that it is not crucial whether the breach was deliberate or accidental: what matters is whether it might materially disadvantage the right-bearer, and it is that disadvantage that should be prevented. There seems to be no difficulty in declining to apply a protective remedy when the right-bearer has suffered no disadvantage as a result of the violation, as where there was merely a 'technical' breach, but this is not to deny that difficult cases would arise – for example, where there was an error in a search warrant that did not mislead anyone.[85] Borderline judgments would therefore have to be made, but the term 'technical' should not be open to any construction at all: it should be defined symmetrically as a breach that did not disadvantage the right-bearer in relation to any criminal proceedings.

NOTES

* I am grateful to my Oxford colleagues and to members of an Oxford/New York University colloquium for their comments on a draft, and also to Eric Colvin and Mike Redmayne for suggesting improvements.

1 Per Lord Hoffmann in *R v Looseley; A-G's Reference (No 3 of 2000)* [2001] UKHL 53, [2001] 4 All ER 897 at [40].

2 Per Lord Bridge in *R v Horseferry Road Magistrates' Court, ex p Bennett* [1994] AC 42 at 67.

3 Police and Criminal Evidence Act 1984, s 78.

4 See the discussion of the principle of non-contradiction by Lon L Fuller *The Morality of Law* (1964) pp 65–70.

5 J Raz *Ethics in the Public Domain* (1994) ch 13, esp pp 290–304.

6 See R Dworkin *Law's Empire* (1986) and S Hurley 'Coherence, Hypothetical Cases and Precedent' (1990) 10 OJLS 221; see generally J Dickson 'Interpretation and Coherence in Legal Reasoning' in *Stanford Encyclopaedia of Philosophy* (2001).

7 For critical discussion, see A Ashworth *Human Rights, Serious Crime and Criminal Procedure* (2002) esp ch 3.

8 The leading decision of the European Court of Human Rights on this conflict is *Doorson v Netherlands* (1996) 22 EHRR 330.

9 *Austria v Italy* (1961) 4 YB 116 at 784, 2 Dig 722. The European Commission on Human Rights acted as a filter for applications to the Court, either declaring an application inadmissible or admissible, and usually delivering a reasoned opinion. The Commission was abolished in 1999, and sections of the Court itself now perform this filtering function.

10 Eg D J Harris, M O'Boyle and C Warbrick *The Law of the European Convention on Human Rights* (1995) pp 244–245.

11 (1988) 13 EHRR 242.

12 (2001) 31 EHRR 1016.

13 [2002] Crim LR 308.

14 At this stage, no stipulation is made as to the appropriate remedy, if it were to be held wrong for a criminal prosecution to proceed when based on evidence obtained through breach of a

Convention right. It is not assumed that exclusion of the evidence would necessarily be the remedy.

15 Compare Peter Mirfield's essay in this volume with, eg B Emmerson and A Ashworth *Human Rights and Criminal Justice* (2001) ch 3.

16 *Allie Mohamed v State* [1999] 2 AC 111 at 123–124.

17 P Mirfield *Silence, Confessions and Improperly Obtained Evidence* (1997) pp 23–28.

18 [1964] AC 1254.

19 The British Crime Survey regularly asks members of the public about their confidence in various criminal justice agencies: in 2000 some 53% thought that the police were doing a good or excellent job, compared with 31% for the prisons, 23% for the probation service and only 21% for the judges. Whereas some 70% thought that the system treats accused persons fairly, some 54% thought that the system was not very effective in bringing offenders to justice: C Mirrlees-Black *Confidence in the Criminal Justice System: Findings from the 2000 British Crime Survey* Home Office Research Findings No 137 (2001).

20 As eg in the House of Lords in *R v Latif and Shahzad* [1996] 1 WLR 104, where Lord Steyn (at 112) stated that, if the courts were routinely to refuse to stay proceedings in such cases, 'that would undermine public confidence in the criminal justice system and bring it into disrepute'. See also the High Court of New Zealand in *R v Dally* [1990] 2 NZLR 184 at 192, referring to 'the rejection of evidence where its admission would be calculated to bring the administration of justice into disrepute'.

21 *Burlingham* [1995] 2 SCR 206 at 270, per L'Heureux-Dube J.

22 See above.

23 For an early discussion, see A Ashworth 'Excluding Evidence as Protecting Rights' [1977] Crim LR 723.

24 This rationale was combined with another strand in the judgment of Stephen and Aickin JJ in the Australian High Court in *Bunning v Cross* (1978) 141 CLR 54 at 75: 'those who enforce the law [must] themselves respect it, so that a citizen's precious right to immunity from arbitrary and unlawful intrusion into the daily affairs of private life may remain unimpaired.'

25 *People v Kenny* [1990] 2 IR 110, discussed by C Fennell *The Law of Evidence in Ireland* (1992) pp 60–71.

26 See the discussion by K Roach *The Supreme Court on Trial* (2001) pp 125–127.

27 T Weigend 'Germany' in C M Bradley (ed) *Criminal Procedure: a Worldwide Study* (1993).

28 See the Supreme Court of Ireland in *State (Trimbole) v Governor of Mountjoy Prison* [1985] IR 550, per Finlay CJ at 573; cf in the US context, Norton 'The Exclusionary Rule Reconsidered – Restoring the Status Quo Ante' (1998) 33 Wake Forest LR 261.

29 This chimes with the oft-repeated statement of the Strasbourg Court that the Convention 'is intended to guarantee not rights that are theoretical and illusory but rights that are practical and effective': *Artico v Italy* (1980) 3 EHRR 1, para 33.

30 364 US 206 (1960).

31 367 US 643 (1961).

32 In this country and many Commonwealth jurisdictions the term 'disciplinary' is preferred. It refers to disciplining the police, but seems to boil down to deterrence, which Peter Mirfield refers to as the prevailing rationale in the US: Mirfield, above n 17, p 321.

33 468 US 897 (1984).

34 Eg M Orfield 'The Exclusionary Rule and Deterrence: an Empirical Study of Chicago Narcotics Officers' (1987) 54 U Chi LR 1016; W Heffernan and R Lovely 'Evaluating the Fourth Amendment Exclusionary Rule: the Problem of Police Compliance with the Law' (1991) 24 U Mich J Law Rev 311.

35 [1980] AC 402; see also the dissenting speech of Lord Oliver in *R v Horseferry Road Magistrates' Court, ex p Bennett* [1994] AC 42.

36 Per Lord Hobhouse in *R v P* [2001] 2 Cr App Rep 121 at [39].

37 H Wigmore 'Using Evidence Obtained by Illegal Search and Seizure' (1922) 8 ABA Journal 479.

38 Eg *Khan v United Kingdom* (2001) 31 EHRR 1016.

39 The statistics show that a majority of defendants in this country and in the United States plead guilty, and thus waive their right to a fair trial. English law offers substantial inducements to defendants to plead guilty, thereby compromising the voluntariness of choices to waive the right to trial. I have elaborated my strong objections to the current English law and practice on guilty pleas at length elsewhere (A Ashworth *The Criminal Process* (2nd edn, 1998) ch 9); to that extent, although the criminal trial ought to be the centrepiece of the English criminal process, in practice it is not.

40 It would be an exaggeration to say 'exclusively', since a fair amount of police questioning may be directed at uncovering information about other offences or other offenders.

41 This much was more or less accepted by the House of Lords in *R v Sang* [1980] AC 402, since it confined the judicial discretion to exclude evidence to 'admissions and confessions and

generally with regard to evidence obtained from the accused after the commission of the offence'.

42 (1999) 28 EHRR 101; see also *Shahzad and KL v United Kingdom* [1998] EHRLR 210, where the relevance of pre-trial events was accepted but the applications were held inadmissible on other grounds.

43 (1999) 28 EHRR 101, para 39.

44 [2001] UKHL 53, [2001] 4 All ER 897.

45 *R v Horseferry Road Magistrates' Court, ex p Bennett* [1994] AC 42.

46 For an exploration of this and other possibilities, see A Ashworth 'Re-Drawing the Boundaries of Entrapment' [2002] Crim LR 161.

47 J Bentham *A Treatise on Judicial Evidence* (1825); for modern discussion, see W Twining *Theories of Evidence: Bentham and Wigmore* (1985).

48 (1783) 1 Leach 263; the rule is preserved by the Police and Criminal Evidence Act 1984, s 76(4)(a).

49 447 US 727 (1980).

50 (1861) 8 Cox CC 498.

51 The small reservation concerns communications between priest and penitent, which he valued so highly as to place under a privilege.

52 *Weeks v United States* 232 US 383 (1914).

53 Above nn 8 and 9 and accompanying text.

54 277 US 438 at 470 (1928).

55 *McNabb v United States* 318 US 332 at 340 (1943) .

56 *Ridgeway* (1995) 129 ALR 41; cf also *R v Horseferry Road Magistrates' Court, ex p Bennett* [1994] AC 42 with *R v Latif and Shahzad* [1996] 1 WLR 104.

57 367 US 643 (1961).

58 A useful formula, invoked by the Strasbourg Court in a series of decisions such as *Artico v Italy* (1980) 3 EHRR 1.

59 *HM Advocate v McGuigan* 1936 JC 16, per Aitchison LJ-C at 18: 'infringements of the formalities of the law in relation to these matters are not lightly to be condoned.'

60 Roach, above n 26.

61 *Ridgeway v R* (1995) 129 ALR 41, per McHugh J at 89, referring to 'the perception that the courts of law condone or encourage unlawful or improper conduct on the part of those who have the duty to enforce the law'.

62 *Elkins v United States* 364 US 206 (1960).

63 This was a well-taken objection to the strong expression of the separation thesis in *Wolf v Colorado* 338 US 25 (1949): see Y Kamisar 'Does (Did) (Should) the Exclusionary Rule Rest on a "Principled Basis" rather than an "Empirical Proposition"?' (1983) 16 Creighton LR 565, 617–618.

64 See eg Justice Frankfurter in *Rochin v California* 342 US 165 (1952).

65 Quoted by Y Kamisar 'Comparative Reprehensibility and the Fourth Amendment Exclusionary Rule' (1987) 86 Mich LR 1, 2.

66 *Cross and Tapper on Evidence* (9th edn, 1999) p 509.

67 By a 'criminal process remedy' is indicated, not merely the exclusion of evidence, but also the stronger remedy of staying the proceedings for abuse of process, and the weaker remedy of mitigation of sentence. It can be argued that mitigation of sentence cannot be sufficiently strong to remedy the violation of a fundamental right. The choice between the others is for discussion elsewhere: see eg A Ashworth 'Re-Drawing the Boundaries of Entrapment' [2002] Crim LR 161.

68 C Tapper 'Trends and Techniques in the Law of Evidence' in P B H Birks (ed) *Pressing Problems in the Law, vol 1: Criminal Justice and Human Rights* (1995) pp 28-29; see also Kamisar, above n 63, pp 646-648, on the misuses of 'balancing'.

69 The decision of the High Court of Australia in *Bunning v Cross* (1978) 141 CLR 54 is a landmark; the Supreme Court of Canada has developed the Charter provisions so as to identify key factors in cases such as *Collins v R* (1987) 33 CCC (3d) 1, on which see D R Stuart *Charter Justice in Canadian Criminal Law* (2nd edn, 1996) ch 11; and the German Constitutional Court has also begun to develop criteria for the admissibility and inadmissibility of unconstitutionally obtained evidence, on which see T Weigend 'Germany' in C M Bradley (ed) *Criminal Procedure: a Worldwide Study* (1993) pp 195–197.

70 Eg *United States v Leon* 468 US 897 (1984), 'minor and not deliberate'; *People v Kenny* [1990] 2 IR 110, exclusion unless the breach of constitutional rights 'was committed unintentionally or accidentally'; Evidence Act 1995 (Cth), s 138(3), 'whether the contravention was deliberate or reckless'; *Bunning v Cross* (1978) 141 CLR 54.

71 Mirfield, above n 17, p 363.

72 Cf the American doctrine of 'harmless error', where the violation was one that did not affect the substance of the right: *Chapman v California* 386 US 18 (1967).

73 Eg *Irvine v California* 347 US 128 (1954), 'the facts in the case before us ... do not involve coercion, violence or brutality to the person.'
74 *United States v Russell* 411 US 423 (1973), per Rehnquist J.
75 Eg *Elkins v United States* 64 US 206 (1960), not 'every finding by this Court of a technical lack of a search warrant', per Frankfurter J dissenting; J Kaplan 'The Limits of the Exclusionary Rule' (1974) 26 Stan LR 1027, 1036; *United States v Leon* 468 US 897 (1984).
76 Eg *Khan v United Kingdom* (2001) 31 EHRR 1016; *PG and JH v United Kingdom* [2002] Crim LR 308.
77 For two judicial statements which fascinatingly avoid the term 'guilty', see those quoted in *Cross and Tapper* at pp 502–503: Barwick CJ in the Australian case of *Ireland* (1970) 126 CLR 321 at 335 ('the public need to bring to conviction those who commit criminal offences'), and Lord Steyn in *R v Latif and Shahzad* [1996] 1 WLR 104 at 113 ('the public interest in ensuring that those who are charged with grave crimes should be tried').
78 Eg Mirfield, above n 17, p 364; Ashworth, above n 7, pp 108–118.
79 Mirfield, above n 17, p 364.
80 On which see above n 68 and text thereat.
81 Per Lord Steyn in *Allie Mohamed v State* [1999] 2 AC 111 at 122.
82 See above n 76 and text thereat.
83 Ashworth, above n 23.
84 In relation to human rights, there are further issues requiring fuller discussion than is possible here. It is one thing to say that deprivation of one of the 'fair trial' safeguards in art 6 should usually have a chilling effect on the trial. It is another thing to argue that a breach of art 8 – which declares a general right to respect for private life, not necessarily related to subsequent criminal trials – ought to be accorded the same effect. The argument from coherence, considered in s 1 above, certainly militates in favour of treating the two violations in the same way.
85 See *Massachusetts v Sheppard* (1984) 468 US 897.

Silence, innocence and human rights

Peter Mirfield *

1 Introduction

The passing into law of the Human Rights Act 1998 (HRA), which gave domestic effect to most of the provisions of the European Convention on Human Rights, was accompanied by acclaim bordering, at times, upon hyperbole. In rather portentous terms, it has been described as 'bringing rights home'[1] and as entailing 'the domestication of freedom',[2] no less. But, who on earth would oppose the citizen being guaranteed certain fundamental human rights? In this essay, I shall seek to confine to the background the point that deciding on the rights to be enjoyed by citizens is a matter of political choice, and, as such, one better made, from time to time, by elected and ejectable politicians than by unelected judges with security of tenure.[3] I shall concentrate on the unsatisfactory nature of the constitutional compromise effected by the HRA itself as the way of protecting those rights.[4] As interpreted, so far, by the higher judiciary, that compromise seems on track to create great uncertainty and confusion in the domestic law, as well as to challenge its integrity. It happens to be the case that it has been in the area of criminal procedure and evidence that much of the judicial hand has first been shown, so that these matters will be of no less interest to Colin Tapper than to the present writer.

In democratic or liberal states, the usual method of giving effect to catalogues of rights is as part of a fundamental constitutional document. Most obviously, the Bill of Rights is part of the United States Constitution by virtue of (very early) amendments to it. There is no statement anywhere in the Constitution that the Supreme Court is empowered to strike down legislation of the United States Congress deemed by it to be inconsistent with some constitutional provision, whether in the Bill of Rights or elsewhere. Of course, it is well known that, in *Marbury v Madison*,[5] that court took unto itself that very power, finding it to be implicit in the greater scheme of the Constitution that it must rest there. It is, perhaps, rather less well known what a wonderful exercise in judicial conceit was Chief Justice Marshall's famous opinion in that case.

There was then, as there is now, a significant time lapse between the election of a President and his assumption of office. The defeated Federalist, John Adams, made good use of that time. Legislation passed by a still-Federalist Congress, enabled him to pack the federal and District of Columbia courts with supporters. The commissions of the new judges were sealed by his Secretary of State, John Marshall, who was then awaiting his move to the Chief Justiceship of the Supreme Court, an office to which Adams had appointed him. Once Thomas Jefferson, a Republican, assumed the Presidency, he instructed James Madison, his Secretary of State, to withhold delivery of all outstanding commissions, including that of one William Marbury. Marbury sought a writ of mandamus from the Supreme Court, basing himself upon the Judiciary Act 1789, s 13, which granted it power to issue such writs, 'in cases warranted by the principles and usages of law, to ... persons holding office under the authority of the United States'. Before the case could be heard, the now-Republican Congress had purported to repeal the Act authorising the creation of new federal judges. There was a tenable argument that that Act was itself unconstitutional, in that it interfered with judicial independence.

Chief Justice Marshall was able to square the political circle by announcing that the court did have the power to declare Congressional legislation void. The reasoning was that the Constitution itself granted the court authority, as a matter of original jurisdiction, only in cases concerning ambassadors or where the state was a party. That being the constitutional *limit* of such jurisdiction, Congress had had no power to extend it to cover other matters. So, the Judiciary Act 1789, s 13 was void, with the result that Marbury had no remedy. In effect, the court was announcing a very grand jurisdiction in the very act of renouncing a much less grand one. Furthermore, the actual result was that which Republicans, and Jefferson in particular, would have wanted, whilst concerns that the court might declare the repealing Act void receded into the background. Two hundred years on, we may reflect that nothing succeeded like success.

Modern constitutional settlements within states embracing the common law have not left judicial review to such 'implication'. For example, the South African Constitution 1996, s 172(1)(a) obliges the courts to declare invalid any law that is inconsistent therewith, to the extent of that inconsistency. In Canada, the Constitution Act 1982, s 52(1) declares the Constitution to be the supreme law, such that any law inconsistent with it is of no force or effect. By s 24(1), anyone whose rights and freedoms, as guaranteed by the Charter contained within the Act, have been infringed may apply to a court for a remedy.[6]

As regards both these states, the key phrase is 'constitutional settlement'. There has been no such settlement in the United Kingdom, only an Act of Parliament, and one passed by the selfsame procedure as any other such Act. Moreover, the Act states, more than once, that the validity and effectiveness of primary legislation that is incompatible with some Convention right is unaffected.[7] In this respect, there is a stark contrast with the European Communities Act 1972, s 2(4) of which states, in effect, that such legislation, whether passed before or after the coming into effect of the instant Act, is to be construed and have effect subject to directly applicable Community law. In *R v Secretary of State for Transport, ex p Factortame (No 2)*[8] the House of Lords held that s 2(4) *did* render valid such Community law in preference to later primary legislation inconsistent with it. At the least, Parliament cannot impliedly repeal such law, with the result that a profoundly significant and novel limitation upon its continuing sovereignty has been imposed. In contrast, not only has Parliament deliberately preserved its continuing sovereignty in the case of Convention rights, it has also declined to exercise its ordinary power of repeal over pre-existing legislation inconsistent with those rights.

As a matter of constitutional law, then, the HRA would seem to be fundamentally different in nature from the Constitutions of the United States, Canada or South Africa, or, indeed, of any other state that has made some general constitutional settlement. None the less, there is a considerable head of steam building up in support of the proposition that the Act should be given a force greater than that of ordinary law made by Parliament. We may take the views of Clayton and Tomlinson as representative.[9] The Act, they say, should be taken to require judges to adopt a 'generous' or 'broad and purposive' approach to its provisions. This is said to be because it is concerned with fundamental rights. Without more, this would be but political aspiration. However, the authors go on to pray in aid statements in a number of Privy Council cases concerning constitutional instruments created for various Commonwealth countries when breaking free of the mother country.[10] Those statements do, indeed, support a generous and purposive approach to the instruments in question, but, notwithstanding that there are dicta of Lord Hope of Craighead supporting a similar approach to the HRA,[11] they should be treated with considerable caution.

One reason for caution is that, unlike under the HRA, those instruments typically entrench the rights in question.[12] Thus, we may note these words of Lord Diplock in *A-G of the Gambia v Momodou Jobe*, itself one of the cases relied upon by Clayton and Tomlinson:[13]

> 'A constitution, and in particular that part of it which protects *and entrenches* fundamental rights and freedoms ... is to be given a generous and purposive construction.'

Another reason, already adverted to here, deserves repetition. The HRA is no constitutional instrument, and is, most assuredly, not the product of any constitutional settlement. Rather, it concerns only one element, albeit an important one, of the subject matter with which constitutions, of the written kind, typically deal. Lord Hoffmann, again in a case relied upon by the authors, makes the point very clearly:[14]

> 'The background of a constitution is an attempt, at a particular moment in history, to lay down an enduring scheme of government in accordance with certain moral and political values.'

In short, a bill of rights is *not* a scheme of government.

So, how does the Act seek to ensure that statutory law is kept on the straight and narrow? First, HRA, s 2(1) instructs courts, in determining questions arising in connection with Convention rights, to 'take into account' any relevant Convention (Strasbourg) jurisprudence. This does not at all mean that the courts must follow or apply that jurisprudence, for Convention rights are now, in a sense, part of domestic law. Thus, though the courts must decide for themselves, they must have had proper regard to the broader picture.

Secondly, HRA, s 3(1) tells the courts that:

> 'So far as it is possible to do so, primary legislation and subordinate legislation must be read and given effect in a way which is compatible with the Convention rights.'

As we shall see later, the extent to which this provision impinges upon future parliamentary choice turns, very largely, on how expansive a view courts are prepared to take of what is 'possible'.

The third device, one needing rather more detailed treatment at this point, is the 'declaration of incompatibility' under HRA, s 4(2). Where a court concludes that a particular statutory provision is incompatible with some Convention right, it may make such a declaration. If it does so, there will be no effect upon 'the validity, continuing operation or enforcement' of the provision in question. Rather, the ball passes from judiciary to executive. Under s 10(2):

> 'If a Minister of the Crown considers that there are compelling reasons for proceeding under this section, he may by order make such amendments to the legislation as he considers necessary to remove the incompatibility.'

HRA, Sch 2 contains the details of how such orders are to be made. In essence, the minister must lay a draft order before each House of Parliament, that draft being subject to the affirmative resolution procedure. Of course, the executive may choose to sponsor primary legislation to cure the incompatibility, and, no doubt, the effect of the 'compelling reasons' qualification is to encourage it to pursue that route in all but the most urgent cases.

Let us imagine a case where a court felt it right to make such a declaration. The litigant will take two things away with him, an authoritative decision of the court that his rights have indeed been transgressed and an equally authoritative decision that he has lost his case. Solace he may find in the possibility that the minister or Parliament may eventually vindicate his rights with retrospective effect. But, what if the executive disagrees with the judicial view of incompatibility? In principle, the minister's decision not to lay a draft order must be subject to judicial review, yet the prospects for getting such a remedy would seem very poor.[15] The remedial order route is intended for exceptional cases, whilst HRA, s 10(2) is couched in thoroughly subjective terms. More practically, will it be appealing to a court to enter into what may well be a highly charged political issue? The route via primary legislation is even less promising; no court would order a minister to author such legislation, for that would be to interfere with proceedings in Parliament.[16]

Presumably, because he will have exhausted his local remedies, the litigant will be able to take his case to Strasbourg.[17] If successful there too, there would be additional reasons for remedial action,[18] but the constraints on his ability to force the pace would remain formidable.

Taking the more cheerful prospect, with remedial action having been taken, it might be assumed that all would then be well for the litigant, for the gap between the law as it is and the law as it should be would have been closed. However, potential problems would remain. A judicial decision interpreting legislation, and describing its incompatibility with some human right, does itself require executive interpretation before the exact wording of the correcting provision can be settled upon. Of course, the declaration itself may, in some cases, specify how the legislation in question needs to be worded in order to be found compatible. But, this will, by no means, always be possible. For example, in *Matthews v Ministry of Defence*,[19] the declaration simply stated that the Crown Proceedings Act 1947, s 10 was incompatible with the claimant's rights under art 6(1). Even if offered wording, the executive might prefer its own. For all these reasons, there is great scope for argument that the change made has failed to remove the element of incompatibility.[20]

Overall, the fundamental difficulty with the whole declaration of incompatibility procedure is precisely that it divides the labour between the judiciary and the executive and/or legislature. The formal doctrine of parliamentary sovereignty has been preserved, but at a considerable potential cost in terms of legal discipline. It may not be idle to reflect that this difficulty might be apt to persuade the courts to seek their way out of some apparent incompatibility through statutory interpretation, mainly, though not exclusively, in the form of the special canon in HRA, s 3(1) itself.

We shall now proceed to deal with cases under the HRA, and in four categories. They concern the burden of proof, strict liability and irrebuttable presumptions, the privilege against self-incrimination and the protection of complainant witnesses in sexual cases.

2 The burden of proof

It is now rather common for Parliament, at least in appearance, to impose a burden of proof upon the accused, on some particular issue.[21] Usually, such provisions are, at least arguably, designed to impose a burden only in relation to some item of affirmative defence, but it is not unknown for one to be imposed as regards some element more obviously part-and-parcel of the offence in question.[22] In *R v Lambert*[23] two such 'reverse onus' provisions were challenged for inconsistency with art 6(2) of the Convention. That provides:

> 'Everyone charged with a criminal offence shall be presumed innocent until proved guilty according to law.'

The two provisions in question, in the Misuse of Drugs Act 1971, s 28(2) and (3), are not entirely similar. Section 28(2) states:

> '... it shall be a defence for the accused to prove that he neither knew of nor suspected nor had reason to suspect the existence of some fact alleged by the prosecution which it is necessary for the prosecution to prove if he is to be convicted ...'

Section 28(3)(b)(i) uses the language of acquittal, not defence; the accused is to be acquitted:

> 'if he proves that he neither believed nor suspected nor had reason to suspect that the substance or product [which was, in fact, a controlled drug] was a controlled drug.'

The House of Lords held, Lord Steyn dissenting, that the HRA did not apply to the case at hand, because not in effect at the date of the relevant events. Nevertheless, the House went on to give answers to the two other questions raised by the appeal, as though the Act had been in effect.[24] First, were the issues dealt with in the Misuse of Drugs Act 1971, s 28(2) and (3)(b)(i) (hereinafter, 'the issues') essential elements of the offence charged, that of possession of cocaine, a class A drug, with intent to supply?[25] Secondly, and in any event, was the legal effect of those provisions to place a burden of proving the issues on a balance of probabilities? The answer to the second question matters most here, but the answer to the first has its own importance.

Four of their Lordships agreed that the issues were not essential elements of the crime. Only Lord Steyn acceded to the contrary submission of counsel for the appellant. That said, for none of their Lordships was any technical distinction between essential elements and defence elements of fundamental significance. For Lord Steyn, what really mattered was whether or not any given 'defence' bore directly upon the accused's moral blameworthiness. These two, he thought, clearly did. For the other judges, the ambit of the art 6(2) presumption of innocence could not properly be restricted to essential elements, in any event.

Turning to the impact of art 6(2), all but Lord Hutton considered that the Misuse of Drugs Act 1971, s 28(2) and (3)(b)(i) must, by reference to the interpretative obligation under HRA, s 3(1), be taken to impose only a burden of adducing evidence upon the accused, and not the full (persuasive) burden of proof. This was so even though, in both provisions, there is a reference to what the prosecution must 'prove', as well as to what the defence must 'prove'. Their Lordships' terminology is not free of difficulty, for they all tend to prefer the term 'evidential burden' to 'burden of adducing evidence', whilst Lord Slynn specifically refers to the 'evidential burden *of proof*'. Orthodox doctrine distinguishes the two burdens precisely because the party that satisfies a burden of adducing evidence does not, thereby, prove anything; rather, he merely does sufficient to require the judge to leave to the jury, for it to decide, the issue to which that evidence relates.[26]

How, then, can it be said that the accused that adduces evidence 'proves' anything? Following on an intimation given in a earlier case in the House of Lords,[27] the House prayed in aid an alluring argument put by Professor Glanville Williams.[28] Answering the objection that one cannot read the word 'prove' to mean two different things in the same sentence, he pointed out that, where relating once to the prosecution and once to the defence, it would have to bear two different meanings anyway, for the prosecution must prove facts beyond reasonable doubt, the defence only on a balance of probabilities. Having, thus, swallowed the camel, why should we strain at the gnat? In other words, let it mean 'unless sufficient evidence is given to the contrary' where applicable to the defence. With respect, this was not one of the distinguished Professor's more cogent points. Indeed, he himself rather gave the game away in a footnote acknowledging the force of Lord Ackner's objection that the discharge of a burden of adducing evidence proves nothing.[29] In truth, we are being invited to swallow the camel *after* the gnat.

It is appropriate to interpolate here that, delivering the judgment of the New Zealand Court of Appeal in *Phillips*,[30] Cooke P stated that the ordinary and natural meaning of 'prove' was incapable of being extended as far as Williams had argued. Yet, as Lord Cooke of Thorndon, sitting in the House of Lords in *R v DPP, ex p Kebilene*, he expressed sympathy for the view that, by virtue of HRA, s 3(1), a *possible* meaning might be the one supported by Williams.[31] In *Phillips*, Cooke P was dealing with the Bill of Rights Act 1990, s 6, which requires enactments to be given meanings consistent with the rights and freedoms therein, wherever they 'can be given' such a meaning. In *Kebilene*, he expressed the view that s 3(1) conveyed 'a rather more powerful message'.[32]

To return to *Lambert*, their Lordships necessarily assumed that, if the accused satisfied his evidential burden, it would fall to the prosecution to satisfy a burden of proof on the issue in question.[33] What they do not seem to have noticed is how hard it is to square this entirely rational deduction with the statutory wording. So, the Misuse of Drugs Act 1971, s 28(3)(b)(i) states that the accused 'shall be acquitted … if he proves …' If he has adduced (sufficient) evidence, he has, according to their Lordships, proved the fact, and he should, therefore, be acquitted as a matter of judicial direction, without the jury ever having the chance to assess that evidence. The same would seem to apply, perhaps a little less strongly, to s 28(2), which is worded, 'it shall be a defence for the accused to prove …' If so, the art of the possible, under s 3(1), is so wondrous that it embraces not only the 'reading down' of the word 'prove' expressly supported by the majority, but also the 'reading in' of a resulting obligation of proof upon the prosecution.[34]

Lord Hutton, in dissent, considered the relevant provisions not to be incompatible with the presumption of innocence. In domestic terms, there were ample grounds for holding it reasonable to require the accused to bear the burden of proving this defence. Furthermore, those grounds could be given a Strasbourg tinge by reference to the leading European Court case, *Salabiaku v France*, which states:[35]

> 'Article 6(2) does not therefore regard presumptions of fact or of law provided for in the criminal law with indifference. It requires states to confine them within reasonable limits which take into account the importance of what is at stake and maintain the rights of the defence.'

Drawing comfort, also, from dicta of Lords Bingham and Hope in *Brown v Stott*,[36] Lord Hutton argued that a reverse onus here would be directed at a clear and proper public objective, given the social evil represented by the use of controlled drugs. In addition, it would be a proportionate response to that problem. He stressed that the defence of innocent possession largely concerns the accused's own knowledge and that a mere evidential burden would be insufficient to ensure conviction of the guilty.

Many will think that there is much force in Lord Hutton's position. The European Court itself has often stressed that it seeks to lay down no legal straitjacket for the signatory states.[37] In addition, English courts must take their own view of what the Convention requires, once suitably aware of Convention jurisprudence. Furthermore, the judgments delivered in a later Divisional Court case resonate much more with Lord Hutton's dissent than with the views of the majority.[38] Pill LJ, identifying himself as a 'dissident', said that to describe satisfaction of the burden of adducing evidence as 'proof' deprived that word, 'as commonly used inside and outside the criminal courts, of any meaning',[39] whilst Poole J said:[40]

> 'It is an interesting consequence of the Human Rights legislation that the same word "prove" must now be taken to mean two wholly different things in one and the same subsection.'

Let us return to the defences under the Misuse of Drugs Act 1971, s 28, to note that they apply no less to charges of simple possession of the least serious (Class C) drugs than to those of possession, with intent to supply, of the most serious (Class A) drugs. It is rather hard to conceive of possession of a small quantity of cannabis (now Class C) as quite the social evil represented by possession of two kilograms of cocaine, as in *Lambert* itself. And it will be obvious that it is much less easy to deem the statutory response proportionate in the former case than in the latter.

One point that does emerge, resoundingly, from both the Strasbourg jurisprudence and *Lambert* itself, is that rights issues are case-dependent. The problem for an English court, dutifully carrying out its task of taking account of Strasbourg jurisprudence, is that they are case-dependent in a quite different way. The job of the European Court is to examine the whole of the domestic proceedings in order to decide, ex post facto, whether the *particular* applicant's rights were properly respected.[41] It has no duty of articulate consistency, to consider the possible effect of its decision upon future cases of a similar kind. It does not seek to interpret domestic law provisions. The English trial judge, by contrast, would be quite wrong to be concerned only with the present accused's rights. Rather, he must interpret both statutes and cases in a way that gives them a more generalised sense. A fortiori, an appeal court is at least as concerned with the law that it lays down for the future as with its decision in the case at hand.

No English court could be persuaded that the word 'prove' at some point in a given subsection, might be taken to refer to a burden of proof in some situations, but only an evidential burden in others. The judgment to be reached is what it must mean for all possible cases in which it might be relevant. In other words, a court's criterion of 'possibility' must have a dimension of scope, as well as one of linguistic meaning.

That conclusion may be entirely consistent with Lord Hutton's position. Were a case to arise in which the reverse onus seemed to apply to simple possession of Class C drugs, his Lordship might find that inconsistent with art 6(2). If so, the reading down device would provide no escape, for the problem would not be with the word 'prove', but, rather, that that onus applied to cases to which it should not apply. Therefore, a declaration of incompatibility would have to be made.

3 Strict liability and irrebuttable presumptions

It is quite possible to take an extensive view of the *idea* of the presumption of innocence, such that it is capable of impinging upon matters beyond (mere) questions concerning allocation of the burden of proof, and, in particular, upon the legitimacy of strict liability offences. However, if one can be forgiven for attending to the actual wording of art 6(2), it does have an exclusively evidential flavour, for one is to be presumed innocent until 'proved guilty according to law'. Equally, the more general art 6(1) places one firmly within the realm of evidence and procedure, in that it guarantees the accused a 'fair *hearing*'.[42]

However, doubt creeps in from two directions. The leading Strasbourg case on art 6(2), *Salabiaku v France*,[43] concerned a somewhat strange provision of French law, to English eyes at least. Salabiaku had been convicted of smuggling drugs. Article 392, para 1 of the Customs Code *presumed* a person in actual possession of drugs, when brought into France, 'legally liable unless he or she can prove a specific event of force majeure exculpating him'. Though phrased as a presumption, this might seem, more appropriately, to be classified as a statement of strict liability, with an exceptional defence of force majeure, on which the accused bears the burden of proof. It is, perhaps, unsurprising that the judgment of the Court rather mixes together strict liability points and reverse onus ones. Thus, it refers to the need to confine presumptions of fact or of law 'within reasonable limits',[44] rather than to keeping reverse onuses within such limits. It also emphasises that, in practice, French courts enjoy 'a genuine freedom of assessment in this area', which allows the accused to be 'accorded the benefit of the doubt, even where the offence is one of strict liability'.[45] This may be read as indicating that the accused's trial had been fair because he had not been subjected to a truly strict liability. Finally, the following statement seems to indicate that strict liability convictions may sometimes fail the art 6(2) test:[46]

> '[T]he Contracting States may, under certain conditions, penalise a simple or objective fact, as such, irrespective of whether it results from criminal intent or from negligence.'

The leading English text relies upon the words 'under certain conditions' in support of the view that art 6(2) *does* embrace strict liability issues.[47]

Those arguing for such a wide reading of art 6(2) may also derive some comfort from two English cases. *R v DPP, ex p Kebilene*[48] dealt with the Prevention of Terrorism (Temporary Provisions) Act 1989, s 16A(1), which rendered a person guilty of an offence:

> 'if he has any article in his possession in circumstances giving rise to a reasonable suspicion that the article is in his possession for a purpose connected with the commission, preparation or instigation of acts of terrorism ...'

Section 16A(3) granted him a defence if he *proved* that the article in question was not in his possession for any such purpose. For the Divisional Court:[49]

> 'The gravamen of the offence charged by s. 16A is the possession of articles, in themselves innocent, for terrorist purposes.'

It followed that, once the prosecution had established the element of reasonable suspicion, s 16A(3) required the accused to disprove an essential element of the offence, namely that the possession had been for terrorist purposes. All three members of the court regarded such a position as inconsistent with the art 6(2) presumption. Though, on appeal, the House of Lords refused to reach a concluded view on the inconsistency point, at least a majority of their Lordships seemed to share the lower court's view of the true gravamen of the offence.[50]

If that analysis be correct, *Kebilene* tells us nothing about strict liability offences, for the art 6(2) objection taken would be wholly evidential in nature. However, Roberts has persuasively argued that, in truth, the Prevention of Terrorisem (Temporary Provisions) Act 1989, s 16A(1) raises no issue about the burden of proof. Rather, it creates a substantive offence of being in possession of any article in circumstances giving rise to a reasonable suspicion of terrorist purpose. Section 16A(3) then grants a defence where it was not the accused's purpose, but requires him to prove that fact.[51] If he is right, s 16A(3) deals with a genuine defence, and not an essential element of the offence itself, with the result that the argument in terms of breach of the presumption of innocence would be rather less compelling. However, if one then switches attention to the substantive law, laid down by s 16A(1), there is a case that what is unacceptable here is that the offence itself is constituted by possession of *any* article *merely* on the basis of reasonable suspicion of terrorist purpose. Whilst rigorous application of the distinction between procedure and substance would lead to the conclusion that these provisions do not conflict with art 6(2), some might say that this would be to prefer technicalities to protection of rights, and would thus be contrary to the spirit and intendment of the HRA.

The second English case is *Parker v DPP*.[52] As regards a number of driving offences involving drink or drugs, the Road Traffic Act 1988 (RTA 1988), s 15(2). provides that evidence of the proportion of intoxicant in a specimen of breath, blood or urine provided by the accused shall be taken into account by the court. It adds that it shall be assumed that the relevant proportion was, at the time of the alleged offence, not less than that in the specimen. By RTA 1988, s 15(3), that assumption shall not be made if the accused proves that he consumed alcohol, *after* completion of the offence, such that, had he not done so, the proportion in question would not have been exceeded. But Parker did not rely on s 15(3). His case was that, because he had consumed a large quantity of alcohol just before he drove, he would not have been over the limit when he did drive, but only later, once the alcohol had reached his bloodstream, and the sample was taken. He argued that the irrebuttability of the s 15(2) assumption rendered it inconsistent with art 6(2). Therefore, he invoked RTA 1988, s 3(1), as requiring the words 'unless proved to the contrary' to be read into that subsection. However, the Divisional Court, believing the assumption to be both reasonable and well within limits, concluded that there was no such inconsistency.

The RTA 1988, s 15(2) assumption takes us to the very edge of the line between procedure and substance. Of course, because that assumption, or, more properly, presumption, was irrebuttable, it imposed no burden of proof upon the accused. Yet, one of the elements of criminal guilt is that the driver was, when he drove, 'over the prescribed limit', so the effect of the subsection is to absolve the prosecution from proving that guilty fact, in that all it need prove is that he was, at a different time, over that limit. Indeed, one commentator has, by reference to *Parker*, suggested that an irrebuttable presumption is *more* difficult to square with art 6(2) than a rebuttable one.[53] If one adverts to the context, there are two additional points to be made, in support of that suggestion. First, in a sense, this presumption is partially rebuttable, because of RTA 1988, s 15(3), but only as to the period between the driving and the taking of the sample; it is irrebuttable as to the period before the driving. Secondly, s 15(2) and (3) represent an evidential 'package', so it would be strange if art 6(2) were to be capable of impinging on the weaker, rebuttable element, but not the stronger, irrebuttable one.[54] On the other hand, an irrebuttable presumption of law, like that in s 15(2), certainly seems to function in exactly the same way as a rule of substantive law.[55] If so, it would appear that we have travelled over the line between procedure and substance, and beyond the territory where art 6(2) holds sway. At all events, it will be plain that there is room for a range of tenable positions with regard to the correct ambit of art 6(2). If irrebuttable presumptions, or even instances of strict liability, are deemed by the courts to be comprehended by it, and assuming, as we must, that *Lambert* sets the standard of possible interpretation under HRA, s 3(1), rather a lot of statutory provisions may turn out to have 'interesting' meanings.

4 The privilege against self-incrimination

In contrast with the presumption of innocence, the privilege against self-incrimination is not explicitly guaranteed anywhere in the Convention. However, the European Court decided, in *Funke v France*,[56] that the general fair trial right under art 6(1) embraces a right to remain silent and not to contribute to self-incrimination. It now seems clear that the right extends to suspects at the investigatory stage, no less than to the accused at trial.[57] There is now a great deal of both Strasbourg and English authority concerning that right or privilege,[58] but attention, here, will be confined to but one aspect thereof.

In *Brown v Stott*, on appeal from the High Court of Justiciary in Scotland, the Privy Council was concerned with the Road Traffic Act 1988, s 172(2)(a).[59] Where it is alleged that the driver of a vehicle has committed any of a number of listed offences, its keeper must, under that subsection, give such information as to the driver's identity as the police may require. RTA 1988, s 172(3) makes failure to comply an offence, potentially punishable with a heavy fine (up to £1,000) and disqualification from driving. But, by RTA 1988, s 172(4), such person:

> 'shall not be guilty of an offence … if he shows that he did not know and could not with reasonable diligence have ascertained who the driver of the vehicle was.'

Miss Brown had been arrested on suspicion of theft from a supermarket. Judging her to be drunk, the police asked her how she had got there. She said by car, and later pointed to one in the car park as being hers. Later, car keys were found in her handbag. Even though the police already had evidence from which an inference could reasonably be drawn that she had driven to the supermarket, they invoked their RTA 1988, s 172(2)(a) power. When she admitted to having been the driver, a breath test, which proved positive, was administered. The art 6 issue was whether or not it would be incompatible with her privilege against self-incrimination for evidence of that admission to be adduced at her trial for driving after consuming excessive alcohol. The Privy Council gave a negative reply. The English Divisional Court later came to the same conclusion about RTA 1988, s 172(2)(b), which imposes a similar requirement upon a person other than a keeper, 'to give any information which it is in his power to give and may lead to identification of the driver'.[60]

In the leading judgment in *Brown v Stott*, Lord Bingham gave three reasons for finding there to be no incompatibility. First, RTA 1988, s 172(2) sanctions the asking of only 'a single, simple question',[61] and not any prolonged questioning. In addition, the penalty for declining to answer is 'moderate and non-custodial'.[62] Yet, the subsection does not say, specifically, that the question may not be repeated, and 'information as to the identity of the driver' seems capable of comprehending information other than simply a name. Moreover, even if simple, it has great potential for generating evidence of one essential element of the offence. As to penalty, it may be retorted that RTA 1988, s 172(2)(a) is available as regards a very wide range of motoring offences, for some of which the penalty is similar to, or even lighter than that for a s 172 offence. His Lordship's second point was that the self-incriminatory potential of the question was neither greater nor less significant than a requirement to undergo a breath test, yet no criticism of the latter requirement had been offered. This argument carries considerable force as a matter of principle, but far less as a matter of precedent, for, whilst there is a *rule* excluding confession evidence in given circumstances, there is merely a *discretion* to exclude other evidence acquired in breach of the accused's privilege against self-incrimination.[63] From the Convention point of view, *Saunders v United Kingdom*[64] clearly states that the right against self-incrimination derived from art 6(1) has no impact upon breath, blood or urine samples acquired under compulsory powers, a point acknowledged by Lord Bingham himself. His final reason invoked public policy and proportionality. The use of motor vehicles, because of their potential to cause grave injury, is, very properly, tightly regulated. In view of that policy, the legislative response found in s 172 was by no means disproportionate. One may agree completely with this sentiment, yet fail to understand how, in giving effect to it, one is not simply *preferring* public safety to the privilege against self-incrimination.[65]

Had Miss Brown refused to answer, she might have been charged with failing to provide the relevant information. It is a defence under RTA 1988, s 172(4) to 'show' that one did not know and could not, with reasonable diligence, have ascertained who was the driver. The court might now be faced with a question about the presumption of innocence under art 6(2). It will be noted that this defence is rather similar in nature to the one in *Lambert*, so an argument that s 172(4) should be interpreted as placing only an evidential burden upon the accused would have considerable force.[66] (On the actual facts of the case, of course, had Miss Brown claimed not to know who was the driver, the prosecution would, because of the circumstantial and other evidence arising from what had happened at the supermarket, have been rather well-placed to rebut her trial evidence.)

It might seem reasonable to conclude that *Lambert* and *Brown v Stott* demonstrate fundamentally different attitudes to the two rights at issue. However, the apparent divergence may hide a common factor, namely the traditional English judicial spirit of pragmatism, a spirit that lies uneasily with the very idea of human *rights*. Thus, a person found in physical possession of large quantities of drugs has his work cut out to win the evidential battle as to knowledge of possession thereof. (One is dealing here with the tactical position, not the strictly legal one with regard to burdens.) The RTA 1988 provision, in contrast, may be thought necessary for the effective prosecution of traffic offenders. If one thinks of the everyday experience, in the United Kingdom, of a car being photographed, exceeding the limit, by a speed camera, it would be virtually impossible for the prosecution to prove the driver's identity if unable to employ either the RTA 1988, s 172(2) devices themselves, or some other, equivalent device. Indeed, the prosecution in *Brown v Stott* offered this to the High Court of Justiciary as support for a conclusion that it should be able to call evidence of Miss Brown's admission. Describing this argument as *in terrorem*, Lord Justice General Rodger deliberately confined the scope of his opinion to the instant facts, whilst making the telling point that that argument:[67]

> 'comes close to saying that certain offences have to be prosecuted in a manner which infringes a central requirement of a fair trial under the Convention.'

The Privy Council itself may well have been keen to decide the consistency point for all purposes, thus *declaring* RTA 1988, s 172(2)(a) 'Convention-safe'.

Once again, one sees the difficulty of applying concepts designed to preserve the Convention rights of the *particular* accused in a jurisdiction where the more important issue is whether or not a given provision would tend, *generally*, to undermine the right in question. There are two further complications. First, some of the Strasbourg authorities indicate that implied rights, like the privilege against self-incrimination, which exist only under the umbrella of the general fair trial right, may sometimes be breached, yet the trial have been fair, overall.[68] Secondly, much may turn on the way in which the right comes to be an issue in the case at hand. Thus, had Miss Brown stood charged with a refusal to answer (under RTA 1988, s 172(3)), it is conceivable that she might have argued that that offence itself is incompatible with the privilege against self-incrimination.[69]

Several members of the Privy Council in *Brown v Stott* adverted to another device that Parliament might have chosen, namely a reverse onus presumption that the vehicle was being driven by its registered keeper.[70] One, Lord Steyn, opined that it had rightly been conceded that such a presumption would have been lawful.[71] Yet, it seems impossible to argue that the identity of the person actually driving the vehicle is other than an essential element of the relevant offence. Moreover, in *Lambert*, Lord Steyn himself stressed that the defence at issue there had a direct bearing on the accused's moral blameworthiness, or the guilt of his mind.[72] It was for that reason that to place upon him the burden of proving that defence would be inconsistent with the presumption of innocence. It would be strange indeed to say that a reverse onus on the very issue of whether or not there was any guilty *act* by the accused were easier to justify. So, one may be entitled to infer that, for Lord Steyn, as well as the other judges in *Brown v Stott*, the notion is that policy, born of judicial pragmatism, and not principle, is what really matters. If so, it is rather hard to resist the conclusion that it is the judiciary, not Parliament, that will be making the policy choices, and thus the law.

5 Protection of witnesses in sexual cases

The Convention recognises that persons other than the accused may have interests, in the criminal process, that are worthy of protection. For example, a person's life, liberty or personal security may be under threat from the accused, such that the witness's art 2 or art 5 rights are at stake.[73] Where a complainant in a sexual case testifies, questions about her previous sexual behaviour seem to impinge upon her right to respect for her private life under art 8.[74] The Strasbourg institutions have shown themselves quite willing to attenuate the apparent scope of the fair trial right, to allow for other Convention rights. In the leading case, the Court, having remarked that individual states should organise their criminal proceedings such that those interests of witnesses are not 'unjustifiably imperilled', continued:[75]

> '... [the] principles of fair trial also require that in appropriate cases the interests of the defence are *balanced* against those of witnesses or victims called upon to testify.'

Against that background, we shall refer to two provisions of the Youth Justice and Criminal Evidence Act 1999 (YJCEA 1999), and to the impact of two recent English cases upon them.

YJCEA 1999, s 41(3)(c) severely limits the admissibility of evidence of the complainant's previous sexual behaviour on an issue of consent in a sexual case, namely to where that behaviour is alleged to have been, in any respect:

> 'so similar—(i) to any sexual behaviour of the complainant which (according to the evidence adduced or to be adduced by or on behalf of the accused) took place as part of the event which is the subject matter of the charge against the accused, or (ii) to any other sexual behaviour of the complainant which (according to such evidence) took place at or about the same time as that event, that the similarity cannot reasonably be explained as a coincidence.'

The effect is to create a 'similar fact' exception to a general rule of admissibility, somewhat akin to that for evidence of an accused's bad character.[76] It is akin to that exception because it undoubtedly sets a threshold significantly above that of ordinary legal relevance. It is only somewhat akin because, in its present-day form, the exception for bad character of the accused has ceased to be technical in nature. Instead, it simply requires that the probative value of such evidence exceed its prejudicial effect. By contrast, the s 41(3)(c) exception is very technical, with the result that it seems apt to deny the accused the use of some relevant evidence of high probative force, notwithstanding the art 6(1) fair trial right.

YJCEA 1999, s 41(4) appears designed to disallow all questions and evidence going to the complainant's credibility. It states:

> 'For the purposes of subsection (3) no evidence or question shall be regarded as relating to a relevant issue in the case if it appears to the court to be reasonable to assume that the purpose (or main purpose) for which it would be adduced or asked is to establish or elicit material for impugning the credibility of the complainant as a witness.'

No doubt, the principal concern here was to prevent the complainant's credibility being impugned by reference to her sexual disposition, for we learn nothing about her inclination to truthfulness from such a disposition. Yet, as drafted, the subsection seems to travel well beyond that mischief, embracing the most pointedly relevant attack on the *specific* credibility of the complainant's present testimony. To take a simple example, the defence might wish to ask her about a previous inconsistent statement in which, say, she accused some third party of the rape now alleged against the accused.

Were there no Human Rights Act, the court's task would simply be to give effect to parliamentary intention, as appearing from the words used. Though this would cut against the grain of ordinary judicial inclinations, in depriving some accused persons of entirely relevant and probative evidence, the (judicial) doctrine of parliamentary Sovereignty would demand it.

In *R v A (No 2)*,[77] the House of Lords used the special canon of interpretation in HRA, s 3(1) to render YJCEA 1999, s 41(3)(c) consistent with the accused's art 6(1) fair trial right. In *R v T, H*[78] the Court of Appeal expressed itself prepared to use that canon to similar effect, as regards YJCEA 1999, s 41(4), but avoided doing so by employing what it claimed to be ordinary canons of interpretation upon the phrase 'sexual behaviour', which phrase trips the special protections for complainants in s 41.

The specific argument put forward in *A (No 2)* may be termed the 'mindset' argument. It proposes that a particular woman may have a disposition to consent to sexual activity with a particular man. If she alleges, say, rape, and his defence is consent, it is relevant thereto that they had been in a long-lasting, intimate relationship. Of course, the matter is very much one of degree, but the argument will have a commonsense appeal, not only for judges, but also for many ordinary citizens.[79] However, it is wrong to imagine that it commands universal support, for there are those who believe it fundamental to the idea of sexual autonomy that a woman be regarded as choosing separately, on each occasion, whether or not to engage in sexual activity, and without reference to any previous occasion.[80]

In *R v A (No 2)*, at a preparatory hearing, the judge had ruled that the accused could not cross-examine the complainant (of rape) about a number of occasions when, he alleged, the two of them had had consensual intercourse. No member of the House of Lords declared whether or not the accused would, thus, be deprived of his fair trial right, yet four concluded that, under ordinary canons of interpretation, YJCEA 1999, s 41(3)(c) was too broad to be compatible, *in general*, with that right.[81] Remarkably, in reaching that conclusion, none of them took any explicit account of the Strasbourg cases, which, as we have seen,[82] support a balancing against each other, of the interests of the accused and the complainant.[83] Turning to the special canon, the four went on to provide a 'possible' interpretation that avoided the incompatibility. In Lord Steyn's words, with which all agreed:[84]

> 'due regard always being paid to the importance of seeking to protect the complainant from indignity and from humiliating questions, the test of admissibility is whether the evidence (and questioning in relation to it) is nevertheless so relevant to the issue of consent that to exclude it would endanger the fairness of the trial under article 6 of the Convention.'

The effect of this 'reading down' is to replace the criterion of sufficient similarity and make inexplicability on the basis of coincidence disappear altogether. It is certainly a compromise, and one attending to the complainant's interests, but surely not that which YJCEA 1999, s 41(3)(c) *really* contemplates.[85] In short, it substitutes practical judicial discretion for a clear and confining legal rule.

An issue of great importance, concerning HRA, s 3(1), is this. Do the courts have power to 'rewrite' legislation even against the intention of Parliament, as currently manifested, or are they confined to divining some 'true' intention behind the more obvious one contained in the words used? A division of opinion emerged in *A (No 2)* itself. Lord Hope of Craighead favoured the more limited view:[86]

> '[T]he rule is only a rule of interpretation. It does not entitle the judges to act as legislators ... The compatibility is to be achieved only so far as this is possible. Plainly this will not be possible if the legislation contains provisions which expressly contradict the meaning which the enactment would have to be given to make it compatible. It seems to me that the same result must follow if they do so by necessary implication, as this too is a means of identifying the plain intention of Parliament.'

Lords Steyn and Hutton favoured the more expansive view. In the words of the former:[87] 'If a *clear* limitation on Convention rights is stated *in terms*, such an impossibility will arise.'

Because of the House's decision in *R v Secretary of State for Transport, ex p Factortame (No 2)*,[88] it does now seem that one Parliament may deny its successors the power impliedly to repeal its own legislation. However, there is a second objection to the expansive view. What reason do we have for believing that the 1998 Parliament *did* intend to deprive its successors of that power, in relation to human rights?

For Lord Steyn, what mattered was what government spokesmen, in both Houses, had themselves said about what became HRA, s 3(1). It was to be so freely used that, in only very few cases would there be need of a declaration of incompatibility under HRA, s 4(2).[89] His Lordship found support for such a use of parliamentary materials *against the executive* in his own extra-judicial writings,[90] by virtue of a proposed limitation on *Pepper v Hart*.[91] The reasoning seems to be that, Parliament having been assured that the courts would enjoy such a very strong power, in protection of human rights, government should be estopped from going back on that assurance.

This argument bristles with difficulty. The spokesmen in question were certainly not explicity declaring successor Parliaments deprived of their power of implied repeal, so it is hard to see why any assurance should be taken to extend so far. Furthermore, whatever one may think about the *particular* government being stuck with its own handiwork, it is hard to see why successor governments, of different political persuasion, should have their hands tied. In any event, one may reject the implied proposition that the rights and obligations of Parliament are properly to be identified with those of government.[92] Overall, the key point is that the HRA is itself a piece of parliamentary legislation, so it behoves the judiciary to fit HRA, s 3(1) into its own statutory context, rather than to extract it therefrom and turn into a free-standing device to protect human rights.[93]

In *R v T, H*,[94] T stood charged with the rape and indecent assault of his niece. At a preparatory hearing, the defence sought leave to question her about two occasions, subsequent to the alleged offences, when the police had asked her if anyone had sexually abused her. Each time, though she had made allegations about another or others, she had made none against T. The judge ruled these prospective questions inadmissible under YJCEA 1999, s 41, because they were 'about any sexual behaviour' of the complainant. His ruling was overturned by the Court of Appeal.

Now, the proposed questions would clearly go to credibility. To delay complaint may itself require explanation but, given the difficulty of the allegation, may be perfectly explicable. It is much harder to explain why the accused was twice omitted from an indictment against others. The evidence would tend to show that the complainant had made up the allegation, which should not be believed. Yet, YJCEA 1999, s 41(4) seems to be firmly in the way of cross-examination of this kind. After *A (No 2)*, it seems entirely tenable to argue that, to adapt Lord Steyn's words, that evidence is so relevant to the complainant's credibility that to exclude it would endanger the fairness of the accused's trial, and, indeed, the court stated that, if necessary, it would have been willing to 'read down' s 41(4), so as to permit the cross-examination.

Instead, the court chose to read the words 'about any sexual behaviour' as not comprehending questions about the witness's earlier failure to complain.[95] Of course, such a failure is not itself about sexual behaviour, but it was not simply the negative that mattered here. Rather, the real strength of the defence's point flowed from the presence of complaints against others. With respect, the court's interpretation is unpersuasive, albeit that it achieves fairness for the accused.

There is danger here of a trickle-down effect of the force attributed to HRA, s 3(1). Resort to that subsection, in assuming at least a prima facie incompatibility, treats the instant legislation as defective, in human rights terms. The attraction is apparent of an argument that no recourse to the special canon is necessary. Yet, the attendant dangers, that words will mean what you or I would not take them to mean, that the penumbra of doubt invades the core of certainty, and that outcomes, in human rights cases, become all the harder to predict, seem to be very much greater than is the advantage gained.

6 Conclusions

It is time to pull together the strands that run through the various issues considered in this paper. Most are constitutional in nature, though not all of them concern matters of classic constitutional import.

(a) The boundaries of procedure and substance

To begin with the non-constitutional strand, arts 6(1) and (2) seem to be concerned only with evidential and procedural matters.[96] One can surely be fairly tried even for the most substantively objectionable of offences. (Of course, other Convention provisions may impinge upon the substance.) Article 6(2) grants only a right to be presumed innocent until *proved guilty* according to law, and so seems to be wholly evidential.

However, even if one discounts the straightforward, not entirely unappealing argument that it is *more* unfair to impose truly strict liability than to qualify liability via some reverse onus provision, and one rejects, along the way, *Salabiaku v France*,[97] there remain some important borderline points to address. If, in truth, *R v DPP, ex p Kebilene*[98] is not a burden of proof case, it is certainly one in which a procedural idea, that of reasonable suspicion, is wound into the definition of the offence. Even more difficult might seem to be the line between rebuttable and irrebuttable presumptions of law.[99] Plainly, art 6 embraces those rebuttable ones that place a burden of proof upon the accused, but what of irrebuttable ones, at least where their effect is evidential, in that they disallow the calling of contrary evidence? In this respect, a tenable line might be drawn between an irrebuttable presumption referring to some fact, such as the concentration of alcohol in a person's blood, and one not so referring, such as the presumption that a child under the age of ten cannot be guilty of an offence.

(b) Differences in judicial function

One of the most surprising features of the HRA jurisprudence is the absence of any explicit reference to the differences in judicial function of the Strasbourg Court and domestic courts. That is especially so, given that the domestic courts must take account of Strasbourg cases.

There are two distinct, though connected, points worth making. More obviously, the trial judge, in deciding some art 6 issue, is in no position to assess the fairness of the trial as a whole. Though this is, of course, not true of the Court of Appeal, its view of a fair trial is not purely a function of what art 6 says, for there is much adjectival domestic law beyond the scope thereof. In short, it is perfectly conceivable that an accused's trial will have been Convention-fair, yet not fair overall.[100]

The second point concerns the tasks that HRA, ss 3(1) and 4(2) assign to the courts. The former requires them to interpret provisions, then give effect to them, consistently with human rights. By the latter, they must decide whether or not some such provision is inconsistent with some right. The enterprise appropriate in Strasbourg is quite different. The court itself has described it, as follows:[101]

> '[T]he Court is not called upon to consider in the abstract whether … [the provisions at issue] … conform to the Convention. Its task is to determine whether they were applied in the instant case in a manner compatible with the presumption of innocence and, more generally, with the concept of a fair trial.'

For example, the court might, quite properly, find that the application of RTA 1988, s 172(2)(a) entailed breach of the self-incrimination privilege in one case, yet not in another, even though, in each, the same offence was charged and the same admission made. In contrast, in applying HRA, s 3(1), a domestic court must read words down, or read them in, for *all* future applications of that provision, if it chooses to do so for this one.[102] In making a HRA, s 4(2) declaration, its judgment will be about the *extent* of the irresolvable incompatibility, so there may well be a range of cases, covered by the provision, in which the right would be breached, but also a range in which it would not.

It does not at all follow that Strasbourg judgments can contain nothing of value for domestic courts. In particular, many contain important statements about the nature and content of the art 6 rights. Still, one must be aware of the danger of failing to place them in their correct context.

Something else of interest emerges. A declaration of incompatibility will describe the precise extent thereof, thus, in principle, enabling the offending provision to be amended such as to remove only that incompatibility. In contrast, a decision under HRA, s 3(1) is capable of being over-inclusive. After *R v Lambert*,[103] 'proves', in the relevant provisions, will always mean 'adduces evidence', notwithstanding that, had some future court been free to do so, it might have decided that imposition of a burden of proof, in some particular category of case, would be consistent with the presumption of the accused's innocence.

(c) Judicial pragmatism

There is little sign of the courts adopting a thoroughgoing rights-based approach to art 6 issues. Even *A (No 2)*, in restricting the ambit of YJCEA 1999, s 41(3)(c), does so to protect the very ordinary, though fundamental, principle of English law that the accused should be able to adduce (highly) relevant evidence. No explicit reference was made to the art 8 aspect, arising from the complainant's privacy right.

It has been argued that the true reason for the different results in *Lambert* and *Brown v Stott* is not that the former favours principle and the latter policy, but that the policy adopted in both, that of judicial pragmatism, points in opposite directions. It is worthy of note that courts have picked up with enthusiasm intimations in Convention jurisprudence that limited qualification by states of art 6 rights is permissible, that individual rights may be balanced against community interests, and that the maintenance of proportionality is the key to reaching the right result.[104]

(d) Judges as legislators

Lambert and *A (No 2)* are both very striking cases. Ironically, perhaps, a literal interpretation of the word 'possible' might suggest a very wide gateway. However, there must still be some constraints upon the criterion of possibility, if we really are engaged in interpretation at all. It is submitted that the two cases stretch that criterion beyond breaking-point. There seems little doubt that both judges in *L v DPP*[105] thought it simply wrong to treat 'proves' as meaning 'adduces evidence'. And, indeed, it is hard to believe that the four judges in *Lambert* that favoured that view really did so for the somewhat unconvincing reasons given. The real division between them and the dissenter, Lord Hutton, may have been as to whether, as a practical matter, it was necessary to impose upon the accused anything more than the burden of adducing evidence of the matters at issue. Yet, this seems, pre-eminently, a question for the legislator, which, as understood by usage inside and outside the criminal courts, had, by the words it selected, chosen Lord Hutton's position. As regards *A (No 2)*, the whole point of enacting YJCEA 1999, s 41 was to redress the balance in favour of complainants, even if it resulted in denying accused persons, on occasions, the ability to ask (highly) relevant questions. That was a true political choice, and *A (No 2)* simply replaces it with a contrary one.

It is certainly not being argued here that unelected judges are illegitimately usurping the function of the democratically elected Parliament. Indeed, it was Parliament itself that gave the judiciary the strong HRA, s 3(1) power that was so marvellously employed in *Lambert* and *A (No 2)*. But, perhaps, the government was keen to embrace the idea of human rights, whilst anxious to retain its ability to respond, politically, to the ideas of the moment. Thus, by the appropriate nod and wink that government gave to judiciary during the course of debate on the Human Rights Bill, formal incompatibility is to be eschewed, and doctoring of statutory provisions embraced. YJCEA 1999 contains, as it must, a statement that, in the view of the minister responsible for it when a Bill, its provisions are compatible with Convention rights.[106] Is it, then, wholly unfair to regard the government as saying:

> 'Because we are human rights-aware, we really do believe that the Act is Convention-safe, but we appreciate that courts, with their great legal expertise, may reasonably think otherwise. If so, they should feel free to rewrite it appropriately, but, on no account, should they leave us with the embarrassment of being told to do that ourselves'?

We may return, finally, to *Marbury v Madison*. There, for entirely understandable short-term reasons, the result suited both the Supreme Court and the President; the broader, more important legal connotations could be left for another day. In the case of the HRA, the reasons for a meeting of judicial and executive minds may be less short-term, but they have the potential for generating a formidable judicial power.

In answer to an expected response, namely that, though formidable, the power falls well short of that of judicial review, it may be permissible to pray in aid another United States legal doctrine, known as 'the rule of constitutional doubt'. It states that:[107]

> 'where a statute is susceptible of two constructions, by one of which grave and doubtful constitutional questions arise and by the other of which such questions are avoided, [a court's] duty is to adopt the latter.'

Unlike the HRA, s 3(1) canon, this doctrine is one minted by the courts themselves. Whilst apparently designed to ensure judicial deference to the legislative branch, a number of modern American commentators have argued that it tends to have the opposite effect.[108] Because, in practice, it leads to recourse to unlikely interpretations, to save the statutory provisions at issue, the courts take effective power to impose their own preferences in substitution for those of the legislature.[109] A power radically to rewrite such provisions, like the one now being adumbrated by the House of Lords, might be thought to have even greater force than one merely to give them the thumbs-up or thumbs-down.

NOTES

* An earlier version of this paper was presented to a Criminal Law Workshop at New York University on 20 September 2002. I am grateful for the helpful suggestions of all who participated.

1 See, in particular, *Rights Brought Home: the Human Rights Bill* (Cm 3782, 1997).

2 Irvine [1998] PL 221 at 225.

3 For a recent and compelling article broadly to this effect, see Griffith (2001) 117 LQR 42.

4 For a description of the political background to the compromise represented by the 1998 Act, see Ewing (1999) 62 MLR 79, 79–82. Others have taken a very different view of that compromise from that expressed in the text. For example, a former Law Lord, Lord Scarman, described it as 'brilliant', during debate in the House of Lords: see HL Deb vol 582, col 1256 (3 November 1997). The reader will form his or her own views.

5 1 Cranch 137 (1803).

6 Perhaps this is, in truth, a case of necessary implication.

7 See HRA 1998, ss 3(2)(b) and 4(6)(a).

8 [1991] 1 AC 603.

9 See Clayton and Tomlinson *The Law of Human Rights* (2000) paras 3.06–3.34. See also, Lester and Pannick *Human Rights Law and Practice* (1999) paras 3.01–3.03; Grosz, Beatson and Duffy *Human Rights* (2000) para 3–13.

10 The leading case is *Minister of Home Affairs v Fisher* [1980] AC 319. See also: *Ong Ah Chuan v Public Prosecutor* [1981] AC 648; *A-G of the Gambia v Momodou Jobe* [1984] AC 689; *A-G of Trinidad and Tobago v Whiteman* [1991] 2 AC 240; *A-G of Hong Kong v Lee Kwong-Kut* [1993] AC 951; *Huntley v A-G for Jamaica* [1995] 2 AC 1; *Matadeen v Pointu* [1999] 1 AC 98.

11 See *R v DPP, ex p Kebilene* [2000] 2 AC 326 at 374–375; *R v Lambert* [2001] UKHL 37, [2001] 3 WLR 206 at 243–244 (para 114).

12 The importance of this distinction is stressed by Gearty (2002) 118 LQR 248 at 269.

13 [1984] AC 689 at 700 (emphasis added). See Clayton and Tomlinson, above n 9, para 3.15.

14 See *Matadeen v Pointu* [1999] 1 AC 98 at 108.

15 Under HRA 1998, s 6(1), a public authority may, when acting in a way incompatible with a Convention right, commit a separable wrong. However, the effect of s 6(6) is that no wrong would be committed by a minister by failing to take remedial action. In principle, this has no effect upon judicial review.

16 See also HRA 1998, s 6(3), which excludes from the phrase 'public authority' any person 'exercising functions in connection with proceedings in Parliament'.

17 See ECHR, art 35(1).

18 Because of HRA 1998, s 10(1)(b) and because of the provisions for enforcement against states contained within the Convention itself: see art 46; and see Emmerson and Ashworth *Human Rights and Criminal Justice* (2001) para 1–159.

19 [2001] EWHC 13 (unreported). Cf *International Transport Roth GmbH v Secretary of State for the Home Department* [2002] EWCA Civ 158, [2002] 3 WLR 344, where the Court of Appeal did enumerate the reasons for finding incompatibility.

20 For further possible difficulties, for the litigant, and, in particular, the accused, arising from the declaration of incompatibility procedure, see Emmerson and Ashworth, above n 18, paras 17-38–17-41.

21 For a revealing account, see Ashworth and Blake [1996] Crim LR 306.

22 The distinction between offence and defence elements is not seen by everyone as either coherent or significant: see, in particular, Zuckerman (1976) 92 LQR 401.

23 [2001] UKHL 37, [2002] 2 AC 545.

24 Lord Slynn based his judgment solely upon the absence of retrospective effect, but went on to give his answers to the other questions raised.

25 See Misuse of Drugs Act 1971, s 5(3).

26 For Lord Slynn's use of the phrase, see [2001] UKHL 37, [2001] 3 WLR 206 at 212 (para [17]) (emphasis added). Lord Devlin, in making this orthodox point in *Jayasena v R* [1970] AC 618 at 624, said that their Lordships did not understand what was meant by that phrase.

27 *R v DPP, ex p Kebilene* [2000] 2 AC 326, on which see below, pp 133–134.

28 See [1988] CLJ 261, 264–265.

29 See [1988] CLJ 261, 265, n 10, referring to *Hunt* [1987] AC 352 at 385.

30 [1991] 3 NZLR 175.

31 [2000] 2 AC 326 at 373.

32 [2000] 2 AC 326 at 374.

33 Lord Hope of Craighead said so explicitly (see [2001] UKHL 37, [2001] 3 WLR 206 at 239 (para [94])) and Lord Steyn expressed his agreement with Lord Hope (see [2001] UKHL 37, [2001] 3 WLR 206 at 224 (para [42])).

34 Of course, where this is *really* what Parliament intended, it will deal with the resulting prosecution duty explicitly, as in the Terrorism Act 2001, s 118(2). In *R v Carass* [2001] EWCA Crim 2845, [2002] 1 WLR 1714 at 1730 (para [62]), the Court of Appeal, applying *Lambert*, described how the provision at issue, the Insolvency Act 1986, s 206(4) should be re-read, and, in doing so, explicitly stated that words should be added thereto to the effect that, if the accused adduced evidence sufficient to raise the issue, the prosecution must then prove the contrary beyond reasonable doubt.

35 (1988) 13 EHRR 379 at 388 (para 28). It has been argued that this kind of balancing, though given the *imprimatur* of the Court in *Salabiaku* itself, is not supported by the bulk of Strasbourg authority: see Ashworth [2001] Crim LR 855 at 865.

36 [2001] 2 WLR 817 at 836 and 851–852. See below, pp 135–137.

37 See eg the discussion in Emmerson and Ashworth, above n 18, para 2–113.

38 *L v DPP* [2001] EWHC Admin 882, [2002] 1 Cr App Rep 420. See also *R v Drummond* [2002] EWCA Crim 527, [2002] 2 Cr App Rep 352 and *R v Daniel* [2002] EWCA Crim 959, [2003] 1 Cr App Rep 99 for an essentially similar approach.

39 See [2001] EWHC Admin 882, [2002] 1 Cr App Rep 420 at 429 (para 23).
40 See [2001] EWHC Admin 882, [2002] 1 Cr App R 420 at 431 (para 29).
41 For a very clear statement of this point, see *Pham Hoang v France* (1993) 16 EHRR 53 at 78–79 (para 3). See also *Salabiaku v France* (1991) 13 EHRR 379.
42 Emphasis added.
43 (1988) 13 EHRR 379. See also *Pham Hoang v France* (1993) 16 EHRR 53.
44 (1988) 13 EHRR 379 at 388 (para 28).
45 (1988) 13 EHRR 379 at 389 (para 29).
46 (1988) 13 EHRR 379 at 387 (para 27).
47 See Emmerson and Ashworth, above n 18, paras 9-64–9-65.
48 [2000] 2 AC 326.
49 See [2000] 2 AC 326 at 344C (per Lord Bingham CJ) and at 356B (per Laws LJ).
50 See Lord Steyn, [2000] 2 AC 326 at 370E-F; Lord Cooke of Thorndon at 373B; Lord Slynn at 362B (expressing agreement with Lord Steyn's opinion). Lord Hobhouse of Woodborough was non-committal (see at 397G–H), Lord Hope of Craighead somewhat equivocal (see at 382C, and cf at 387A–B).
51 (2002) 118 LQR 41.
52 (2000) 165 JP 213.
53 Munday *Evidence* (2001) para 2.33.
54 In *R v Drummond* [2002] EWCA Crim 527, [2002] 2 Cr App Rep 352 the reverse onus clause in RTA 1988, s 15(3) was itself challenged by virtue of art 6(2), but was found not to be inconsistent with the presumption of innocence.
55 See *Cross and Tapper on Evidence* (9th edn, 1999) p 66; Dennis *The Law of Evidence* (2nd edn, 2002) p 421.
56 (1993) 16 EHRR 297.
57 See, in particular, *Murray v United Kingdom* (1996) 22 EHRR 29. In the leading English case, *Brown v Stott* [2001] 2 WLR 817, though the Privy Council overturned the decision of the High Court of Justiciary 2000 SLT 379, it cast no doubt on the latter court's view that the right against self-incrimination comprehended both aspects.
58 See Emmerson and Ashworth, above n 18, paras 15-63–15-107.
59 [2001] 2 WLR 817. The provision applies to England and Wales, as well as to Scotland.
60 See *DPP v Wilson* [2002] RTR 37.
61 See [2001] 2 WLR 817 at 836H.
62 See [2001] 2 WLR 817 at 837A.
63 Police and Criminal Evidence Act 1984, s 76 and cf s 78.
64 (1996) 23 EHRR 313 at 338 (para 69). See also *Heaney and McGuinness v Ireland* (2001) 33 EHRR 264 at 278 (para 40).
65 There is a strong argument that the Convention jurisprudence does not allow Convention rights to be 'balanced' away in this fashion (see *Doorson v Netherlands* (1996) 22 EHRR 330; *Heaney and McGuinness v Ireland* (2001) 33 EHRR 264) even though it is accepted that the implied right not to incriminate oneself is not absolute in nature.
66 It is reasonable to assume that nothing turns on the fact that the word here is 'shows', not 'proves'. In addition, RTA 1988, s 172(4) contains that word only once, and applicable to the defence, unlike *Lambert*, where it was used twice, and applicable to both prosecution and defence.
67 2000 SLT 379 at 391.
68 See *Miailhe v France (No 2)* (1996) 23 EHRR 491, esp at para 43, for a possible example. On implied rights, in general, see Ashworth [2001] Crim LR 855, 865–866.
69 Cf *Tora Tolmos v Spain* (1995) 81 DR 82.
70 See [2001] 2 WLR 817 at 836F (per Lord Bingham of Cornhill), at 842B (per Lord Steyn), at 856F-G (per Lord Hope of Craighead), and at 863E–864A (per the Rt Hon Ian Kirkwood).
71 See [2001] 2 WLR 817 at 842B.
72 [2001] UKHL 37, [2001] 3 WLR 206 at 220 (para [35]).
73 See *Doorson v Netherlands* (1996) 22 EHRR 330.
74 See *Baegen v Netherlands* (1995) A.327-B.
75 *Doorson v Netherlands* (1996) 22 EHRR 330 at 358 (para 70) (emphasis added).
76 See *DPP v Boardman* [1975] AC 421, but see now *DPP v P* [1991] 2 AC 447.
77 [2001] UKHL 25, [2002] 1 AC 45.
78 [2001] EWCA Crim 1877, [2002] 1 WLR 632.
79 See eg Berger (1977) 77 Col LR 1, 58–59; Galvin (1986) 70 Minn LR 763, 807; Birch [2002] Crim LR 223, 247–249.
80 See eg Schwartz (1994) 31 CR (4th) 232, 233–235; Boyle and MacCrimmon (1999) 41 Crim LQ 198, 229.

81 Lord Hope of Craighead was not prepared so to conclude, for he thought that it was not for the House to deal with YJCEA 1999, s 41(3)(c) in the abstract: see [2002] 1 AC 45 at 86 (para [106]).
82 See above, p 137.
83 Several of the opinions do refer to the significance of the interests of the complainant, but a more pressing concern of their Lordships seems to be that the accused's fair trial right should be balanced against the general interest of the public: see, in particular, Lord Hope of Craighead [2002] 1 AC 45 at 81–82 (para [91]).
84 See [2002] 1 AC 45 at 69 (para [46]). Lord Hope of Craighead joined the rest on this point: see at 87–88 (para [110]).
85 Not everyone regards this as a *possible* interpretation, having regard to the words of enactment Parliament actually chose: see Mirfield (2002) 118 LQR 20. See also Spencer [2001] CLJ 452.
86 [2002] 1 AC 45 at 87 (para [108]). See also *R v Home Secretary, ex p Simms* [2000] 2 AC 115 at 131F-G (per Lord Hoffmann).
87 [2002] 1 AC 45 at 68 (para [44]) (emphasis is original). See also at 106 (para [162]) (per Lord Hutton).
88 [1991] 1 AC 603, referred to above, p 127.
89 See HL Deb vol 585, col 840 (5 February 1998); HC Deb vol 306, col 778 (16 February 1998).
90 (2001) 21 OJLS 59.
91 [1993] AC 593.
92 Lord Steyn himself rejects this kind of identification, at least where it *favours* the executive: see (2001) 21 OJLS 59, 68.
93 See, for a similar general point, Gearty (2002) 118 LQR 248.
94 [2001] EWCA Crim 1877, [2002] 1 WLR 632.
95 See [2001] EWCA Crim 1877, [2002] 1 WLR 632 at 639 (para [33]).
96 The same applies to art 6(3), which has not been dealt with in this paper.
97 (1988) 13 EHRR 379, considered above, p 133.
98 [2000] 2 AC 326, considered above, pp 133–134.
99 See *Parker v DPP* (2000) 165 JP 213, considered above, p 134.
100 This question is separate from that of whether or not, if the accused's trial was unfair by Convention standards, his conviction must necessarily be unsafe, for the purposes of the Criminal Appeal Act 1968, s 2(1)(a) (as amended), on which question see *R v Davis, Rowe and Johnson* [2001] 1 Cr App Rep 115; *R v Francom* [2001] 1 Cr App Rep 237; *R v Togher, Doran and Parsons* [2001] 1 Cr App Rep 457; *R v Forbes* [2001] 1 AC 473 at 487; *R v Craven* [2001] 2 Cr App Rep 181; *R v Doubtfire* [2001] 2 Cr App Rep 209; *R v Botmeh* [2002] 1 WLR 531.
101 See *Pham Hoang v France* (1992) 16 EHRR 53 at 78–79 (para 33).
102 It is not even necessary that the rights of the accused in the case at hand have been breached: see *R v A (No 2)* [2001] UKHL 25, [2002] 1 AC 45, considered above, pp 138–140.
103 [2001] UKHL 37, [2001] 3 WLR 206.
104 This is not to say that any such intimations represent the true thrust of that jurisprudence: see Ashworth [2001] Crim LR 855, 864–868.
105 [2001] EWHC Admin 882, [2002] 1 Cr App Rep 420.
106 HRA, s 19(1)(a). See also, HL Deb vol 598, col 1221 (23 March 1999).
107 See *United States, ex rel A-G v Delaware & Hudson Co* 213 US 366 at 408 (1909).
108 See, in particular, Schauer [1995] Sup Ct Rev 71; Kelly (2001) 86 Cornell L Rev 831.
109 An excellent example is *United States v X-Citement Video, Inc* 513 US 64 (1994), which involves a departure from ordinary canons of linguistic interpretation of a kind similar to that in *R v Lambert* [2001] UKHL 37, [2001] 3 WLR 206.

The policies of legal information services: a perspective of three decades

Jon Bing[1]

1 Introduction[2]

Today, online legal information services are tools of the legal working environment for lawyers in many countries, certainly those in North America and Europe. They are to some extent trivial, and used as a matter of course, which may make us forget that they really have been developed by lawyers still active as researchers, not part of our history, but part of our own times.

Colin Tapper is a prime example of this. In introducing this essay, it may be permitted briefly to review the development of which he was such an important part in Europe. Many pursued the objective of designing computerised systems to enhance legal research in the 1950s and 1960s. John F Horty of the University of Pittsburgh is usually named as the person successfully demonstrating a system for retrieving sections from a database of statutory texts at a conference of the American Bar Association in 1960. This initiated further research, and caused optimism (in hindsight, quite unrealistic optimism) regarding the use of the new information technology to solve the research challenges faced by lawyers.

The method used by Horty is often called – somewhat misleadingly – 'full text retrieval'. In principle, an input text was processed to create two files. One was a 'text file', containing the original text with an additional index, which gave an internal address for each element of the text – like 'section 2, paragraph 3 starts at location *n* on the magnetic tape'. The other was a 'search file',[3] where all the different words occurring in the text were sorted in alphabetical order, giving for each occurrence the internal address of the word.

The search file could be used as a very extensive index to the text itself: looking up any term in the search file, the internal address was specified, and the computer system could use this in accessing the index of the text file, and retrieve the word in context from the text file. The user had the impression of searching the 'full text'; specifying a word like 'privacy', the system would return with the information that this occurred in, for instance, two sections of the statutory text in the database. And if the user asked to have these displayed, they would be retrieved, using the internal addresses as the key linking the search and text files.

This may seem rather simple and straightforward. It is still the basic principle for searching natural languages texts, demonstrating that principles may survive longer than technological solutions. But to appreciate the system demonstrated by Horty, one should take into account the technology available for realising the solution. He was using an IBM 650, which was based on vacuum tubes and a drum storage of 2,000 words, and the IBM 7070, which was a transistorised version of the IBM 650, having a magnetic core storage containing 9,990 numbers of ten digits each. One may compare the capacity to current examples of information technology, like a digital watch or a pocket calculator. Random access memory units like magnetic disks were not available; data not placed into the central storage units mentioned above, had to be read to and from a sequential tape. Sorting the words of a text in alphabetic order could be compared, perhaps, to arranging books by authors' names in a book case. Anyone who has ventured to do this will know that new books frequently have authors with last names starting with a letter early in the alphabet, requiring you to move the last books, working yourself back towards the place where a space for the new book is needed. This metaphor may give some indication of the practical problems facing the early developers. And, of course, they did not have online systems, but had to deal with batch processing, using punched cards for input and printouts for output.

Horty's early work was done on statutory texts. The really dominant challenge to legal research, especially for the common law lawyer, would be case material. The one really to explore this challenge was Colin Tapper, in the work which came to be known as the 'Oxford Experiments'. The work produced very important results in two respects.

As an example of the first kind of result, one may mention his conclusions regarding the use of manual indexes of case law material. At the time, a database for case law would represent a huge amount of data; the systems available (at the end of the 1960s) could hardly cope with such volumes and the storage media necessary implied costs of a corresponding order. Therefore many, not least in Europe, were tempted to experiment with retrieval based on abstracts or indexes of each case established by an experienced indexer.[4] Tapper also tried this approach, but to check consistency he let the same document be indexed by different indexers. He found that the consistency was less than satisfactory, and to check further, he gave back the same documents to the original indexer. His finding that intra-indexer consistency was little better than inter-indexer consistency was a major argument in favour of discarding intellectual indexing or abstracting as a viable solution for retrieval of case law. In order to give the user – a lawyer with a real problem – a chance of finding possibly relevant cases, the user would have to be working on the authentic text of the case: the filter of indexers would reduce performance unduly.

This is only one example of the results which were important for the design of computerised systems for legal research that emerged through his work. The second result is also exemplified by the first: he brought a scientific method to the field. He was not mainly concerned with getting a system up and running with a view to launching a commercial venture; his interest was academic, an interest in how systems worked, what influenced their performance, etc.

Through the Council of Europe, and its Committee of Experts on the Harmonisation of the Means of Programming Legal Data into Computers (later renamed with the slightly less confusing title Committee on Legal Data Processing), which met for the first time in 1969, Tapper was very influential in disseminating the results from projects and research among European countries, and thus contributing to developments in Europe.

In this essay, some characteristics of the developments of the three decades following the 1960s will be sketched. The situation on which the development was based has been indicated above. In simplifying, one will also be guilty of misrepresentation. The author offers his excuses for this, but hopes that the simplification may bring out some policy issues that otherwise might be less visible through the mass of details.

2 Europe's problem in 1970: the information crisis of the law

In an important book published in 1970, *Informationskrise des Rechts und Datenverarbeitung*,[5] Spiros Simitis analysed the current status in Europe. This analysis had a wide scope, but some of the observations were as follows.

During the previous decade, European countries had established welfare systems; a change had been made from welfare that rested purely on the appraisal of need, to systems based on rights to social benefits. In these systems, embedded in administrative law, there had emerged certain appeal institutions or tribunals, or established agencies for reviewing administrative decisions, which had been given increased responsibility. These agencies were not necessarily courts, but were at least similar to courts in the respect that they adhered to the same ideals as a court, and defined their function to guarantee 'due process', 'rule of law' or *Rechtsicherheit.* The legal sources on which these agencies based their decisions, were – also in the Continental European systems – to some extent their own previous decisions; at the very least, they wanted to appear consistent in their application of law. At that time the number of appeal cases increased rather sharply. As appeals generally were free of charge and part of the administrative procedure, those who felt they had not received the benefits to which they had a right (or a hope), would be inclined to appeal negative decisions. Therefore, a rather high proportion of the negative decisions was appealed. At the same time, the number of decisions increased due to demographic factors. The appeal agencies could not always screen cases (though strategies for this were soon developed), and backlogs mounted. Backlogs could only be reduced by two strategies: either by increasing the resources for case processing, or by reducing the resources necessary for process an average case.

Manpower for increasing resources was not forthcoming. Therefore, the alternative was to cut down on the resources necessary to process an average case. As research of the prior decisions of the agency was time-consuming, a possible solution appeared to be the application of computerised systems to make this more efficient.

Looking at the initiatives taken in different European countries, one may see a tendency for agencies or institutions such as those characterised above to be prominent. In Italy, the Corte Suprema di Cassazione took an initiative as early as 1963–64; this was central in establishing the information system Italgiure, initially concerned with the dissemination of the *massime* of the court itself to subordinate courts or agencies. In France, an initiative was taken by the Conseil d'état in 1967, the result being the creation of Centre de recherche et développement en informatique juridique (CEDIJ) in 1969, with strong links to the Conseil d'état and administrative courts, but also the Ministry of Justice. In Sweden, the Directorate of court administration (established 1975) started with the decisions of the administrative courts, and in Finland, the Supreme Administrative Court at the same time took the lead.

These are examples characterising a trend. Obviously, there are examples of other types of initiatives, but it is maintained that it is typical for the initiative to be taken by a national court or other appeal tribunal within the sector of public administration. It may also be maintained that the investments were typically justified by arguments that they would reduce costs in the legal research associated with an average case, but that the expected economical benefits were not realised. If challenged, the argument would be amended: the better research facilities improved the quality of the decisions, and as the investments should be seen in the perspective of 'due process', an economical analysis was inappropriate. The emphasis was thus shifted from a reduction of cost to an increase in quality. One should, perhaps, see this not only as a tactical dodge, but also as reflecting the real concerns of these institutions in meeting the standards set by 'due process' for their operation, standards which were derived from those applied to the general courts working under rather different constraints.

Germany is an interesting example. In 1967 the Ministry of Justice started planning a legal information system, the preparatory work resulting in a report for the establishment of Das Juristische Informationssystem[6] (JURIS) in 1972. For the impatient, the plan seemed to take a very long view; it started with a 'development phase' in the period 1973–82. The system was launched within two areas, decisions in social law (based on the Bundessozialgericht) and tax law (based on the Bundesfinanzhof). In this way, the plan fits well with the premises indicated above, reacting to the pressures brought to bear on administrative courts.[7] But during the development phase, new databases were continually added.

Also, the only really detailed study of the business economics of such a plan was undertaken for the JURIS system, concluding that for the public sector, an average time reduction of 1.4 hours could be realised, corresponding to 54.60 DEM per week in 1976.[8] Though the study is rather theoretical, and based on presumptions that are hardly valid,[9] the study illustrates how the necessary investment in the legal information service is based on a 'rational' and economic argument.

But the plan also contained the concept of an 'extended JURIS system', which would be a general national legal information service for all federal legal sources; and the material for the different states is now being completed.[10]

In JURIS we have exemplified another major characteristic of the development of the European systems that were initiated in the 1970s. Though their start typically was limited to a certain court or agency within the public sector, and justified by the needs of this institution, their ambition was soon escalating into a vision for an integrated legal information service for the whole jurisdiction. This service would offer case law, statutes and regulations. It would require an effort over time, incrementally building up the databases. But in a few years (and the JURIS example illustrates that we are talking about a decade or more), a general service for professional users of legal sources would be available – a user group often characterised as 'lawyers', though it would include professionals without formal legal education in public administration and private organisations. This in contrast to a service which would have a more general target group: the public at large or the 'layman'.

One of the reasons why the vision of the national legal system extended only to professionals was the technological environment. At the time we now are looking at – the end of the 1970s – the information systems were accessed by terminals. These were comparatively expensive, and there were few terminals at a user site. The communication relied often on dial-up lines with a rather low baud-rate for transmission. The user interface was line-oriented, one line was communicated, a new line received – the user could not edit the screen. And communication relied typically on commands in certain formalism. Though attempts generally were made to make such commands easy to understand and remember, it was nevertheless rather cumbersome. Such systems could cater for professionals, but could not obviously be offered for general use.[11]

European legal services were therefore, it may be argued, at the end of the 1970s poised to grow into general services for the different national jurisdictions. The vision was there, and perhaps also some impatience with users not realising the potential benefits of the systems, and therefore rather slow on the up-take. The Commission of the European Communities launched a technical study in the use of the different national legal services,[12] and this reported on the problems of user friendly interfaces, lack of availability etc, indicating many of the reasons for the services not taking off in the way predicted by those (the author included) who were looking for general use of such services by professionals.

Then came the unexpected arrival of the personal computer and office automation.

3 The 1980s – the decade of distributed computing

In 1981, IBM launched its first 'personal computer', based on the Intel 8088 microprocessor, and this became the start of a revolution in office automation. In the context of this essay, it is important to indicate the shift in focus that the introduction of PCs represented. In a surprisingly brief time, typewriters were lifted from the desks in all sorts of offices, leaving a free space in which a PC could be placed. These had software that was much more user-friendly than that available on the typical terminal linked to a time-share mainframe – one should recognise that even the MS-DOS operating system was comparatively user-friendly. But they were very modest in today's terms: a typical PC featured a monochrome monitor, 16K of RAM and one 5.25-inch diskette drive (hard drives were not commonplace for another three years).

The change in focus was then from the services available from mainframes through terminals, to the services offered by the PC on the user's own desk. In many respects this made services more available, one become less dependent on third parties, one got better and more direct control over the programs and the tasks, etc. But despite the many advantages, there also was one major disadvantage: PCs were initially stand-alone equipment. Even sharing peripherals like printers was not trivial. As a consequence, the vision of the integrated national legal information service suffered – such services assumed communication to a common database, and PCs simply did not initially, support this.

Speaking in broad terms, one may maintain that the distribution of computing, symbolised by the PC, demolished the vision of users connected to a common legal database. Slowly, PCs were connected in Local Area Networks, and one could – perhaps – see that the foundation was rebuilt for an enhanced situation, where the user did not have to walk up to a terminal in order to link to the computerised legal service, but would be able to access that service from his or her own desktop computer. But it took considerable time to realise this new development.

Solutions therefore were sought for this new situation. In 1980, Phillips and Sony had proposed a standard for a machine readable compact disk (CD), and in 1983 prototypes of compact disks for read-only-memory (CD-ROM) were demonstrated. Compared to the storage capacity of the current magnetic disks, the CD-ROM of 650 MB was impressive. It was also sufficient to offer legal information services. The early CD-ROM of the Norwegian Lovdata foundation offered consolidated statutes in force and all national and local regulations in force on the same platter.[13] This disk could be inserted in a station of the user's own PC, and make the material available in the same environment as the other office tools.

But even if the new, compact storage medium had a relative high capacity, it did not measure up to what was necessary for a national legal information service – again, the requirement to represent the volume of case law easily exceeded what was available on one CD-ROM. There were experiments offering services on several CD-ROMs, but this proved inconvenient – the user had to juggle between the different disks, hyperlinking across disks was awkward, and if the disks were made available on a local area network, the server would have to support several disk stations. Therefore, there was a tendency to define services which could be supported by a single CD-ROM, containing both the retrieval program and the legal data. These tended to be specialised services. There were many business opportunities for such services; perhaps the most popular was services for tax law, but there were many other variations: building and planning law, intellectual property law, European directives etc. However, these services were more clearly focused on market segments, and the users within a particular segment had to be able to pay for the service. Therefore, sectors of the law which offered less of a business opportunity would not be covered by the specialised services – for instance, social security law, where the legal advice to clients was mainly offered by agencies within the public sector rather than lawyers in private practice.

Another feature also made the CD-ROM proposition attractive. They could be marketed as physical objects in the same way as conventional printed books. Therefore, traditional publishers could easily see how their marketing channels and strategies could be adapted to offer this new form of 'electronic publishing'. For online services, however, these strategies could not be easily adapted.[14]

The retrieval software was also different. In the days of batch-processing systems, much emphasis had been placed on the construction of the search request, and strategies optimising retrieval performance. When online systems came along, making it less of a practical problem to rephrase a request that did not perform as expected, there was somewhat less concern with preparing the request, as users would work more on a trial and error basis. But still tradition prevailed; the systems often had possibilities for making complex queries, and strategies might include ranking of results. This was especially important for case law, where documents were long and where the search requests often would try to express rather subtle issues of law.[15] The systems of CD-ROMs, however, typically supported rather simple search strategies, often only allowing the user a search request of one term, or a few terms combined by Boolean operators.

One may mention in passing the important distinction between fact and interest retrieval. In fact retrieval, the user may define the criteria for 'relevance'.[16] For instance, if a user looks for a book by a certain author, the user expects the name of the author to appear in the field of the document defined as 'author's name'. If the system gives a negative response, this is interpreted as there not being any documents by the specified author. Compare this with a user looking for a case on a certain subject, for instance 'liability of the owner of a house when a person is injured by a loose brick falling from a balcony'. It is obvious that the user could not conclude that if the case did not contain the term 'brick', it would not be relevant – if the falling object was a tile from a badly maintained roof, the case concerning this damage may easily be deemed relevant. Lawyers, especially when working with case law, need systems to support interest retrieval; the strategies supported by most CD-ROM-based systems had been developed for fact retrieval.

Taken together, the CD-ROM-based services emphasised the fragmentation encouraged by the nature of the early office automation. The old paradigm had been that of a centre reaching out through telecommunication lines (admittedly often offering communication of low quality), interconnecting all users through a central computer facility from which the services were offered. The new paradigm was that of a large number of self-sufficient islands. The idea of the integrated national legal information service was perhaps not lost, but certainly downgraded. Computerised legal research become more common, but the services offered were typically specialised or limited in scope.

4 Networking and web services

In the early 1990s, a latent situation had been created by two somewhat different developments.

The first was the distribution of computer power outlined above, which had resulted in placing a workstation or PC on the desk of most lawyers. At this time, these were also linked together in local area networks.

The second was related to the Internet, a solution for interconnecting computer facilities in universities and research institutions. This had originally been sponsored by the Advanced Research Program Agency (ARPA) of the US Department of Defence, but had by 1980 been split into two separate networks, military (Milnet) and civil (Internet). The National Science Foundation (NSF) operated the latter, and enforced the policy that only research institutions could be linked into the net. The email service supported by the Internet became very popular, and was certainly the feature within the network which attracted new institutions, and secured its growth. Around 1990, NSF also discontinued its support to the Internet, leaving this infrastructure in the hands of the self-regulatory bodies that had grown up in the Internet community, and the national organisation co-operating with these.[17] As the NSF relaxed its control, other organisations than those charged with research and development, were allowed to connect to the Internet, mainly to get access to the email services. The foundation for a commercialisation of the Internet had been laid.

The catalyst exploding the latent situation into a feverish development was the World Wide Web. The Web was originally conceived and developed for the large high-energy physics collaborations which have a demand for instantaneous information sharing between physicists working in different universities and institutes all over the world, by Tim Berner-Lee of the European Organization for Nuclear Research (CERN).[18] Together with Robert Cailliau, Berner-Lee wrote the first WWW client (a browser-editor running under NeXTStep) and the first WWW server along with most of the communications software, defining URLs, HTTP and HTML.[19] In 1993, Marc Andreessen released the first web browser, Mosaic – at the end of 1993, only 50 servers worldwide could access the Web. This increased sharply, as the new mass-medium for communication and electronic trade was developed.

As has been indicated, the development of office automation had the drawback that the importance of communication between users and a central facility had been somewhat downgraded. But as local area networks were hitched onto the Internet, and the Web service became available to the local workstation of any user, communication was given priority. But the structure of this communication network was very different from what had been common at the end of the 1970s. At that time, one would draw a centralised network around a main hub, linking all users to this facility; this made communication between users possible, but only through the central hub. The Web and Internet was more of a distributed network, any node could communicate to any other node, and it did not have an obvious hierarchical structure. One could, of course, create such within the net – a popular service would attract users, and within the distributed network the service could function like a central facility shared by a large number of users.

One of the fascinations with the new technology was the ease and low cost of establishing home pages, enabling institutions to present themselves and to provide information on them. Rather than using the technology to collect information from many sources, presenting them in a co-ordinated and integrated way, a profusion of initiatives was taken – each court, each agency, each institution presented their own site to the public. Initially, therefore, the tendency to fragment was further emphasised.

The user who wanted to search for national sources was presented with a rather differentiated, if not confused, situation where the different sites might have different standards for updating response, document design, retrieval strategies etc. Also, the services offered at web sites generally adopted the standards for retrieval which are common for search engines, and which support very simple strategies, mainly based on single word or phrases, occasionally supplemented by simple Boolean operators – and clearly insufficient for the support of interest retrieval.

This new technology created a tension between the older commercial services and the new possibilities. Legal sources such as statutes, regulations and decisions are, in most jurisdictions, not subject to copyright,[20] and it might be seen as a paradox that the user would have to pay to access this material. It was tempting to set up alternative services competing with the older.

One of the major examples is provided by Legal Information Institutes (LIIs). In 1992, the LII of Cornell Law School[21] was launched by Peter Martin and Tom Bruce, co-directors. 'The legal information industry in the U.S. in the mid-'90s had focused totally on judges and lawyers and hadn't paid attention to the information needs of others', Peter Martin has stated. 'One of our powerful early discoveries was how much demand outside those professional sectors there was – ordinary citizens trying to make sense of laws that impinge on their lives.'[22] The site offers the United States Code, an organised compilation of current federal laws; and the collections of all recent opinions of the US Supreme Court and New York State Court of Appeals. The site also provides topical overviews of such areas as banking law and employment discrimination law and organised collections of links to sites offering court decisions, statutes, regulations and other legal materials. Making information accessible on the Web in a manageable format has been a challenge – there are 13 US Circuit Courts, each putting its decisions on the Web. The problem is that data structures and formats differ from site to site: researchers need some solution, for instance, a search engine, that reaches across those structures.

The Cornell Law School LII may have been the first site of its kind on the Web,[23] but LII has become a generic term indicated a certain type of operation on the Web,[24] and there are namesakes as far-flung as New Zealand, Zambia and Kazakhstan.

One of the more remarkable LIIs is the Australasian Legal Information Institute (AustLII), jointly established by the University of New South Wales and the University of Technology, Sydney, with Graham Greenleaf and Andrew Mowbray taking the initiative. This is an effort with an impressive ambition, and a background in the policies of legal information services in Australia, where the doctrine of 'Crown Copyright' prevails. AustLII argued that unless governments and agencies positively co-operate with non-commercial bodies that wish to provide information via the Internet by providing them with raw data in computerised form, non-commercial bodies are unlikely ever to be able to publish the data in any form.[25] There are several characteristics of the AustLII that make the service remarkable – the scope of the database is one thing, the programs developed to enhance the service, and support search strategies is another. But perhaps most important are the standards AustLII sets itself for making legal sources available in a complete and authentic form, a service to integrate material and to be trusted.[26]

AustLII has also many offspring, one of them being the WorldLII, a co-operation between itself and British and Irish Legal Information Institute (BAILII), Canadian Legal Information Institute (CanLII), Hong Kong Legal Information Institute (HKLII), Pacific Islands Legal Information Institute (PacLII) and including databases provided by Wits Law School, South Africa. This is an attempt to create a truly international information resource; not only are the materials made available by the LIIs listed, but a search engine has been developed to index legal sites around the world.

The story of the LIIs has still to be written, and this essay can hardly do more than indicate the important policy implications of this movement. But some tentative issues can be discerned.

First, the initiatives are typically associated with universities and law schools. This is by no means the first time that policies have sprung from this source. The first documentation centre to emerge in France was the Institut de recherches et d'études pour le traitement de l'information juridique (IRETIJ), the result of an initiative taken in 1965 by Professor Pierre Catala at the University of Montpellier. Their main focus was initially on the decisions of the 32 French appeal courts, which were not subject to systematic publication.[27] This was a problem that researchers at several universities set out to address, though IRETIJ remained one of the few centres throughout the 1970s to pursue this policy.

Second, there is the indication of a tension with respect to the objectives of the services of the LII. As stated by the co-directors of Cornell LII, legal information services were mainly concerned with the needs of the professional user of legal sources, perhaps even limited to those with a formal legal education. The ideal of *publicatio legis* requires that the law is available to all, and this certainly can be perceived as a necessary foundation of a democratic state. Therefore the limited publishing through specialised services may be seen as too restrictive to provide the necessary legal information for the citizens of a modern state. In the last part of the nineteenth century, many jurisdictions changed their system of communicating statutes and other important legal instruments to the public, adopting some form of printed gazette to replace, typically, the public reading of texts from the steps of the church. It would seem appropriate that, given the possibilities of new information technology, these were exploited to give the public better access to the law.

And this has happened in many jurisdictions. France has, from 15 September 2002, been reforming its legal information services from the commercial service Jurifrance,[28] to the free service Legifrance. Norway changed its principle for the official publication of statutes, regulations etc from the printed version (*Norsk Lovtidend*) to the Web publishing of Lovdata on 1 January 2001; the printed gazette is still being published, but is no longer the official publication. The former system made the official printed version available to a few thousand subscribers, the new system reached through the Web the approximately the two thirds of the Norwegian households having access to the Internet.

But one should not confuse the policy of *publicatio legis* with the needs of the professional user of legal sources for an efficient research tool. The public should undoubtedly be given as easy access as possible to statutes and other important legal instruments. But use of the authentic legal sources is certainly not trivial. The public should, ideally, have a problem-oriented gateway to the material, where the authentic instruments are commented and explained. This is often done within specialised areas where there is a perceived need for legal advice, typically by public agencies through guides, popular presentations etc, and by doing this on the Web, the material may be presented hyperlinked into a rich environment of other material. But this strategy requires resources for presenting the law and keeping the presentation current – there are, to this author's knowledge, no examples of such a service covering the whole area of law; they remain specialised. If all authentic sources – statutes, regulations, court decisions etc – were made available, this obviously would not satisfy the needs of the lay user.

The services offered by the LIIs are often buffered by the policy of *publication legis* and a reference to the basic right of all citizens to know the law. This justification is *not* challenged here. But it is challenged that it is wise, or even possible, to satisfy *both* the needs of the lay user *and* the needs of the professional user by the same information service. Even though much of the authentic material would be identical, the user requirements for a friendly service would differ. Possibilities for sophisticated search requests would not necessarily be helpful to an occasional user of the system; the semantic of hyperlinks, at least, would have to be explained, the principles for interpretation of decisions from the different courts; the harmonisation of the results both when decisions were not consistent, and with respect to statutory rules, with different application in time, would be complex and – as we too often have reasons to consider – not at all easy, even for an experienced lawyer.

The tension between these two objectives can be discerned in several aspects of services from LIIs. For instance, Cornell LII integrates its services with legal education, and AustLII has several features to help lay users.[29]

5 Completing the jigsaw

The first Web browser was called Mosaic. In art, mosaic is a decoration of a surface with designs made up of closely set, usually variously coloured, small pieces of material. In this essay, it has been argued that the vision of a coherent, integrated national legal information system emerging during the 1970s was smashed to pieces by the technological characteristics of the systems for office automation in the 1980s. When the Web technology became available in the 1990s, this led initially to a further profusion of specialised and separate systems.

However, the possibilities of the Web also gave birth to the LIIs, which challenged the organisation of traditional computerised legal information services.[30] The LIIs were to some extent themselves suspended between the objectives of serving the public at large, and offering an alternative service to professional users of legal sources.

But the developments are still in the making. Looking ahead, it would seem that an attempt may be made to use the available technology to integrate the separate services into something that – from the user's point of view – may serve as an integrated, national service. There are no real examples of this currently, though there are indications – like the search strategies made available by WorldLII mentioned above. There are also many practical issues to be solved, for instance hyperlinking across sites in order to represent the rich hyperstructures of legal material,[31] structures which the categories of documentation in the separate legal sites typically cut across.

In this is also a re-affirmation of the belief that integrated, national legal services are what the legal profession needs. Few jurisdictions have achieved this, the European development staggered under the reconsiderations made necessary by technological development. But there are those which have achieved national solutions – Germany's JURIS system has been mentioned.[32] And in the further development of Web-based solutions and technologies, we may see a possibility of the sites making up different tiles of the mosaic, being fitted together to form a coherent picture.

This requires, however, a policy dedicated to achieving this result, which may be beyond the business objectives of the separate services making up the whole. And it also presumes that someone accepts responsibility for establishing services covering those areas of law, or those types of legal material, that are not offered by existing services.

As so often with respect to computerised legal services, the major challenge is not the technology, but agreeing on the policies for the use of the technology, and establishing the organisational basis to implement such policies. The LIIs may prove to be such organisations, but will then probably have to reconsider the consequences of their origins at law schools and universities[33] – or there may emerge other organisations taking on the role as 'integrators'.

In this paper, the 1970s have been characterised as the decade of building the vision of integrated, national systems; the 1980s as the decade of the distribution of computer power; the 1990s as the decade of networking – we still have to learn which characteristic to award the first decade of the new millennium.

NOTES

1 The author would like to thank Roger Smith, fellow and tutor in law of Magdalen College, Oxford for his generous assistance in making the English language of this essay more readable, the responsibility of the content obviously rests with the author.

2 The historical background is set out in Jon Bing et al *Handbook of Legal Information Retrieval* (North-Holland, Amsterdam 1984), also available at http://www.lovdata.no/litt/index.html.

3 Also known as 'inverted file' or 'concordance'.

4 This demonstrates why 'full text retrieval' may be a misleading term: Horty's the method was used not on the 'full text' of the cases, but on the 'full text' of the abstracts or indexes.

5 Karlsruhe, 1970.

6 *Das Juristische Informationssystem – Analyse, Planung, Vorschläge* (Bonn, 1972). The Germans chose the same acronym for their service as the US Justice Retrieval and Inquiry System, with the consent of the US Department of Justice. Juris is, by the way, also the name of an Austrian wine and snapps.

7 One may note that Professor Spiros Simitis was part of the three-man committee contracted by the Ministry of Justice to suggest the design of a computerised system in 1969 (the two other members were the Professors Klug and Fielder).

8 Cf Reinhold S Gluck *Wirtschaftlichkeit juristische Informationssysteme* (S Toeche-Mittler Verlag, Darmstadt).

9 Cf Jon Bing *Rettslige kommunikasjonsprosesser* (Scandinavian University Press, Oslo 1982) pp 265–266.

10 The home page of JURIS is http://www.juris.de/produktion/juris/WebSite/juris/juris.htm.

11 But at this time, videotex systems emerged, using a television set and a dial-up modem as user interface. Many of these were rather successful, a couple in the UK, home of the Prestel services (like Infolex or Lawtel). And in France, the Minitel was a success, to such a degree that it is argued that it held back the deployment of the Internet.

12 Cf *Technical Study in Legal Information Retrieval,* vol I-III (Commission of the European Community, Brussels, 1977) and *Technical Study in Legal Information Retrieval,* vol I-V (Commission of the European Community, Brussels, 1978).

13 This is a pun: the CD-ROM was using the technology of Silver Platter.

14 This is not say that some traditional publishers did not take an interest in online services. The Thompson group was very active in several countries, and today owns one of the major US services, Westlaw, while the other major service, Lexis, is owned by Reid-Elsevier. In this essay, however, the pricing issue will not be pursued as such, though there may be a few notes like the one above.

15 Referring back to the initial experiences of Tapper, we see a connection. The fact that the consistency in indexing was less than satisfactory is perhaps best explained by the indexer seeing different facets of a case in different contexts. Likewise, the legal argument using analogous reasoning may utilise a case of a horse injuring a pedestrian when arguing the liability of the owner leading his or her dog down the street.

16 This term is in itself an issue, but in the context of this essay, the possible definitions of relevance will not be pursued.

17 The historical sketch above is rather rough, but in the context of this essay, it is sufficient to make the point.

18 CERN is an acronym of Conseil Européen pour la Recherche Nucléaire, the official name of the organisation until 1954.

19 Abbreviations for 'Uniform Resource Locator' (the address of a web site), hypertext transfer protocol and hypertext mark-up language (for page definition and description).

20 And in most jurisdictions where the state in principle retains copyright to such sources, the exclusive rights are not used to control third-party use of this material.

21 Cf http://www.law.cornell.edu/.

22 Cf Linda Myers 'CU Law institute web site has latest legal information, from Miranda to Elian', http://www.news.cornell.edu/Chronicle/00/4.27.00/Legal_Info_Inst.html [25 July 2002].

23 One will appreciate that 1992 was very early indeed for such a service.

24 The term 'Legal information Institute' (LII) refers to a provider of legal information that is independent of government, and provides free access on a non-profit basis to multiple sources of essential legal information, cf Graham Greenleaf, Philip Chung http://www2.austlii.edu.au/~graham/publications/2002/HKLII_WorldLII_Jan02/HKLII_WorldLII.html - fn1#fn1http://www2.austlii.edu.au/~graham/publications/2002/HKLII_WorldLII_Jan02/HKLII_WorldLII.html and Andrew Mowbray 'Free access to law via Internet as a condition of the rule of law in Asian societies: HKLII and WorldLII' http://www2.austlii.edu.au/-~graham/publications/2002/HKLII_WorldLII_Jan02/HKLII_WorldLII.html#Heading3 [25 July 2002].

25 Graham Greenleaf, Andrew Mowbray, Geoffrey King and Peter van Dijk 'Public access to law via internet: the Australasian Legal Information Institute' http://www.austlii.edu.au/austlii/articles/libs_paper.html#RTFToC11 [25 July 2002].

26 Also other LIIs have similar standards, for Cornell LII see Thomas R Bruce 'Some Thoughts on the Constitution of Public Legal Information Providers' http://www4.law.cornell.edu/working-papers/open/bruce/warwick.html [26 July 2002].

27 There existed only two reporters, one for the Paris and one for the Grenoble appeal courts.

28 Cf http://www.jurifrance.com/ [26 July 2002].

29 One of the innovative features of AustLII is an expert system integrated in the information service, when the user has identified a provision in a statute, the user may (where available) switch to an expert system mode that will guide the user through a series of questions in order to advice the user whether the provision will apply to the problem of the user.

30 The author believes that the discontinuation of the Department of Justice JURIS service may be an example of the consequences of this, with the LIIs and other organisations related to the freedom of information interest groups taking issue with the dominance of West Publishing Company, including its computerised service, Westlaw. But there are no studies available on this fascinating piece of recent history, so this is only a hypothesis based on the insufficient knowledge of the author.

31 Structures which, incidentally, Colin Tapper has pioneered in utilising for legal information retrieval: see *An Experiment in the Use of Citation Vectors in the Area of Legal Data* (CompLex 9/82, Scandinavian University Press, Oslo, 1982).

32 And the Norwegian Lovdata system is another example.

33 One will note that, for instance, AustLII is an organisation independent of the universities from which the original imitative was taken.

Information technology and the criminal justice system

Richard Susskind[1]

There are surely very few scholars of the law who can be said to have attained international recognition in three different legal disciplines. But Colin Tapper is one such academic. Best known today perhaps for his encyclopaedic contribution to the law of evidence, Colin is also widely regarded, by specialists around the world, as the father of computer law. Forgotten by many, and never known by some, is the fact that Colin made a seminal contribution in a third and distinct field – computer applications in the law.

In the first instance, Colin injected unprecedented rigour into the investigation of the potential and limitations of the use of computer technology in the law.[2] Combining his formidable knowledge of analytical jurisprudence with his deep appreciation of the methods of the social and natural sciences, Colin single-handedly carved out a domain of his own. Indeed, he devoted much of his professional life in the 1960s and 1970s to demonstrating, with clinical precision and compelling argument, that legal data retrieval technology could operate to good effect on case law.[3] Hitherto, researchers had focused on the application of such systems on statute law. Colin's research laid the foundations for the vast, global information systems (such as Lexis and Westlaw) that are now at the heart of legal practice and legal research in most advanced legal systems. Only a handful of legal academics can be said to have exerted such influence on the very fabric of legal life.

My own personal debt to Colin is profound. He supervised my doctoral research at Oxford University from 1983 to 1986, doing so with unerring good humour, a fly's eye for detail and by bringing to bear a wealth of experience that was second to none. Invariably we agreed on matters of theory but we were sometimes at odds when it came to speculating about the practicalities of overhauling advanced legal systems through the deployment of IT. Then and now, I was optimistic and bullish (probably naïve) and supposed that the undeniable benefits that technology could bring would translate, in short order, into excitement, political will and then action. Colin was more sceptical (realistic, in the event), cautioning that I should not underestimate the many obstacles that stood, or might be erected, in the way, amongst which he would itemise technical complexity, political inertia, indifference and indolence, fiefdom mentality and general lack of vision.

Looking back, Colin was not far wrong in his admonitions but, more than 20 years after our early discussions on computerisation of the justice system, it is fair to say that, in England at least, things are now beginning to move.

The branch of the English legal system that is currently enjoying the most IT funding, and so attention and activity, is criminal justice. In my view, this is not because the criminal system is more amenable to the application of IT than other parts of the justice system but because the tackling of crime is highest of all legal items on the political agenda of the current government. The public understands more about criminal law than civil law. Serious crime seems to be on the increase. Current working practices across the criminal justice system, from policing through the courts to prison, appear to many to be unacceptably antiquated. And victims are said to be treated poorly, if not institutionally neglected. Demand for change, improvement and modernisation is widespread. Funds are being made available for transformation. In this context, IT is held by many to be if not the panacea then at least a fundamental building block in any credible attempt to reform the criminal justice system.

These strong expectations that IT should be able to come to the rescue of a groaning criminal justice system have no doubt been fuelled by the pervasive influence of personal computers and the Internet – there is growing anticipation, in many quarters (both in the public and private sectors; and both informed and unenlightened), that these tools should unquestionably be put into action in all areas of public life which suffer from perceived inefficiency.

In passing, it is unnerving in many ways to note as a sign of just how rapidly information technologies have developed that, when Colin and I first met in 1982, the personal computer had just been invented, but the extent of its take-up was beyond either of our imaginations. And it would be ten years before the now pervasive World Wide Web came into being. During the two decades in question, we have seen a steady progression from personal computing to inter-personal computing to inter-organisational computing. The computer is no longer an isolated island of processing and storage activity. Nor is networking within organisations the full story. It is the ability now, courtesy largely of the Internet, of organisations to communicate and collaborate electronically, to work together under the one virtual roof, that is transforming our social and economic lives. And nowhere do onlookers see this more clearly demonstrated than in the criminal justice system.

The irony here is that, in terms of technical complexity, likely organisational upheaval and sheer scale and expense, IT for the criminal justice system is one of the hardest nuts to crack. None the less, the potential impact is profound.

With the potential and yet the undoubted challenges in mind, the purpose of this paper is to begin to explore the impact of IT (by which I mean, broadly, computer and communications technology, including the Internet) on criminal courts specifically and across the criminal justice system more generally. The paper is conceived as an introduction, a first rather than last word.

Taking a helicopter view, IT can have considerable impact on the criminal courts in two quite different ways. First, there is the use of IT in support of the operations and management of the courts themselves. There are, of course, numerous systems already working in the courts (in ways mentioned in section 2 of this paper) but there is no doubt scope for improving these systems and ensuring that the systems of different courts work better alongside one another, where appropriate.

The second way in which IT can have an impact is in its use across an entire criminal justice system – not just in the courts, but by the police and prosecution, and in the prison and probation services as well. The emphasis here is on sharing information amongst, or on passing information between, parts of the criminal justice system.

This paper looks at both types of system. At the outset, I endeavour to highlight the general relevance of IT for the criminal justice system and the benefits that technology might bring (section 1). Thereafter, I lay out the current uses of IT in modern criminal courts, following that with my predictions of longer-term applications of IT that can be expected in the criminal courts of advanced legal systems in five to ten years (section 2). Moving beyond the confines of the criminal courts, I then seek to clarify the main challenges and issues that arise from attempting to introduce IT across an entire criminal justice system (section 3). I go on to consider the options open to policy-makers who are seeking, in some sense, to bring together, through IT, the work of criminal justice agencies; explaining in this connection Lord Justice Auld's proposals for criminal justice technology in England and Wales and the government's response to them (section 4). Penultimately, I draw attention to relevant work that is being conducted in other jurisdictions (section 5). And, finally, I offer some summary thoughts on the way ahead (section 6).

1 The relevance of IT for criminal justice and criminal courts

Today, the criminal justice system in England and Wales, to take an example, is a massive, document-intensive and labour-intensive operation, most of the administrative and management systems of which were developed at a time when the throughput and workload of the courts and lawyers were far smaller than they are today. Many of the systems are crude, paper-based, orientated towards the process of administration and not the community, and not all are able to cope with the increasing demands placed upon them. This can currently bring high staffing costs, inefficiencies, error, delay, poor reputation and dissatisfaction.

Although few judges, lawyers or officials would put it in these terms, the criminal courts (taken together for now as one phenomenon) can be regarded, in large part, as a huge information system – an entity that receives, processes, stores, creates, monitors and disseminates large quantities of documents and information. The court system currently employs large numbers of clerical staff to maintain and run a very large document management capability, which is partly computerised (and the dependency on IT is already great) but is still very much paper-based too. Experience from other industries and other jurisdictions strongly suggests that the systematic and widespread introduction of better, more integrated systems would bring huge efficiencies and major cost savings.

The direct savings might be achieved through staff reductions, more widespread delegation to less costly personnel and, gradually, in property (IT-based court systems do not need to be located in costly sites). The cost savings need not stop at the administration of the courts – the legal aid bill could itself be reduced if the same kinds of efficiencies proposed for the courts were *required* of legal aid practitioners as well. Imaginative solicitors and barristers have already shown, in all sizes of case, that the use, for example, of case management systems, electronic communication and systems for document storage and retrieval (all categories of systems discussed below) can bring quicker and better service at lower cost.

The technologies in question could give rise not only to cost savings but also to a more productive, responsive and effective court system with swifter and cheaper disposal of individual cases. With improved methods for filing, communicating, document production and the management of cases, reduction of delays would follow. The productivity gains would *not* necessarily lead to costs savings to the state, however. Instead, for the same expenditure, the system could process a larger number of cases more swiftly.

In summary, it can reasonably be expected that the following benefits might accrue from improved use of IT within the criminal courts:

- *a more efficient criminal justice system*, by making what is a highly information-intensive system more productive and less costly (in terms of the unit costs of transactions within the system if not the overall cost);
- *reduction in the delays, costs and time,* associated with criminal matters, by equipping the courts, judges and officials with systems which will manage resources and documents more effectively, enhance productivity and reduce the length of hearings;
- *more productive use of human effort,* by releasing police, prosecutors, judges and prison officials, for example, from excessive administrative burdens and putting the information they need at their fingertips, these individuals will be afforded more time to apply their own respective substantive skills and knowledge; and
- *stimulation of greater confidence in the criminal justice system*, in individuals, for whom the law is too often regarded as antiquated; and for the community at large whose dissatisfaction with delays is compounded by exposure to court practices that are primitive in comparison to those found in most modern offices.

However, IT is relevant for criminal justice not only because there is already considerable dependency upon technology and there is widespread feeling that there is scope for major improvement in existing systems. More than this, IT must also be taken seriously because, first, the Internet is rapidly changing so many aspects of society and, second, technology might afford new opportunities for the criminal justice system.

Looking at each of these two factors in turn, let me turn for a short while to the Internet. If we project into the future, whether as academics, law reformers, politicians or policy-makers, we must surely anticipate a society that will have been radically altered by information technology. Many commentators (of whom I am one) maintain that we are on the brink of a fundamental revolution in society – a set of changes as far-reaching as the industrial revolution of two centuries ago. We are moving rapidly from a print-based industrial society to a technology-based information society. This upheaval will bring changes that are so fundamental for modern society and modern legal systems that the practice of law and the administration of justice will be radically affected in the coming decade. The dominant technology here will be the Internet, a global network with hundreds of millions of users today and one billion users, it is probable, by 2005. The Internet is becoming a mass medium that is putting information and services at people's fingertips on a scale that was inconceivable just ten years ago. By 2005, certainly if the government achieves its objectives,[4] the overwhelming majority of people in Britain will have easy access to the Internet (through the next generation of televisions and through hand-held machines, as well through conventional computers) and will come to expect many services, both public and private, to be delivered through technology. A modern criminal court system and criminal justice system will need to have firm roots in Internet technology, especially if it is going to remain coherent and contemporary for the emerging, so-called 'net generation'.

More generally, looking at the second factor flagged above, it is clear that IT can have impact in two quite different ways. First, IT can be used to *automate*, streamline and improve existing practices, activities and organisations. Second, IT can be used to *innovate*, and so to bring about change and introduce new ways of working and carrying out tasks and managing organisations, ways that were either not possible in the past or even not conceivable in days gone by.

Beyond law, this distinction is seen clearly when one thinks of IT-based cash dispensers. That technology did not automate pre-existing domestic banking practices. Instead, it provided the basis for an entirely new way of conducting banking business. In the criminal justice system too, it can be expected that IT can be used not only to streamline current practices and institutions and render them more efficient but also to *change* many aspects of the way in which the law is practised and justice is administered today.

2 Current and future applications of IT within the criminal courts

It is not the purpose of this paper either to set out detailed descriptions of existing systems or to review the latest specifications for future applications. Instead, by way of context, it is intended in this section, first, to point to the broad categories of use to which IT is currently put and then to make some predictions about systems that are likely to be in use in, say, five to ten years' time.

It might be said in passing that it is a safe assumption in many criminal justice systems today that the various applications discussed are implemented in entirely different systems in different courts, so that the systems in use in the lower courts are different from those in the upper courts which, in turn, will be different from those in appeal courts. Further, even within each category of court, the applications tend not to be held together in integrated systems but are spread across a variety of packages and systems.

The basic categories are as follows:

- *Diarying* – the use of IT to automate the scheduling (calendaring) of courts, judges, officials and parties. This includes the listing function. The term 'case load management' is sometimes also used as a generic term for diarying, listing and allocation of resources.
- *Management information systems* – those that provide statistics and reports relating to the work of the courts, individually and collectively, in terms of throughput, costs, time scales and so forth.
- *Document production systems* – from word processing to automated document production, in respect of letters, directions, rulings, forms, judgments, publications and more.
- *Document management* – systems that capture, store and offer access to documents and files, including indictments, case summaries, applications, pre-sentence reports, expert reports etc. This category includes electronic case files (as discussed in section 3(e) of this paper) and litigation support systems.
- *Access to external information services* – for example, the World Wide Web or subscription-based services (whether on CD or online).
- *Access to shared internal know-how* – to allow judges and officials to share their collective experience of substantive, procedural and organisational issues. (In England, Felix, the judicial email and conferencing system, is such a system. Indeed, it is a precursor of a Judicial Intranet.)
- *Electronic communications* – links (data, video, audio) between courts; between courts and other public agencies, and between courts and other participants in a case.
- *Case management* – including case tracking and access to and creation of electronic case files.
- *Courtroom technologies* – the range of systems that are already deployed in the courtroom itself, including computer-assisted real-time transcription, digital audio recording, laptop or desktop facilities for the taking of notes, document and exhibit display technology, video simulations and IT-based demonstrative

evidence (used especially in serious fraud trials), and video-linking for remote evidence.

- *Judicial technologies* – the variety of systems and services that are for direct use by judges (or magistrates) themselves.[5]
- *Provision of information about the courts* – using IT, and especially the World Wide Web, to disseminate details about the daily work-load, organisation, management, operations and procedures of the criminal courts.

Turning now to future applications, if we project ahead five or ten years (or more), there are many emerging technologies that should also be borne in mind. A variety of these are set out below (in no particular order).

(a) An entirely networked criminal justice community

With many hundreds of thousands of users, secure, confidential, reliable networking/ communications will be in place within a few years, linking together everyone who works in the criminal justice system. This is the context in which tomorrow's criminal justice system will operate. It will be a telecommunications infrastructure not just for conveying conventional messages and documents but will be able to carry video conferencing, databases, bundles of document images, video recordings and voice messaging as well. The technology will link all users to one another, whether in court, chambers, law offices, at home, travelling and so forth. Much of the business of the courts and of legal practitioners will be carried on this network and it will be accessible both by physical connections and by wireless technology too.

(b) Sentencing systems

Considerable research and development work has already been undertaken around the world in the field of sentencing information systems. Some systems simply provide judges with a convenient body of legal, factual and statistical information, while others go much further and are able to make specific suggestions as to sentences, based on the knowledge and data built within them. Thought has also been given to the relationship between sentencing systems and sentencing guidelines.[6]

(c) Virtual hearings and meetings

Video conferencing and telecommunications can enable the conduct of certain court hearings and other legally oriented meetings without all the parties needing to assemble in the one physical location. (A virtual meeting or hearing is one where people do not actually meet face to face but IT reproduces many of the features of such physical meetings.) As legal standards and procedures emerge, virtual hearings and meetings could come to play a major role in the criminal justice system, not only displacing some forums of today but also enabling more frequent and greatly improved communication where, hitherto, face-to-face meetings have not been feasible. In turn, this may enable a reduction in the number of court buildings across the country. In the criminal context, video technology has already been used for remand hearings and to minimise the trauma of court appearance for child victims/witnesses.[7]

(d) Multi-media and hyperlink-based legal bundles

In due course, the preferred and perhaps required format for the lodging of documents in the courts or the exchange of documents amongst parties will be in electronic form in accordance with some pre-specified formats or standards. Electronic document bundles will thus be created and supplemented as they are used at each stage in a legal process. Whereas document bundles today come in the form of discrete and invariably printed documents, with occasional internal cross-references which readers themselves have to pursue while reading, document bundles in the future will be electronically linked to one another (using technology such as hypertext), so that users will navigate around electronic bundles as though they were single sets of information. And the information itself will no longer simply be text-based but will be presented using other media as well, including video, images, sound and animation. Thus, an electronic bundle of legal documents will be more usable and more expressive than their paper counterparts of today.

(e) Multi-media transcripts

With technologies available to capture, and later provide, information in multi-media format, multi-media transcripts – of meetings and hearings – could also come to be available, thus providing a record not just in textual form, but with accompanying sound and video as well, for example.

(f) Promulgation

Promulgation, the formal mechanism by which the public is informed of new laws (or changes in old), may soon be possible using IT – from tailored legal news services to the automated uploading of decisions onto the Internet. As elsewhere, however, this will require some broader changes in law reporting, especially in the need for medium-neutral citations and paragraph marking.

(g) Legal guidance systems

Alongside all sorts of other types of information, legal guidance, legal knowledge, legal expertise and legal experience is gradually coming to be available on the Internet, offering non-lawyers (individuals and organisations, for social and business purposes) access to structured, practical guidance on legal affairs. These systems do, and will continue to, vary in complexity, from electronic check-lists to automated document assembly. While they may not replace conventional legal services, such systems can provide affordable, easy access to legal help (on issues of substance or procedure) where this may have been unaffordable or impractical in the past.

(h) Case tracking

Where case tracking and case management systems in the past have been the exclusive province of court administrators, and more recent proposals for civil reform suggest their extension to judges and lawyers as well, access to information about the status of particular cases (both civil and criminal) may be extended still further, beyond the court system and legal profession to private individuals (including victims) and organisations who have legitimate interests in the progress of their own cases. This could even be achieved, for example, across the Internet directly from the homes of users.

(i) Public administration systems

Routine public administration and related form-filling will gradually be enabled and undertaken electronically. The submission of tax returns and the granting of licences, for example, will be possible online, as will the payment of social security and benefit claims and the provision of grants. With all such services, there might be focused guidance available for users with immediate assessment, explanation and payment, where appropriate. Such public administration systems will extend to areas as diverse as obtaining passports and driving and television licences (all probably in the form of smart cards) as well as numerous business-oriented pieces of administration, including the many formal requirements of disclosure and management imposed on those running companies. Thus, it can reasonably be expected that form-handling in respect of criminal proceedings will come to be an online activity.

(j) Electronic transcription

With the advent of 'speaker-independent, continuous speech, large vocabulary' voice recognition systems, today's techniques for recording and transcribing – including shorthand writing, tape-recording and even computer-assisted real-time transcription – may (in, say, ten years) no longer be needed. Thus, proceedings in court may instantaneously, and in real-time, be captured in electronic form, thereby revolutionising court reporting. So too with meetings and, for example, the taking of witness statements. Voice recognition technology could immediately deliver polished transcripts, in printed or electronic form.

(k) Standards for litigation support systems

As ever more powerful document management systems and electronic communication systems operate together, the document loads for litigation will increasingly be stored, managed and distributed around the justice system in electronic form. Whereas there are currently many different approaches and formats used in criminal litigation support (broadly, the use of database technology to handle documents), it would be preferable to establish and even require that these systems correspond to a set of standards and formats, which could be articulated in a number of protocols appropriate for different classes of case or court (following the example in the civil world of the TeCSA Protocol, for users of the Technology and Construction Courts in England – formerly, the standards set by the former Official Referees' Solicitors' Association in England).[8]

(l) Various applications of IT in the court-room

Where dedicated court-rooms are used for the hearing of cases (as distinct from virtual courts, as discussed above), IT will come to play an ever more dominant role. With voice recognition technology capturing the proceedings, judges or magistrates will no longer need to hand-write notes or type on their own machines, but instead may annotate and comment upon the text as it appears before them (in the manner of real-time transcription of today).

There could be immediate access from the court-room to all primary and secondary source material, entire document sets may be made easily accessible in the court with individual pages capable of presentation on all participants' screens, some evidence may be taken remotely by video-linking, and computer and video simulations could be deployed in the presentation of evidence. Oral evidence might be supplemented by multi-media techniques which could take the court graphically through the evidence and legal arguments, while case management systems may be immediately to hand, enabling decisions or directions to be implemented on the spot, with relevant documentation directed electronically to all relevant parties and bodies across the justice system.

3 IT across criminal justice systems – issues and challenges

Turning away now from current and future applications within the criminal courts, my purpose in this section is to consider the issue of long-term strategy for the use of IT across an entire criminal justice system of an advanced jurisdiction. My approach acknowledges that although new and improved IT can indeed bring considerable benefits within the criminal courts (as suggested in sections 1 and 2 above), the far greater potential for IT lies in its more coherent exploitation across an entire criminal justice system. While this topic has been addressed around the world for at least 20 years, most practical efforts to implement appropriate technical solutions have not succeeded. It is unquestionably a difficult area – technically, culturally, organisationally – and it is costly too. In that context, I would not want to claim too much for any proposals that I make. They should be seen as a tentative hypothesis rather than a definitive, final specification.

In setting out my suggestions, I take a long-term perspective, unlike many politicians and senior officials who are often, not always without justification, impelled to introduce changes that can be characterised as 'quick wins'. In passing, it might be noted that most quick wins invariably turn out to be neither swift nor victorious. They are often no more than superficial packaging that may attract favourable yet transient media coverage; but they tend to detract from the serious business of making progress.

At the same time, my proposals are vision-based and not legacy-based, by which I mean they are inspired by my ideas of how the criminal justice might be about ten or fifteen years from now – with strong management, sufficient investment and a bit of luck. They are not constrained and contained by current systems, problems and incompatibilities. I am provoked by the idea of designing a criminal justice information system from scratch; and in that context, of one thing I am sure – that, given a blank sheet of paper, my blueprint would look nothing like the wide range of more or less ineffective and incompatible systems that currently sit across most modern criminal justice systems.

Although my intention is to adopt a vision-based approach, it is none the less instructive to reflect, in the first instance, on the current position: assuredly, not to be driven by legacy systems while thinking ahead; but to understand just how formidable are the challenges that we face.

Traditionally, the criminal justice system has been regarded by most participants and commentators as a series of loosely related *functions*; a scarcely connected collection of departments or agencies (for example, police, prosecution service, courts, prison and probation), each with its own IT (information systems and services), often idiosyncratic and partly home-grown. The systems of the various departments tend to be at different stages of technical development. Some are more sophisticated than others. Moreover, the systems of each body are generally run under different management regimes, each with its own director of IT and teams of IT managers, for example. At the same time, the financial and contractual bases of the systems of each department also will vary radically – some will have funded the technology themselves, others will have drawn deeply from other government sources and still others may be the subject of some public and private sector partnership (so-called). Underpinning these quite different deals will be a diverse set of contractual arrangements with suppliers, each giving rise to quite different liabilities, obligations and entitlements and each set to run for timescales that do not align. And finally, in this brief catalogue of differences, I invariably see that the operational systems in the various departments share little or no infrastructure (telecommunications, for instance) and were not designed or developed to be interoperable, that is, to work alongside and interact happily with one another.

In summary, I find across every criminal justice system that I examine a set of separate technologies, separate data and separate management. Further, it is generally the case that there is a rather poor track record of collaboration amongst the IT teams of the various departments. The 'not-invented-here syndrome' that characterises many IT functions is far from absent in the criminal justice system, so that, at best, I observe reluctant co-operation, often fuelled by unspoken competition but marred not infrequently by outright hostility.

Another way of characterising the current position, as suggested earlier, is by regarding the criminal justice system as a type of information system. Bizarre though this may sound to many criminal justice workers, it cannot be seriously doubted that a criminal justice system is indeed, in large part, a huge information system, a collection of entities that create, process, share, transmit and in numerous ways manage vast bodies of data, documents, files and information.

However, a systems analyst or business process specialist, when confronted with any modern criminal justice system would say immediately that what is in place is not one criminal justice IT system. Rather, they would identify a collection of loosely connected systems. For the criminal justice system to be regarded as a system, in systems terms, would require a degree of coherence, consistency, rigour and commonality that is simply absent today.

Equally, although the subject is taught at law schools and is referred to as such in ordinary language, the systems specialist would inevitably question whether there is in fact a single criminal justice process to speak of; instead, we find a collection of businesses and operational processes, at least one (and often many more) for each department or agency involved. I accept there is some degree of co-ordination but not enough, in my view, to say, in business or systems analysts' terms, that there is one single process. Evidence of this can be found in connection with case management. While the discipline of case management (a type of project management) is indeed brought to bear in individual agencies, it is a rare criminal justice system that has cradle-to-grave, end-to-end, case management, whereby one case or accused is progressed and monitored by one individual or group from start to finish. On the contrary, a case is handled much like a baton in a relay race on the track – when one participant has done his bit, he passes the case along to the next in line. The best effect a smooth hand-over, while the less impressive tend to fumble and even drop the case.

This lack of genuine system and process is brought sharply into focus when considering a traditional case file. The following is an oversimplification but the general thrust is accurate. An incident occurs. The police open a file or series of files. If the evidence if sufficient, the police will copy part of the file and pass it to the prosecuting authorities. They in turn will add to the file and make a decision as to whether or not to prosecute. If they do, they again will copy a select part of their file to the court. On this model, we now have three files with some considerable overlap. When the file or part of the file is transmitted in electronic form, sometimes the format in which a file is handed along cannot be handled by the recipient's systems, in which event re-entry of the data (time-consuming and, frequently, errorful) is necessary. Note that if a key detail changes (for example, the address of the accused), the necessary update needs to be made to the three hypothesised systems. The administrative and management processes are thus determined in very large part by current organisational and departmental structures and not by the need for optimum case management.

Along with various other factors, IT is leading some enlightened individuals (within and beyond the system) to look forward to days when we can regard the criminal justice system not as a set of overlapping but loosely co-ordinated tasks and events, but instead as a *single process*, made up of a variety of overlapping and interrelated *phases* and supported by one *information system.* This aspiration raises five sets of fundamental issues; relating to organisational integration, incompatibility, common systems, telecommunications infrastructure and the electronic case file, each of which is considered below.

(a) Organisational integration

Those who wish to regard the criminal justice system as one single process are troubled today, as outlined above, by the collection of more or less incompatible systems that are the legacy of the traditional approach. There are three broad strategies that might be adopted to overcome this legacy:

- Assume that current organisational structures (government departments and other agencies and bodies, as currently constituted and empowered) are unalterable, keep and make the most of the existing systems but strive to make them as interoperable and compatible as possible. Until recently, this was the spirit, in England, of what was known as 'CCCJS' (see section 4(a) below).[9]
- Assume that current organisational structures are unalterable, but redesign and introduce some new systems which will enable seamless operation across traditional boundaries. Systems will then come to perform as though they were single, coherent systems. In this way, many of the anomalies and incompatibilities of today will gradually be removed. Working practices would change on this model, as would relationships between agencies. One illustration of this approach, again in England, was that embodied in the IBIS initiative.[10] More ambitious versions of this strategy are also possible (for example, Lord Justice Auld's recommendations, as described in section 4(a) below).
- Take nothing for granted, develop new IT and information systems to support a redesigned, single, integrated and coherent criminal justice system and expect that traditional organisational structures will be broken down entirely in the process. This is genuine business process 're-engineering'. It is long term (say ten years) and revolutionary in nature and I doubt it has been embraced anywhere.

(b) 'Incompatibility'

For sake of completeness, it is worth taking a short detour to clarify the notion of 'incompatibility', a term that rears its head in most discussions of criminal justice technology. On almost any view of the future of the IT underlying the criminal justice system, some rationalisation is required, so that the same information is stored as few times as possible and so that all major systems can operate alongside one another as though they were one system (remembering also that, for reasons of security and confidentiality, the systems must also allow strict access control as well). This requires some level of compatibility.

On one analysis, there are four different levels of compatibility between systems:

- *Incompatible* – the different systems (which can mean either the applications themselves (for example document production) or the underlying database technology) cannot share one single body of data or operate together.

- *Technically compatible but not interoperating* – the different systems may be able to operate together but do not as a matter of fact; and they cannot share one single body of data.
- *Interoperating* – the different systems do actually operate alongside one another and can readily exchange data but they do not share one single body of data.
- *Unified* – the different systems do actually operate alongside one another and can share one single body of data. There is also a version of unification that entails the systems themselves coming together to become one system (as discussed later).

The above classification is deployed later in this paper in the context of Lord Justice Auld's fundamental review of the criminal courts of England.

(c) Common systems

If either of the second or third strategies for organisational strategy noted earlier is adopted, it is important also to have in mind the various elements which might be common to the many information systems across the criminal justice system. This is a challenging area, both in theoretical and practical terms.

It is often said, by those who have an interest in IT usage in the justice system generally, that there should be 'common systems' across all courts and tribunals in a given jurisdiction. Sadly, this is rather simplistic thinking and often presupposes that the computer systems of respective justice agencies are monolithic entities that might usefully be brought together to constitute one, much larger, monolith. The reality is far more complex and subtle. To be sure, a crucial task for any contemporary policy-maker in the justice field is indeed to identify the wide range of interrelationships amongst the various systems and technologies that underpin, say, the civil, family, criminal and tribunal systems. However, to talk starkly of interrelationships between 'systems' does not shed much light. Most computer systems are made up of quite separable component parts and it is entirely meaningful to propose that some parts might be common across a legal system, while others need not be conjoined. The following categorisation (and this is one of many possible ways of cutting the cake) pinpoints various components of systems that might, on the face of it, be developed or maintained in common across the justice system.

(i) The information and data itself

Across the criminal justice system, the same data about individuals, cases, courts, paper files and so forth are needed over and again. It is hard to argue against the proposition that duplication of data, re-keying of information, and transfer from one data format to another, for example, should be eliminated in so far as possible. It follows that, in the criminal system, the main systems (those of the police, the prosecution services, the courts, the prisons and so forth) should, ideally, share a common pool of information and data (this is much more than mere interoperability where one part of the system passes materials electronically to another). However, the need for this 'unification' of data is less obvious as between, say, the civil and tribunal jurisdictions. But it is a clear task for policy-makers in the justice arena, I suggest, to identify those parts of the system where the overlap and sharing of data is so pervasive that common data should be advocated. Sometimes, when there is a need to pass data between systems, trying to establish common data is going too far. Instead, what is needed is interoperability – the capability of systems to pass information easily between one another.

(ii) The user interface

From a judges' point of view, it is obvious that there should be a common judicial user interface, so that the part of the computer system that the judge actually looks at and uses is not different across different jurisdictions. Indeed, all data from all jurisdictions should feed automatically into this single interface. This leads naturally to the concept of a 'judicial portal'. (I suspect a common user interface for many court and tribunal officials would be similarly appropriate.)

(iii) The infrastructure

Some infrastructure should surely be shared, if possible, across all jurisdictions, such as telecommunications, major file servers, relational database management systems and technical support. It would be potentially very inefficient for a justice department (or equivalent) and its agencies to run similar services (in different jurisdictions, such as civil and family) using different infrastructure. This is partly an economy of scale issue, and partly a question of setting up systems so that when interoperability or common data is wanted, then having common infrastructure increases the chances of successful operation. With regard to the telecommunications infrastructure specifically, at the very least, agencies should be able to transfer computer files amongst one another – simply, swiftly, securely, reliably and confidentially.

(iv) Applications

Some applications should be common. It is often argued in England, for example, that case management systems for civil and family should be the same. I am not convinced that they need also be the same as those for criminal but this needs much more analysis and discussion to determine the overlaps, the synergies and the justifications. There are clearly strong arguments, however, for diarying/listing systems to be common – this would help officials with their case load management and, of course, judges who will want one integrated diary (although I accept this could be achieved less elegantly through interoperable systems). The challenge for policy-makers is to identify those applications (software systems, other than operating systems) that, for policy, economic or operational reasons should be common. With regard to the criminal justice system, if it comes to be managed as a unified process, technology that enables cases and files to be accessed and progressed seamlessly from one phase (or agency) to another would become the glue holding the whole system together (see the discussion of the electronic case file below).

(v) Management information

While this is less obviously relevant across the justice, court and tribunal systems generally, it is increasingly important to be able to assess the performance of the entire criminal justice system (productivity, throughput, cost, resources and time scales) with reference not just to individual agencies but across the life of individual cases and groups of cases.[11]

In short, we should be very precise about what systems and what components of systems can and should be common across the different jurisdictions and across the criminal justice system. Do we really mean that entire systems need to be unified? Or are we just referring to the data; or to the user interface; or to the infrastructure; or to the applications; or indeed to the management information systems?

While there are general demands for common systems, there has been little real analysis yet in most advanced legal systems of the nature of that commonality nor justifications for the claim that systems should indeed be common. A powerful set of arguments surely needs to be advanced – on grounds of efficiency, quality, productivity or justice – before it can be said to be imperative to ensure there are common systems (whatever that might mean in any given circumstances).

(d) Telecommunications infrastructure

The issue of telecommunications infrastructure is of particular concern and deserves a little further attention. There are a number of considerations here. In the first instance, without full interoperability or unification of systems (as introduced earlier) across the criminal justice system, little progress can be made in streamlining or indeed re-engineering the system as a whole, if that is indeed wanted. To be realistic, however, it is almost inconceivable in any modern legal system that all agencies and systems could simply jump over onto a new, single telecommunications platform.

In England, the implications of the Government Secure Intranet (GSI) should always be considered, given that it has been conceived precisely as a secure infrastructure to support work across different departments. The GSI, and its equivalents in other countries, supports the government's use of Internet email as well as the secure sharing of information amongst government departments.

The GSI (or equivalent) aside, the reality is that many agencies are already committed to particular networks or infrastructures of their own. At the same time, under private finance agreements, some agencies are essentially outsourcing their infrastructure, although it is unlikely they will have managed to have anticipated all the requirements of a unified criminal justice system. Indeed, their contracts may – directly or indirectly – discourage communications across systems. Similarly, the underlying commercial arrangements (such as a private finance scheme) may preclude the migration of current systems onto some common platform within the life of the contract. In fact, many private finance arrangements, as they have been drafted so far, have not allowed sufficiently for use and access to the systems by agencies beyond those who are parties to the contracts.

(e) The electronic case file

By way of clarification of much of the above, it is instructive to look at the idea of the 'electronic case file', thought by many to be central to the operation of the criminal justice system as a single process. Once created in the first instance, usually by the police, such a file should contain and record all documents and information about each particular case and be able to be available quickly and cheaply across the entire justice system.

Once one part of the system has finished its work on the case (for example, the police), then appropriate parts of the file can either be (a) *passed* or (b) *shared and so made available*, in electronic form to the next part – as an accurate, complete and up-to-date record, ready for attention by the next set of professionals. If it is passed, we are witnessing interoperability of systems that contain the data. If it is shared and so made available, we are seeing unification of data.

On either model, for example, a file might be opened by the police, passed or shared and so made available to the prosecution service, thence to the courts and thereafter to the prison service, each using the information as necessary and contributing additional documents along the way.

Not all parts of the files, of course, could be allowed to travel throughout the system or be shared and so be available to all users – there are certain materials to which the courts should not allow access by the prosecution, for example. And, in due course, when such a system is used for case tracking (so that interested parties can, at the touch of the button, monitor progress on any particular case), again there will be strict access controls, so that, for instance, an accused or his advisers only have access to certain authorised categories of information.

Whether underpinned by interoperability or unification, electronic case files should save costs (for example, by avoiding the costs of duplicate entry of common data); it should increase throughput and productivity (for instance, by reducing delays and loss of files); and promote justice, by ensuring that all relevant information is always at the disposal of decision-makers across the system.

4 Options for the future

In the previous section, I introduced a wide collection of issues and challenges that face anyone trying to introduce IT across a criminal justice system. My purpose now is to show how all of these factors bear on the practicalities of policy-making in the criminal justice sphere. By way of case study, I consider the recommendations on IT made by Lord Justice Auld (Sir Robin) in his Criminal Courts Review.[12] I had the good fortune to be appointed as Sir Robin's 'expert consultee' and so can claim to have some insight into the thinking underlying his recommendations and conclusions.[13]

At an early stage of Sir Robin's investigation of the criminal courts, I placed before him much of the analysis and argument laid out in this paper. His response, as embodied in his seminal and monumental report, was bold, vision-based and, in my view, as correct as one can be in the uncertain world of legal and court technology. He immediately recognised that the greatest possible impact for IT would be across the criminal justice system, although he was supportive of greater investment in various court technologies. He was realistic about the extent of organisational change that was feasible; and so his recommendations, in so far as IT is concerned, do not require any fundamental restructuring of the departments and agencies of the current criminal justice system. Nor do they preclude major change, however. He was keen that IT should encourage rather than hinder progress.

He faced, as all others do when they seek to introduce technology across the criminal justice system, a limited range of options.

(a) The options facing Lord Justice Auld

Five main options were put before Sir Robin.

The first was to encourage or tolerate each department or agency across the criminal justice system to have incompatible systems, with no aspiration to share data amongst one another. This was the situation throughout most of the 1980s and in the very early 1990s as well. This option is now really of historical interest only in England and no step backwards in time was ever contemplated by Sir Robin.

The second option was to encourage or tolerate each department or agency to have technically compatible systems but to have them neither interoperating nor sharing data. This was the position through most of the 1990s – much of the effort of what was known as 'CCCJS' was devoted to achieving technical compatibility.[14] On this option, computer files from one system (for example, documents or databases) can transferred (by email or disk) from one agency to another but there is no attempt to stitch the systems together.

The third option was indeed to set up links between the various systems, so they could indeed be said to be interoperating. The systems are still separate but they are tailored to dovetail with one another. Crucially, however, they do not share one body of data: each has its own files, which are passed along from one department to another. This was the approach adopted by the IBIS.[15]

The fourth option requires that the systems of the various departments do not simply pass data and files from one to the other, like the aforementioned baton in a track event, but share a common body of data. Thus, each department retains separate technology but each draws from and contributes to, under conditions of strict access control, a single body of data and information. This data and information may be held centrally but it might equally be distributed across various systems. From the point of view of users, however, their systems behave as if they are operating on one central store of information. For this reason, I call this option 'virtual unification' – it does not create one monolithic system for the criminal justice system but it behaves as though it is. The underlying systems are interoperating but they are still separate systems. Reflecting back on the distinctions drawn earlier in relation to common systems, this fourth option therefore requires that the data and information are common but not necessarily the user interface, the infrastructure or the applications.

The fifth and final option is what I term full unification. There is one common system (infrastructure, applications and interface) and one shared body of data.

Sir Robin considered each. The first option, as I have said, was not considered as a sensible option. The second option also looked unattractive. Although it prevails in most contemporary criminal justice systems, it is inefficient (given the inevitable duplication and redundancy of much of the data input and maintenance); unreliable (data is often lost, not passed along entirely and mistakes are made); potentially costly (in terms of parallel licensing arrangements and having more than one body of database specialists); non-strategic (in that it prevents information and knowledge being at the fingertips of all conceivable users); restrictive (may obstruct rapid growth or development of the systems of the criminal justice systems in the event of radical reform); and rarely conducive to external confidence in the underpinning technologies.

More than this, Sir Robin was attracted to the idea of the electronic case file and this could not be delivered through the second option. Yet the third option did not seem to make sense either. It has some superficial attractions. It seeks to 'join up' the systems of the various departments and agencies and 'joined-upedness' is something to which the current government in the UK strongly aspires. It also seeks to achieve, as is often said, 'whole system benefits', that is to say, it is beneficial to the criminal justice system as a whole, as well as to (or maybe notwithstanding) the individual departments. This, as mentioned, was the preferred option for IBIS.

On analysis, however, this option is little better than the second option. Precisely because it falls short of unification (virtual or otherwise) and strives only for interoperability, it still suffers from all the drawbacks and problems just outlined in respect of the second option (save for reliability, because the chances of lost data, misplaced data and the creation of new errorful data are greatly reduced). It is hard to resist the conclusion that option three is a medium-term, tactical and often cosmetic fix, driven too frequently by a hankering after a 'quick win' rather than a thoroughgoing improvement to criminal justice technology. It is not a step change. Sadly, it tends to be a step sideways.

This leaves the fourth and fifth options. The fourth was seen by Sir Robin as the minimal solution for the level of integration, efficiency, reliability, cost effectiveness, long-term sustainability and flexibility to which he aspired. The fourth and fifth also passed 'blank sheet of paper' test – if you were asked to design, from scratch, a set of systems to underpin the criminal justice process, what would they look like? If, without the worries of legacy systems, you came up with the first, second or third options, your sanity could reasonably be called into question. But the fourth and fifth options were plausible blueprints.

The fifth option was thought on its own to be unrealistic, however, given the systems, organisations and contracts currently in place; and given also that any attempt to jump, in one single bound, to the single new master-system is, the history of IT projects tells us, doomed from the start.

In the broadest of terms, and leaving aside his numerous suggestions regarding particular technologies (such as video conferencing), Sir Robin made the following recommendations. First, within the court system he argued that the magistrates' and Crown courts should use the same basic systems rather than continue with separate court administration technologies. Second, in relation to the central issues discussed in the current and previous sections of this paper, he advocated and envisaged a 10–12 year programme for the introduction of a new approach to IT across the criminal justice system. Within ten years, he recommended the virtual unification of the systems across the criminal justice system (the fourth option discussed above); and he expected full unification to follow – within 12 years in all (the fifth option). The resultant set-up, he recommended, should support case management (essentially project management) across the entire system: cases would not just be managed within individual departments but would be progressed through the entire system. Further, he recommended that management information systems should operate across the whole system and not just in particular departments – only then will we be able reliably to measure the performance of the criminal justice system as a whole. He also advocated far wider access to the systems, suggesting that lawyers and victims, amongst others, should be able to track the progress of cases across the Internet. He recognised, however, the need for a new body to support the new approach – a Criminal Case Management Agency (discussed below).

Central to all of his recommendations for IT across the criminal justice system, of course, was the fundamental principle – anathema to many justice workers but axiomatic for most systems analysts – that there should be one shared body of data and information from which all departments could draw and into which they would contribute. In proposing unification of data, Sir Robin is sometimes misunderstood. The most fundamental misconception is the belief that he supports the introduction of one huge system in one 'big bang' – a single information system to replace all current systems. Careful reading of his report and examination of the various diagrams reveals the reverse. What is envisaged is, in my words, an evolutionary approach, moving towards a ten-year goal of what I term virtual unification (the fourth option above). The ten-year period, however, is subdivided into five controlled phases, each delivering major benefits in its own right. In other words, having set a point on the horizon, it is not being suggested that nothing happens at all until ten years hence. On the contrary, a series of stepping stones are proposed and, on arrival at each one, new features and benefits will result. Clear progression towards a well articulated goal is the order of the day with a series of substantial and interim deliverables along the way. For example, Sir Robin advocates the introduction of case management across the criminal justice system as one stepping stone and the imposition of management information systems embracing all relevant departments as another. Each of these will clearly bring benefits and improvements in their own right, while simultaneously moving towards the agreed ultimate goal. The contrast here is with an IBIS-like approach which expressly sought incremental improvements for the short and medium term with no longer-term objectives in mind. This is akin to starting a car journey with no destination: you might make good time, enjoy a comfortable ride and avoid bottlenecks but these benefits may or may not contribute to the generally agreed goal of travelling, namely, getting to where you want to be.

Without delving into any technical discussion, it should be noted in passing that the staged progression that is proposed presupposes the division of each departmental computer system into basic building blocks (user interface, enabling technologies, the data and information, communications, and management information systems case management – an approach that echoes the earlier discussion in the context of common systems).

I am often asked about the step from virtual unification to full unification, as anticipated by Sir Robin as a two-year phase following the initial ten-year transition to virtual unification. Two simple points can be made. First, once the data has been virtually unified and so can be shared (and this is no trivial task, requiring a common data standard across all systems[16]), then the job of unifying the technologies is relatively straightforward and will, in my view, follow naturally. And, second, this would make commercial sense – why have duplicating systems, people and licences operating on a shared body of data? The savings could be enormous.

A final recommendation worthy of mention is perhaps one of the most controversial – Sir Robin's suggestion that a new body needed to be set up to support the implementation and ongoing management of his IT proposals. This was his proposed Criminal Case Management Agency.

(b) The government's response

The British government's response to Sir Robin's review should be seen in the context of its wider commitment to modernisation of the public sector generally and to electronic government in particular. In *Modernising Government*, a White Paper published in March 1999,[17] the government set various ambitious IT-related targets: that 25% of dealings with government should be deliverable electronically by 2002; 50% by 2005; and 100% by 2008 (unless there are policy or operational reasons for not so doing).[18] These targets have undergone some refinement since then, as is explained on the *UK online* web site – the current commitment seems to be to have all government service delivered electronically by 2005 and, moreover, to have everyone with access to the Internet by 2005.[19] In a sense, the precise targets are less significant than the overall policy thrust, which is unambiguously in the direction of the deployment of IT in government wherever possible and desirable. Clearly, this commitment to technology applies as much to the delivery of court services as it does to other areas of government. There are some other relevant themes in the Modernising Government programme. One is the commitment to ensuring that public services are genuinely citizen-facing (designed to support the community and not for the convenience of the service provider). Another is the theme of 'joined-up government' in accordance with which government departments and agencies should work together far more closely in the delivery of citizen-facing services.

If one adds these themes of modernisation and of electronic government to the proposition put forward at the outset of this paper, that criminal justice is high up the government agenda for action and investment, one can see that the criminal justice system is an ideal test-bed for the introduction of IT. Thus, in the government's formal response to Sir Robin, in expressly supporting him, it is clearly stated that:

> 'Making the best possible use of IT is fundamental if we are to have a modern joined up system that delivers fast, effective justice. We agree that lack of common IT is one of the main impediments to achieving better overall management of the CJS.'[20]

As to Sir Robin's specific recommendations, the government is also in agreement with his proposal for a single system in the magistrates' and Crown courts.[21]

When it comes to Sir Robin's more ambitious recommendation – for unification – this is rejected by the government, whose preference is 'to join together existing and developing IT systems in a staged development'.[22] This is expanded upon in their White Paper, *Justice for All*,[23] para 9.57 of which reads:

> 'Sir Robin Auld proposed building a new integrated IT system. However, whilst recognising some advantages, our preferred approach is to join together the existing and developing IT systems in a staged development, using an "information walkway" to link individual systems.'

This is not an easy paragraph to follow, not least because, contrary to what is said: (a) Sir Robin did not in fact advocate a 'new' system and (b) Sir Robin did in fact recommend a staged development. Similarly mystifying, I am afraid, is para. 9.58 of the White Paper, which rightly (in my view) goes on to recommend a modular and evolutionary approach as an alternative to Sir Robin's alleged 'big bang' approach. And yet, once again, given that Sir Robin's recommendation was clearly not to adopt a 'big bang' tack and was expressly modular and evolutionary, it is all but impossible to follow the drift of the government's argument. In the end, it may not matter, because the substance of the government's policy thus far articulated seems, in my view, entirely sensible. The fact that it accords with Sir Robin's thinking and yet there is a reluctance to acknowledge this is a matter over which others may care to speculate.

More importantly, it is not easy to offer a definitive view on the government's position on criminal justice IT because no details are offered about the 'information walkway' that would allow readers to judge what is envisaged here. If the walkway is no more than a metaphor for greater interoperability, then I would be hugely disappointed because this would constitute no more than a glorified Option Three and would suffer from the various shortcomings that I outlined earlier. This would be IBIS II, which would not be welcome; it would be a massive opportunity missed. However, as I dearly and optimistically hope, if shared data and information might sit on the walkway, then what is in mind is an Option Four solution which would be very encouraging indeed.

There is cause to be optimistic because various other vital signs are positive. In the White Paper, for example, it is confirmed (para 9.47) that a budget of £600m is being allocated to criminal justice IT over the next three years; for the first time, a Minister for Justice Systems Information Technology has been appointed (para 9.59) and he is supported by a full-time Director General of Criminal Justice Information Technology); and three, practical targets for improvement have been set: by 2003, secure email should be in place across the criminal justice system – by 2005 all criminal justice organisations will be able to exchange case file information electronically – and victims will begin to be able to track the progress of their cases online (para 9.48).

Moreover, useful web sites have already been launched to improve information to the public and practitioners.[24]

Finally, on the government's response, Sir Robin's proposal for a Criminal Justice Case Management Agency was rejected.[25] While this was never likely to have been popular with the Home Office, the Lord Chancellor's Department and the Attorney General, my prediction is that, if there is indeed virtual unification of systems and, further, case management across the criminal justice system is introduced, then some new body will in due course come into being. I say this if only because it is hard to imagine how any existing department could uncontroversially and with complete propriety (a) take on the task of managing (for example, maintaining the integrity and security of) criminal information created and used exclusively by another department (even if it does sit in some central pool) and (b) assume the responsibility of managing cases through other departments. Time will tell.

(c) Problems and obstacles

In England and elsewhere, of course, there are many obstacles in the path of introducing IT across a criminal justice system in the way envisaged by Sir Robin and in this paper generally. Some are technical. The projected systems are complex and large scale. Governments, the world over, have lamentable track records for delivering, on time and within budget, complex large-scale systems that actually do what is wanted. While poor project management can be said to explain many classic failures, the reality is that major IT projects are, simply, difficult.

There are commercial obstacles too. Big systems cost big money. That said, as in England, if crime is high on the political agenda, cash will be tend to be found in the unfathomable depths of the public purse. And if not, there is still life left, in my view, in public/private joint financing schemes.

Concerns over privacy should not be underestimated. Proposals to create vast, unified bodies of crime-related data rightly set off alarm bells in the ears of those who worry about technology encouraging the impingement of the liberties of citizens. I have not found the objections I have heard voiced on grounds of privacy to be entirely compelling in this context but there is unquestionably a case to answer and the need for some crisp argument and frank debate.

The biggest obstacle, I fear, is organisational-cum-cultural. More specifically, I am pessimistic about the willingness of government departments to collaborate – to work together productively, to cede responsibility and resource even if this makes sense from a 'whole system' perspective, to avoid departmental turf wars, and to eschew 'not-invented-here syndrome' when appraising the systems of others. In support of my pessimism, one need look no further than the nervousness across key departments engendered by Sir Robin's proposal for the establishment of a Criminal Case Management Agency. More lamentable still, one can but wonder, but in a different context, at the hostile resistance of central government to the entirely sound proposals of Sir Andrew Leggatt for the rationalisation of the tribunal system of England (even if his suggestions did demand the shrinking of some departmental empires).[26]

5 What relevant work is going on in other jurisdictions?

There is much to be learned from the many initiatives in other jurisdictions that are seeking to exploit IT for their criminal justice systems. The aim here is not to undertake a detailed review or analysis of all the systems in other jurisdictions but to point to some instructive efforts and provide some references for further reading. The following, then, is by way of snapshot of some of the most promising and interesting initiatives in other jurisdictions:

1. Project Pathfinder, commissioned by the Victorian Department of Justice in Australia, seems to be one of the most thoroughgoing attempts to 're-engineer' a criminal justice system. IT seems to be at the heart of this major integration exercise, especially the proposed JIX (Justice Information Exchange) system, which is a form of electronic case flow system of the sort envisaged in this report.[27]

2. In Ontario, Canada, the IJP (Integrated Justice Project) is along similar lines to Pathfinder and has been described as one of the largest justice modernisation projects in the world.[28] This project is run as a partnership between the provincial government and a consortium of four, private sector companies; and the partners share the risks and the profits.[29] Also in Canada, in Alberta, interesting work has been done on electronic appeal books.[30]
3. In the USA, a considerable amount of work has been done on the integration of justice information systems.[31] Activity at federal court level seems less relevant than progress in the state courts, although interesting work is going on in related areas.[32]
4. Colorado is said to be the first state to have introduced an integrated justice information system. It is described as: 'an integrated computer information system that links the five state-level criminal justice agencies – law enforcement, prosecution, courts, and adult and juvenile corrections – creating one virtual criminal justice information system. This enables all criminal justice agencies to track offenders through the criminal justice system from arrest and prosecution to adjudication and incarceration.' In light of the earlier analysis in this paper, it is interesting to note that the system 'is a virtual database because it provides access to information contained on each of the five systems without unnecessary data duplication between the agencies' legacy systems'.[33]
5. In Scotland, the ISCJIS programme (Integration of Scottish Criminal Justice Information Systems) is progressing well, offering a live example of what can be achieved within the UK.[34] Further, progress on sentencing information technology in Scotland has been considerable.[35]

Note, however, that while many other, smaller jurisdictions will report successes, it has to be emphasised that it is far easier to achieve change through technology in jurisdictions of more manageable size (England suffers from 'supertanker syndrome' – it is hard to stop or change direction).

More generally, any reports of successes must always be viewed with caution. It is only once one has spoken with users and seen demonstrations of live systems that firm conclusions can safely be drawn. It may even be that, since the research underlying this paper was conducted, some of the above projects have become unstuck.

6 The way ahead

Finally, it is worth considering, by way of conclusion, some broad requirements for the successful introduction of IT into the criminal courts in particular and across the criminal justice system more generally. Experience from other industries, other governments, and other jurisdictions suggests that the productive deployment of IT in a modern justice system requires the following:

1. a clearly articulated *vision* of the criminal justice system itself – a high level, unwavering view of the end result of any proposed reforms, without which any introduction of IT is likely either to be rather unfocused or brought into play for the sake of technology rather than in support of some broader aim;
2. an approach to the use of IT that is vision-based and not legacy-based, that is, driven by a medium- to long-term vision of what it is intended that the technology should achieve, rather than a desire for 'quick wins' or for incremental improvements on today's systems (in summary, not 'staggering backwards into the future');

3. a centrally co-ordinated IT strategy (short, medium and long term) for the entire criminal justice system, developed in conjunction with all relevant interest groups, indicating what investment is necessary, identifying the anticipated benefits and embracing the vision of how the criminal process will function with the new technologies in place;
4. unambiguous and explicitly articulated support for an IT-based criminal justice system, from relevant, senior political figures and civil servants as well as judges and lawyers;
5. recognition that substantial financial investment is vital if the vision is to be realised and yet acknowledgment that this funding may not always need to be sourced directly by central government;
6. commitment to ongoing, well targeted research and development programmes, aimed at generating results which will ensure that the available IT is being exploited to the full and that technical innovations are being recognised and deployed as early as possible – just as has always been the case in many hi-tech industries, research and development initiatives will become far more important in the legal world, not just for commercial organisations seeking to achieve competitive advantage and good practice in their sectors, but also in government and in the court system as well, where it will be increasingly important for IT to be (and be seen to be) used efficiently, productively, and competitively too (in international terms). At the very least, it will be vital to maintain ongoing research into progress in other jurisdictions and into emerging mainstream technologies;
7. acceptance that many of the most substantial and beneficial influences of IT will come from *innovation* rather than *automation*; and
8. realisation that the Internet and the World Wide Web especially (the global information infrastructure) are fundamentally changing the nature of communications and information dissemination in society and so are likely to exert a massive influence on the development of criminal justice.

One formidable, additional challenge in this context is to persuade senior individuals, in a variety of bodies and agencies, of the advantages of the use of IT and of collaboration and standardisation. It is unlikely that this can or will be done solely by written papers or through oral discussion. It is invariably helpful to accompany these with a few simple *demonstrator systems,* which can show, in straightforward terms, what the police, prosecutors, judges, officials, or prison staff (as the case may be) could actually have at their fingertips, on their screens, in a few years. This could be very persuasive and help create a genuinely shared vision.

NOTES

1 Email richard@susskind.com.

2 See Jon Bing and Trygve Harvold *Legal Decisions and Information Systems* (Universitetsforlaget, Oslo, 1977), pp 67–68.

3 See Colin Tapper *Computers and the Law* (Weidenfeld and Nicolson, London, 1973).

4 See www.ukonline.gov.uk.

5 A fuller discussion of the many categories of application was laid out by Richard Susskind in 'Information Technology for the English Judiciary – Notes of a Presentation to the Judicial Technology Group' 13 July 1999 (unpublished).

6 A special issue of the International Journal of Law and Information Technology, (1998) 6 (2) IJLIT, is devoted entirely to judicial sentencing support systems.

7 For detailed analysis, see 'Speaking Up for Justice' (Report of the Interdepartmental Working Group on the treatment of Vulnerable or Intimidated Witnesses in the Criminal Justice System, Home Office, June 1998). Also see Plotnikoff and Woolfson 'A publication arising from section 57 of the Crime and Disorder Act 1998' (Video Link Pilot Evaluation, 1999).
8 See www.tecsa.org.uk/tecsa/itprotoc.htm.
9 CCCJS stands for Co-ordination of Computerisation in the Criminal Justice System. See Robin Page 'IT Technical Standards Policy for the Criminal Justice System' in (1992) 2(6) Computers in the Law 8.
10 IBIS (Integrating Business and Information Systems in the Criminal Justice System) was the major initiative that aimed towards 'joined-up' IT systems for case handling in England and Wales. It replaced CCCJS, a programme which ran during much of 1990s without great practical impact. IBIS produced its Medium Term Strategic Plan, which sought to set out 'what can be achieved by better sharing of information between the organisations in the CJS' (police, CPS, magistrates' courts, Court Service, probation and prison services). See 'Medium Term Strategic Plan for Information Systems in the Criminal Justice System' (Home Office Communications Directorate, 1999). IBIS has since been disbanded, not least (in my view) because there was always an inherent tension in pursuing short/medium-term plans which might have taken the criminal justice system in a direction that would later make it impractical to pursue some desirable longer-term approaches.
11 Cf Audit Commission *Route to Justice: improving the pathway of offenders through the criminal justice system* (2002) p 71: 'The sharing of performance and management information between CJS agencies and areas is severely hampered by out-of-date and non-integrated information technology.'
12 Rt Hon Lord Justice Auld *Review of the Criminal Courts of England and Wales* (The Stationery Office, London, October 2001) especially pp 304–308, 353–366, 500–503.
13 I am extremely grateful to Lord Justice Auld for allowing me to discuss our work together in this paper.
14 See above, n 9.
15 See above, n 10.
16 Valuable unpublished work by the Home Office has been undertaken in this direction.
17 See www.cabinet-office.gov.uk/moderngov.
18 See www.cabinet-office.gov.uk/moderngov.
19 www.ukonline.gov.uk.
20 Appendix to the White Paper *Justice for All* (Cm 5563, July 2002) entitled *Responses to the Auld and Halliday Reports* p 24.
21 P 24.
22 P 27.
23 Cm 5563, July 2002.
24 www.cjsonline.org and www.juror.cjsonline.org.
25 Above n 20, p 27.
26 This is a story for another time. See Sir Andrew Leggatt *Tribunals for Users* (The Stationery Office, 2001).
27 See *Technology and the Law*, Report of the Victorian Law Reform Committee (May 1999) pp 81–85, at www.parliament.vic.gov.au/lawreform/tech. This report is an important document. Generally, Australia is the home of many of the world's most interesting applications of IT in the law.
28 See (1998–99) 26 Computer News for Judges 8–10 at www.cjc-ccm.gc.ca.
29 The address of the project is www.integratedjustice.gov.on.ca.
30 See www.ncsc.dni.us/NCSC/TIS/CTC5/102.HTM.
31 See eg www.integration.search.org.
32 See eg the comprehensive analysis in 'Privacy and Access to Electronic Case Files in the Federal Courts' at www.uscourts.gov/privacyn.htm.
33 See www.state.co.us/gov_dir/cicjis/index.html as well as an article on the systems at www.govtech.net/publications/gt/1997/oct/jandt/jandt.shtm. For information on state courts generally and their use of technology, there are useful links leading from www.ncsconline.org.
34 The regularly published 'ISCJIS Bulletin' is a convenient source (obtainable through The Scottish Office Home Department).
35 See above n 6.

Defining and rewarding invention: a review and a modest proposal for patent law

David Vaver*

Professor Colin Tapper was a member of the electoral board that in 1997 appointed me to my present position at Oxford as Reuters Professor of Intellectual Property and Information Technology Law. He also introduced the inaugural lecture I delivered in May 2000. I therefore have my own reasons to be grateful to him. More importantly, Colin Tapper continues to play a central role in the research and teaching of intellectual property and information technology law within the university.

His interest in those fields goes back some time. He has published widely in them but, for me, his most important sustained work is the monograph he published 25 years ago, *Computer Law*. Just under 200 pages long, it was the first monograph on the subject and told all there was then to know about the law relating to computers. The complexity of the subject belied the simplicity of the title. Appropriately enough, the first chapter dealt with intellectual property rights for computers, and the first possibility discussed was that of patenting. The prominence devoted to patenting, particularly for computer programs, continued throughout the three later editions of *Computer Law*.

In the first edition, Tapper introduced the topic by saying: 'Patenting computer programmes is an inherently controversial topic.'[1] Controversy has dogged the issue ever since, even though that sentence had been dropped by the time the fourth edition of *Computer Law* came out in 1990. That edition was over twice as long as the first; so, correspondingly, was the discussion of patents and other intellectual property rights.

A central doctrinal question with which Tapper dealt was the very basic issue of whether or not a computer program could technically qualify at all as an invention under patent law. Tapper had little doubt that it could, although he displayed more ambivalence about whether, as a matter of policy, patenting or some *sui generis* scheme was the best means by which to provide appropriate protection for the programming industry. *Sui generis* protection for computer-related inventions continues to have it adherents. Nevertheless, the idea that a computer program can and should qualify as an invention under patent law has come to dominate the field internationally. This paper will not enter the lists of *sui generis* protection *vel non*. Rather, in the absence of a fifth edition of Tapper's *Computer Law*, I shall update the discussion of the notion of invention in patent law for emerging technologies generally.

Following Tapper's non-Panglossian spirit,[2] I shall suggest that the way in which inventions are currently screened for patentability may not be the best of all possible worlds, and that a more publicly accountable scheme of patenting merits consideration.

1 Preliminary

The patent system is based on the theory that people should be granted an exclusive time-limited right to encourage them to produce, or to reward them for having produced, certain results that are thought to be socially beneficial. The results typically stem from experiments and research to solve a problem in the industrial sphere, and produce some new and unobvious solution to that problem – be it a new article, substance or method, or an improvement on previous technology. Without the prospect of such a grant of rights, fewer people and resources would, it is generally believed, be attracted to such activities, and consequently fewer solutions would be sought or discovered. A lower rate of social progress and less social well-being would ensue – at least, so the standard story goes.[3]

The beneficial results for which society rewards such researchers with a patent are called inventions. The important question is, of course, what results should be so classified. Anything outside that category will not be patentable and so will fall into the public domain once it is marketed or becomes otherwise publicly available. The product or process can then be freely copied (or independently created) without tribute to the patent holder – at least, unless some other intellectual property or unfair competition law, or binding obligation of confidentiality, intervenes.

The question of what subject matter falls under the concept of invention can be conveniently separated from other qualities the invention must have. Analytically, this proposition exemplifies the familiar Aristotelian dichotomy between essence/kind on the one hand, and attributes/quality on the other, also reflected in other intellectual property laws. Thus, in copyright law, what qualifies as an artistic work (its 'essence' or 'kind') is analytically distinct from the question whether the work is 'original' or not (its 'attribute' or 'quality'). Similarly, in patent law, what qualifies as an invention – the 'subject matter' of the grant – is distinguishable from other criteria of patentability, ie that the invention must be (1) new, (2) not obvious, (3) useful, and (4) adequately disclosed in the specification.[4]

These preliminary observations bring us to the question: 'what is an invention'?

2 The definition of invention

(a) Who defines 'invention'?

'Invention' is not a self-defining concept. Etymologically, the modern verb 'invent' comes *via* Middle English from the Latin *invenire*, meaning to find or contrive. *Inventio* is the noun form. According to English language dictionaries, 'to invent' tends to be defined as to create by thought, to devise or originate (for example a new method or an instrument). 'Invention' correspondingly means 'thing invented', and is often accompanied by the further explanation: 'especially something for which a patent is granted'.

Neither the etymology of the word 'invention' nor its modern usage reveals the precise parameters of the concept – nor should we expect them to, for the notion of invention is a legal term of art. It is defined by legislatures, and the legislative definitions are interpreted according to legal criteria by courts, tribunals and officials such as patent examiners and patent office appeal boards. Like other terms of art, the definition and interpretative contours of 'invention' are not immutably fixed: they have changed over time and have often differed – and may still differ, at least marginally – among jurisdictions. The term of art meaning of 'invention' has naturally affected, and continues to affect, the concept's popular meaning, but popular meaning cannot determine the meaning of a legal term of art.

It is entirely proper for 'invention' to be considered as a legal term of art, for the purposes of the patent law. In that way, its definition may be shaped by the policies espoused from time to time by the patent legislation as interpreted by courts and tribunals. The difficulty is that invention is something which, by its nature, cannot be fully known or defined in advance. The concept is dynamic, not static. Were the same legislators who voted for a piece of patent legislation 20 years ago now faced with the question whether or not a newly emergent technology should be patented, their views might very well differ today from those they may have held 20 years ago. Of course, their world view may have progressed meanwhile. But, just as likely, the new technology may present them with issues which were barely perceptible or not conceived of at all earlier.

This truism is evident worldwide from recent disputes about whether any and, if so, which biotechnologies should be patented. Part of the dispute revolved around the ontology and teleology of 'invention': for the purposes of the patent law, can some or all of the products of genetic engineering properly be classed as 'inventions' rather than 'discoveries'? But the perhaps more important part of the debate has been deontological: *ought* this result, patentable in law, be patentable *in fact*? As importantly, who decides?

Currently such decisions are made by patent offices, patent office appeal boards, and courts. Legislators may become involved, but a long period of uncertainty often ensues as they debate the issues and their involvement ceases once the legislation is passed. The result may not prove particularly satisfactory and may need to be revisited: the technology or public opinion may have shifted even during the period of the legislators' debate. The legislation may well look obsolete as soon as it is passed; but thereafter patentability is treated as a technical question for specialists in patent law. The public has no continuing input on the point. Moreover, once the specialists have interpreted the legislation to encompass a new technology, it proves hard to go back. The courts rarely 'disrupt the settled expectations of the inventing community' by reducing extensions to patent scope;[5] nor will legislatures.

Public input here is critical if the patent system is to command public respect. Patenting is not just a matter between a particular industry (or industry in general) and the patent office, nor even between an industry and the government ministries responsible for patents and innovation policy. How to provide such input is an issue which will be considered in the concluding section of this paper.

(b) International usage

The legal definition of invention is not left solely to the discretion of national legislatures or of supranational law-making institutions such as those of the European Union.

(i) TRIPs and 'invention'

Since 1994, 'invention' has acquired an international dimension through art 27.1 of the TRIPs Agreement.[6] That provision requires member states of the World Trade

Organization (WTO) to make patents available 'for any inventions, whether products or processes, in all fields of technology', if they are 'new, involve an inventive step and are capable of industrial application'. The proposed European Patent Convention of 2000 (proposed EPC) virtually repeats this definition, with the immaterial substitution of 'susceptible' for 'capable'.[7] The same article of TRIPs emphasises that patents should be available 'without discrimination ... as to the field of technology'.

The TRIPs language reveals little else about what qualifies or should qualify as an 'invention'. The phrase in art 27.1 – 'any inventions, whether products or processes' – includes the main examples of invention, seemingly without attempting to be exhaustive. European patent law has long treated both products and processes as patentable, and this position undoubtedly will continue under the proposed EPC.[8] Similarly, inventions must fall within a field of 'technology' but this advances thought very little: 'technology' as a concept seems as elusive as 'invention'. The main idea behind including 'all fields of technology' in the TRIPs language is to prevent states from excluding any area of human endeavour – for example agriculture or medicine – from patentability for national sectoral public policy or economic reasons. What constitutes the outer limits of 'technology' is left open for discussion or interpretation.

(ii) TRIPs and exceptions to patentability

The obligation under TRIPs, art 27.1 is qualified in three ways:

(A) PUBLIC ORDER EXCEPTIONS

First, TRIPs recognises that states may wish to discourage certain activities because of their perceived adverse social consequences. It may seem inconsistent, on the one hand, to discourage such matters by a state's social laws while, on the other, encouraging new forms or means of producing or exploiting them by offering the opportunity of reward through the patent law. TRIPs, art 27.2 therefore allows states to exclude certain inventions from patentability, namely, those –

> 'the prevention within their territory of the commercial exploitation of which is necessary to protect *ordre public* or morality, including to protect human, animal or plant life or health or to avoid serious prejudice to the environment, provided that such exclusion is not made merely because the exploitation is prohibited by their law.'

This provision reflects a similar provision in the present and proposed EPC,[9] but is not always present or explicit in other laws.

(B) SOCIAL OR ETHICAL EXCEPTIONS

Secondly, TRIPs recognises that states have historically excluded certain categories of things from patentability for a variety of social or ethical reasons. States may wish to continue these exclusions until a different social or ethical consensus emerges in their territory. Article 27.3 accordingly provides a closed list of permitted exclusions: diagnostic, therapeutic and surgical methods for treating humans or animals; plants and animals other than micro-organisms; and essentially biological processes for the production of plants or animals.

The reasons for excluding these items are not always the same. One may infer that the items are all capable of being classified as 'inventions' but that some other reason may dictate their exclusion. Thus, the present EPC excludes medical and diagnostic treatments because these are considered not to be 'inventions which are susceptible of industrial application'. In other words, a new treatment may involve invention but surgery, diagnosis and the like are professional individual skills that are, or should, not be 'susceptible of industrial application.'

The proposed EPC continues the exclusion, but this time without providing any specific reason[10] – as is permissible, since TRIPs lets states choose how to implement its provisions.[11] The proposed EPC does confirm the patentability of 'products, in particular substances or compositions, for use in any of these methods',[12] ie the current European practice (sometimes followed outside Europe) of allowing Swiss-type claims for new or old substances for use in medical treatment where the inventiveness lies in their particular medical application.

Other states apply the TRIPs medical treatment exception in different ways. Thus, in Canada, surgical treatment is not specifically excluded from patentability but Canadian courts have interpreted 'invention' in the Canadian Patent Act to apply only to inventions in the field of trade and industry, not for professional skills. Such skills are to be exercised in the interests of a particular client or patient and not traded as a commodity. Thus, advocacy is among the skills that are unpatentable: 'a barrister who has devised a particular method of cross-examination [cannot] obtain a monopoly thereof so as to require imitators or followers of his methods to obtain a licence from him.'[13]

'Cannot' in this quotation imports a legal decision, but one partly influenced by a mixture of ethical and public policy reasons. These include the fact that professionals, often already benefiting from a state-granted monopoly to practise their skills for the public benefit, should not seek to enclose their skills through monopoly or other means, but should rather share them as widely as possible for the public benefit. Professionals, moreover, do not need the spur of a patent to do their best for their clients; professional codes of conduct require that of them in any event. Nor should they be prevented by a patent from acting in the best interests of the client or patient – particularly important when life-saving surgery is being undertaken.

(c) PLANTS AND SEEDS

Thirdly, TRIPs, art 27.3(b) lets WTO members choose how they wish to protect plant varieties: 'either by patents or by an effective *sui generis* system or by any combination thereof.' The provision reflects the fact that many states have passed plant breeders' rights legislation pursuant to a version of the international plant variety protection treaty, UPOV. Article 27.3(b) does not mandate UPOV-style legislation: any *sui generis* system that protects plant varieties effectively in a non-discriminatory way suffices under TRIPs. Developed states may let plant breeders acquire patent and plant breeder rights cumulatively if they wish, so long as the product may be described in a way that falls within the subject matter definition of both statutes.[14] Alternatively, they may (as in the EU) allow partial cumulation: a patent if the technology applies to more than one variety, a plant breeder right where the technology produces only a single new variety of plant.[15]

More recently, the TRIPs review at Doha, Qatar, in November 2001 produced a ministerial declaration requiring a broader consideration of plant variety protection issues that would take into account the concerns relating to biodiversity and the protection of traditional knowledge and folklore particularly for developing countries.[16]

(D) EPC EXCEPTIONS NOT REPEATED IN TRIPS

Exceptions in the present and proposed EPC, not mirrored specifically in TRIPs, are the following:[17]

> '(a) discoveries, scientific theories and mathematical methods;
> (b) aesthetic creations;
> (c) schemes, rules and methods for performing mental acts, playing games or doing business, and programs for computers;
> (d) presentations of information ...
> ... only to the extent to which a European patent application or European patent relates to such subject-matter or activities as such.'

These things may presumably be excluded, consistently with TRIPs, art 27.1, as being neither 'inventions' nor concerned with some 'field of technology'. Whether business methods and computer programs, now patentable in the United States, may properly be excluded under the EPC for such reasons is a question currently under debate.

(c) Teleology of 'invention'

Historically, the concept of invention has been inextricably tied to the purpose of the patent legislation as it has developed and been perceived over time.

(i) Old UK law: 'any manner of new manufacture'

In 1623, the English Parliament passed the Statute of Monopolies to curb profligacy in the exercise of the royal power in granting monopolies. An exception was, however, made by s 6 of the Statute for 14-year grants:

> 'of the sole working or making of any manner of new manufactures within the realm, to the true and first inventor and inventors of such manufactures, which others at the time of making such letters patent and grant shall not use, so as also they be not contrary to the law nor mischievous to the state, by raising prices of commodities at home, or hurt of trade, or generally inconvenient ...'

This language of 'any manner of new manufactures' remained part of the British patent law as a de facto definition of invention until the United Kingdom enacted the Patent Act 1977 to implement the EPC of 1973. We may note that, right from the start, British patent legislation accepted that not all manufactures were thought worthy of patenting. Those that were 'mischievous to the state' in the three stipulated ways, including broadly being 'generally inconvenient', would not be patented.

(ii) Other countries continue old UK law

Even today, some countries maintain the 1624 formula. Australia's completely remodelled and revamped Patent Act 1990 provides that: '"invention" means any manner of new manufacture the subject of letters patent and grant of privilege within section 6 of the *Statute of Monopolies* ...' Australia's deliberate retention of a formula introduced in its early days as a British colony reflects its relative satisfaction with the way in which the courts had treated the term over the years.

The leading Australian decision is that of its High Court in 1959. The court unanimously reversed the Patent Office's refusal to accept claims for a method of deploying a known chemical for a new use as a selective herbicide. The court held that it was wrong to conduct, as the Patent Office had, a purely linguistic analysis into whether or not the claimed method was a 'manner of manufacture'. The Office should have delved 'not into the meaning of the word[s] so much as into the breadth of the concept which the law has developed by its consideration of the text and purpose of the *Statute of Monopolies*'. In a much quoted passage, the court observed:

> 'The purpose of s. 6 [of the *Statute of Monopolies*], it must be remembered, was to allow the use of the prerogative to encourage national development in a field which already, in 1623,[18] was seen to be excitingly unpredictable. To attempt to place upon the idea the fetters of an exact verbal formula could never have been sound. It would be unsound to the point of folly to attempt to do so now, when science has made such advances that the concrete applications of the notion which were familiar in 1623 can be seen to provide only the more obvious, not to say the more primitive, illustrations of the broad sweep of the concept.'[19]

Since then, the Australian courts have accepted that computer programs, methods of medical treatment, and possibly even business methods may qualify as patentable subject matter.[20] At one time, patenting any of these inventions might have been considered 'generally inconvenient'. The New Zealand Court of Appeal thought this to be so for medical treatment, which, after a full review of the Commonwealth jurisprudence, it held to be unpatentable in 1982.[21] More recently, Australian courts have taken a different view, holding that it is not 'generally inconvenient' to patent medical treatments.[22]

The recent trend, both in Australia and New Zealand, is to read this exception narrowly.[23] In short, the courts themselves now find the qualification itself to be generally inconvenient. Previously, Australian and New Zealand courts tended to retain judicially created exceptions to patentability, saying that any change to long-established exceptions should be made only by Parliament. The contrary presumption now seems more prevalent: the courts can and do eliminate exceptions for which they claim to see no justification, saying that Parliament can always correct them if they are wrong.[24]

(iii) US and Canadian definitions of 'invention'

United States courts and the US patent office have similarly taken the view that 'anything under the sun that is made by man'[25] is patentable. The case in which that somewhat hyperbolic statement (from the *travaux préparatoires* of the 1952 US patent amendments) was approved involved the grant of a patent for a genetically modified bacterium which degraded fuel oil.[26] Computer programs, business methods and genetically modified animals (excluding humans) have progressively been swept within the language of 'anything under the sun that is made by man'. This process has occurred even though the wording of the US patent law, in this respect little changed from the early nineteenth century, is rather different. The US Patent Act allows inventors to patent only 'any new and useful process, machine, manufacture, or composition of matter, or any new and useful improvement thereof'.

Canada has a provision similar to that of the United States, except that the US wording, with the addition of 'art', appears as a definition of 'invention' in the Canadian Patent Act:

> '"invention" means any new and useful art, process, machine, manufacture or composition of matter, or any new and useful improvement in any art, process, machine, manufacture or composition of matter.'

Canadian courts have, however, been more reluctant than their US counterparts to allow patenting, particularly for more contentious new technologies. Thus, computer programs, computerised business methods, cross-bred plants, and methods of medical treatment have not been accepted as falling within the definition of invention.[27] Even more interestingly, the Canadian Supreme Court, by a narrow 5:4 majority, recently rejected an application to patent the Harvard onco-mouse. The court said that the new genetic technologies were not intended to, and did not, fit well within Canada's patent legislation; it was for Parliament to amend the law, if it wished, to cater specifically for these new technologies. The fact that the United States had interpreted the concept of invention broadly was no reason why Canada should do so in this instance.[28]

3 Different approaches to patentability

It is useful to compare the United States and European approaches to deciding whether or not an invention is patentable as a prelude to considering the difficulties arising from each approach and possible reforms. The US approach embodies one end of the spectrum; the European is towards the other.[29] The operation of these two approaches may then be conveniently considered by reference to two technologies: genetically modified animals and business methods.

(a) Current differences between US and European approaches

The United States patent system, in accepting that anything under the sun that is made by man is patentable, firmly takes the view that any advance, good or bad, deserves the reward of a patent. The patent system is there to grant property rights. Property is thought to be good in itself and therefore deserving of encouragement: the more property there is, the greater the incentive to use and profit from it, and the better off society will be as a whole (ignoring distributive effects – which is to ignore a lot). Under this conception, the grant of property is sharply distinguished from its use. Just as a gun can be used for good or ill, so may a property right. Just as any quantity of guns can freely be made, so may any quantity of patents be created. Just as it is the job of other laws – tort or criminal law – to regulate the use of guns, so it is the job of such other laws – including competition law – to regulate the use of patent rights.

Patent law in Europe has developed differently. Patents are indeed property rights but their grant is not automatic. Technology may be good or bad; if bad, it should be discouraged at the earliest point. Certainly, there should be no incentive to develop anti-social technologies by offering the prospect of a patent, or indeed any other privilege or subsidy.

The European sentiment is deeply-rooted. In the UK, patents started off as monopolistic privileges that were granted at the discretion of the monarch. They were not available as of right. That view prevailed in its strongest form before the passage of the Statute of Monopolies in 1623. Battles in the seventeenth century before the courts and in Parliament led to curbs, contained in that Statute, on both the type of monopoly granted and also the circumstances in which that type could be legitimately refused. Patents thenceforth could be granted by the Crown for, inter alia, manners of new manufacture but only if the patent would not, in the words of the Statute, be 'mischievous to the state by raising prices of commodities at home, or hurt of trade, or generally inconvenient'.

The first and second of these grounds were probably always thought of as window-dressing: monopolies inevitably raised prices and, by suppressing competition, hurt someone's trade. The third was potentially more significant. It signalled that the decision to patent could take into account contemporary economic and social policies. In the sixteenth century, for example, the social disorder which high unemployment might bring was widely feared; it was therefore deemed 'inconvenient' to patent machines that would throw workers out of jobs. This view fell into desuetude: progress, not employment, was a right; social disorder could be repressed in progress's name. The proviso in the Statute was reinterpreted with the times, without completely losing force. Thus, in the twentieth century, as noted earlier, the question whether medical or surgical treatments can be patented has been decided partly by reference to whether patenting them would be 'generally inconvenient'.

The current references in European law, reflected in TRIPs, to refusing patents where the exploitation of an invention would be 'contrary to '*ordre public*' or morality',[30] continue to emphasise that patenting is not a morally neutral act. Patents may no longer be refused in the state's general discretion, nor are the EPC/TRIPs grounds potentially as wide as the old 'generally inconvenient' ground. Nevertheless, as Cornish puts it: 'The state, as granting authority, cannot disclaim responsibility for the inventions for which it grants protection.'[31] Inventors can claim no natural right to benefit from immoral or socially disruptive activity, however ingenious.

(b) Patenting animals

The differences between the United States and Europe are well exemplified in the case of the Harvard onco-mouse. When the application to patent this genetically engineered animal came before the EPO, the EPO explicitly weighed the benefits and burdens of patenting the animal to determine whether the grant would be against *ordre public* or morality.[32] The reasoning used by the EPO to decide in favour of patentability may not be to everyone's inclination, but at least the morality of exploiting animals as research tools to improve the quality of human life was considered – and will continue similarly to be considered under the EU Biotechnological Inventions directive.[33]

In the United States, on the other hand, once a man-made bacterium was accepted as a 'manufacture' even though it was a living thing, the patenting of man-made multicellular life forms (excluding, supposedly for constitutional reasons, humans) seemed to follow inexorably.[34] The US Supreme Court said that courts deciding issues of patentability had no mandate to weigh the potential hazards involved in genetic engineering, including such risks as that 'its practice may tend to depreciate the value of human life'.[35] The US patenting of the Harvard onco-mouse in 1988 was thus treated as a relatively routine matter.

This is not to say that the EPC '*ordre public* and morality' exception operates satisfactorily. It does not. Patent examiners and the technical boards of appeal which review their decisions are little equipped by training or inclination to give the exclusion much substance.[36] A different body to deal with such matters is suggested below in the concluding section of this paper.

(c) Business methods

It is also instructive to look at a case where the patent application does not apparently raise any issue of *ordre public* or morality: the patenting of business methods.

Just five years ago, few people would have predicted that a new method of doing business method, whether computerised or not, might qualify as a patentable invention. Presumably, it was thought that such methods were more mental than technological, were in large enough supply without needing the incentive of a patent, and could unduly inhibit ordinary business competition.

But once the US Court of Appeals for the Federal Circuit directly admitted a computer program as patentable subject matter ('any new ... machine') in 1994,[37] it was only a matter of time – viz 1998 – before it also admitted a computerised business method on the same basis and suggested that an uncomputerised business method was equally admissible ('any new ... process').[38] Australian courts took a similar line.[39] Technically, both countries could act this way without fanfare because their courts treat potential constraints on patentable subject matter as flowing from the language of their patent legislation and the prior judicial interpretations of it. In the US Patent Act, any subject matter that is 'any new and useful process, machine, manufacture or composition of matter, or any new and useful improvement thereof' is patentable; in Australia, it is 'any manner of new manufacture etc.' tracking, as we have seen, the language of the old Statute of Monopolies. Neither country needs to follow the European preoccupation with finding a workable modus vivendi between patentability and exceptions to patentability – because (apart from a ban on patenting human beings) there are virtually no exceptions written into either Patent Act. US and Australian courts and their patent offices thus welcome virtually anything into the patent fold today.

It was not always so. The US patentability of a computerised method of running a machine remained in doubt until 1981 when the US Supreme Court (by a slender 5:4 majority) accepted it as 'any new ... process'.[40] It then took over a decade more for a new computer program as such to be accepted as a patentable machine, but thereafter only four more years for business methods to be similarly admitted. As previously noted, 'anything under the sun that is made by man' has become the paraphrastic rallying-cry of patentability in the US courts and patent office. The actual language of the Patent Act seems now relevant mainly when the scope of the invention is considered: a technical issue of how the claims are drafted and of what acts later may infringe the patent.

In Europe, the question seemed closed by the present and proposed EPC's ban on patenting 'methods for ... doing business [and] programs for computers .. as such'.[41] An application claiming a computerised business method should therefore fail before the EPO on two grounds, not merely one. Such is the view taken in the UK, under which claims which are 'in substance' for a method of doing business or for a computer program must be rejected even though they 'in form' cover an apparatus programmed to execute a defined task.[42] Under the UK approach, the exceptions are treated seriously as statements of legislative policy.[43]

The EPO, on the other hand, seems to find the EPC's exceptions to patentability embarrassing to its perceived task of rewarding inventiveness through the patent system, and seems willing to accept any superficially plausible theory to avoid them. Thus, a recent EPO board of appeal was willing to accept a claim for a programmed computer as a patentable invention, even though the computer was designed and used to execute a business method. In the board's view, the computer, being a concrete apparatus, had the 'technical character' necessary for an invention. Since exceptions to patentability are interpreted narrowly, the finding that a piece of hardware is neither a method for doing business nor a program for a computer inexorably follows on the EPO's reasoning. Thus, the EPC exceptions can be avoided simply by clever (though uninventive) drafting.[44]

This approach echoes that taken place in the US since 1994 and in the UK pre-EPC.[45] It assumes that patents, being property, should be encouraged and that disallowing them interferes with the right to acquire property. The use of property language here stultifies rather than advances clear thinking. An equally plausible, possibly preferable, approach is to say that:

> 'it is as important not to patent anything on [the EPC's list] as it is to patent things that are off it. On this approach, any doubts about whether or not a patent application claims a mere "discovery" rather than a true "invention" – something found in the natural order rather than man-made change to the natural order – should be resolved by dismissing the application. [The opposite approach assumes that] when in doubt, create and reinforce property; do not deny or cut it back.'[46]

This heresy has not yet struck the European Commission. In February 2002, it proposed a directive that admitted all computer-related inventions (except those for business methods) to patentability and that allowed both process and product claims for them. Since harmonisation EU-style inevitably means harmonising in favour of more protection, the Commission unsurprisingly preferred the approach taken by the EPO (endorsed by the German courts) over that taken by the UK courts. The usual flim-flam about legal certainty and more jobs for Europe was trotted out, with about as much conviction as for prior directives in the intellectual property field.[47]

4 Some further trends

The foregoing discussion reveals that the forms of wording used to signal what items are patentable inventions varies among states. Nevertheless, what is and is not a patentable invention is today remarkably quite similar worldwide. Perhaps paradoxically, newly emerging activities with potential economic significance – for example business methods, genetic engineering, computer programs – are more readily classified as inventions in states whose legislation is couched in terms of seventeenth- and eighteenth-century concepts of invention, than in states using twentieth- and twenty-first-century definitions such as those found in the present and proposed EPC.

(a) International control of the meaning of 'invention'

International homogeneity is less surprising as a phenomenon today than it may have been even a decade ago. TRIPs has effectively imposed a worldwide standard under which the availability of patents for inventions in all fields of technology has become the norm. States may choose what exceptions to make from a short closed list. They may expand the range of items for which patents are granted[48] – for example, to include discoveries or pure mathematical ideas – in which case, they must make such patents available on identical terms to other WTO states.[49] They cannot, however, unilaterally add to the list of exceptions that TRIPs allows. Nor may they, through legislation or judicial decision, restrict the meaning of invention – at least, not for long. If another WTO member state complains, the WTO may, through its dispute resolution procedures, require the offender to discard any unacceptably narrow meaning of invention or any unacceptably broad interpretation of a permissible exception. WTO trade panels have found states in breach of other patent obligations under TRIPs (for example India, 1999; Canada, 2000) and would no doubt police with equal vigour attempts to avoid TRIPs obligations on patentable subject matter.

(b) Reduction of exceptions to patentability

A further development that should be noted is the clear trend since TRIPs towards the progressive elimination of many, perhaps even all, exceptions from TRIPs, art 27.1. Apart from the common tendency in human affairs towards simplification and generalisation, two specific phenomena contribute to this trend.

(i) Bilateral 'TRIPs-plus' treaties

First, the United States has embarked on a programme of bilateral negotiations, particularly with developing countries, under which the contracting parties undertake obligations beyond those required by TRIPs – so-called 'TRIPs-plus' treaties. Thus, the US-Jordan Free Trade Agreement of 2000 eliminates all the exceptions mentioned in TRIPs, art 27.3(b), imposes UPOV obligations for plant variety protection, and commits Jordan to granting patents for business methods and computer-related inventions by ensuring that these items are not caught by the 'mathematical methods' exception in Jordan's patent law.[50]

Treaties such as this, while nominally bilateral, have multilateral effects because TRIPs requires any advantage extended by one WTO member to another to be extended to all.[52] States that are bound to extend special advantages to others may fairly demand reciprocal treatment from them. Moreover, the more bilateral agreements impose obligations on states to grant patents for, say, business methods, the more likely it is that a WTO panel may interpret TRIPs itself as requiring business methods to be treated as an 'invention' and a 'technology': state practice may 'clarify' the meaning of TRIPs, art 27.1. A nominally bilateral obligation may thus become quickly multilateral in practice, and gradually universal in tendency.

(ii) Common law trend towards more patenting

Secondly, common law courts have shown themselves willing to follow the trend towards wider patentability spearheaded by United States courts and the European Patent Office. It is not surprising that European (including UK) courts have followed the EPO's lead, given the pressure towards harmonisation exercised by the EPC and the centrality of the EPO in the EPC's scheme. Less inevitable has been the trend of common law courts in jurisdictions such as Australia and New Zealand to reverse or whittle away at long-standing exceptions to patentability created by earlier courts in interpreting their respective patent statues. The recent allowance of a patent in Australia for computer programs and medical treatment, and in New Zealand for Swiss-type claims covering the use of known compounds to produce pharmaceuticals for medical treatment,[52] are examples of this phenomenon.[53] In each case, the courts followed United States or European developments, ostensibly in the desire to keep their innovation policy up to date and not to let their country feel left behind in the technological race. Only Canada has, by refusing a patent for genetically engineered animals, not joined the crowd, but then only narrowly and in a decision that may ultimately prove quixotic.

(c) Cumulative protection

As intellectual property rights have proliferated and expanded, instances of multiple intellectual property protection have increased.[54] For example, a firm's logo may be registered or protected at common law as a trade mark, a textile pattern may be registered as an industrial design, a computer program can be protected by a patent; yet copyright protection for all three is often cumulatively available. Patent and design right holders also strive to create trade mark rights over aspects of their product and so lessen free competition on expiry of the patent or design registration. As noted earlier, in some jurisdictions plant breeders may acquire both patents and plant breeder rights over their new seeds and enforce the rights cumulatively, thereby circumventing any inconvenient user exemptions found in one Act but not the other.[55]

Sometimes intellectual property legislation itself partly discourages multiple protection. Thus, the EPC excepts, inter alia, aesthetic creations and computer programs 'as such' from cumulative patent protection, largely because these items are adequately protected by copyright automatically without any formality or registration.[56] Yet, as earlier noted, the EPO has undercut the full force of the computer program exception by interpreting it narrowly and has allowed patents for a wide range of computer programs. A copier may therefore be liable for either or both patent and copyright infringement as a right holder decides. Indeed, the rights may be transferred and held by different entities, subjecting the copier to double liability and double damages.

Intellectual property rights are here treated like products in a supermarket: a shopper with enough money and information can acquire as many items as she wishes. Innovation levels are hardly enhanced by the prospect of adventitious multiple protection. Whether the rule of 'take as many as you can carry' could be replaced by a rule of 'only one per customer' is worth investigating further. If an 'only one per customer' rule were adopted, then seeking or obtaining a patent for a technology could bar reliance on any right which attaches without registration (for example copyright or common law trade mark) and which substantially corresponds with the registered right, both during the pendency of the registration and also on its expiry. Current common law jurisprudence shows some tendency in this direction,[57] but the rule that cumulative protection may be obtained unless legislation positively forbids it is more prevalent.[58]

One may also look at the matter from the patents end. Patents should be awarded to encourage desirable inventiveness. Therefore, where the activity is adequately encouraged and would occur even without the prospect of a patent, patenting is unjustified. This consideration suggests that the EPC exceptions to patentability for aesthetic creations, computer programs and presentations of information should be interpreted more broadly than they are now by the EPO. Indeed, a more general exception may be warranted to exclude all material that is susceptible of being adequately protected by copyright, database or design rights.

5 Reform suggestions

The foregoing discussion suggests a pressing need to reform the notion of patentable invention. The conflict between the UK courts and the EPO on how exclusions from patentability should be interpreted is serious and basic. The growing irrelevance of the '*ordre public* and morality' exception, as applied by the EPO and national patent offices, is troublesome. The propensity of the EPO, in common with other patent offices, is to grant patents, not reject them; it is not institutionally equipped to make judgments on whether, in the public interest, a patent should be issued or continued. The point is tentatively recognised in art 7 of the EU Biotechnological Inventions Directive,[59] which states neutrally – without imposing any obligation on the EPO or national patent offices – that the EC's European Group on Ethics in Science and Technology 'evaluates all ethical aspects of biotechnology'. Other jurisdictions also implicitly recognise that intellectual property offices do not necessarily possess institutional competence to deal with broader public policy issues.[60] With growing public concern about new technologies and the pace of their introduction and dissemination, it is increasingly important for the public to be involved on an operational level in the grant of patents and not merely to be consigned to a sideline role.

Patents should work manifestly in the public benefit – the ultimate justification for the system. The public pays a high price for patents. It must get, and be convinced that it is getting, correspondingly high value from it. Greater public involvement and hence understanding would help attain this goal. Without such involvement, the system may not muster the public support it needs to survive.

Public input, to be meaningful, requires a broader ability than currently exists to decide on which inventions deserve a patent. The old idea of patenting as a privilege rather than a right has much to commend it. The idea lost currency through being too intermeshed with royal patronage and, later, bureaucratic discretion. But these objections would lose force if the body that granted patents were more representative of the public, and if the grounds for grant or rejection were more firmly linked to the perceived benefits the invention would potentially confer on the public. In short, a 'generally inconvenient' invention should not be patented, but the question of general inconvenience should be resolved by a more widely representative body than one comprising merely lawyers or technical experts.

Colin Tapper is equally troubled by 'the shackles of the established law of intellectual property in relation to computer-related areas', noting the need for 'an increased dimension of flexibility'.[61] In *Computer Law* Tapper did not map out any scheme that would advance this goal while maintaining the appropriate stimulus to inventiveness. I suggest the following, which focuses on the European system while being easily adaptable (at least in theory) to other systems, and which may meet some of Tapper's concerns:[62]

1. The European practice of not defining 'invention' in legislation is sound.
2. The practice of excluding firm categories of items is unsound except for categories that, on any view, fall outside the concept of 'invention'. So 'discoveries . . . as such' may reasonably continue to be excluded, because any decision to expand the patent legislation to include discoveries is a major structural decision – akin to the decision to establish a *sui generis* database right – that would require legislation. The line between discovery and invention would still need to be continually policed and clarified.
3. The EPO practice of construing patentability exceptions narrowly and allowing their avoidance through simple drafting means is unsound. The UK practice of treating the exceptions as embodying expressions of substantive policy is preferable.
4. A technology should not be protected under more than one intellectual property law. Thus, if the technology is protectable by copyright, no patent should be awarded. All plant technologies should be protected under more precisely targeted plant breeder laws, rather than by patents.
5. The decision to award or refuse a patent requires greater flexibility than presently exists. Unforeseen technologies and issues may require broader consideration than technically oriented patent examiners are equipped to give them. Therefore the legislation should be amended to exclude inventions

that it would not be in the public interest to patent – in effect, a return to the principle of excluding 'generally inconvenient' patents, but one where the issue of 'convenience' or 'public interest' is seriously weighed and considered. Inventions could be excluded by categories but, more importantly, there should also be a general discretion to exclude any particular invention whether or not it presently falls within a specific category.

6. Among the non-exhaustive reasons of public interest to exclude an invention might be that:
   (a) its production was already adequately encouraged (ie supply was sufficient);
   (b) it was already adequately protected under another intellectual property law or by the general law (for example by unfair competition or trade secret law);
   (c) its patenting would discourage biodiversity, contrary to the Convention on Biological Diversity 1990;
   (d) current ethical concerns rendered it, on balance, inadvisable to patent. This view could be modified from time to time to render patentable what currently is not, and unpatentable what currently is.
7. A special Ethics and Public Interest Panel should be established independently of the patent offices.[63] The Panel would comprise both experts in law, ethics and technology, and also ordinary members of the public, with power to co-opt other persons (including experts) from time to time as it thought fit.
8. The Panel would:
   (a) decide what categories of inventions should not, in the public interest, be patentable;
   (b) add to or subtract from those categories from time to time;
   (c) exclude a particular invention in the Panel's discretion;
   (d) issue advance rulings on potential patentability of particular new technologies, and repeal or amend those rulings from time to time;
   (e) decide issues of ordre public or morality – a subset of public interest – currently decided by the EPO and national courts;
   (f) advise the EPO and national patent offices on what categories of applications should be referred to the Panel (an examiner could always refer any application to the Panel for its opinion, whether it fell within a stipulated category or not);
   (g) request the referral of any application to it at any time;
   (h) revoke, after a hearing, any patent on the ground that its grant was against the public interest, or that its continued exploitation was against the public interest, *ordre public* or morality;
   (i) commission studies on any patent issue (including patentability) to assist it in its decision-making.

Charles de Gaulle is reputed to have said that politics were too serious a matter to be left to politicians. A similar sentiment holds true for patent law. It is too important to be turned over to the specialists, be they patent lawyers, patent judges, or even patent law professors. Patent laws are there for the whole of society. Not every member of the public may read patent laws or patents as avidly as they read literature, but they are nevertheless touched by those laws at least as significantly, whether they know it or not. They therefore deserve a greater role in the way patent laws operate than the laws currently allow them. The modest proposal of this essay is that the public be allowed that greater role.

NOTES

* An earlier version of this paper was written in the context of a wider project on patentability in the light of current technological innovation ('La brevetabilité face à l'innovation technique contemporaine'), directed by Professor Michel Vivant at the Université de Montpellier, France. Another version will be published in 2003 in the International Journal of Law and Information Technology, on the board of which Colin Tapper has fittingly served since the journal's inception.

1 C Tapper *Computer Law* (London and New York: Longman, 1978) p 1.

2 I do not, of course, presume to suggest that Tapper would agree with all my suggestions, although I suspect he would agree with at least some.

3 How much activity is spurred by the patent system, and in what spheres, are empirical questions on which research is sparse and on which opinions accordingly differ. This study notes, but does not enter, that debate.

4 The distinction between kind and quality cannot be pressed too far. For example, one might fairly argue that novelty and non-obviousness are part of an invention's essence. It is unnecessary to pursue that point here. Rather, we shall assume, safely, that the essence or quality of a thing is not established *a priori* but is the product of common social understandings and practices. Since it is universal practice and understanding (including within the EPO and its boards of appeal) to treat the elements of novelty, non-obviousness, utility and adequate disclosure separately from the element of subject matter, that convention will be followed here.

5 *Festo Corpn v Shoketsu Kinzoku Kogyo Kabushiki Co Ltd* 122 S Ct 1831 at 1841 (2002), rejecting a rule of patent interpretation which had been proposed by the lower court for the sake of greater certainty, but which reduced the breadth of patent claims.

6 Ie Agreement on Trade-Related Aspects of Intellectual Property Rights (TRIPs), annexed to the World Trade Organization Agreement 1994 (WTO Agreement).

7 Proposed EPC, art 52(1). This version of the EPC, rather than the EPC 1973, is often referred to in this paper on the basis that it is likely to be adopted in the near future.

8 Neither the present nor the proposed EPC refers explicitly to 'products or processes' but the omission is unimportant. To have expressly included the TRIPs language in the proposed EPC would have been not only tautologous, but may also have cast doubt on previously well-established European jurisprudence.

9 Proposed EPC, art 53(a). Art 53(a) omits the inclusory examples found in TRIPs, art 27.2, again essentially for the reasons mentioned in n 8 above.

10 EPC, art 51(4); proposed EPC, art 53(c).

11 TRIPs, art 1.1: '... Members shall be free to determine the appropriate method of implementing the provisions of this Agreement within their own legal system and practice.'

12 Proposed EPC, art 53(c).

13 *Lawson v Comr of Patents* (1970) 62 CPR 101 at 109 (Ex Ct); see also *Tennessee Eastman Co v Commissioner of Patents* [1974] SCR 111.

14 Eg as in the United States and Canada: *JEM Ag Supply Inc v Pioneer Hi-Bred International Inc* 534 US 124 (2001); *Monsanto Canada Inc v Schmeiser* 2001 Fed Ct Trial Lexis 174 (Fed TD); affd [2002] FCA 309 (Fed CA).

15 See art 4(1)(a) and (2) of the EU Directive on the legal protection of biotechnological inventions of 1998, 98/44/EC; *Novartis II/Transgenic plants* (G1/98, 1999).

16 Doha WTO Ministerial Declaration, art 19 (WT/MIN(01)/DEC/1) adopted 14 November 2001, www-chil.wto-ministerial.org/english/thewto_e/minist_e/min01_e/mindecl_e.htm.

17 Taken from art 52(2) and (3), as amended by the proposed EPC 2000.

18 1623 was the year when the Bill which led to the passage of the *Statute of Monopolies* was introduced; 1624 was when it passed. (*My comment.*)

19 *National Research Development Corpn v Comr of Patents* (1959) 102 CLR 252 (HC Aust).

20 *International Business Machines Corpn v Comr of Patents* (1991) 33 FCR 218 (computer program); *Bristol-Myers Squibb Co v FH Faulding & Co Ltd* [2000] FCA 316 (medical treatment); *Welcome Real-Time SA v Catuity Inc* [2001] FCA 445 (business method).

21 *Comr of Patents v Wellcome Foundation Ltd* [1983] NZLR 385 (CA).

22 *Bristol-Myers Squibb Co v F H Faulding & Co Ltd* [2000] FCA 316, following the majority view in *Anaesthetic Supplies Pty Ltd v Rescare Ltd* (1994) 28 IPR 383 (Aust Fed Ct); Pila 'Methods of Medical Treatment within Australian and United Kingdom Patent Law' (2001) 24 UNSWLJ 421.

23 *Pharmaceutical Management Agency Ltd v Comr of Patents* [2000] RPC 857 (NZCA) para 20 (obiter): 'It has been doubted whether it forms part of our definition of invention that the manner of new manufacture "be not contrary to the law nor mischievous to the state by raising prices of commodities at home, or hurt of trade, or generally inconvenient"': Blanco White *Patents for*

Inventions (4th edn, 1974) para 1-212. There is some support for this view in the fact that when the Act was passed in 1953 it included also in s 17(1)(b) the power for the Commissioner to refuse an application if it appeared to him '[t]hat the use of the invention in respect of which the application is made would be contrary to law or morality; . . .'

24 Reversing the presumption may not be neutral on the likelihood of parliamentary intervention: 'when lawmakers are lobbied for new intellectual property rights, [i]t seems easier to justify widening an existing right and eliminating an exception, than it is to justify inserting an exception or widening an existing exception': Vaver 'Intellectual Property Law: The State of the Art' (2000) 116 LQR 621, 635. Re-introducing an exception is akin to eliminating a property right, especially if applications or grants have occurred before Parliament acts. The move a few years ago by the American Medical Association to have medical treatments held unpatentable resulted only in Congress' narrowing the range of people who might be liable for infringement: see now US Patent Act, § 287(c), applying only to patents with a priority date after 30 September 1996 (the date when the amendments took effect).

25 The only exceptions are 'laws of nature, natural phenomena, and abstract ideas': *Diamond v Diehr* 450 US 175, 185 (1981).

26 *Diamond v Chakrabarty* 447 US 303 (1980).

27 Eg *Schlumberger Can Ltd v Comr of Patents* (1981) 56 CPR (2d) 204 (Fed CA) (computer program); *Imperial Chemical Industries Ltd v Canada (Comr of Patents)* [1986] 3 FC 40, CA (method of medical treatment); *Re Application for Patent of Pioneer Hi-Bred Ltd* [1987] 3 FC 8, CA, affd on other grounds sub nom *Pioneer Hi-Bred Ltd v Canada (Comr of Patents)* [1989] 1 SCR 1623 (cross-bred soybean plant).

28 *Harvard College v Canada (Comr of Patents)* [2002] 4 FC 528, CA.

29 The Australian-New Zealand approach, with its broad exception for 'generally inconvenient' inventions, ought theoretically to be at the complete opposite end of the spectrum, compared to the United States. However, as has been noted, this exception is little applied today, partly under the influence of TRIPs, art 27.

30 Present and proposed EPC, art 53(a).

31 Cornish *Intellectual Property: Patents, Copyright, Trade Marks and Allied Rights* (4th edn, 1999) p 228.

32 *Harvard/Onco-Mouse* [1991] EPOR 525.

33 This 1998 directive (above n 15) continues the EPC's '*ordre public* or morality' exception and explicitly deems various genetic engineering practices to be unpatentable under this head, including modifying an animal's genetic identity if that is 'likely to cause [it] suffering without any substantial medical benefit to man or animal': art 6(2)(d).

34 *Re Allen* 2 USPQ 2d 1425 (PTO Bd App & Int 1987) (genetically modified oyster).

35 *Diamond v Chakrabarty* 447 US 303 (1980).

36 Eg Beyleveld, Brownsword and Llewellyn 'The morality clauses of the Directive on the Legal Protection of Biotechnological Inventions: conflict, compromise and the patent community' in Goldberg and Lonbay *Pharmaceutical Medicine, Biotechnology and European Law* (Cambridge University Press, 2000) ch 7.

37 *Re Alappato* 33 F 3d 1526 (Fed Cir in banc, 1994).

38 *State Street Bank & Trust Co v Signature Financial Group Inc* 149 F 3d 1369 (Fed Cir 1998).

39 See the pre-*Alappat* Australian decision in *IBM v Comr of Patents* (1991) 3 FCR 218, followed by *Welcome Real-Time SA v Catuity Inc* [2001] FCA 445.

40 *Diamond v Diehr* 450 US 175, 185 (1981).

41 EPC, art 52(1)(c). Similarly proposed EPC, art 52(2)(c).

42 *Merrill Lynch's Application* [1989] RPC 561, CA. The UK Patent Office, faced with the apparent conflict between *Controlling pension benefits* (below n 45) and *Merrill Lynch*, initially followed *Merrill Lynch* in *Pintos Global Services Ltd's Application* (6 April 2001) and then threw in the towel in a Practice Notice issued on 24 April 2002: 'inventions *which involve a technical contribution* will not be refused a patent merely because they relate to business methods and mental acts.' How this practice will fare in the UK courts remains to be seen.

43 Cf the UK Patent Office's Practice Notice of 24 April 2002, above n 42.

44 *Controlling pension benefits system/PBS Partnership* [2001] OJEPO 441.

45 *Re Alappato* 33F 3d 1526 (Fed Cir in banc, 1994); *Re Burroughs Corpn's (Perkin's) Application* [1974] RPC 147.

46 Vaver 'Intellectual Property Law: The State of the Art' (2000) 116 LQR 621, 633–634.

47 *Proposal for a Directive of the European Parliament and of the Council on the patentability of computer-implemented inventions* (COM(2002) 92 final, 2002/0047 (COD)), 20 February 2002. One is reminded of the EC's Copyright Term Directive, which extended the standard period of copyright protection by 20 years, to 70 years after the death of the author. The reasoning

underpinning this directive was called 'disgraceful' by the authors of a leading text on copyright: Laddie, Prescott and Vitoria *The Modern Law of Copyright* (2nd edn, 1995) p vi.

48 TRIPs, art 1.1: '... Members may, but shall not be obliged to, implement in their law more extensive protection than is required by this Agreement, provided that such protection does not contravene the provisions of this Agreement.'

49 TRIPs, art 4.

50 Agreement Between the United States of America and the Hashemite Kingdom of Jordan on the Establishment of a Free Trade Area, arts 4.1(b) and 4.18; Memorandum of Understanding on Issues Related to the Protection of Intellectual Property Rights Under the Agreement Between the United States of America and the Hashemite Kingdom of Jordan on the Establishment of a Free Trade Area, art 5. Both documents were signed on 24 October 2000, and took effect on 17 December 2001.

51 TRIPs, art 4, so-called 'most-favoured-nation treatment'.

52 See above nn 20 and 22; *Pharmaceutical Management Agency Ltd v Com of Patents* [2000] RPC 857, NZCA, deliberately avoiding the medical treatment exception affirmed in *Comr of Patents v Wellcome Foundation Ltd* [1983] NZLR 385 (CA).

53 Such moves may prompt civilian lawyers to reconsider their preconceptions of what precedent and *stare decisis* mean in practice in modern common law jurisdictions.

54 This section draws on Vaver *Copyright Law* (Toronto: Irwin Law, 2000) pp 16–18.

55 See the US and Canadian cases cited in n 14 above. Thus, in *Monsanto Canada Inc v Schmeiser* 2001 Fed Ct Trial Lexis 174 (Fed TD); affd 2002 FCA 309 (Fed CA), the court enforced a patent for genetically modified seed against a farmer who had saved seed, holding that the exemptions for saving seed under the Plant Breeders Rights Act was irrelevant to a patent infringement action.

56 Proposed EPC, art 52(2)(b) and (c).

57 Eg *TrafFix Devices Inc v Marketing Displays Inc* 532 US 23 (2001), barring trade dress protection for a functional design feature covered by the claims of an expired patent. Tapper rightly calls problems of overlap 'ugly' and favours at least some form of election of remedies: *Computer Law* (4th edn, 1990) p 132.

58 Eg Canada: *Apple Computer Inc v Mackintosh Computers Ltd* (1986) 10 CPR (3d) 1 (Fed TD); affd [1988] 1 FC 673, CA; affd [1990] 2 SCR 209 (copyright for computer program even if it could be patented); United States: *Krueger International Inc v Nightingale Inc* 915 F Supp 595 (SDNY 1996) (trade dress, ie unfair competition, protection for stacking chair even after expiry of design patent).

59 Above n 15.

60 Consider, eg the Trade Marks Bill introduced into the New Zealand Parliament in 2001. In the Bill as reported out of Committee on 1 March 2002, the Commissioner of Trade Marks must reject an application if he 'considers that, on reasonable grounds, its use or registration would be likely to offend a significant section of the community, including Maori': Bill, s 17(1)(b)(ii). A committee will advise the Commissioner on such issues. Originally, the advisory committee's role was limited to advising whether a registration 'that is, or appears to be, derivative of Maori imagery or text is, or is likely to be, offensive to Maori'; but this clause was struck out during Committee consideration of the Bill. The new committee would have a general advisory role on all matters: Bill, s 178. Presumably the Commissioner may accept or reject the committee's advice. Adverse advice would constitute 'reasonable grounds' on which the Commissioner could refuse registration under s 17(1)(b)(ii) of the Bill.

61 *Computer Law* (4th edn, 1990) p 134.

62 The suggestions take no account of political or other possible obstacles to implementation such as those presented by international conventions, eg TRIPs or the EPC.

63 This suggestion builds on one contained in the Westminster Institute for Ethics and Human Values & McGill Centre for Medicine, Ethics and Law *Ethical Issues Associated with the Patenting of Higher Life Forms* (Ontario, London, 1994) p 103ff.

Cumulation and convergence of intellectual property rights

William Cornish

Colin Tapper has pioneered the study of computers and the law from their earliest maturity to their extraordinary multiplicity today. In Britain our perceptions of the subject have been formed by his keen and accurate eye. His interests have lain both in the potential of computers as informational, drafting and other aids for legislators, judges and practitioners and in the need for legal frameworks which can help to condition their use. Not least among the latter has been the adaptation of intellectual property rights to encompass the new technology.

The commercialisation of computing led eventually to demands for rights against imitation of products, and indeed against the adoption of certain ideas even though they have been independently conceived, that will be broadly equivalent to those in operation for other, longer established industries. What the pattern should be, particularly in respect of software and firmware, has been the subject of unending controversy. In some respects, digital technology has delivered greater shocks to established intellectual property systems than anything in their history, save perhaps the initial decisions to adopt them at all. Accordingly, in a volume which celebrates Tapper's deeply satisfying contribution to British legal scholarship, here is a brief essay which reflects upon the ways in which intellectual property rights (IPRs) go forth and multiply as technology wills. It aims to stress two characteristics of this almost biological drive: the tendency to cumulate and the tendency then to converge; and to ask what megacephaloid may ultimately evolve.

1 Cumulation

The opposite of cumulation is separation and most specific IPRs are initially conceived as separate by virtue of their subject matter. Patents are for inventions, copyright for aesthetic work and its production, trade marks for the signs by which the origin or products and services are designated, and so on. The cumulation question then arises where the subject matter or elements within it in some degree overlap. What I shall be mainly concerned with are cases where a person who makes a single intellectual or marketing effort giving rise to the subject matter (invention, work, mark etc) becomes entitled to more than one IPR. This should be distinguished from circumstances where different activities lead to parallel rights, very often accorded to different people – as with the authorial copyright given to a composer for creating a work, and the entrepreneurial copyright given to the record producer for recording it. The consequences of the cumulation of rights vary from one case to the next, so let us move straightaway to some examples.

(a) Industrial design

The British have experienced wild swings in the protection available to the design of industrially produced goods. In Victorian times, the designer of an industrial product was accorded a registered design right in the features of appearance that were incorporated into it.[1] The system was established by statute and with time acquired features not unlike an invention patent. However, in 1911, when all copyright was drawn together in an Imperial Copyright Act, it became arguable that copyright in two-dimensional artistic works could be infringed by reproduction in three dimensions. If so, a drawing of Peter Pan could not be made into a statue without permission of the copyright owner. What then, if a manufacturer turned out Peter Pan lamp-standards? There would be a direct overlap with registered design rights.

Accordingly, a provision against cumulation was included in the Act.[2] If the subject matter could be protected by a registered design, then it could not enjoy copyright as an artistic work. The distinction turned principally on the intention of the designer: if the design was initially drawn for a mass-produced product then only a registered design would be available. That distinction, however, ran into difficulties over designs that were originally for exploitation in cartoons and book illustrations. If the designs were then used for merchandising – as decoration on clothing, or for toys, figurines, cutlery and so on – could the only rights in the appearance of these things be registered designs? Often a registration had not been applied for in time, and in any case the term would be much shorter than that for copyright. The House of Lords insisted that the designer's initial intention alone was relevant; otherwise there would be cumulation to start with, and exclusion once the designer had agreed to the making of the industrial product.[3]

Cartoon producers thus secured a right which in many respects gave them an advantage over product designers in general. In the upshot, a comparative unfairness emerged, which the next investigators of the issue decided to rectify.[4] In the Copyright Act 1956, the non-cumulation provision ceased to operate on a division of subject matter and instead invoked a division within the types of act constituting infringement: copyright would have effect only for those types of exploitation outside the sphere of industrial products.[5]

All attempts at a properly stratified regime of non-cumulation were soon enough to collapse in Britain. Absentmindedly, in 1968, Parliament allowed the application of artistic copyright to the actual application of industrial designs so that it could supplement any registered designs that there might be.[6] But, while this copyright was given a 15-year limit, there proved to be an exception. Where the product elements were purely technical, and so could not have a registered design, they could have copyright protection for the designer's life and 50 years thereafter.[7] This explosion of rights made for disturbing inconvenience in industry. Those who produced a large array of industrial items had been in the habit of taking new inspiration or detailed specifications from previous models, whether they were their own or a competitor's. Suddenly they found it necessary to abandon free borrowing in face of the need to make cautious inquiry into the provenance of what they were copying. Otherwise they might face accusations of copyright infringement.[8]

Within a few years there were persistent demands to cut this rampaging copyright down to size. But there were powerful groups among the new right-owners. Particularly prominent were vehicle manufacturers, who found in artistic copyright a means of preventing the imitation of their spare parts.[9] The eventual outcome was a new IPR – unregistered design right (UDR), introduced in the Copyright, Designs and Patents Act 1988 (CDPA 1988), Pt III.[10] It provides a new cumulation with registered designs. UDR does not depend upon registration and extends to purely technical shapes. There is therefore a second cumulation with patents. But the legislation setting up UDR is abtruse and it can be interpreted to the business world only by expensive specialists.[11]

The 1968 and 1988 adventures have together made British views on protecting design features of industrial products quite incomprehensible to our European partners. In the new EU dispositions in that field, the British form of UDR now bobs as an embarrassing piece of flotsam across our island lagoon.[12] In the upshot, this country is hard put to stand as the voice of reason and experience in setting limits upon the range of any intellectual property. Already with this first example, we can observe that attempts to avoid cumulation lead all too readily to difficulties over boundaries between the separated rights. The way to avoid borderland trouble is to cumulate, and so it becomes ever more common.

(b) Plant varieties, plant patents

Next, some examples concerned specifically with technological developments. As the generation of new plants from cross-pollination, grafting and the cultivation of 'sports' grew into an industry, there were demands for protection of the resultant varieties. In the United States, the patent system was extended in two stages to give plant patents, thus drawing the new field within an established type of right.[13] However, in Europe after Hitler's War, industry pressures gave rise to a distinct plant variety right. The British version was established in 1964. The right was shaped to give a moderate balance. The incentive to plant breeders was qualified so as to allow other growers a certain commercial independence. Rights were granted only after official testing determined that there was a variety that was distinctive, uniform and stable. Each genus within the scheme had to be covered by a separate regime which allowed for variations in such matters as the term of the right. Exceptions might restrict the right so that it did not apply to flowers or fruit of the variety, and farmers were allowed to re-sow from their own seed. The whole is an unusual instance of a right which is nuanced to fit particular subject matter. By contrast, most IPRs have a 'one-size-fits-all' character, and that is often their prime inefficiency in the eyes of an economist.

A plant variety right of the European type was initially treated as non-cumulative. The patent system was excluded as any sort of alternative. The international convention, UPOV,[14] which provided for mutual recognition of rights for producers from the member countries, insisted upon this; and the European Patent Convention of 1973 duly so provided. But seeds and plant stock became the stuff of massive investment, particularly as genetic manipulation gained a place alongside traditional breeding methods. The limited PVR in each variety was not what the new agro-giants wanted. The campaign to lift the embargo on patents became insistent. If a whole genus or species could be genetically manipulated so as, for instance, to make any constituent variety resistant to a weedkiller, then a patent for the procedure across the whole range was the demand.

UPOV was amended so as to remove the non-cumulation embargo in 1991. But in the European patent system the ban on patents for plant varieties as such remained in place.[15] Appeal Boards in the European Patent Office took the view that patent claims upon a genetically varied species related to each variety in the species and thus fell within the exclusion covering plant varieties. Eventually this position was overruled by the enlarged Board of Appeal. At much the same juncture, the result was in effect confirmed by a provision in the EC's Biotechnology Directive.

The upshot is an uneasy compromise which could well prove to be transitional. Breeders whose activities follow the old path of development, variety by variety, can still obtain a PVR. Biotechnology enterprises, with their sights on wider-ranging changes, can have their patent. The rights may appear to provide for different cases, but it is easy to suspect that the line is even now being blurred. It is not difficult to suppose that there is already a creeping cumulation, which may soon enough be driven further toward convergence. To this case we shall return.

(c) Petty patents, full patents

More and more IPR regimes in Europe and elsewhere have established a subsidiary regime alongside the regular patent system, with its pre-grant examination and its 20-year term. In the EU, only Sweden and Luxembourg, as well as the United Kingdom, do not adopt this course. This secondary right is known by such titles as utility model, petty patent, short-term patent, innovation patent etc. It varies in detailed structure from country to country, but typically it is granted without preliminary examination of the substantive claim to novelty etc; it lasts for a lesser period (perhaps six years, perhaps ten); it may well not have to satisfy a test of inventive step as severe as that required for a full patent; and it may perhaps cover subject matter which is not regarded as patentable, such as a business method. A petty patent system alongside a full patent system presents an obverse case to that of PVRs and patents. Beginning from the limited instance of machines and other mechanical technology in which distinctive shapes expressed the novel concept, they were introduced as a simpler, cheaper and less demanding type of limited protection. They were aimed at small inventors and investors in order to help them on to a first rung of enterprise.

Rather than there being any separation of the rights, a petty patent or utility model often provided an initial guard which, when the idea proved to be of real commercial value, could later be replaced by a full patent. As they were extended to more of the same territory as patents, they became an interwoven part of the same texture.

The result seems a precocious instance of cumulation tending towards convergence. There is no formal limitation in these systems restricting the lesser right to enterprises below a certain size or market share. Equally it is inevitable that large businesses will turn to them as a way of securing their initial interests. Thus they can be used for valuable advances that are evident early on, and also for fringe novelties which may not survive patent office examination or opposition. It is in the latter case that one can see the least desirable aspect of this double-bonding approach. The proprietor of a petty patent will only have an unexamined claim. That may well be waste paper when waved before a determined competitor. But it is the small business which may be unable to fight that sort of disdain, while the large establishment may succeed in getting a licence and a measure of control over competitors when it is the proprietor of the dubious right.

This is the principal reason why the United Kingdom continues its refusal to introduce a secondary right in inventions, insisting instead that it is the patent system itself which deserves to be made attractive enough that it does not frighten away small businesses with good new ideas. The European Commission, however, keeps a model ready on its shelves against the day when such hostility may lessen. In the end it may become politically feasible either to harmonise national laws in EU states or to introduce a Community Petty Patent covering the whole territory.[16] The

Community would be better advised to be examining full patent systems hard in order to see how they can be made more attractive to start-ups and similar businesses. These should undoubtedly include the actual introduction of the Community patent. The project for it has been almost at the ready since 1975, when the Community Patent Convention was originally signed.

(d) Trade secrets, patents

To some extent, the nature and objective of one particular right necessitates its separation for another. Thus it is an essential object of patent protection that, in return for the grant, the inventor must disclose his invention to the public in his patent specification. He cannot at the same time continue to claim protection of the invention as a trade secret. Modern systems, such as our own, have tended none the less to say that this logic applies purely to the invention claimed in the patent. Surrounding know-how which relates to production techniques and the like may still be the subject of obligations of confidentiality, if they are discrete.[17] For the most part this neat balance satisfies industry, since modern technology tends to surround core concepts with a penumbra of technical additions. The licensor of a technology can therefore offer the patent as the kernel of a licence, while the supply of detailed, confidential know-how will contain the real flesh of an essentially confidential collaboration.

What is overlooked in this practical outcome is the larger question: if the very object of a patent system is to induce invention and consequent innovation as quickly as possible, should trade secret protection be available as an alternative or supplement?[18] This issue was debated extensively in the United States in the context of the federal pre-emption of state law powers. Since the United States had the constitutional power to protect inventions under a patent law, how could individual states maintain common law or statutory rules governing trade secrets? Arguments in this form had already been used to strike down state statutes which protected the design elements of industrial products.

Eventually the Supreme Court ruled in favour of a broad cumulation of patent and trade secret protection.[19] It considered that major inconveniences would follow from substantially precluding trade secret protection for technology which was patentable. What can be patented requires an investigation into whether there is an invention and whether it is already known at the priority date of the patent. That can be a very complex and costly inquiry in its own right. To posit it as an incidental question that would be entangled in trade secret litigation would be a major inconvenience and evidently one that would set the law at variance with standard practice in technology transfer. Hence the outcome. At least one can say of it, that the cumulation relates in principle to discrete pieces of knowledge and so therefore deserves to survive.

(e) Computer programs: copyright, patents

In the first generation of main-frame computers, the industry's leaders were opposed to IPRs in programs. They supplied programs as part of large-scale installations on a bespoke basis that entailed contracts and consequent confidentiality. The dominant producers (notably IBM) considered that IPRs would tend to go to smaller competitors and merely be a nuisance. Hence, in the European Patent Convention of 1973, computer programs were declared to lie beyond the patent system, along with methods of doing business, at least 'as such'. The exclusion was not apparently introduced in order to leave space for copyright or any *sui generis* provision that might be designed for the case.

The arrival of the personal computer and computer games and their consoles changed the industry's attitude at top speed. Imitators of mass-produced programs were everywhere – in pirate outlets, in commercial firms and institutions, which bought one copy of a program and installed it endlessly on hard disks, in private hands everywhere. No hesitation was allowed. Programs must be protected by copyright as literary works, even though the purpose was purely to make a machine function, not directly to pass information or entertainment to humans. So it came to be in most court decisions, in national legislation, in the EC Software Directive and ultimately in the TRIPs Agreement, art 10 and the WIPO Copyright Treaty of 1996, art 4.

Copyright was indeed a useful tool in the hard business of chasing of direct copyists and to some extent it was available against those who reworked programs in order to introduce varied functioning.[20] Copyright meant that there was infringement when only quite small portions of the original program were taken. That appeared a real advantage to the largest software producers who wanted to prevent competitors from linking their application programs into the producer's operating system. Such a naked move to exclude small operators from providing interoperable programs was considered to be highly monopolistic in motivation. The EC's Software Directive of 1991 was enacted only with a set of hotly contested defences. In particular, competitors were permitted to decompile a program back to as much of its source code as could be recovered, in order to devise the necessary link-up of other programs.[21]

Without this exception, which is not open to abrogation by contract, copyright would have underpinned a powerful binding of user to machine. Just at this time, the dominant suppliers of systems accordingly turned back to the prospects of patenting programs. While copyright began its protection from the detailed programming which expressed its basic ideas, the tendency of a patent was to define whatever could be treated as inventive in the programming and give an exclusive right in as many of its applications as could be defined in the patent claims. Within relatively few years, in the European system, and even more expansively in the United States, the old embargoes have been undermined. Novel and inventive ways of programming, whether for operating systems or applications can, with a degree of subtlety from the patent attorney, be patented. A separation has become a cumulation. Yet, so familiar is the process of eliding overlapping rights today that the cumulation of patent with copyright in this field is at most remarked upon in passing.[22]

2 Convergence

When can it be said that the process of cumulating rights reaches a further stage which deserves to be labelled convergence? The latter phenomenon is not easily defined. We have already noted examples where one IPR available to an individual in respect of given subject matter threatens to overrun others, thus, as it were, producing a take-over rather than a merger. That, for instance, would be the effect of extending patents to plant material, if in the end it overwhelms plant variety rights. We have also seen cases where the overlap in protection of the same element in a product or service makes the rights differ largely in procedures and scope of protection: that is the difference between petty and full patents and UK design rights and patents.

There is a different situation where individuals may have separate rights for distinct contributions to a final composite work. Consider, for example, the music and the lyric which together make a song. Whether a particular system treats the resultant copyright as being a joint interest in a single work, or allots separate copyrights to the words and music, the copyright results from distinct aesthetic contributions which make up the whole. Many copyright productions today are much more elaborate than that example: encyclopaedias, newspapers, stage presentations, films and so on. In particular, over the course of a century, copyright has been given not just to authors in the classic sense (giving 'authors' rights') but also to investors who finance the production of films, sound recordings, published editions and now databases (giving so-called 'related' or 'neighbouring rights').[23] In the case, therefore, of a film, elaborate licensing arrangements have to be negotiated before all the distinct rights which go into making the ultimate product are secured.

There is no cumulation of rights over any one contribution and no convergence in the sense that only one IPR exists at the end of the day. But in the crafting of the separate rights there is always some tendency to equalise the scope of each. Authors' rights are accorded the long, individualistic property of life plus 70 years (as it has now become in the European Union and the United States). While related rights are for somewhat shorter terms, they have stretched up towards those of authors: thus in Europe, record and film producers now enjoy protection for 50 years from their own first exploitation. Had they not been able to make the analogy, they would likely have enjoyed something like a patent or registered term – perhaps half of what they enjoy today.

When modern copyright began some three centuries ago, the entrepreneurs of the day – the book publishers – secured legislation in the name of their authors, because it was the latter who had the morally convincing case for protection against piracy. Over time, authors learned to cling to their characterisation as the fertile embryos of copyright, because they thereby gained some hope of independence within the commercial organism as a whole. For the few who became a great success, this independence gave them a real chance to demand rewards related to their rentable reputation. For the general run, the hope was largely ephemeral, but at least it was something. And it remains the longer term of authors' rights, which restrains producers from demanding that those rights be absorbed into their own producers' rights, much as they would like a legal scheme in which the only protection would be for the capital investment which makes the whole thing happen in a commercial sense.[24]

If then the convergence of IPRs has any significant meaning, it is best thought of as relating to those cases where a collection of rights relating to different aspects of a product or service, possibly originating in the same, possibly in different, hands, can be positioned in some synergistic way. The protection against competition from equivalent production is then able to expand, not least in duration, so as to give an enhanced area of exclusivity.

One example, now of great commercial importance to the organisers of films, books, sporting events, museums and the like, as well as advertising and branding more generally, are the conjoint activities of promotion through the endorsement of celebrities and the merchandising of things bearing the names, symbols or pictures of individuals, fictional characters, clubs, universities, municipalities and so on. The European Court of Justice has had no compunction in stretching the new law of registered trade marks to cover the use of a mark upon the goods for it is registered even where purchasers do not think it is being used to indicate the source of the goods.[25] Thus the Arsenal Football Club can use its registrations against small-time clothing sellers even where 'Arsenal' and team logos are used as decorations which fans will wear to show their loyalty to the club, not because they think the clothes come from it. The club gets an exclusive right to stop competitive copying which will last as long as it does. The result will inevitably be monopoly pricing and other ways of attacking that consequence – most obviously through competition law –

will have to be taken up.[26] Such mindless stretching of IPRs can only bring the whole panoply into disrepute.

There are examples of the successive roles which patents and designs, and then trade marks and product and packaging get-up (perhaps with associated copyright), may play in building up and sustaining popularity of a novel product line. Of all the elements which may go into this, the most interesting are those concerned with shape. A mechanical or electrical article may contain shapes within it which cause it to function and it may have others which are purely to make it attractive to the eye of the purchaser. In between are the shapes of functioning parts which are also a pleasure in themselves. The functional aspect can, when it is a novel invention, be protected by a patent for up to 20 years, or else by some petty patent or unregistered design right, where a country makes it available for a lesser term.[27] If the shape gives a novel and distinctive appearance to the article, it will be entitled to a design registration for up to 25 years. But here one meets a first element of non-cumulation: registered designs are not available upon shapes that are purely functional; and courts are left to settle how wide this exclusion is.

Whether or not such initial rights are secured at the outset, the EC's new law for trade marks again provides some supplement. The producer of a market success may now seek to register a mark consisting of the particular shape either for the product or for a picture of the product. As with registered designs, however, the law accepts that there is a danger of undue cumulation. No registration is permitted of a product shape which results from the nature of the product, when it is a technical necessity or an addition of substantial value.[28] The Court of Justice has at least accepted that these limitations are to be read in a way which gives them real substance. The positioning of the rotary shaving heads on the 'Philishave' electric razor, well known though they may be, are adopted for technical reasons. They cannot be treated as acquiring trade mark distinctiveness just because rivals could put the rotary heads in a different configuration.[29]

None the less, the test is one of necessity, not of mere desirability. There will be many circumstances where a shape mark will confer useful protection against the copying of popular products without any limitation of time, because the shape is not technically *necessary*. The day may well come when it must be considered whether such marks ought at least to be open to a licence on statutory terms after a given period. A patent or copyright in the shape is limited because only a limited term of protection is considered necessary to induce the initial creation and development of the product; a point is reached in which the public benefit of competitive pricing and the general desirability of free access to ideas should take precedence. Should these limits be in effect obliterated by virtue of a trade mark right? For such cases, there really is a case for a single right protecting the investment needed to encourage the introduction of the product. Its main characteristic would be a short-term industrial property right.[30]

3 Cumulation, convergence and unfair competition

How far does it matter that there are cumulations and convergences of various kinds occurring in the forward march of intellectual property? That question takes one to a fundamental difference of attitude towards the extent to which industrial producers and marketers should be left free to take ideas from other sources. Whether from a root sense of equity or from a calculation of economic efficiency, individual IPRs mark off situations where particular factors should be wrapped in exclusive protection:

inventions, aesthetic works, marks and signs, and so on, are so treated, sometimes for as long as they are needed, more for only a limited duration. To those who see considerable public benefit in leaving the remaining seas free for competitive navigation, IPRs should always be treated as exceptions confined to the objective which suffices for their creation. Each should be created only by legislation which has considered that justification and has shaped the right in detail to cover it but to go no further.

In most developed countries there is a flow of demands for new IP. In the United Kingdom this has occurred recently over the general format of television shows and over 'lookalike' products in stores which customers are unlikely directly to confuse with a well-known brand but which they may nevertheless be drawn to select. Neither of these has so far succeeded, whereas there has been protection for semi-conductor chip layouts, as well as the extraordinary case of copyright in industrial design already outlined. For those whose instinct is formed, there is much sense in seeking to prevent cumulations of different rights and in examining with considerable asperity any case that in some sense amounts to a convergence of rights.

The contrary attitude manifests far greater sympathy for those who, having initiated some development for goods or services, are then subject to free riding. People most readily convinced of a property rights approach to capitalist investment because of its unique ability to realise economic potential are ready to provide legal redress that will stop others gaining something for nothing. For them, cumulation and convergence give rise to nothing like the same suspicion. They are likely in any case to have little difficulty in accepting that the general law of obligations should recognise a wrong of unfair competition. This they would conceive as not limited to cases where competitor and consumer interests align; rather it should be available wherever there is some undue misappropriation of an element in production or distribution.

As is well known, by restricting passing off and related torts to the first of these categories, Commonwealth law tends against any catch-all view of unfair competition. In varying degrees, civil law countries show a tendency the other way, and this may spill over into specific IP regimes, as has been the case with the new EU law of registered trade marks. The opposing positions are unlikely ever to resolve themselves, nor should they. Some degree of balance emerges from the continual contest. We would be far worse off if it could no longer be demanded that extensions of intellectual property be shown to have a sufficient justification and if earlier and wider rights of this type were taken to be presumptively justified. At times, such as during the drive to implant the TRIPs Agreement within the World Trade Organization, it appears that such a presumption is riding forward in triumph. It is always healthy to observe a public reaction calling for a halt, such as is occurring in numerous forms at present. Long may such innate sense prevail!

NOTES

1 For the emergence of industrial design protection, see B Sherman and L Bently *The Making of Modern Intellectual Property Law* (1999).
2 Copyright Act 1911, s 22.
3 *King Features Syndicate v Kleeman* [1941] AC 417.
4 Gregory Committee on Copyright (Cmd 8662, 1952) Pt X.
5 S 10.
6 Design Copyright Act 1968 – a private member's Bill given a small measure of government time.

7 This should have been apparent to the Legislature in 1968 from the Court of Appeal's decision in *Dorling v Honnor Marine* [1965] Ch 1; but the case went unregarded.

8 These were at the time the more threatening because a severe copyright law made an infringer liable for conversion damages related to the value of the items embodying the copyright work. With jewellery, furniture and the like, suddenly damage awards could be stratospheric. (This basis for assessment of damages was repealed in 1988.)

9 The Whitford Committee on Copyright and Designs Law (Cmnd 6732, 1977), set up very largely to resolve the controversy, was unable to reach a unanimous recommendation, though it showed some sympathy for the car manufacturers' case: see ch 3.

10 In many respects still a form of copyright, which explains why there is no cumulation of the two: see CDPA 1988, s 236. UDR was not treated as copyright in order that the UK could establish limited international reciprocity for the new right beyond the constraints of the Berne Convention. The German government, however, reminded the British that there might be a breach of the national treatment principle applying to designs in the Paris Industrial Property Convention. For the upshot, see CDPA 1988, s 221.

11 For the complexities in full, see eg Laddie, Prescott and Vitoria *Modern Law of Copyright* (2nd edn, 1995) chs 40–44.

12 The utter oddity of its appearance lies in this: UDR gives a limited term protection – generally of ten years – to shapes in products, however purely technical they are. It is an equivalent, but without any formality whatsoever, to the old version of utility model (a type of petty patent) which German and other systems recognised many years ago: a form of protection over the shape which elements in machines had to assume into order to perform their function. Most other countries in Europe now favour a more broadly based petty patent of some kind, but Britain stands rigidly against, arguing that a registered but unexamined right will prove to be so uncertain in its validity and scope as to be a totally unpredictable instrument. What then of the unregistered design right – for all that it is infringed only by copying?

13 Plant Patents Act 1930 and the Plant Variety Protection Act 1970. The constitutional limits upon the powers of Congress tend towards an expansion of existing rights. The same is true in protecting investors in the copyright industries.

14 Union pour la Protection des Obtentions Végétales, 1961.

15 Indeed a Community PVR was introduced in 1995, as an alternative to the national systems of Community states: see reg 2100/94.

16 For its latest proposals, see the Commission's Consultations on the Impact of the Community Utility Model in order to Update the Green Paper on the Protection of Utility Models in the Single Market (SEC (2001) 1307) and the Summary Report on the answers received of 1 March 2002.

17 See further, eg Cornish *Intellectual Property* (4th edn, 1999) para 8-14.

18 It will, of course, only be available for such information as need never be revealed about the technology. Much, inevitably, will become apparent through reverse engineering once the end-product is on the market.

19 *Kewanee v Bicron* 416 US 470 (1974).

20 See eg Cornish, above n 17, paras 13–29/35.

21 Directive 91/250, arts 4–8. For decompilation, art 6.

22 Thus the European Commission, in its proposed Directive on the Patentability of Computer-implemented Inventions (COM (2002) 92 final) pp 8-9, has no difficulty in treating the two forms of protection as 'complementary'. Indeed, perhaps disingenuously, it dwells upon the very limited defences to copyright in programs when compared with those for private and experimental purposes in European patent law. But that is very little when compared with the strategic difference in scope of protection of the two rights.

23 The case which falls between the two is that of the performer. Where actors and musicians have their own property against imitation it is commonly classified as a 'related right'. But the performers' contribution is aesthetic rather than financial so their case is something of a bridgehead.

24 As somewhat prematurely announced on behalf of the record industry by Turkevich 'Authors' Rights are Dead' (1990) 38 J US Copyright Soc 41.

25 *Arsenal Football Club v Reed* [2002] EWHC 2695 (Ch), [2003] 1 All ER 137; but see the reaction of Laddie J: [2003] 1 All ER 137.

26 The price of sports club merchandise is already being investigated by the Office of Fair Trading.

27 If there is no satisfactory substitute for it during that time, there will be a chance to lodge its trade-marked name in the public's mind so as to carry it forward into the era of competition with a massive advantage, since rivals will not be able to use the mark. It will, of course, be necessary to establish a generic description of the thing, which is different from the mark; otherwise the mark will be open to attack as having itself become generic.

28 In the UK, see the Trade Marks Act 1994, s 3(2).

29 *Philips v Remington* [2001] RPC 745.

30 Cf Jacob 'Trade Marks and the Olympic Games throughout the Years' [2001] EIPR 1. There would then be an analogy to the limited duration rights to publicity for celebrities introduced by legislation in various American states.

Works by Colin Tapper

Books

Computers and the law (London: Weidenfeld and Nicolson, 1973), pp xvi and 314

Computer law, (London: Longman, 1978), pp xxv and 190

Computer law, 2nd edn (London: Longman, 1982), pp xxvi and 221

An experiment in the use of citation vectors in the area of legal data NORIS (36) (Norwegian Research Center for Computers and Law, COMPLEX No 9/82, Oslo, 1982)

Computer law, 3rd edn (London: Longman, 1983), pp xxvii and 242

Cross on evidence, 6th edn (London: Butterworths, 1985), pp xcvii and 663

Outline of the law of evidence, 6th edn (London: Butterworths, 1985), pp xxix and 307 (with Nancy Wilkins)

Computer law, 4th edn (London: Longman, 1989), pp xlvi and 449

Cross on evidence, 7th edn (London: Butterworths, 1990), pp cx and 757

Handbook of European Software Law (Oxford: Clarendon Press) co-ed with M Lehmann Part I (1993), pp ix, Tables 77, and pp 216; Pt II (1995) pp 771 and Index 5

Cross and Tapper on evidence, 8th ed (London: Butterworths, 1995), pp cxxv and 845

Cross and Tapper on evidence, 9th ed (London: Butterworths, 1999), pp cxxx and 725

Contributions to books

Criminal Law, Evidence and Procedure chapter (with various co-authors), Annual Survey of Commonwealth Law:1966–1969, 1973–1974

'Powers and Secondary Rules of Change' (pp 242-277) in Simpson (ed) *Oxford Essays in Jurisprudence (Second series)* (Oxford University Press, 1973)

'Legal remedies for misrepresentation of software' in *Performance Evaluation of Numerical Software* ed Fosdick (Amsterdam: North Holland 1979)

'Citations as a Tool for Searching Law by Computer' in Niblett (ed) *Computer Science and Law* (Cambridge University press, 1980)

'The meaning of section 1(f)(i) of the Criminal Evidence Act 1898' (pp 296–322) in Tapper (ed) *Crime, proof and punishment: essays in memory of Sir Rupert Cross* (London: Butterworth, 1981)

'Proof and prejudice' (pp 177–210) in Campbell and Waller (eds) *Well and truly tried, essays on evidence in honour of Sir R Eggleston* (Law Book Co, Sydney &c, 1982)

'An experiment with citation vectors' (pp 90–109) in Campbell (ed) *Data Processing and the Law* (Sweet & Maxwell, 1984)

'Legal problems posed by computers: international considerations' (pp 3–20) in Hughes (ed) *Essays in Computer Law* (Longman Cheshire, 1990) 3-20

Chapter on Evidence in Saxby (ed) *Encyclopedia of Information Technology Law* (Sweet & Maxwell, 1990, with updates)

'The European software directive: The perspective from the UK' (pp 143–161) in Lehmann & Tapper (eds) *A handbook of European software law* Pt I (Oxford: Clarendon Press, 1993)

'National Report: United Kingdom' (pp 1–122) in Lehmann & Tapper (eds) *A handbook of European software law* Pt II (Oxford: Clarendon Press, 1995)

'Evidence: Trends and Techniques' in Birks (ed) *Pressing Problems in the Law: Volume 1: Criminal Justice and Human Rights* (Oxford: Clarendon Press, 1995) 13–34

'Some aspects of contractual licences for software' (pp 282–296) in Rose (ed) *Consensus ad Idem: essays on the law of contract in honour of Guenter Treitel* (London: Sweet and Maxwell, 1996)

'Crime and Evidence' in Stephens (ed) *Information Technology Law* (2000) (London: Informa) (CD ROM CL 21)

Articles and notes

'A case of privilege' New Left Review (1961)

'Legal Analogy' The Listener (1961)

'No parity for peers' (1961) 24 Modern Law Review 757-762

'Finance Acts 1961 and 1960' (1962) 25 Modern Law Review 64-68

'Insanity and drunkenness' (1962) 25 Modern Law Review 238-242

'Revelation and relevance' (1962) 25 Modern Law Review 576-580

'Lawyers and machines' (1963) 26 Modern Law Review 121-137

'Freedom and privilege' (1963) 26 Modern Law Review 571-574

'R v King: a small jump sideways' (1964) 27 Modern Law Review 222-224

'British experience in legal information retrieval' (1964) 5 Modern Uses of Logic in Law 127-134

'Mechanised methods of documentation of interest to criminologists' (1964) ASLIB Proceedings 17

'Austin on sanctions' [1965] Cambridge Law Journal 271-287

'The uses of computers for lawyers' (1965) 8 Journal of the Society of Public Teachers of Law 261-274

'The case of the hysterical victim' (1965) 28 Modern Law Review 359-361

'Criminal Injuries Compensation Board releases' (1965) 28 Modern Law Review 460-463

'Are the judges necessary?' (1965) New Society

'Computers for solicitors?' (1966) 110 Solicitors Journal 181-182, 203-204

'Hearsay evidence in civil proceedings' (1966) 29 Modern Law Review 653-656

'Satisfaction Onus or incidence?' (1966) 29 Modern Law Review 692-695

'Research and legal information by computer' (1967) 48 Chicago Bar Record 226 – 238

'The second report of the Criminal Injuries Compensation Board' (1967) 30 Modern Law Review 319–321

'Instant law in the Court of Appeal (Criminal Division)' (1967) 30 Modern Law Review 441–445

'Information retrieval for international law' Computer Weekly 1968

'The solicitor and the computer' (1968) 118 New Law Journal 55–56

'Law Reform Committee: Sixteenth report on privilege in civil proceedings' (1968) 31 Modern Law Review 198-202

'Legal information and computers: Great Britain' (1968) 1 Law & Computer Technology Issue 1, 18-19

'World co-operation in the mechanisation of legal information retrieval' (1969) 9 Jurimetrics Journal 1–11 (reprinted from Chicago Bar Record June–July 1967)

'Feasibility study on retrieving legal information from two types of natural language texts' (1969) OSTI Research report 5062

'Computers and legislation' (1970) 23 Alabama Law Review 1–42

'Blood test evidence' (1970) 33 Modern Law Review 202–205

'Survey of recent developments in North America (1970) Council of Europe EXP/Ord Jur (70) 41

'Survey of recent developments in North America (1970) Council of Europe COM/Informatique Jur (74) 2

'Council of Europe and the computerisation of law' Computer Weekly 1970

'Note on principles' (1971) 34 Modern Law Review 628–634

'Legal information retrieval' (1971) 2 The Law Librarian 8–9, 15

'Computers and privacy' (1971) Proceedings of the UNIVAC Users Association

'The retrieval of legal information by computer' (1972) Computer En recht

'An experiment in the retrieval of British case law by computerized methods' 12 (1972) Jurimetrics Journal 122–125

'Privilege and confidence' (1972) 35 Modern Law Review 83–87

'Evidence (general) Eleventh report of the Criminal Law Revision Committee' (1972) 35 Modern Law Review 621–624

'Criminal Law Revision Committee 11th report: character evidence' (1973) 36 Modern Law Review 56–64, 167–174

'Corroboration from an independent source' (1973) 36 Modern Law Review 541–545

'Privilege and policy' (1974) 37 Modern Law Review 92–96

'Evidence from computers' (1974) 8 Georgia Law Review 562–613

'Computers and case law' (1974) 14 Jurimetrics Journal 249–253

'Legal information retrieval by computer: applications and implications' (1974) 20 McGill Law Journal 26–43

'Similar facts: peculiarity and credibility' (1975) 38 Modern Law Review 206–209

'Case Law and Computers' (1975) Issue 4 Computers & Law 7

'Letter from America, July 2, 1975' (1975) Issue 5 Computers & Law 9

'Letter from America, 23 September, 1976' (1975) Issue 6 Computers & Law 10

'Letter from America, 1 January, 1976' (1976) Issue 7 Computers & Law 9

'Letter from America, 31st March, 1976' (1976) Issue 8 Computers & Law 6–7

'Citation patterns in legal information retrieval' (1976) Datenverarbeitung im Recht 5 Heft 3, pp 249–275

'Computers and privacy' (1977) 40 Modern Law Review 198–200

'Privacy at work' (1977) Personnel Management

'Legal information retrieval' (1978) 128 New Law Journal Office and equipment and services supplement (May 4) 7–8

'The open society and its enemy' (1978) 41 Modern Law Review 192–195

'Legal information retrieval: its past, present and future' Computers and the Law (Conference Proceedings 30 June–2 July 1978) 2–4

'The Computer Revolution' (1979) 76 Law Society Gazette 1–2

'Citations as a tool for searching law by computer' in *Proceedings of International Conference on Literary and Linguistic Computing* ed Malachi (1979)

'New frontiers of legal information' (1980) 130 New Law Journal 1153–1156

'Microform publishing: too little and too late?' (1981) 1 Oxford Journal of Legal Studies 123–125

'Information retrieval: full text and citation vectors' (1981) 30 Computers and the Law November 6–8

'Copyright protection for computer programmes' (1981) 2 Business Law Review 357–360

'Closed or open information retrieval systems' (1981) Aslib Proceedings

'Computer output as evidence' (1982) 2 Oxford Journal of Legal Studies 128–130

'Copyright in judgments' (1984) 1 Computer Law and Practice 76–80

'Computer output and the law' (1984) 6 Information Age (Issue 3, July) pp 131–133

'Use of Computer Printouts in Criminal Cases' (1985) 2 Applied Computer and Communications Law 3

'Mackenzie Patten v British Olivetti: Buying a computer – a dreadful precedent' (1985) 6 European Intellectual Property Review 182–183

'Genius and Janus: information technology and the law' (1985) 11 Monash University Law Review 75–96 (Fullager lecture)

'Copyright in computer programs: an international perspective' (1985) 1 Santa Clara Computer and High Technology Law Journal 13–25

'"Computer crime": Scotch mist?' [1987] Criminal Law Review 4–22

'An aspect of copyright in data bases' (1987) 14 Northern Kentucky Law Review 169–210

'The revelation of Jones v DPP' (1988) 51 Modern Law Review 785–789

'Copyright in databases' (1988) 5 Computer Law and Practice 20–23

'Judicial attitudes, aptitudes and abilities in the field of high technology' (1989) 15 Monash University Law Review 219–228

'Hillmon rediscovered and Lord St Leonards resurrected' (1990) 106 Law Quarterly Review 441–468

'Discovery in modern times: a voyage around the common law world' (1991) 67 Chicago Kent Law Review 217–271 (Charles Green lecture)

'Discovery of documents' (1991) 107 Law Quarterly Review 370–376

'New European directions in data protection' (1992) 3 Journal of Law and Information Science 9–24

'The Probative Force of Similar Fact Evidence' (1992) 108 Law Quarterly Review 26–30

'Hearsay and Implied Assertions' (1992) 108 Law Quarterly Review 524–528

'Evidence: reform in an international context' (1992) 22 University of Western Australia Law Review 31–51

'New European directions in data protection' (1992) 3 Journal of Law and Information Science 9–24

'Evanescent evidence' (1993) 1 International Journal of Law and Information Technology 35–58

'Impact of computers upon law in an international context' (1993) Proceedings of Biennial Computer Law Conference

'A suitable case for treatment' (1993) 109 Law Quarterly Review 48–51

'Freedom of information: a conceptual mess' (1993) Information Technology and Public Policy

'Law Commission's Report on the reform of the hearsay rule: Its impact upon the reception of computer output' (1994) 10(2) Computer Law and Security Report 86–88

'Corporations and the privilege against self-incrimination' (1994) 110 Law Quarterly Review 350–353

'Commentary on *Intergraph Corp v Solid Systems CAD Services Ltd*' [1994] Masons Comp Law Rep 8

'The erosion of Boardman v DPP' (1995) 145 New Law Journal 1223–1225; 1263–1264

'Dissimilar views of similar facts' (1995) 111 Law Quarterly Review 381–385

'Reform of the law of evidence in relation to the output from computers' (1995) 3 International Journal of Law and Information Technology 79–93

'Commentary on *East-West Transport Service Ltd v Crown Prosecution Service*' [1995] 4 Masons Comp Law Rep 11

'Prosecution and Privilege' (1996) 1 Evidence and Proof 5–24

'Commentary on *Glencore International AG v Bank of China*' [1996] Masons Comp Law Rep 3–4

'Commentary on *In the matter of Patent App 92049592 in the name of Fujitsu Ltd*' [1996] Masons Comp Law Rep 22

'Hearsay in criminal cases: an overview of Law Commission Report No 245' [1997] Criminal Law Review 771–784

'Overhearing and oversight' (1997) 1 Evidence and Proof 162–173

'Evidential privilege in cases involving children' (1997) 9 Child & Family Law Quarterly 1–16

'Commentary on *Standard Bank London Ltd v The Bank of Tokyo Ltd; Sudwestdeutsche Landesbank Girozentrale v The Bank of Tokyo Ltd*' [1997] Mason's Comp Law Rep 8–9

'Commentary on *Amstrad plc v Seagate Technology Inc*' [1998] Masons Comp Law Rep 87–89

'Commentary on *Bramall v DPP, DPP v Ward, R v Aylesbury Crown Court, Reid v DPP*' [1998] Masons Comp Law Rep 233

'Commentary on *Re Market Wizard Systems*' [1999] Masons Comp Law Rep 23

'Commentary on *Microsoft Corporation v Backslash Distribution Ltd*' [1999] Masons Comp Law Rep 40

'Commentary on *R v Taylor-Sabori*' [1999] Masons Comp Law Rep 79

'Commentary on *Taylor v Cox*' [1999] Masons Comp Law Rep 85–86

'Commentary on *Microsoft Corporation v Plato Technology Ltd*' [1999] Masons Comp Law Rep 100–101, 379

'Commentary on *Morgans v Southwark Crown Court*' [1999] Masons Comp Law Rep 114–115

'Commentary on *Pierce v Promco SA*' [1999] Masons Comp Law Rep 134

'Commentary on *Cantor Fitzgerald Ltd v Tradition (UK) Ltd*' [1999] Masons Comp Law Rep 265–266

'Commentary on *Godfrey v Demon Internet International*' [1999] Masons Comp Law Rep 278–279

'Commentary on *Re IBM's Application*' [1999] Masons Comp Law Rep 295

'Commentary on *Intelsec Systems Ltd v Grech-Cini*' [1999] Masons Comp Law Rep 320–321

'Commentary on *Mars (UK) Ltd v Teknowledge Ltd*' [1999] Masons Comp Law Rep 333–334

'Commentary on *Mercury Communications Ltd v Communication Telesystems International*' [1999] Masons Comp Law Rep 368–369

'Commentary on *R v Bow St Mag Ct and Allison ex p USA*' [1999] Masons Comp Law Rep 390–391

'Commentary on *R v Marcolino*' [1999] Masons Comp Law Rep 395

'Commentary on *R v Waddon*' [1999] Masons Comp Law Rep 398–399

'Clouded acquittal' (2001) 117 Law Quarterly Review 1–5

Reviews

Review of David Yardley *The Future of the Law* (1965) 8 Journal of the Society of Public Teachers of Law 243-244

Review of G Hughes and A Sharp, *Computer Contracts: Principles and Precedents* (1993) 23 University of Western Australia Law Review 186–188

Review of Stanley Lai, *The Protection of Computer Software in the United Kingdom* (2000) 2 digital technology law journal

Review of Richard Susskind, *Transforming the Law: Essays on Technology, Justice and the Legal Marketplace* (2001) 117 Law Quarterly Review 515–517

Index